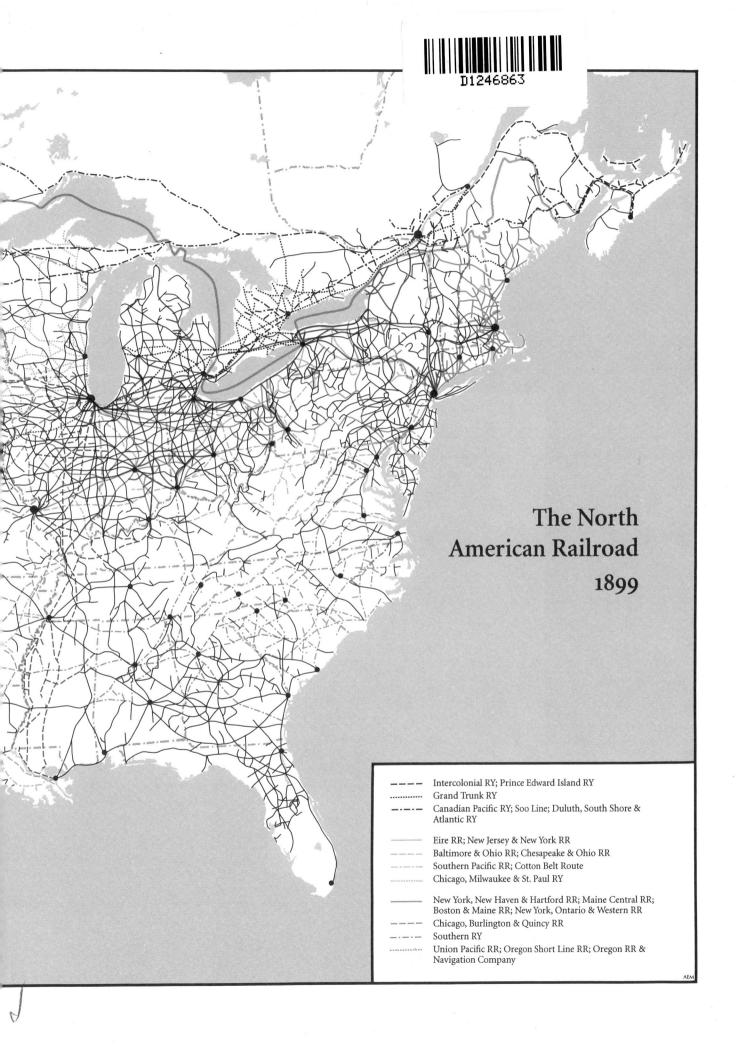

The North American Railroad 1899

– – – –	Intercolonial RY; Prince Edward Island RY
···········	Grand Trunk RY
–·–·–·–	Canadian Pacific RY; Soo Line; Duluth, South Shore & Atlantic RY
———	Eire RR; New Jersey & New York RR
– – – –	Baltimore & Ohio RR; Chesapeake & Ohio RR
–·–·–·	Southern Pacific RR; Cotton Belt Route
··············	Chicago, Milwaukee & St. Paul RY
———	New York, New Haven & Hartford RR; Maine Central RR; Boston & Maine RR; New York, Ontario & Western RR
– – – –	Chicago, Burlington & Quincy RR
–·–·–	Southern RY
··············	Union Pacific RR; Oregon Short Line RR; Oregon RR & Navigation Company

AEM

12.5.95

The North American Railroad

CREATING THE NORTH AMERICAN LANDSCAPE

Consulting Editors
Gregory Conniff   Bonnie Loyd   Edward K. Muller   David Schuyler

Published in cooperation with the Center for American Places,
Harrisonburg, Virginia

The North American Railroad

Its Origin, Evolution, and Geography

JAMES E. VANCE, JR.

The Johns Hopkins University Press • Baltimore and London

Illustration for title page spread: Thomas Moran's painting of Weber Canyon on the Union Pacific. *Source:* Henry T. Williams, *Pacific Tourist.*

© 1995 The Johns Hopkins University Press
All rights reserved. First Edition
Printed in the United States of America on acid-free paper
04 03 02 01 00 99 98 97 96 95   5 4 3 2 1

The Johns Hopkins University Press
2715 North Charles Street
Baltimore, Maryland 21218-4319
The Johns Hopkins Press Ltd., London

All original cartography, including endpaper maps, by Adrienne Morgan, Berkeley, California.

ISBN 0-8018-4573-4

Library of Congress Cataloging-in-Publication Data will be found at the end of this book.
A catalog record for this book is available from the British Library.

FOR JEAN

not because she would have chosen its subject, but because she appreciated
the pleasure it gave me to write it and to present it to her as a gift on the day
before her untimely death

CONTENTS

PREFACE AND

ACKNOWLEDGMENTS

The unquestioning acceptance of plausible but unestablished "truth" may well have contributed more to human error than forthright ignorance has; the latter quite commonly indicts itself, whereas the former is often exculpated by a simple "right-soundingness." Thus, it is custom to hold that steam transport on rails began in Britain and, therefore, that all later rail development was also rooted in British soil.

Such a conclusion presupposes a differentiation among countries that limits innovation and technical advance to only one or two nations, with all others following the course of the initiator. If we seek to understand experience rather than to assert merely plausible tradition in rail development, we find that there are two basic stimulants of that experience, with two distinct geographical environments: the British railway arose because of the crowding and stressing of existing transportation, found concentrated on canals, whereas the North American railroad grew in a very different soil, as a new development in the absence of any good prior transportation.

There is obviously an important distinction to be found between these two: the conditions inducing development under stress of business will be sharply separated from the conditions of true innovation responding to an absence of prior development. Much has been written about the British railway, its origin and wider geographical adoption. Its spread has been great, though far from universal, and it is of critical importance to analyze where it is. Attempts to explain the nature of the North American railroad directly in terms of derivation from the British railway have led more to confusion than otherwise. When we reflect on the considerable difference between the history and geography of rail formation in Britain and in North America, we should not be surprised that such sharp distinction is the case.

This book grew out of a search that long ago wandered from its original course. The economic concept of the "best and highest use" as applied in the nineteenth century suggested that the objective of rail building should be to reproduce the most developed and demanding aspects of the railroad wherever it was constructed, on the assumption that progress would ultimately demand the best. If all construction had finally led to the shaping of "main lines," this would have been sound long-term practice. But many lines never rose much above the most modest traffic, leaving the problem more one of overbuilding than of too mean provision. This failure to predict accurately or to plan differentially meant that few areas could afford the gamble of slavishly following British practice. Thus, there were large areas of the world where existing or potential markets were hopelessly too small for high-level rail development, and even in western Europe only relatively few lines should have been built to such standards if cost recovery were to be found in traffic potentials.

The search that I abandoned would have involved using the historical geography of British rail building to attempt to explain such activities in North America and less economically developed regions. Any detailed account of rail development quickly makes it evident that there are other strains of evolution not comprehended by the British system of rail building. This fact has been acknowledged for many years. What has not been done is to provide an integrated account of this parallel rail evolution to stand alongside that based in Britain. It often seems as if America's parallel history was late in starting, minor in extent, and of little technical importance. As none of those is the case, the time has certainly come to write an analytical historical geography of the most important of the alternatives to the British version of rail development.

Without here unduly elaborating the point, we should note that something we might call the "North American railroad"—to contrast it with the very earliest railways as evolved in Britain before 1850—was undertaken within less than a decade of the opening of the world's first railway as found in the Stockton and Darlington Railway of 1825. By the early 1830s several American railroads of considerable length were open and operating. In 1833 the South Carolina Railroad was operating over 135 miles between Line Street in Charleston and the Savannah River Bridge at Augusta, Georgia, making it the world's longest line. Boston was served by three separate radiating rail lines in 1835 to become the world's first rail junction city. A number of technical accomplishments—the four-wheel swivel truck, reliance on leveling rods, the use of the Morse telegraph, and demonstration of the advantages of high-pressure steam, for example—came first on the North American railroad. There can be no doubt that that medium of transport was fully a peer of the British railway, and ever remained so. During the First World War, usually cited as the period of the greatest relative importance of rail transport, a quarter of all the world's rail mileage was in the United States—a full third in North America—with the greatest numbers of passengers and freight loadings also found there.

There is no question that though used as a technical system on all the world's settled continents, this railroad was genetically and culturally North American. In all its characteristics it was a railroad seeking to promote rather than simply responding to development. The fact that no railroad can exist with less than a single track is obvious; less obvious is the fact that a single-track railroad places a strict limit on traffic that would not be tolerated if actual business were available to support a second track. In the beginning no more than a handful of rail lines in the United States had more than a single track, in contrast to Britain where relatively few did not have such provision. Other measures of the high hopes in Britain appeared in the presence of separated grades on those lines, of "flyovers" to allow unimpeded right turns to be made on double lines, and of "escape tracks" at large stub-end stations to allow more efficient operation of locomotives. Most of the operating practice on American railroads stemmed instead from conservatism in terms of investment or labor. The common rail spike was devised in the New World almost at the very beginning because it greatly conserved labor and material. It remains in use a century and a half later because it still has those virtues.

In the course of our discussion many contrasts will be drawn between the British-style railway and the American-style railroad. These are intended to signal differences rather than to award differential virtue. It is true that an initial line such as England's Great Western Railway was so superbly constructed that in the 1960s it could be operated in 125 mph service with little change. But it should not be thought that the British solution to a problem is always superior. Transcontinental railroading came to the United States just forty-one years after the first significant construction of railroads began. Given British practice and American capital resources, one wonders how long that line would have required for construction if the British system of railways had been introduced.

It should be reiterated that this is not a historical geography of world railroads; it is a book specifically about the North American railroad. How and why it differs from the British railway is discussed, but no attempt has been made to give equal treatment to the initial system, as the literature is already disproportionately rich along that line. References are made to the employment of North American rail practice outside North America, but there is no attempt to produce a gazetteer here. This is an account of why North America developed its own form of railroad and how that development led ultimately to the distinctive historical geography of railroads on that continent.

Any study of a major industrial activity carried out over a wide geographical and temporal span involves many events and places. I grew up in the hearth of American railroading, so its landscapes are vivid for me. This was in one of the world's first railroad suburbs, seventeen miles west of Boston, where as early as the middle of the nineteenth century men and women used the wonderful new mobility of the steam train to open a widened employment field for the enhancement of their material life. When I arrived in the 1930s this was still a world that through commuter trains offered to suburban adolescents the chance to experience and begin to understand a great city, something now largely withheld from them. The connection between the suburb and the city also had a geographical locale, a *signum urbis,* in the great city station; the example I knew, South Station in Boston, had been the greatest of them all in numbers of passengers passing through its doors on an ordinary day in 1917. I left by train from my local station in 1944 as a member of a group sent for army induction; I returned from Europe in August 1945 on a special train that reached that same South Station before breakfast four days after the atomic bomb was dropped and the war disappeared. A world of mobility was then a realm of train travel. An old house in the country for the summer was reached most easily on the *Blueberry Special* of the Boston and Maine. Even getting to my first teaching job, in the heart of the Ozarks, required only two trains from Framingham in Massachusetts next door to my home. Connection came by the *Southwestern Limited* to the world's largest station, still an important articulation point in St. Louis, and the St. Louis and San Francisco's *Meteor* essentially to my back doorstep in Fayetteville, Arkansas. My fascination with the world could never have arisen independent of railroads.

It was not until I became the first geographer to teach the field in Wyoming that my interest in and initial understandings of the North American railroad began to crystallize. The construction of the first transcontinental railroad brought out signal qualities of the developmental railroad and strongly suggested that it had played the major role in the rapid growth of the North American economy. This experience with the pioneering line, the Union Pacific Railroad, demonstrated that the standard historical view of rail transportation has been unduly influenced by the British experience, which I discovered had rather little importance in the analysis of American railroading.

In attempting to understand the North American railroad, a fresh viewpoint was needed; the idea had to be to look at the railroad *in* North America and as a system devised to seek the economic development of that continent. Foremost was the shaping of its large political units, brought together and integrated by what was fundamentally a long-distance form of transportation. This effort was much the same in the great republic that arose in 1783 as in the dominion formed in 1867. In the first case the railroads can be said to have grown in part from that republican independence; in the second case they produced the core for a separate and distinct independence and nationhood. Different though a republic and a royal dominion are, a similarity of demography and economic stage allowed the United States and Canada to share the same type of railroad. And as we shall see, to carry our analysis from the creation of that distinctive American rail technology around 1825 down to the present, we need to deal with both the American and the Canadian experience.

As this is a book in geography, it should be understood that the main body of observation and information that informs it is the geographical pattern of the regional, corporate, and national rail system that evolved in the United States and Canada. The monographal literature in history is the most wide-ranging source to be had, and the one offering the most comparable coverage of the United States and Canada. To pin down observations to the land a great deal of map analysis is carried out, and the records of engineering operations are given major consideration. It is intended that this book should leave the reader with a fairly detailed survey of where and why rail lines were placed on the ground in various regions and at different times.

In a study as dependent on field observation as this, many people have given their time and understanding under circumstances that make individual thanks impossible, though most deserved. Trainmen, conductors, car attendants, and others working on both passenger and freight trains have demonstrated that railroads can still capture the loyalty of their better workers, those who richly convey their enthusiasm to the outside observer. Even in an era of jumbo-jet pilots and astronauts, working for the railroads still makes small boys envious. To all who have so generously shared with me their knowledge, understanding, and affection for railroads, I send deep and sincere thanks.

Several railroads in particular have been generous in aiding my understanding of the North American railroad. From 1955 to 1957 the Union Pacific Railroad, both at its headquarters in Omaha and along the line in Wyoming, was in many ways tolerant of my ignorance in the interest of promoting my ultimate knowledge. More recently some Canadian railroads, notably the British Colum-

Preface and
Acknowledgments

bia Railway and the Canadian Pacific Railway, have kindly rescheduled freights to work in daylight hours or have in other ways been most generous with time and resources. This generosity has allowed me to see that the characteristics given to the North American railroad earlier in the nineteenth century remain with it today, right down to the most recently constructed lines in Alberta, British Columbia, and the Northwest Territories. To those occupants of the cab and the caboose who have patiently borne my insatiable curiosity expressed over long hours, I send my greatest thanks. They could have served me no better than they did in approaching the edge of stalling on the slippery track of a snowy Crowsnest Pass, in demonstrating the reason for the derailer in the descent therefrom, and in giving me use of a "speeder" (handcar) and the freedom of the road for a day on the Tumbler Ridge line.

Because an account of the planning and construction of the North American rail net depends on material now available only in libraries, I wish to thank a number of such institutions for their assistance: the Love Library of the University of Nebraska, Lincoln; the Transportation Library of the University of California, Berkeley; the Union Pacific Railroad Museum and Library, Omaha, Nebraska; the University of British Columbia Library, Vancouver; the Museum of New Mexico Library, Santa Fe; and the Baltimore and Ohio Museum, Baltimore, Maryland. For pictures and the permission to reprint them I wish to thank the following: the Canadian Pacific Railway Archives (and Mr. Shields), Montréal; the Canadian National Railway Archives (and Ms. Connie Romani), Montréal; the Library of Congress, Pictures and Map divisions, Washington; the Public Affairs Department, British Columbia Railway, North Vancouver; the Massachusetts Historical Society, Boston; and the Southern Pacific Railroad, San Francisco, California.

I wish particularly to thank Charles Hadenfeldt for numerous kindnesses at all stages of the preparation of this manuscript. The completion of this while I was isolated on "Canada's western frontier" was made possible by Charlie's kindness and repeated attentions. Doty Valrey and Anne Matthews helped importantly in typing the final manuscript. In drafting most of the original maps contained in the book, Adrienne Morgan showed her usual skill and common sense on my behalf. And the Hon. Victor Ryerson of the California Public Utilities Commission was of great help in establishing the present-day pattern of North American railroads.

From the very beginning George F. Thompson, president of the Center for American Places and my editor at the Johns Hopkins University Press, has both encouraged and advanced this work. He has handsomely contributed that bit of enthusiasm each of us needs to overcome self-doubts.

Mary Yates continues in this book as that paragon in publishing, the ideal copy editor, who for me has the great good fortune of being interested in the same curiosities I am. And I wish to thank Kimberly Johnson for being a paragon without limit in the production of books.

Financial support from the Committee on Research of the University of California, Berkeley, has repeatedly made it possible to continue what cannot remain solely a labor of love. In the same way, the Institute for Transportation Studies in Berkeley has played a crucial role in supporting the costly cartography and picture searching that have made this a better and clearer book. The generosity of a small grant from the Canadian Consulate General in San Francisco, and of travel support from the Canadian Pacific Railway, the Canadian National Railway, and the British Columbia Railway, has made it possible for me to look seriously at the truly North American railroad.

Innumerable people have helped importantly in this work, and for that I thank them most sincerely. The failings must be mine, the strengths are clearly theirs. To all of these true friends I send my deepest appreciation.

The North American Railroad

The North American Railroad

A Relative in Little More Than Spirit

As more time passes, allowing us to reflect on the truly fundamental transformations worked by our ancestors during the nineteenth century, the more most of us come to appreciate that it was our lives that experienced the greatest change of all. Discoveries and innovations in medicine—particularly those associated with the acceptance of the germ theory of disease—began to lengthen life and improve its quality. The lighting of that life—first by illuminating gas, and even more fundamentally by Edison's successes with electricity— was truly emancipating (as I am directly reminded while I write these words in a cabin facing the Gulf of Alaska, which lies beyond the net of electrification and is favored only by the kindly short nights of the subarctic summer). We have inherited many such favorable changes from the last century, but for the geographer perhaps the most beneficent was the vast expansion of mobility, for persons and for goods, that transformed our culture as much as our material life. The breakfast banana of the prairies and plains, the popularization of fresh milk in the South, and the replacement of crudely preserved meat by fresh chilled beef in the diets of the working class in eastern cities reflected the shifts in material culture brought on by this enhanced mobility for goods.

For persons, the changes wrought by enhanced mobility were equally legion. It became possible for manufacturing to be massed in existing cities, commonly within or near their greatest market and source of labor even when raw materials had to be brought from afar. Personal migration tended to lose its terrors and finality when the steam train became the medium of the trek. With improved transportation, news traveled faster, first in written communications carried in stagecoaches and steam cars and subsequently on the telegraph wires first strung along the tracks and made integral to the operation of the trains moving along them. The general spread of interest that resulted from enhanced mobility came to be expressed first in a lengthening of and increase in the frequency of business travel, but ultimately in a rapid rise in discretionary travel for pleasure and education. The summer resort became the first commercial expression of the "head of iron" in the Adirondacks, the White Mountains, and the mountains of Pennsylvania and Virginia, even well before the Civil War. After that conflict was ended, the greater personal knowledge of subtropical America brought home by returning Union soldiers, as well as the strengthening of rail ties between the North and the South, made the development of "winter resorts" a reality (first in North Carolina, but ultimately ever farther south until Key West was reached by rail at the end of the century).

The greater truth was discovered that more extensive geographical experience tends to whet spatial curiosity, leading to greater totals of movement and thereby ever pushing the frontier farther away to or beyond the most distant end-of-track. In 1914 the last totally separate North American transcontinental railroad, the Grand Trunk Pacific Railway, was completed to Prince Rupert, a new port hacked out of the forest at the 54th parallel of latitude in western Canada. Land on that coast and its offshore islands was thus the westernmost patch of potential cultivable country in a band that had first been plowed by Europeans in the early seventeenth century in Nova Scotia and Massachusetts, at Port Royale and Plymouth respectively. To the west of Prince Rupert lay the vast Pacific, and to the north the subarctic with agriculture restricted to little more than scattered meadows and garden patches. The homestead in the northern Queen Charlotte Islands, now long abandoned, where I write this introduction is within a tiny cluster of pioneer farms that became the ultimate, the westernmost geographical frontier opened by the railroad in North America. In the second decade of the twentieth century it could be believed there that livestock raising would be facilitated once a railroad reached the region, providing economic access to distant markets. But distance finally defeated those pioneer farmers even when possessed of a rail line at Prince Rupert. The cost of reaching the railroad from fields on an island sixty miles off the coast had to be added to narrow options there as to agricultural production (due to chilly climate) and a journey to market eastward measured in the thousands of miles. In the end this combination could not permit a viable agricultural frontier to come into existence; instead, only spatially unusual products such as the cut from huge cedar forests, the world's greatest halibut fishery, and a rare ecology could bring European-American settlers to this area and justify its being attached to the North American rail net. What began as a geographical abstraction—Canada's closest possible port to the Orient, used to justify building the Grand Trunk Pacific Railway to Prince Rupert—has recently become a true asset. Now that transpacific trade exceeds transatlantic, potential markets in the growing ports of the Pacific coast or even westward across the ocean itself may ultimately remove the "isolation" that defeated the earlier agricultural frontier sought here in the first decade of the twentieth century. Where that market is and how we may reach it have remained the most important questions that have arisen in the settlement and growth of economic activity in North America ever since the planting of European settlers on this continent began in the seventeenth century.

Enhanced mobility is an objective that most societies have sought as far back as recorded history gives us any idea as to the nature of human desires. But it was with the great push of European plantation of colonies overseas that a general urge became a historical imperative. Areas of colonization were distinctive, though hardly unique, in being characterized by directed expansion, usually from one or a few points of coastal attachment (entrepôts) toward a hinterland emerging as the developing colony grew inward into a large area of little or no previous economic development (as that term was understood by Europeans). Because the outward economic thrust of Europe across the world's oceans was engendered by primarily mercantile objectives, we usually seek to analyze its economic geography through reference to the tenets of a mercantilist system. In such a mercantilist model of settlement it is assumed that from initial points of attachment of the colonial system—located on the coast most easily reached from the colonizing mother country—a network of trading places is pushed outward into an economically underdeveloped interior, a network tied together by transportation routes and a system heavily emphasizing the externalization of commercial association. Improvements in mobility would automatically be expressed through enlargement of the economy. Similarly, the migration of individuals outward from the initial entrepôt would normally grow through a desire for some form of personal economic "growth"—perhaps originally merely in an individual's gaining his first in-fee-simple ownership of land, but subsequently in his gaining possession of better or more land. Because the frontier of exploration moves ahead of the frontier of settled experience, perceptions of the possible benefit to be secured from moving onward to a new settlement band could be in error. When mobility is not backed up by local resources, as in northern New England in the early nineteenth century or on the edges of subarctic Canada even today, experience often disappoints anticipations that further migration will be beneficial. But still, the advancing frontier is an integral necessity of such a mercantile model of settlement, and to secure it, improvement in transportation becomes a particular strong objective in vigorous and materially advancing societies, and an earnest of any serious settlement frontier.[1] Ultimately, on a frontier where resources are of limited distribution and are often concentrated at widely separated points, no more than linear settlement occurs in lengthy corridors of exploitation.

Certainly there is far more to the operation of transportation than simply facilitating human migration and extending mercantile frontiers. My initial attention to these limited aspects of a more complex activity grows out of a fundamental dichotomy in transportation experience that is frequently overlooked. This split lies between an *operational* and a *genetic* consideration of the activity, with the operational gaining ever greater interest the longer a form of transport has been in existence. There is now much concern for the recent growth of the civil aviation industry in North America, whereas far less attention is given to the fundamental transformations taking place in North American railroading. The assumption seems common that the railroad is a nineteenth-century creation wherein little has changed since 1945. Because the genetic is downplayed in current writing about railroads, I seek here to right the balance a bit, particularly as the future sound operation of railroads will be advanced by a better conception of why lines came into existence and why and how they have changed during their century and a half of existence.

Another dichotomy that has characterized our common consideration of railroad evolution lies in the specific concerns that have been attacked. Railroad history lies well within the general field of history and thus is most commonly written by professional historians, who have a methodology described by the term *historiography*—literally the writing of history, but in practice the "proper" approach to that activity, implying measures of appropriateness for the sources used to reconstruct the past. Most historiography greatly favors the written record from the past as the source for reconstructing those times, for patent reasons. The result has been a skewing of interest toward those past acts that tended to be recorded and against those that may be equally or even more fundamental in the subsequent operation of a railroad, but that are recorded only in engineering works (though these can be as readable as epigraphy or texts). For the geographer this skewing shows up in the historians' failure to attend to the actual location of rail lines. The nature and placement of the route often seems in the writing of historians to be determined by actions taken in the boardroom and recorded in the minutes, rather than stemming from terrain, settlement fabric, economic activity, and operating characteristics of locomotives and other equipment. Assembling a "system" from the bits and pieces of rail line, often built for initially quite distinctly different purposes, is important —and there is a legitimate interest in analyzing that activity—but how can we go on commencing genesis only when records begin?

Here we discover the fundamental distinction between *history* and *historical geography*. The latter is not merely history placed on the landscape; it is instead the study of the continuing interaction between human beings and the land on which they live and act. Since the Italians in the Middle Ages first devised a system of book- and record-keeping to administer economic activity conducted significantly elsewhere, space and place record-keeping has sought to downplay geographical concerns, thus encouraging through sound historiographic practice a similarly aspatial history. For the historical geographer this practice is not only unfortunate but also obstructs his fundamental purpose. Thus, the aspects of railroad history that have an innate need to consider space and its highly differentiated nature must turn in addition to historical geography, which may use observation of terrain characteristics, of mappable (but not often specifically recorded) distribution patterns, and of spatial interactions to make its broader form of analysis.

It is from looking at the geographical aspects of railroading that we ultimately become aware of perhaps the most significant of all dichotomies associated with railroad history, that between the spatial aspects of the railway as it emerged in England and Wales in the first quarter of the nineteenth century and those of the railroad as it emerged less than a decade later in North America, particularly the United States. Simply stated, this contrast lay between the *railway* (using that term specifically to designate the British technology and its associated geographical expression) and the *railroad* (restricting that term to the North American technology and geography). In Britain the railway came in to provide additional capacity and cheaper transportation in an already well-developed economy that had affected all but a few peripheral areas of the nation. The market was in existence, and the prospect of substantial earnings from the conduct of transportation was clear if private investors undertook the construction of a rail line.

The Geographical Background of the British Railway

There had already been fairly lengthy "plateways," "railways," or "tramways" built in Britain to carry heavy commodities, most notably coal. The influence of grades opposing the direction of loaded movement was well understood in an economic sense, as was the benefit to be secured from using iron rails to guide and support the wheels of the wagons used in transport. For fifty years in the earlier installations these various (commonly gravity) railways had demonstrated the economic advantages they offered and the fundamental geographical features involved. The influences of grade and curvature on the cost of operating a rail line were well understood several decades before there was any thought of employing mechanical and animal traction—even human haulage, in several instances—rather than gravity propulsion. The geography of the railway was established in the very earliest years of operation in the late eighteenth century. The desiderata were determined by the use of the guideway, particularly the iron "edge rail" that both supported and led the wheels of the wagon. The broader the curves, the less problem was posed by the fact that the inner rail was shorter than the outer, and thus that the fixed wheels typical of wagons had to travel different distances. On curves of a mile radius or more there was such a small percentage difference between the length of the two rails that there was little dragging of the longer-running wheel by the shorter. Thus, friction was greatly reduced and tractive effort held to a minimum.

A second concern rested with the effort to overcome gravity. It was easily demonstrated that the least tractive effort was needed for a track descending with the direction of goods flow. Most early coal-carrying plateways were built with such descending track—facing an opposing grade only in the return of empty wagons to the top of the "battery" or "bank"—and in that way actually used gravity to cheapen the cost of operation. Where gravity could not be harnessed, the effort turned toward minimizing its adverse impact through the development of a level line, even at the considerable cost of bridging intervening valleys so that the line could avoid dropping into the valley and having to climb out of it on the other side. Some truly substantial arch bridges were thrown across valleys well before steam ever came to the railways. Experience taught that a level, or nearly level, track greatly reduced the economic cost of providing transport.

Given that grade and curvature affected the cost of operation, it seems accurate to argue that geography, in the sense of terrain, became a determinant of the location of railways from the earliest years of their construction. Where markets for their use were large and prospective earnings substantial, as they were in England and Wales, it became sound business practice for investors to expend considerable sums to improve on natural terrain. If embankments, cuts, and tunnels could reduce the sharpness of curves or the steepness of grades, prudence called for making larger investments to gain those benefits for future operation. As Britain was in the early railway era the source of capitalist investment ahead of all other countries, it is axiomatic both that the early railways built there had access to the capital needed for such amelioration of the terrain, and that they used it. Thus, in its geographical features the early British railway was highly ameliorative, this even in a landscape of no true mountains and mostly maturely graded streams flowing in normally wide valleys.

What controlled the broad-scale location of rail lines was, of course, the geography of the major settlements. Because in Britain the railway was introduced after the onset of the Industrial Revolution, with its great emphasis on the production of coal and iron ore and the manufacture and shipping of goods, it was the major manufacturing and trading towns, and the ports for the overseas shipment of manufactures and the receipt of raw-material "returns," that gave the primary triangulation to the rail net. Bristol to London, Liverpool to Manchester, and Birmingham to London were predictable termini of early lines. Pioneering on these lines consisted of trying to determine the existing size of the market, to see if it would support the private investment involved, rather than testing the likelihood for settlement and its possible size and scale of development and employment. The fact that the true railway towns of Britain, those actually created by the railway, can be tallied on one hand gives us a clear perspective on the direct effect rails have on settlement. To borrow Fred Nussbaum's distinction, rails in Britain were almost never "city founding," but they were importantly "city filling." Thus, the early locating engineers almost never had any problems determining where the railways were going; in fact, the government gave the Board of Trade the major say on that question. Rather, those engineers had to find routes that could be laid out to gain the best conditions of grade and curvature possible between the existing termini.

Because a well-developed economic geography predated even the earliest common-carrier rail lines, the site for major settlement was heavily influenced by local, preindustrial conditions. That site might prove awkward for rail access; it was up to the locating engineers to find an economically usable route. If that took money, there was money to accomplish the job.

It was the necessity to accept and make useful for rails an established settlement pattern that defined the major qualities of the British railway. Within an existing market these lines had money to expand generously. Only where the settlement fabric was niggardly—as it was, for example, when Isambard Kingdom Brunel insisted on pushing an early line into the narrow confines of Cornwall—was investment capital in short supply. In that case what resulted was an acceptance of the cheaper expedients—wooden bridges and steeper grades—that characterized established North American practice. Another quality of the British railway was the clear anticipation of the ultimate benefit to be gained by large initial investments that would secure more economical operation of the line. The canal and the turnpike had shown British investors the ultimate profit to be secured from reducing line operating costs within a well-developed market. And on the horse-drawn tramways that were the ancestor of the British railways, light grades and broad curves had been shown to be the key to low operating costs. Those tramways had shown that a single horse could move many tons, given the best possible track on which to do the job. It became established wisdom in Britain that with a "properly" built line, a small tractive force could show up to good effect.

The last point needs some further discussion, for it helps to explain yet another aspect of the transatlantic contrast in rail development. The Newcastle "railways," as the originally horse-drawn coal-transporting lines were called in the Northeast of England, and the "tramways" of the South Wales coal field were the site of early experiments looking toward the application of steam power to traction. Because in each of these areas gravity had earlier been harnessed to provide part of the pull for the trains of coal wagons heading for staiths for loading on schooners, and because engineering had been called upon to provide the best possible conditions of curvature and grade, little tractive effort was in fact called into use. In some places boys were used on these trains, mainly as brakemen to constrain the roll down to the loading port. I would argue that geography and engineering thus accustomed British railway builders to unpowered or underpowered operating conditions. Where gravity and good track were not to be had—and where canals were impracticable because of cost or terrain—coal simply did not move beyond the range of economically supportable wagon transport. Given that experience of transport by rail at the cost of small tractive effort, the early attempts at substituting steam power for animal traction were less demanding than might have been the case in other areas and different societies. Starting in 1804, with Richard Trevithick's experiments in South Wales, small "locomotive engines" were used on the tramways. By the close of the Napoleonic Wars these primitive engines had come into moderate use in Britain. The fact that most were of very low steam pressure, and thus mechanically most inefficient, was not critical. They were not asked to provide that much traction. George Stephenson, whose work as an engine wright on the Newcastle railways fell into this pattern of low-pressure, low-powered locomotives, thought this the way matters should be. Low-pressure engines were safe, less demanding in manufacture, and already fully in hand. Stephenson did, however, equally fully understand that one had to have the location engineering to go along with such engines. Curves must be made wide, grades kept well below 1 percent, and tunnels and viaducts constructed wherever needed to gain those objectives.

It is impossible at this remove to solve the problem of whether the generally weak locomotives characteristic of early rail operations in Britain brought about the practice of heavily engineered lines or whether the heavy-built lines simply permitted locomotives to be less powerful. In any event, the functional association of less powerful engines and superbly engineered lines became established. What this meant economically was that initial investments had to be very considerable indeed, whereas operating cost could be kept rather low. This seemed sound practice to the British mind, and in truth it would have been elsewhere if all the world had been like Britain. North Americans, however, realized as early as the late 1820s that British conditions were not universally the case, though many later-day Britons have been slow in accepting that fact. What I wish to suggest is that the British railway was an economically sound design and is an enduring solution to the mechanical transport of masses of people and large quantities of goods when, genetically, the market is well-developed. It has become a truism of transportation theory that it pays to substitute money in early investment in facilities for continuous later expenditure in operation. The capital used for the construction of facilities is invested once, while the charge for expensive operation is incurred each time the train passes by.

Like many "truths," this one has geographical limits. In the developed market under capitalism, it is a truth; in the no more than emergent market with little capital accumulated and the ultimate economic geography still undetermined, it is a dogma at best. It would have been irrational, probably economically impossible, for British railway practice to have been adopted at all widely. History tells us that where conditions were most like Britain's, British railway technology was rapidly—and normally effectively—adopted. Belgium shared with the United States the designation as the second country in time to experience the Industrial Revolution. There is, however, a sharp geographical distinction between the two. Belgium had been well settled and economically developed since the High Middle Ages; the United States had neither of those qualities when railroads were first built. Only a tiny part of the United States was affected by industrialization for some decades. The technical and social organization characteristic of an industrial society was known in America, but only narrowly. Even though industry in Belgium was not widespread at first, being restricted mostly to the former prince bishopric of Liège, dense settlement and highly evolved economic development characterized most of the components of the kingdom as it rose in 1830. Because of its highly developed economy found within a densely settled area, Belgium was able to make the investment necessary to follow British railway practice.

After 1830 George Stephenson was invited by the new king of the Belgians to locate and supervise the construction of a basic "cross" of British-style lines reaching from Ostend in the west to the German border at Aachen in the east and intersecting at Malines (Mechelen) a north-south line from Mons to Antwerp. Because of the split between the Netherlands and Belgium in a civil war in 1830, the Dutch denied the brand-new kingdom use of its traditional routes to the sea via the Meuse (Maas) and the Scheldt, the mouths of which remained in Dutch hands. If Belgium was to survive economically at the advanced level it enjoyed, a new route to the sea would have to be found for it, just as a new port would have to be developed in the dunes of Ostend. This was an archetypal situation for British-style railway development—a highly developed market, with a basically capitalist economy well provided with investment funds, that faced an immediate and massive need to enlarge or replace the traditional transportation system. Thus, it is in no way difficult to explain why the new kingdom was the first to develop a national plan for railways and the first to complete that construction as the state actually undertook the financing of the trunk-line system.

The Geographical Background of the North American Railroad

We have considered the nature of that British railway system and the reasons for its coming into existence. Now we must describe the type of North American rail facility that stood in broad contrast. The need for improved mobility approached universality; but actual rail construction necessarily reflected sharp regional differences in developed economic geography, settlement pattern, and terrain. Western Europe was long and densely settled, generally quite flat or gently rolling in landscape, and more industrialized than any other area on earth. In northeastern North America economic development was far less advanced than on the other side of the Atlantic, towns were smaller and farther apart, and the terrain was widely mountainous with both deep valley dissection and heavy glaciation—difficult country for highly engineered rail lines. As new

8

THE NORTH
AMERICAN
RAILROAD

lands, Canada and the United States had low levels of capital accumulation attached to high levels of uncertainty about the ultimate pattern of settlement and industrialization. No tradition of public expenditure in aid of transportation had been transferred from Britain, where the leading forms of transport were the canals, essentially all privately built, and the "turnpike trust," similarly the product of capitalist investment in facilities to aid the transport of goods in return for the payment of tolls. In an area where terrain was difficult, money was scarce, practice was against any governmental support for the construction of transportation facilities, and the patterns of settlement and economic geography were still in doubt, the British system of rail design and operation was fundamentally irrational; certainly it was unaccomplishable. There had to be a different system, one responding to North American conditions, if there was to be any rail construction.

The nature of the North American system of railroad development was shaped mainly by the geography of the area a century and a half ago. The settlement fabric of the new republic was still quite limited once one traveled any great distance back from the Atlantic coast, and even on the coast the level of industrialization was low save in a few valleys adjacent to Providence, Boston, the Hudson River, and Philadelphia. Capital was accumulating in the northeastern ports, though it remained scarce elsewhere and was none too plentiful even in the Northeast. Between that coastal development and the vast interior of the country, extending politically then to the crest of the Rocky Mountains, lay first the deeply dissected Appalachians with their steep slopes and narrow valleys, and then the vast plains, in some places fully fifteen hundred miles wide. What towns existed west of the Atlantic coastal plain were small and were located almost entirely in relation to navigable rivers and the Great Lakes. It seemed that there were neither the markets, the settlements, nor the goods moving that had called British railways into being. Yet Americans felt a tremendous need for transportation development. In 1808 Albert Gallatin, then secretary of the treasury, had submitted to Congress a significant report calling for an extensive and integrated effort at improving on the natural waterways and trails that had been the only routeways available for the first two centuries of European-American existence. Written just before the railroad came to be perceived as a practicable common carrier of goods and people, Gallatin's report proposed a series of canals across the Appalachians as well as what later developed as a second set connecting the Ohio and Mississippi rivers with the Great Lakes. Before the railroad became a seriously considered alternative form of routeway, as it did just after 1825, a number of canals had been undertaken, some even in the trans-Appalachian West. There could be no doubt that Americans saw both the need for improved transportation—even in a pioneering time and in frontier areas—and the great support such improvement would offer to the economic development of the areas away from the Atlantic coast.

It is necessary at this point to recall that the basic nature of North American settlement by Europeans was different from some of the earlier stages of European economic evolution. The Old World had a long tradition of autarky and the localized economy. The manor had a localized economic geography, which tended to reduce trade with its peers to the very restricted scale of an exchange of luxuries. The labor practices of the attendant serfdom created

Introduction

personal immobility, which meant that few people indeed ever ventured beyond the immediate horizon of the place where they had been born. Of course, there would have been no Europeans in North America—Canada fully as much as the United States—in the first place if such a localization of economy and immobilization of people had remained dominant. And as the early settlers from Europe increased in numbers with the passage of generations, their descendants may have moved out to new frontiers, but they had no notion of there engaging in the subsistence agriculture that would have prevailed without improvements in transportation.

If the North American dream was to be realized for Europeans, there had to be continuing improvements in transportation so as to achieve the commercial agriculture, the capitalist mining, fishing, and lumbering, and the distant trading that promised rapid economic advance to the successive generations of settlers. In this situation the urge for transportation development was fully as strong in the New World as it then was in the Old; the main difference lay in the practical ability to advance along the lines of the building of British-style railways. Neither the construction skills nor the requisite amounts of capital were available. The two choices open to the North Americans were either to restrict their transportation improvements to the small reasonably developed region of the continent, or to devise a rail technology that could be utilized near the economic and settlement frontiers (which in North America advanced rapidly, and in harness). Being both ingenious and enterprising, those Americans took the basic idea of the railed route and turned it into an almost entirely indigenous creation. As we shall see, British engineering technology in most of its details and the British locomotive in all but its most basic concepts were abandoned, and an autochthonous style of location, engineering, propulsion, and operation was devised for New World use. It seems that little more than the track gauge was successfully carried across the Atlantic, much to our ultimate disadvantage in that case.

This book, then, is about the railroad that is native to North America, and thereby distinctly different from the slightly earlier British creation. That North American railroad lacked the long, slow evolution that railed ways of one sort or another had had in Europe. These railed ways first appeared during the late Middle Ages in mining operations in Germany, Bohemia, and Austria, where horse or even human traction was used. Only in the seventeenth century did evolution begin to proceed most strongly in Britain, because of the expansion of coal mining there. And only at the very beginning of the nineteenth century did steam power come to be associated with the hauling of trains on these "railways" or "plateways." These mineral lines were known to a number of migrants to the New World, and we can lump within a general transferred European heritage the notion of the rail-guided and rail-supported way for the transport of heavy products.

Because the New World settlements were mainly planted along the rivers that gave shelter to transatlantic ships landing migrants and taking raw materials eastward in return, there was almost no provision made in colonial times for costly improvements to natural transport routes. It came to be seen that settlement would be made only where nature provided a costless route. Only later, as industrialization was introduced—based almost entirely on waterpower gained at falls or rapids—and general economic development brought about a geographical expansion of trade, did money have to be spent to gain a usable route. At that juncture the best European practice called for canal building, so North America began to build canals to gain the cheapest general improvement in its transportation by adding no more than small artificial increments to its magnificent natural waterways. Thus, the earliest railways built were small, localized, and specialized installations.

In the United States early railways were built in Boston to aid in the removal of the top of Beacon Hill to provide fill for the Back Bay, and at Great Blue Hill in Quincy for use in a granite quarry. In Canada it was transferred Royal Engineers who built early works-railways used in the construction of the Citadel in Québec City and other defense installations on the Canadian side of the Niagara Gorge. These direct borrowings from European railed transport were so limited as not to prove too costly for the New World in the years around 1825. But when larger applications of rails to movement were envisaged, as they were around that year, no direct implementation of British practice came to anything. It waited upon the development of an autochthonous railroad system for any significant construction to take place.

Initially, of course, there was no specifically "American practice." Printed materials and visits by American civil engineers to Britain at first proceeded along the assumption of the superiority of British practice. Healthy American skepticism, however, was soon called into play, and after a period of experimentation a widely adopted American practice was established. By 1850 that practice was set in its general characteristics. I set out here to look into the evolutionary elements that brought a distinctive North American railroad into existence within a period of no more than a decade—and did so in such a way that by the middle of the nineteenth century, any modest element of imported British railway practice had usually become submerged in indigenous practice. This was almost entirely true in the United States by that time, and it became increasingly true in Canada (save on the Grand Trunk Railway, which was operated from London until it disappeared in bankruptcy at the time of the First World War).

Before setting about this historical geography of the North American railroad, we should take brief note of the organization of our search. Chapter 1 considers the period when North Americans, particularly citizens of the United States, sought to create a railroad that they could afford to build, and one suited to the very particular demands for transportation in the new land. History provides a convenient breaking point, the close of the year 1852: within about eighteen months of that time, six railroads were completed across the Appalachians, dramatically overcoming what had until then remained the great barrier to European settlement and mercantile expansion. It was in this trans-Appalachian advance that the form and characteristic geography of the North American railroad were established. The railroad as an expression of hope and confidence was first fully demonstrated in this surmounting of the mountain barrier; thereby an instrument of national growth was created.

With that instrument in hand, what became the world's most effulgent agricultural region grew up "on the railroad," stretching uninterrupted from the backslope of the Appalachians in Québec, Vermont, and upstate New York to the edge of the Great North at Fort Vermilion in the Peace River Country of northern Alberta, and to the Great West in the Rockies at the spine of the continent. This simultaneous shaping of the world's most extensive integrated railroad system—over three hundred thousand miles of line, which stood as nearly a third of all such rail line on earth—and its greatest of all agricultural realms shows most conclusively that the North American railroad served as the instrument of geographical development of a previously inconceivable scale. Chapter 2 examines the shaping of that partnership in the American Middle West, as well as the creation of the practices and limits that were to determine the further evolution of the North American system. Because this middle-western experience made further expansion a matter for public participation, the chapter also describes how a plan of national support was established, and it details the great surveys undertaken in the United States in the 1850s and in Canada in the 1870s to establish a geography of publicly aided railroads.

These lines were built mostly beyond the settlement and economic frontiers of their time. Thus, once construction was completed, the need arose to create systems determined not, as the construction had been, by the national pattern of transportation sought by public investment, but instead by the shaping of private companies that could survive profitably, as had been the objective of the private investors engaged in this "mixed private-public investment." This effort toward "survival" of railroads in the two North American democracies forms the tale of chapter 3, in which the geographical strategy of railroad corporations is assessed. As there had been a quite complex evolution of that strategy, some of the ground covered in the earlier chapters is necessarily repeated here. The conclusion, however, is carried down to the last few years with the creation of some seven massive semicontinental companies in the United States and two truly transcontinental companies in Canada.

In order to remain economically sound, the railroad companies attempted to transform and enlarge ownership patterns previously worked out in small, initial-stage intercity railroads. This integration was achieved by assembling small first-stage companies and by filling gaps through construction and consolidation into regional rail systems. But the influence of the frontier on railroad development has not totally disappeared. Yet another stage of development is being shaped, this time on the resource frontier of Canada, where actual field observation can be made and works either under construction or recently completed can be studied.

Chapter 4 examines the active creation of railroad geography since the Second World War, essentially entirely in Canada. There we can observe the persistence of practices and geographical patterns formed early in the history of the railroad in North America. The railroad thus remains a major instrument of economic development, just as it was a century and a half ago. Many practices remain the same; what differs are the much larger pool of capital now available in North America and the existence today of an actual, approachable world market whose satisfaction can be translated into investment and physical construction on the North American economic frontier in northern and western Canada.

CHAPTER ONE

The North American Railroad Rises in the East

An Instrument of National Development

W hen word reached North America of the technological improvement of the older horse-drawn railways through the use of steam traction, European settlement in that vast developing land was only two centuries old. For the first of those centuries the major effort had gone into gaining a foothold on the shore; for the second the undertaking had been to use the rivers to advance the mercantile frontier into the body of the continent. By the early nineteenth century American economic development had, through these pioneering technologies, become sufficiently advanced to encounter stresses of the sort that engenders innovation in transport. The first of these stresses was typical of growing capitalist economies, particularly those experiencing the strains of industrialization, wherein the facilities of transport adequate for less geographically extensive and integrated systems simply became clogged by the increasing demands for movement. The solution to the problem so much the *raison d'être* of railroad building in western Europe was made as necessary in the northeastern United States not by equivalent volumes of trade, but rather by the seasonality of river and canal transport in a cold continental climate, where ice impeded navigation for four to five months a year. For Europe and the northeastern United States, the railroad came to give relief to a maximally taxed system of movement inherited from an earlier, less active economy.

The second stress found in North America was particular to its history as the first of the areas of mercantilist development projected outward from a hearth in northwestern Europe. As such, the new lands of Canada and the United States had no transportation patrimony, although they did have an inheritance from nature that was fully exploited during the seventeenth through mid-nineteenth centuries. But where waterways shoaled because of aridity or ramification into headwaters too minute to have water for more than canoes— America's first great contribution to early inland navigation, as the flatboat became later—some alternative transport became critically desirable. Geographically, that need for a new transportation beyond the frontier of the devel-

13

oped economy, the *oecumene,* took two forms: the search for a solution to the watershed problem, and the search for a solution to the aridity problem.

Save in the Far North, where the Erie Canal can be thought a successful and enduring "development," the Appalachian barrier thwarted effective waterway construction, leaving to the later technology of the railroad an immediate field of endeavor. At the Rocky Mountain backbone of the continent, that necessity of crossing a water parting was ever more obvious and extended, as well as being tied fairly directly to the second of the geographical expressions of American railroad building—that is, the creation of transportation in arid regions. It was as American interests in transportation first came to be focused on the Great Plains that this particularly North American purpose for the railroad emerged. In the watershed railroads of Europe—the lines from St. Etienne to Lyon, from Linz to Budweis, from Liège to Cologne—there had been a conditional expression of "aridity" wherein the higher ground at the edge of the basins was insufficiently watered to make canal building economical, a situation also encountered in the Appalachian crossing; but it was only when the climatic and regionally extensive dryness of the Great Plains was encountered that the problem was expressed in earnest.

This is all analysis after the fact, with the neatness and clarity such appraisals confer on what were originally rather inchoate-seeming events. Developers of rail lines in the 1820s and the 1830s hardly sat at their drawing boards reminding themselves that they now faced a watershed and a railroad was therefore in order. Rather, they were aware of the existence of a specific situation in which traditional waterborne transport simply would not do the job. At that time the roads were so poor and the animal traction available on them so inefficient and limited that the only rational alternative—that is, supplement—to waterways was the steam locomotive running on an iron-rail pavement and guideway. Word of this technology had come from two sources: the increasingly successful efforts of Richard Trevithick and other English mechanics to create mining railways, and the stillborn proposals for steam traction on a railway made by Oliver Evans in the United States in 1812.[1] A year earlier Colonel John Stevens of Hoboken had applied to the New Jersey legislature for a charter to permit him to build a railroad, and in 1812 he published perhaps the first railroad tract to be issued in America, *Documents Tending to Prove the Superior Advantages of Steam Railways and Steam Carriages over Canal Navigation.*[2]

Stevens, a man of some inherited wealth, had combined an interest in public office with an avocation for practical science akin to present-day engineering. In 1804 he had constructed a boat using a screw propeller, which missed by only a few weeks being the first steamboat successfully demonstrated in the United States and practicably employed in the world. When Robert Fulton gained a monopoly for navigation by steam in the waters of New York State for his *Clermont* of 1804, Stevens turned his efforts back on his pioneering *Propeller,* making improvements that were to be found in the *Phoenix* launched soon thereafter. Ships of Stevens's design came into use on the Connecticut and the Delaware, outside the Fulton monopoly area. Thus, the New Jersey colonel had experience with steam-powered vessels when a serious proposal for a canal across New York State was broached around 1812. Perhaps it was the economic and operational realities of inland navigation already clear in his mind that

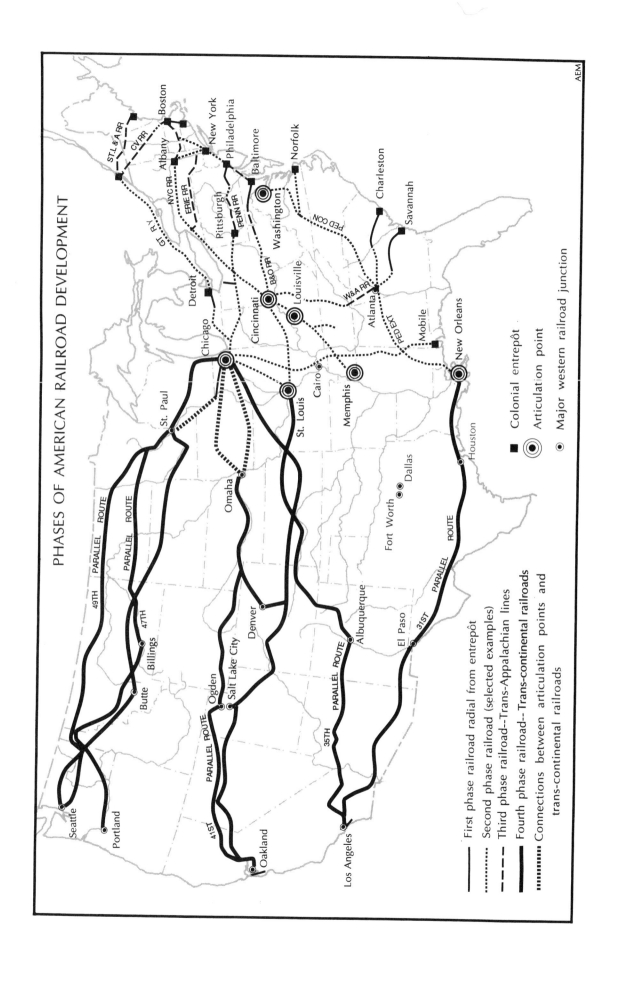

PHASES OF AMERICAN RAILROAD DEVELOPMENT

First phase railroad radial from entrepôt
Second phase railroad (selected examples)
Third phase railroad—Trans-Appalachian lines
Fourth phase railroad—Trans-continental railroads
Connections between articulation points and
trans-continental railroads

■ Colonial entrepôt
◉ Articulation point
⊙ Major western railroad junction

caused the commodore of this river fleet to urge upon the New York Canal Commissioners the substitution of "rail-ways and steam carriages" for the canal and horse-drawn barges. In proposing a substitution Stevens propounded a number of assumptions that came to be borne out by experience in the American historical geography of transportation.

In calling for the building of railroads even where canals might have their most practicable application, Stevens argued cogently for a national system of integrated transportation whose construction lay within the financial and technical competence of a largely undeveloped nation:

The extension and completion of the main arteries of such a system of communication would by no means be a work of [an extended] time. It would be exempted totally from the difficulties, embarrassments, casualties, interruptions, and delays incident to the formation of canals. Requiring no supply of water—no precision and accuracy in levelling, the work could be commenced and carried on in various detached parts— its progress would be rapid, and its completion could be ascertained with certainty. Innumerable ramifications would from time to time be extended in every direction. Thus would the sources of private and public wealth, going hand in hand, increase with a rapidity beyond all parallel. For every shilling contributed towards the [public] revenue, a dollar at least would be put into the hands of individuals.[3]

This appeal to the national desire to create capital was linked to an obvious geographical need to integrate economically a domain that extended from the Atlantic seaboard to the Rocky Mountains. Of the railroad Stevens noted,

The celerity of communication it would afford with the distant sections of our wide extended empire, is a consideration of the utmost moment. To the rapidity of the motion of the steam-carriage on these rail-ways, no definite limit can be set. The Flying Proas, as they are called by voyagers, belonging to the natives of the Islands of the Pacific Ocean, are said at times to sail at the rate of more than twenty miles an hour. But as the resistance of the water to the progress of a vessel increases as the square of her velocity, it is obvious that the power required to propel her must also increase at the same ratio. Not so with a steam-carriage—as it moves in a fluid 800 times more rare than water, the resistance will be proportionably diminished. Indeed the principal resistance to its motion arises from friction, which does not even increase in a direct ratio with the velocity of carriage. If, then, a Proa can be driven by wind (the propulsive power of which is constantly diminishing as the velocity of the Proa increases) through so dense a fluid as water, at the rate of twenty miles an hour, I can see nothing to hinder a steam-carriage from moving on these ways with a velocity of one hundred miles an hour.[4]

In an interchange of proposals he conducted with the New York Canal Commissioners, reprinted in his pamphlet, Stevens argued several basic points that were ultimately to prove fundamental in American transportation geography. Responding to Robert Livingston's objections that railroads would be more costly than canals, he held that "the expense of rail-ways [will be] one-fourth that of a canal."[5] But even more, he argued the general utility of the railroad in a developing country where capital was scarce, construction expertise was limited, and the ultimate geography of economic activity and settlement was still to be shaped. "It cannot be denied then, that these circumstances must render the travel on these rail-ways *very convenient*."[6] The commissioners interposed the objection that it was impossible to assume that such heavy tonnages as Stevens

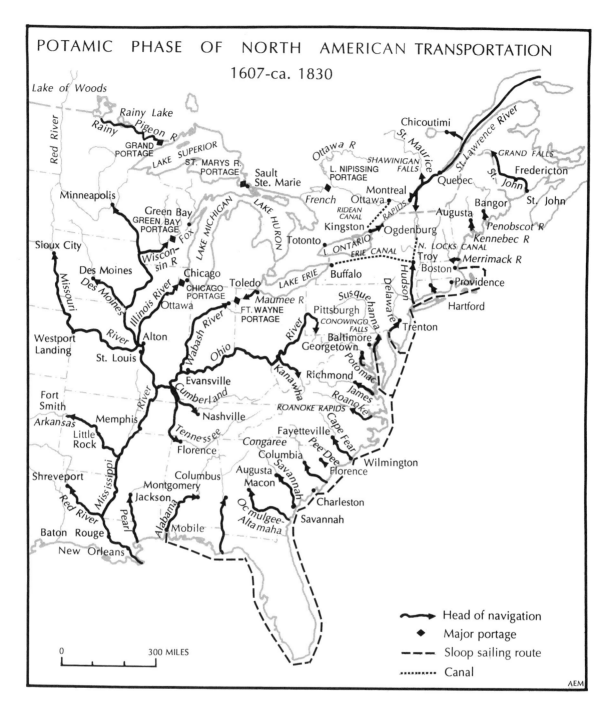

POTAMIC PHASE OF NORTH AMERICAN TRANSPORTATION
1607-ca. 1830

Head of navigation
Major portage
Sloop sailing route
Canal

0   300 MILES

AEM

predicted could be drawn by steam engine, to which he responded with a clear
and concise statement of the advantages that rails held over roads in the transport of goods of great weight.

Probably the weakest point in Stevens's proposal was the infrastructure of
the line. The colonel envisioned a set of wooden rails of pine topped with a
cladding of oak, carried as stringers on posts raised several feet above the
ground. Thus, there would not have been the rock ballast that came to be
standard on American as well as British lines. Quite possibly it was because of
Stevens's proposal that two of the pioneering American lines—the South Caroli-

na Railroad, the first long line to open, and the New York and Erie, the first expression of the line across New York State that Stevens sought—started building on such a raised structure. The argument that the snow would blow under the tracks rather than lying on them had validity in the Southern Tier of New York State where the Erie was commenced; but between Charleston and Hamburg the utility of this fabric is harder to establish, though it was seen in the absence of any need to build culverts or bridges where the rails crossed small streams. There was some notion of placing iron straps on the pine stringers, but Stevens tended to resist that plan because of the high cost and scarcity of iron in the United States. One can only wonder if the Jerseyman's proposal would not have been given more attention if he had grasped the nettle directly and called for iron rails. But in America in 1812 the notion of iron in such abundance seemed too uneconomical to be entertained.

The fact that finally worked most heavily against Stevens was that "the great utility of canals is 'sanctioned by experience' whereas the practical utility of rail-ways, on the proposed construction, remains to be ascertained by actual experiment." Calling for such experimental testing of his ideas, he still foresaw probable defeat. But "sooner or later, . . . the improvement now proposed will be brought into general use, and, if I mistake not, long before the projected canal will be completed."[7] Stevens was off by about a decade, but the force of his argument was vastly greater than he could imagine.

This 1812 proposal seems to me to demonstrate that American railroad development was not merely derivative from British practice, as was the case in Europe where the Belgian lines were heavily influenced by the work of Stephenson in particular. In the United States, Oliver Evans, John Stevens, Gridley Bryant, and others interested in "internal improvements" and mechanical development created an independent tradition of railroad construction that was insulated from British practice by distance and by a deficiency of financial support. Only in the earliest locomotives was there much borrowing, and Americans very quickly found that they could make much better engines than they could import. It seems accurate to hold that Europe's main contribution to American railroad building came from the general awareness of rail-guided ways brought across the Atlantic by immigrants from the mining districts of Germany, Wales, and England. In the late eighteenth century such light railways had been used to good effect in the transport of riverboats, at the inclined plane constructed at the South Hadley Falls of the Connecticut River, and probably at construction and industrial sites. An inclined plane on Beacon Hill in Boston was constructed in about 1795, to be followed in 1807 by a short railway near the same site. Philadelphia had such a short wooden-railed route in experimental form in 1809. Quarries soon adopted rail pavements and guideways, so by the time Stevens wrote his tract, the European technology was fairly widely known and had been applied in the more settled parts of the Northeast, as well as in Britain's Canadian colony.[8]

Gridley Bryant's Granite Railway

All the very early experimental lines in the United States were short, were constructed for a most limited private purpose, and used wooden rails, as envisaged in Stevens's proposal to the New York Canal Commissioners. In this they differed not importantly from the medieval lines of German miners. The great shift toward the railroad as we know it came near Boston in 1826, when the first American line to employ ironclad rails was constructed. Clearly, this construction represented a direct borrowing from British practice on the "Newcastle mineral railways," but as we shall see, almost immediately the realities of American resources forced a radical transformation of that infrastructure to conform with an emerging American purpose that called for the use of railroads as a direct element in the effort toward regional development.

Before looking at the general situation, it is well to examine the Granite Railway, the first direct ancestor of what came to be the world's most extensive rail system. In 1825 it was decided to commemorate the Battle of Bunker Hill on the occasion of its fiftieth anniversary. The monument decided upon was the first of a series of obelisks that came to be the *signa* of patriotic virtue in nineteenth-century America. Classicism in Boston was of a higher order than elsewhere, so this obelisk had to be shaped from granite, preferably the syenitic granite the ancient Egyptians had quarried at Aswan and other places in Upper Egypt. In the neighborhood of Boston good-quality syenite was to be had in Quincy, so the monument trustees bought the ledge and set out to get the stone out. Fortunately, in 1803 local men in Quincy had discovered how to split the syenite through the use of wedges, so massive dressed blocks for use in the monument could be produced.9 What remained was to move the huge blocks the dozen miles to Breed's Hill in Charlestown where the battle had been fought and the 220-foot monument was to be built. Boats could be used from a wharf on the Neponset River (three miles from the ledge) to the foot of the drumlin where the patriots had inflicted such losses on the British. That three miles from the wharf to the ledge posed the problem, which the developer of the quarry, an ingenious Yankee builder named Gridley Bryant, proposed to solve by building a "rail-way." In this he departed little from what had been done earlier at mineral sites; what lent distinction to his efforts was the relatively generous financial backing he gained, most notably from Boston's premier merchant, Thomas Handasyd Perkins.10

With funds probably amounting to some $50,000, Bryant was well able to build whatever his inventive mind might devise. He is generally credited with the invention of the eight-wheel freight car—an indication that from the very beginning, the scale of transport here was much larger than in Europe. Because knowledge of British mineral railways was quite unspecific in America, Bryant simply set about designing most of the features of his railroad for himself. Switches, turntables, and mobile cranes were of his own devising. Even the rail responded to the availability of resources in America. The heavy frosts of Massachusetts worried the early advocates of railroads, so Bryant had his line laid on a foundation "formed by digging a trench two feet wide and about the same depth, which was filled with stone, compactly laid, without mortar." Across these parallel trenches were laid granite crossties, which in turn carried pine beams ("rails"), six inches thick and twelve inches high, that were capped by a strip of oak, three inches wide and two inches thick, clad on top for the full width by a quarter-inch-thick strap of iron. As time passed granite "rail" capped directly by iron straps came to be substituted for much of the pine.11 The

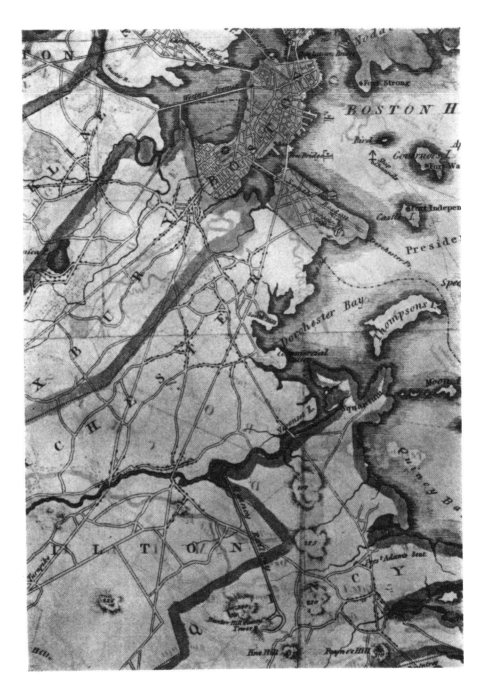

Map of the first North American railroad, Quincy, 1825. *Source:* Granite Railway Co., *The First Railroad in America.* Privately printed and published, 1926.

essential point is that in this earliest phase of railroad development in America, even on such a well-financed line as the Granite Railway, builders found it necessary to develop a distinctive fabric better suited than any "British model" to local capital limitations and the high cost of iron. Even Edward Kirkland, who sees a stronger tie between early American and British rail-building practice than I do—mainly because he is mostly concerned with written records and history rather than geographical patterns—refers to Gridley Bryant as being in the "Massachusetts-English school of railroad engineering."[12] Certainly much in that school, as indicated by Bryant's work, was sharply different from English practice even in the very earliest years. The swivel truck (four-wheeled), the generous loading gauge, and the strongly experimental nature of much of

Bryant's work make too close an attribution of British precedent quite unfair to a man who could ably think for himself.

The most interesting feature of the Granite Railway, and the aspect that more than anything else justifies calling it "America's first railroad," came as a result of the town of Milton's approval of its construction. The ledge to be quarried lay within that town, so its approval had to be gained, along with that of Quincy where the Neponset wharf was located. The two-mile line was sufficiently long that a right-of-way could hardly be secured without engendering intractable opposition from some landowners, objections that might be resolved only through purchase under the principle of eminent domain. To exercise that aspect of sovereignty, the approval of the commonwealth of Massachusetts— and indirectly, of its basic subdivision, the town—had to be sought. On April 3, 1826, the Milton town meeting voted "unanimous and cordial consent so long as said corporation [the Granite Railway] indemnifies and protects the town against charge, prosecution or damages caused by said railway's crossing the public highways." In return for "said Town offer[ing] the corporation its best wishes for the success of the enterprise," the town meeting inserted a provision that "any person shall be entitled to have stone carried in the said cars and vehicles at [their] pleasure, on payment of toll."[13] In this simple way was established the principle of public access to what had previously in America been considered a private undertaking for private ends. With that practice established, the railroad became rather quickly the common carrier we think a railroad should be.

The Granite Railway was a resounding success, operationally and financially, in an area where the desire for better transportation was rapidly becoming importunate. By 1825 Massachusetts had taken the lead in the industrialization that was sweeping the Northeast. To the extent that the railroad became the backstay of such factory development, it was in Massachusetts that most of the significant first efforts took place. It should be appreciated, however, that this quasi-English rationale for rail lines was less frequently a justification in the New World than in the Old, and it tended to be geographically rather localized. Far more widely "American" was the use of the railroad as an instrument of regional or interregional development, and it was for that purpose that the first important lines were proposed. We shall look again at the southern New England railroads, with their "Massachusetts-English engineering," but it is best to maintain some chronological fidelity by first turning to those lines of regional development that came next in the historical geography of American railroads.

The Railroad, Urban Mercantilism, and Misplaced Cities

History and geography had become so interwoven in colonial America that the new republic found itself divided into thirteen former colonies now considered the basic sovereignties from which the new union was to be formed. It should be remembered that each of those states was coastal and possessed at least one adequate port from which trade with the former mother country, and now the world, could be conducted. When we examine the history of this settlement, we find that it is intricately tied to the projection of mercantile interests onto the Western Shore of the Atlantic by the English merchants of the seventeenth and eighteenth centuries.[14] Because those merchants were numerous, the English sovereign was induced to grant to different groups at successive times charters to establish trading colonies in coastal North America. Extending from Newfoundland to the borders of Florida, all but the northern three (Newfoundland, Nova Scotia, and New Brunswick) joined in the revolt that shaped the new republic.

Geography had contributed to this segmentation of settlement. From New Brunswick southward to Georgia considerable rivers flowed from the Appalachian highlands down the slope toward the sea, at the same time giving access to the interior by river for the spread of the mercantile settlement pattern while insulating one drainage basin from the next along the divides between basins. In the colonial potamic transportation pattern there were no sizable towns not located directly with reference to this interaction of the mercantile port and its upriver collecting points for the staples of transatlantic trade. There were, however, some geographical misperceptions that tended to become more awkward with the growth in the economy—particularly with its transformation when the new United States became the first mercantile-industrial capitalist state outside northwestern Europe, and the first without a large metropolitan population. It was for those towns of geographical misperception that the railroad assumed unusual importance and was assigned the first distinctly American purposes.

The main colonial misperceptions came as a result of exclusively maritime exploration. From 1497 on, English navigators had visited the North American coast, the Western Shore, gaining increasing knowledge of that littoral and building assumptions about conditions in the interior based on the size of the river mouths. We all know the tale of a Hudson or a Cartier sailing up his particular river in search of a passage to China; we tend to overlook the fact that later explorers had probably long since given up Oriental goals, searching instead for likely sources of timber, minerals, and furs, the specie of colonial trade. In any estuarine coast, such as that of North America, the chance for disappointment was considerable. The fjorded Hudson and Connecticut's Thames did not in nature match the Mississippi, though they were equally open to the sea. And from Portland in Maine southward to Charleston there were ample bays that gave little actual access to the interior. Portland never actually deceived, because it was obviously located merely on a bay, but Portsmouth in New Hampshire seemed by the Piscataqua's broad lower course to have an entrance to the interior more useful than the vigorous but foreshortened Salmon Falls River headwaters actually afforded.

In Massachusetts the classic deception was encountered. When Captain John Smith visited and named the Charles River at the innermost reach of Massachusetts Bay in 1614, he gave it the name of the then prince of Wales. But like that unfortunate man, it proved a sad disappointment. Its forty-seven miles were so coiled in meanders that the seemingly regal stream soon narrowed to a large brook and extended only some twenty-five miles inland from its impressive mouth. When Boston grew, intended from the very beginning as the metropolis of New England, this poor access to the hinterland became a problem. Similarly, in Carolina in 1670 when an entrepôt town was to be established, Charleston was sited on the Ashley River, later to be moved to the Cooper, on what appeared to be a great harbor watered by two broad streams. Only as the interior was explored was it revealed in both cases that the master stream of the region was other than the Charles or the Ashley-Cooper.

Several other colonial towns had, like Portland, sites that at first seemed tolerable but ultimately were found to be otherwise. New Haven in 1638 had been the best site available for an offshoot Puritan colony near Dutch New York, but no river of size emptied into its harbor. As the city grew and sought to develop a productive hinterland, it was forced to seek to "shift" nature toward the west by redirecting the flow of trade along a canal dug in the Connecticut River graben away from both that stream and from Hartford. When the Calverts were allowed to substitute a site on the Chesapeake Bay in return for their original proprietorship on Newfoundland's "Southern Shore," they encountered two problems: first, that their feudal efforts seemed to stunt town development; and second, that the two major rivers flowing through the colony, the Potomac and the Susquehanna, led (more important) to the interior of other colonies, Virginia and Pennsylvania respectively. Thus, when urbanization finally came to Maryland with the founding of Baltimore in 1729, a site at the mouth of the short Patapsco River but on an excellent harbor seemed acceptable. So long as the adjacent Manor Counties sufficed to support the colony's trade, the restricted hinterland of the splendid harbor did not become apparent. Even Philadelphia partially shared this plight. When that town was established in 1681, the valley of the Delaware River seemed to offer sufficient scope for trade with England. But as the proprietorial colony grew mostly westward, into the grant the Penns had received, it became a great commercial nuisance that the main river of the interior, the Susquehanna, flowed to the sea within Maryland. It became a frightening fact when the much younger Baltimore grew so fast, reaching Philadelphia's size—to share honors as America's second city—in 1820 and actually outdistancing the Quaker City in 1830.

The coming of the railroad for the first time seemed to offer those "badly located" mercantile centers a chance to gain ground lost to the ports at the mouths of the larger streams. Some efforts had already been made in the canal era. Improvement was sought by the construction of the Middlesex, Santee, and New Haven and Northampton canals. But each of these was small and awkward to navigate, so the misplacement problem remained for Boston, Charleston, and New Haven respectively. Philadelphia had attempted to open a waterway to the Susquehanna by means of the Schuylkill Navigation and the Union Canal, but these very narrow and difficult waterways proved of relatively little value, save in the transport of coal to the metropolis.

For Baltimore the geographical problem was even more aggravated. Interest in tying its fine port to a larger hinterland had brought local financial support for the construction of the Susquehanna and Tidewater Canal within Pennsylvania, which served to open navigation of that river over the rapids at the Fall Line to reach the Chesapeake Bay at Havre de Grace. That tie is thought to have sparked much of Baltimore's growth in the early nineteenth century. Wheat from the Middle Atlantic states, and later the Middle West, began to be milled into flour here for distribution across the Atlantic by the famous Baltimore clippers. Access remained a problem, however, because Pennsylvania actively sought to divert the trade of its own interior away from the Chesapeake port. At the same time efforts to build the Chesapeake and Ohio Canal tended further to divert the flow of interior products, notably wheat, toward Georgetown and Alexandria at tidewater on the Potomac. It was in this context that the extremely active merchant group in Baltimore sought to overcome the "locational mistake" that had sited the city on an excellent harbor but one without natural routes to more than its immediate environs.

We shall examine each of these "misplaced cities" in due course, so it is appropriate here to ask why and how they came to be the first developers of railroads in the United States. The misplacement referred to was quite relative as to time. In the colonial period, when the towns were established, they were exceptionally *well* located, given the littoral settlement and economic pattern of the British colonies. Because prosperity and continued existence then depended upon maritime trade with England, and because the area necessary to supply the staples for that trade was at first quite small and within relatively easy reach of the harbors that had brought the towns into existence, finding the "right location" for a town could be confined to discovering a fine port. Only as the mercantile settlement frontier was pushed inland, as happened particularly in the early nineteenth century, did the misplacement begin to show up. Once the interior assumed greater economic importance, the colonial ports began to seek a new role for themselves. These ports had been founded as entrepôts on the Western Shore for the direct conduct of English mercantile development; but the Revolution sundered that necessary tie, and the Peace of 1783 made free access to the British market quite difficult. In this situation the colonial entrepôts themselves revolutionized their own role, coming to take the place of the British metropolis in a newly articulated American mercantile system. One of the outcomes was the rapid rise of industry in the United States, a development that was particularly instrumental in shaping a form of railroad distinctly American in its infrastructure and purposes. Because this revolution in the American mercantile system took place within the parceled political geography of the thirteen original mercantile colonies, there were a number of former entrepôts each seeking a share in world trade to use the changed conditions for its own direct benefit. We should not forget that it was considerably the trade conflicts between Maryland and Virginia that six years after the peace led to the search for a new structure of government to replace the particularist qualities of the Articles of Confederation.

The rivalry among the colonial entrepôts meant that national mercantilism, as practiced by the British crown, came in America to be expressed at first largely as urban mercantilism practiced by some fifteen entrepôts now seeking metropolitan status.[15] In New York, Virginia, and Georgia inland navigation was adequate for the early years of this urban mercantilist competition, but in Maine, Massachusetts, Pennsylvania, Maryland, and South Carolina, as we have seen, it was not. So when this urban mercantile competition took shape after 1783, alternative efforts at transportation improvement were required. It is in this context that we can most easily understand the Turnpike Movement that swept the infant United States between 1790 and 1830. These improved roads were built extensively around the colonial ports, most notably Boston, Philadelphia, Baltimore, and Alexandria (where the first turnpike in the country was opened in 1786).[16] But those turnpikes were hardly a substitute in economic terms for the waterways of New York. Tolls were considerable, and in addition the cost of hauling by wagon remained high. [Thus, any town finding a better way to move goods overland could anticipate stealing a competitive march on its mercantile rivals.]

This was a reason for railroad development entirely different from that responsible for the "railway revolution" in Britain and on much of the Continent. This contrast is graphically borne out in the effect rail building had on the settlement fabric in Europe and in America. In Britain, for example, railways created no new towns larger or more significant than Crewe, Swindon, and Middlesbrough, hardly world-renowned places. In France not even such extremely parochial places can be assigned to rail creation. In America, however, as we shall see, we are not restricted to an Altoona, Ayer, or Huntington; we have places like Atlanta, Charlotte, Omaha, and Albuquerque to serve more adequately as examples of railroad towns. It is generally true that in Europe the railroad systems were laid out to enhance the existing settlement pattern, whereas in the United States they were laid out only to enhance the urban mercantile status of the relatively few original colonial entrepôts, leaving the effect on the settlement fabric of their hinterlands to be worked out as much by competitive success or failure as by design. In the Middle West the existence of a series of small towns dependent upon river and canal transportation—Cleveland, Columbus, Toledo, Fort Wayne, Chicago, and Milwaukee, among the more significant—meant that the rail lines projected westward from the competing coastal entrepôts could look toward an actual destination, even where there were no considerable places to be served. In the end, of course, the previously more important river towns—Cincinnati, Louisville, and St. Louis—lost out to these new railroad termini that transformed the transportation geography of the United States from its potamic beginnings.

Baltimore and Urban Mercantilism

The rise of Baltimore in the postrevolutionary years was remarkable. "Before and during the War of 1812, the commercial and general prosperity of Baltimore advanced with great rapidity and afterwards seemed as suddenly arrested. The system of turnpike roads which centered on the city enabled it to compete successfully [at first] for the Ohio trade, but [after 1811] the introduction of steamboats on the Ohio and Mississippi Rivers . . . diverted the trade to New Orleans."[17] The War of 1812 had considerably enriched the merchants of the Chesapeake Bay city, for the privateering ships that were under their ownership had taken rich prizes. For a decade after the war, however, the city's trade languished as Pennsylvania increased its efforts to keep the trans-Appalachian trade north of the Mason-Dixon line. In 1825, with the opening of the Erie Canal, the Keystone State began actively to undertake its own internal improvements, which were opened as the Pennsylvania Mainline Canal System between Philadelphia and Pittsburgh. Part of that effort was also expressed in a resistance to a lateral canal along the lower Susquehanna between Columbia (Pennsylvania) and Port Deposit (Maryland), at the head of navigation on the Chesapeake Bay. It was only in 1839 that this stretch was first opened, thus permitting trade passing across the Appalachians toward the seaboard to reach the Chesapeake Bay, and possibly Baltimore rather than Philadelphia. The victory for the Mary-

The North American Railroad Rises in the East

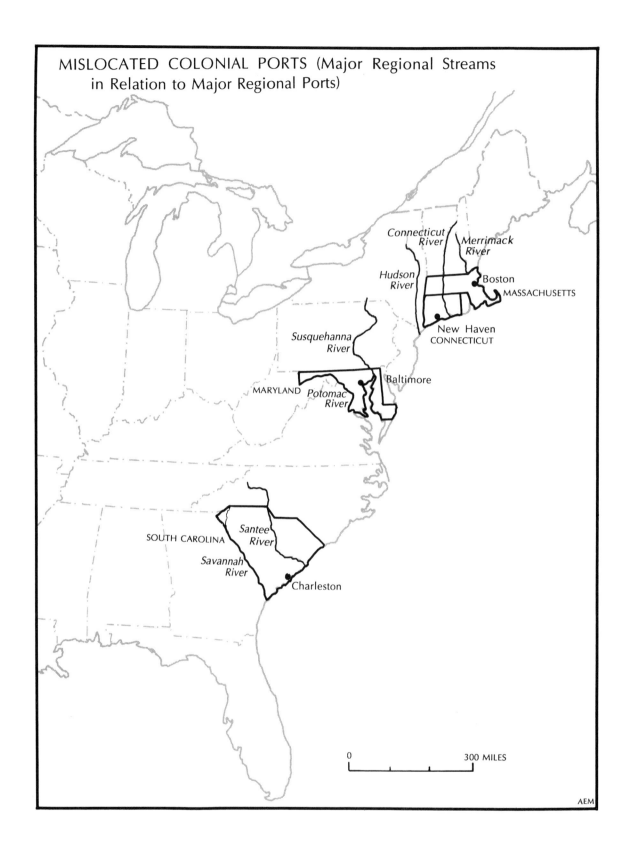

MISLOCATED COLONIAL PORTS (Major Regional Streams in Relation to Major Regional Ports)

Connecticut River

Merrimack River

Hudson River

Boston

MASSACHUSETTS

Susquehanna River

New Haven
CONNECTICUT

MARYLAND

Baltimore

Potomac River

SOUTH CAROLINA

Santee River

Savannah River

Charleston

0   300 MILES

AEM

land port was largely countered by the completion in 1829 of the Chesapeake and Delaware Canal across the thirteen-mile neck of the Delmarva Peninsula. It soon developed that trade coming by waterway from the west could reach Philadelphia still in boats by using the lower Susquehanna, the bay, the Chesapeake and Delaware Canal, and the Delaware River in place of the awkward transshipment necessitated by Pennsylvania's use of the Philadelphia and Columbia Railroad as the easternmost segment of the Mainline System. In that situation the Pennsylvania legislature agreed to complete its longstanding commitment to the improvement of the lower Susquehanna, and for a few years in the 1840s and 1850s Baltimore managed to divert quite a bit of this Pennsylvania trade to its own docks.

In general, though, Baltimore felt desperately cut off from the western trade as the Chesapeake and Ohio Canal was built up the Potomac toward the Allegheny Front and the Mainline System was carried across that barrier in Pennsylvania. The boom atmosphere in the Chesapeake port, once American ships gained access to the world at the close of the Revolution, had encouraged the active pursuit of urban mercantilism. Thus, the stagnation after the War of 1812 created an urgency for improvement that seemed thwarted under the geographical realities of inland navigation. In such a context it was entirely logical that American proselytizing for railroads—and word of the small actual experiments in England—led to specific proposals for a railroad to attempt to solve Baltimore's mercantile "misplacement."

The relative merits of canals and railroads was a general question in the efforts at transportation improvement in the 1820s. Massachusetts and Pennsylvania were particularly vexed in making a choice between the two; neither commonwealth had the ideal conditions for canal development, lacking the clear low route across the Appalachian structures that New York possessed, and Massachusetts would need to cross two divides, one over two thousand feet in elevation, to reach the interior by canal. Yet the railroad was still too experimental, even in England, to give Americans confidence that such lines could become the sinews of national existence and trade in substitution for canals.

In 1825 the Pennsylvania Society for the Promotion of Internal Improvements sent the distinguished architect-engineer William Strickland to England to investigate the relative merits of canals and railroads. The next year he published his results in an elaborate volume, *Reports on Canals, Railways, Roads, and Other Subjects, Made to the Pennsylvania Society for the Promotion of Internal Improvement,* that served to bring the alternative of the railroad under active discussion. In Pennsylvania the canal forces were most unfortunately successful in persuading the state legislature to go ahead with the mainly canal solution found in the Mainline System, but for Massachusetts and Baltimore, Strickland's report seems to have tipped the balance toward rail solutions. Because the situation in the Bay State was less clear-cut in favoring the iron rail, several years were taken up in finally defeating the canal proponents. In Maryland the interests of the state and the city tended to be expressed separately. The state promoted the Chesapeake and Ohio Canal while the city did not, as it led trade away from the turnpikes that converged on Baltimore toward the ports at tidewater on the Potomac—Alexandria and Georgetown. For Baltimore there was no reasonable alternative to the railroad, and so in the late winter of 1828 the city merchant

27

The North
American Railroad
Rises in the East

group secured a charter from the state permitting them to build a rail line.

This charter was the outcome of speculations by a group of some twenty-five merchants and city leaders who had met first on February 2, 1827, on a call to "take under consideration the best means of restoring to the city of Baltimore that portion of the western trade which has recently been diverted from it by the introduction of steam navigation and by other causes."[18] Their conclusion, certainly influenced by Strickland's analysis, came finally in strongly geographical terms. A subcommittee of the first meeting was deputized to investigate the practicality of a railroad to the Ohio River. Reporting back promptly, the subcommittee first noted Baltimore's weak position with respect to the Susquehanna and Potomac canals, and the trade they might funnel to the Chesapeake port. Then came the main argument:

But important as this trade is to Baltimore, it is certainly of minor consideration, when compared with the immense commerce which lies within our grasp to the West, provided we have the enterprise to profit by the advantages which our local situation gives us in reference to that trade. Baltimore lies 200 miles nearer to the navigable waters of the West than New York, and about 100 miles nearer to them than Philadelphia, to which may be added the important fact, the easiest, and by far the most practicable route through the ridges of mountains that divide the Atlantic from the western waters is along the depression formed by the Potomac in its passage through them. . . . The only point from which we have anything to apprehend is New Orleans; with that city, it is admitted, we must be content to share the trade, because she will always enjoy a *certain portion* of it in defiance of our efforts; but from a country of such vast extent, and whose products are so various and of such incalculable amount, [t]here will be a sufficient trade to sustain both New Orleans and Baltimore; and we may feel fully contented if we can succeed in securing to ourselves that portion of it which will prefer to seek a market east of the mountains.[19]

If urban mercantilism was accepted as the main guiding objective of such a line of inland transport, its technology still had to be agreed upon. The subcommittee's report analyzed turnpike roads and canals as well as railroads, concluding as follows:

Railroads had upon a limited scale been used in several places in England and Wales for a number of years and had in every instance been found fully to answer the purposes required. . . . The idea of applying them upon a more extended scale appears, however, only recently to have been suggested in that country; but notwithstanding so little time has elapsed since the attempt was first made, yet we find that so decided have been their advantages over turnpike-roads, or even over canals, that nearly 2000 miles of them are actually completed or in a train of rapid progress in Great Britain, and that the experiment of their construction has not in one case failed, nor has there been one instance in which they have not fully answered the most sanguine expectations of their projectors. Indeed, so completely has this improvement succeeded in England that it is the opinion of many judicious and practical men there that these roads will, for heavy transportation, supersede canals as effectually as canals have superseded turnpike-roads.[20]

The account of British railroad construction seems highly exaggerated. In 1827, save for the admittedly considerable mileage of horse-drawn mineral railways, only the Stockton and Darlington had been completed and opened, and only the Liverpool and Manchester was actually under construction. Even these latter lines were so short as hardly to be a practical demonstration of the use of rails for a line as long as one from Baltimore to the Ohio. The thirty-two miles that separated Manchester from its port represented less than a tenth the rail distance separating Baltimore from Wheeling on the Ohio (379 miles). And even the Ohio was considered by some as only an intermediate objective. Still, the sub-committee heartily recommended the building of a "double railroad," two tracks, between the Chesapeake port and the readily navigable course of the Ohio. In a peroration the report noted that nearly a fifth of the Republic's population would live adjacent to this route with its river extension, whereas only a tenth lived similarly with respect to the Erie Canal. The specifically American purpose of such rail building, in comparison with that found in Britain, is particularly well recounted in the following argument:

The country around Chesapeake Bay was first settled by Europeans about the year 1632 and in the year 1800 the white population had barely reached as far west as the Ohio River; that is to say, in 160 years it had advanced westward about 400 miles, or at the rate of two and a half miles per year. There is now [in 1827] a dense population extending as far west as the junction of the Osage River with the Missouri; which is about 900 miles west of the Ohio River at Wheeling; of course the white population has, within the last thirty years, traveled that distance, or more than thirty miles each year and is at this time advancing with as great, if not greater impetus, than at any former period; and according to all probability, if not checked by some unforeseen circumstances, it will, within the next thirty years, reach the Rocky Mountains or even to the Pacific Ocean.[21]

The railroad was foreseen as encouraging this growth by lowering the cost of transport for the agricultural and mineral products expected to be produced within the spreading oecumene. "The expense of conveying cotton upon the proposed railroad from the Ohio River to Baltimore, including all charges, may be estimated at one-quarter of a cent per pound, certainly not more than half a cent per pound; and coal from the Allegheny Mountains, near to Cumberland, including its cost at the pits, could be delivered at Baltimore at from 11 to 12 cents per bushel." And in the competition with New Orleans it was argued, "We should not lose sight of the important fact that the productions of these extensive regions, excepting only tobacco and cotton, being breadstuffs, provisions and other perishable articles, cannot be exposed to the deleterious [summer] climate of New Orleans without the hazard of great injury; [as] we find that considerable portions of the flour and provisions which go by the way of the Mississippi are often so much damaged as to be rendered unfit for exportation to a foreign market."[22] In any notion of developing the Middle West as a granary and pasture for the support of the growing cities in eastern North America and western Europe, this trans-Appalachian artery was seen as a national essential—and one, it was pointed out, that could operate year-round rather than seasonally, as did the Erie Canal.

The subcommittee called for "immediate application [to] be made to the Legislature of Maryland for an act incorporating a joint stock company to be styled 'The Baltimore and Ohio Railway Company'; and clothing such company with all the powers necessary to the construction of a railroad, with two or more sets of rails, from the city of Baltimore to the Ohio River."[23] In this the subcommittee was accepting the modest but firm judgment William Strickland had expressed in his report to the Pennsylvania internal improvements society: "The

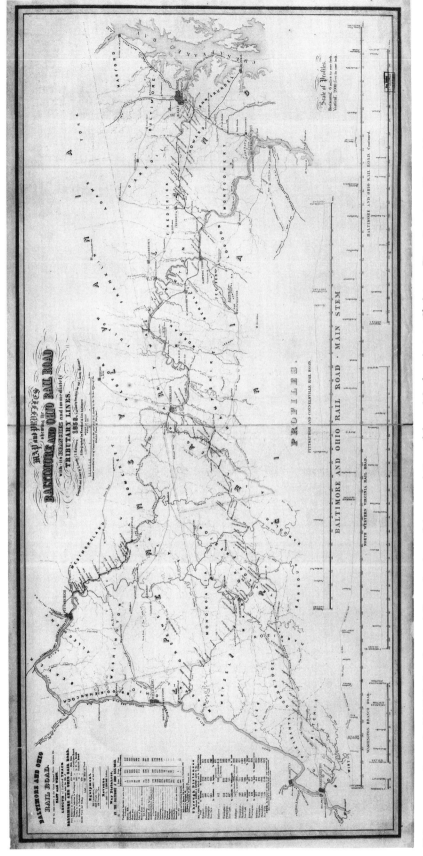

This 1853 map shows the B&O Railroad essentially at the time of the completion of the original project on Christmas Day, 1852. *Source:* Library of Congress map.

introduction of the locomotive engine has greatly changed the relative value of railways and canals; and where a communication is to be made between places of commercial or manufacturing character, which maintain a constant intercourse, and where rapidity of transit becomes important, it cannot be doubted that railways will receive a preference, in consequence of this very powerful auxiliary."[24] But the incipient Baltimore and Ohio Railroad, as it came to be known, differed in its geographical location from the situation envisaged by Strickland. It was built from such a commercial city but not to another of similar stripe—instead, into what by English standards would have been a virtual wilderness. The promoters of, and the early engineers for, the B&O were thus faced with far more perplexity than the cool rationality of Strickland's report would seem to imply. I think it is fair to say that the report and the English experience on which it was based were crucial to the development of railroads in the United States, but only in a very specific and limited way. The English had found (1) that the mineral railways could be effectively and economically worked, and (2) that the steam locomotive engine and the edge rail were practical features of that system; and this meant that American promoters, facing a far more uncertain prospect in economic and geographical conditions, could have the courage to set about the task. The limitation in applicability comes even more from a fact of American experience: the more slavishly the Americans applied English practice, the less successful their rail lines were likely to be beyond the direct geographical analogue as stated by Strickland ("where a communication is to be made between places of commercial or manufacturing character, which maintain a constant intercourse"). This is the Massachusetts-English engineering that Edward Kirkland noted and, we might add, a distinctly English economic geography. Where the distinctly American economic geography ruled, as it did over most of the Republic's space, an American system had to be devised if the obvious benefits of the railroad were to be enjoyed by any but a few.

When we consider the construction of the Baltimore and Ohio we witness the emergence of that American system—not, let it be emphasized, a true diffusion of British practice beyond the dual concepts of the rail-guided way and the use of steam locomotives. Ultimately, even those seeming "borrowings" were so transformed as to be parallel rather than derivative developments.

The School for American Railroad Engineering and the American System

Once the charter for the Baltimore and Ohio had been secured in 1827, the promoters set about taking subscriptions for stock. To begin with, no trouble was encountered—partly, we must suspect, because the charter specified that no more than one-third of the subscription was to be demanded during any one year and no actual payment called for without sixty days' notice.[25] In this manner the considerable capital requirements of the company, $3 million, were to be spread over so long a period that a capital-poor country might meet the call. Of course, Baltimore was far from the poorest of the poor, so self-financing, with a reasonable spacing of such calls, seemed possible. The success of the subscription suggested to the promoters that a true English rail line might be constructed. Directly following Strickland's description of the Newcastle railways, they set about locating the line in the prescribed manner. In his report Strickland had placed great emphasis on shaping as level a line as possible and had referred indirectly to the British practice of concentrating grades so that they might be located at one place and be served by steam winding engines rather than locomotives:

Previously to the survey of the route, upon which the general railway is to be formed, it is proper to ascertain, as accurately as possible, the amount of lading that may be expected to traverse it in each direction. This will determine, in one particular, the character of the work; for if the lading in the two directions approaches an equality of bulk and weight, the road must be set out in lines as nearly level as possible; while in other cases, it is proper to give it such an inclination as may most facilitate the heavier trade.

This preliminary having been determined, surveys should be made of the different routes of which the country is capable, and plans and profiles drawn of them all. These will enable the engineer to determine the position and extent of his different levels, and the best position for his inclined planes. Of course, as in canalling, the engineer, where there are valleys rising to high ground, will endeavor so to arrange his line, as that the earth excavated from the hill, shall supply the material for the adjoining embankment. If creeks or brooks are to be encountered in such situations, he will support his railway on a platform of wooden sleepers raised on stone piers, or will form an aqueduct bridge or culvert, as circumstances suggest.[26]

No doubt the engineers of the B&O followed such a plan. They were generous in the use of stone viaducts—the term that came into use for such bridges on rail lines rather than Strickland's *aqueducts*—and concentrated grade into inclined planes. At least in the beginning, their intent was to use the fish-belly edge rails then currently the best practice in Britain.

The beginning of the construction was scheduled for July 4, 1828, with the last surviving signer of the Declaration of Independence, Charles Carroll of Carrollton, Maryland, to lay a First Stone—a simple rectangular monument donated by the "Stone Cutters of Baltimore" and placed alongside the line between Mount Clare and Gwynns Falls. Some years later this relic disappeared, and it was only in 1898 that it was found by returning to the original surveys and then digging down some six feet to where the several reconstructions of the line—typical of nineteenth-century American railroading—had buried it.[27] The construction of the line actually commenced on July 7. Captain William Gibbs McNeill and three assistants, Lieutenants Cook, Hazzard, and Dillahunty, were loaned to the enterprise by the United States Army, the sole source of trained engineers in the country in 1828 (West Point being the first engineering school established in the Republic). These men investigated possible routes out of Baltimore. In beginning the gentle ascent of the Piedmont, the valley of the Patapsco River as far west as Mount Airy (43 miles) was used, and the contracts for twelve miles, as far west as Ellicott, were almost immediately let.[28] This construction, on the English pattern, soon rocked the company even despite its success in raising capital: "The average cost per mile for grading and masonry alone ran about $17,000; in those days to be regarded as an excessive figure. The fourth and fifth contracts, which included the 'Deep Cut,' west of Gwynns Run (78 feet deep and some 1300 yards long), alone came to about one-third of the total cost of preparing the line for the rails, all the way to Ellicotts Mills."[29] This high level of cost came from the obsession for an absolutely level line that copying British practice induced. Alexander Brown, one of the great Baltimore merchants, finally persuaded the engineers not to make the Deep Cut so deep, in fact to fill up a bit that had already been excavated, so that it would have the barely perceptible grade of seventeen feet per mile, both to save costs and to assure some drainage within the actual cut.[30] In such practical ways did the American system of railroad building evolve.

The need for that particular system arose from the increasing difficulty experienced in securing construction funds. Calls, after the first, for stock subscriptions began to reveal how little capital was available in America for such costly and uncertain enterprises. Within what is now metropolitan Baltimore, the problems had to be faced quite directly. In passing to and then up the Patapsco Gorge, to use that river valley to gain an easy route across the Piedmont, bridging was necessary. As the company's finances were being strained, Lieutenant Colonel Stephen H. Long, one of the engineers, proposed wooden structures to lower costs; but British practice was still too compelling in the minds of most of the directors, so stone arches were decided upon, save for the overpass carrying the Washington-Baltimore Turnpike over the line. There Long was permitted to construct a wooden structure, which he did with considerable flair, shaping a thin-membered wooden truss of which he was sufficiently proud to secure a patent and name it for the serving president, Andrew Jackson. The other bridges came as large stone arches, as at Carrollton and in the Thomas arch that bore the Washington branch of the B&O across the Patapsco. These had arches of eighty-foot span and were built so well that they still serve today, when locomotives weigh more than ten times what they did in 1829 when the arches were built.[31]

The actual track for the B&O brought quickly to the fore a discussion of diffusion versus independent development; and as might be expected, at first there was a compromise. Captain McNeill, Major George Whistler, and a Quaker engineer who long served the company, Jonathan Knight, were sent to England to examine the question on the Stockton and Darlington and the Liverpool and Manchester. Upon their return, track laying began close to the Mount Clare terminus in Baltimore. The very substantial track carried on stone blocks was seen as the ideal, but the high cost of iron in America had caused the company to adopt the expedient of wooden stringers, usually capped by straps of iron and borne and kept in gauge by wooden crossties. Thus, in 1829 the crosstie had already been introduced to railroading, and in America. Jonathan Knight's report to president Philip E. Thomas of the B&O in 1830 laid out the problem succinctly and in actual comparison:

Two plans for the laying [of] the rails on the Baltimore and Ohio Railroad have been in contemplation; the one with wood sleepers [crossties] and string pieces surmounted with the iron rail; the other with the continued stone sill, or string piece on which the iron rail should bear throughout. The English methods, which would have required about three times as much iron, were excluded on account of the great cost in this country of that material. The stone sills were considered next in cost to the English railway, but preferable. The method with wood was adopted on account of its still greater cheapness, especially on the parts where it would have been attended with very great expense and where the roadbed had not been sufficiently settled and firm for the more permanent work. . . . It was determined that in laying the part of the track from the city to the Patapsco . . . a distance of about 7 and one half miles, it should be done

The North
American Railroad
Rises in the East

with wood sleepers and string pieces [capped with iron rail], but that the residue of the distance to Ellicotts Mills . . . about 5 and one half miles, should be laid with stone blocks and wood string pieces [again with iron rails on the surface]. The track has been so laid, accordingly. The comparative advantages of the two methods will of course now be tested by experience.[32]

The company finally settled upon wrought-iron rail in the familiar fish-belly pattern. At least while the line was being laid down, the vexing question of motive power was held in abeyance; horses were used for construction "trains," so it was assumed that they could also draw the occasional directors' train that traversed the line. On January 7, 1830, the company responded to expressed demand by introducing public trains between the Mount Clare terminus in Baltimore and the Carrollton viaduct, thus initiating the first public rail service in America and only the second outside Britain (the other was on Marc Seguin's line from the Rhône to St. Etienne in France). The traction question was still in abeyance; horses were used for this essentially sightseeing operation.

To prepare for passenger service, the railroad directors sought to build an efficient passenger car. Rather by chance, the problem was presented to one of the suppliers of horses, Ross Winans from New Jersey, who came forward with one of the great innovations of railroading: unlike all previous road vehicles, wherein the wheels revolved individually on fixed axles, with four or more separate bearings that were likely to give considerable friction, the B&O cars would have the wheels and axles rigidly fixed one to the other, and the whole axle assembly would be attached to the car body in a bearing outside the wheel, whereby ease of maintenance would be assured. This Winans (or friction) wheel was rapidly adopted in America and was introduced in Britain, though Winans was never given due credit for it.[33] In this way the American system of railroading was made cheaper to operate and less demanding of labor.

That principle of ease of operation was further advanced when, again on Winans's advice, the flange of the wheels was moved from the outer to the inner side of the wheel tread. Yet another improvement came when these wheel-axle assemblies were combined into two-wheel "trucks" that might be pivoted so as to reduce friction when cars operated over the tighter curves found on American railroads. It became the axiom of American railroad practice that *practicality* was the overriding objective. That practicality came to be assured through the strength of locomotives, measured both as machines themselves—they had a simple and reliable brute force not so commonly found in British locomotives— and in their usable tractive effort. Stephenson had crept into the shelter of the winding engine whenever any sizable hill was seen on the horizon. The B&O was at first blinded by "British bestism"; an upswell in the surface of the eastern Piedmont frightened the company into making the deep cut at Gwynns Falls, and a residual terrain divide at Parr's Spring Ridge on the Piedmont, a bit to the west, was planned to be surmounted by the use of a winding engine at its crest. But the brute qualities of the locomotives that the railroad had built in America were such that the early driving "engineers" stormed up the eastern slope of Parr's Spring Ridge using their relatively powerful engines successfully to engage in ordinary adhesion working of the line.

In his seminal study of the American locomotive, John H. White, Jr., clearly accounts for the employment of this brute force. He notes that by 1850

Britain had spent a billion dollars, then a truly vast sum, in the construction of five thousand miles of rail, whereas the United States had spent only about a quarter that sum ($265 million) for sixty-five hundred miles. The savings were made particularly in the matter of curves and grades. "Many roads had 600-foot curves, and the Beaver Run Railroad had one as sharp as 250 feet. Grades were also severe; an incline of 30 to 50 feet per mile [0.56 to 0.94 percent] was not unusual. The Baltimore and Ohio's seventeen-mile grade (near Piedmont, West Virginia) of 116 feet per mile [2.2 percent] is an extreme example of the steep incline intended to challenge locomotive power." Observing the experience with Stephenson locomotives imported into North America, White continues: "The first concern of early railroad mechanics was the development of a dependable locomotive that would not break down [or go off the track] when sent out on the road. Such a machine was perfected by the early 1830s. It would consume more fuel than theory permitted but it wouldn't forever be in the shop for repairs." Putting firmly to rest any too casual assumption that America waited upon British experience and practice to gain its railroad, White deals forthrightly with the question: "It is not surprising that the first locomotives in [the United States] were imported from Britain, but it is surprising how quickly they were found unsuitable for American roads and how quickly our rural nation launched its own locomotive establishment. This is not to say that we are not enormously indebted to the British builders. . . . American improvements—mainly in running gears—were hardly as fundamental or as far-reaching as the work of the British designers who had perfected their basic design by 1830." But because the American concept of the railroad's essential purpose was a strongly developmental one, we quickly created an American-type locomotive to go with that purpose. White explains: "Imports fell rapidly after 1837. . . . In 1841 the Philadelphia and Reading received the *Gem,* which is generally considered the last locomotive to have been imported from Britain. In all between 1829 and 1841, about one hundred and twenty locomotives were imported. Assuming that nearly all were still in use in 1841, they would constitute about 25 percent of the locomotives in service in the United States at that time."[34]

Accepting that it was practicality and brute force that distinguished the American locomotive and quickly caused it to be substituted for the small number of British locomotives that were actually imported, we must ask why the first American locomotive was built as early as 1830 (when the West Point Foundry Association of New York City constructed the engine the *Best Friend,* commonly referred to as the *Best Friend of Charleston,* for the South Carolina Railroad), and parenthetically why the export of American locomotives to Europe came as early as 1836 or 1837 (when Ross Winans's *Columbus* was sold to the Leipzig and Dresden Railroad). In other words, why and how was the American locomotive developed? Arthur M. Wellington explains:

The distinctive peculiarities of the running gear of American locomotives, as compared with foreign, are two: the swivelling *truck* in front (in England called "bogie"), and the *equalizing levers* by which the load is kept uniformly distributed on the four or more drivers, and the effect of any chance irregularities in the track reduced to a minimum. The first was invented by John B. Jervis in 1830, soon after the trial of the *Rocket* took place; the second was invented by Ross M. Winans, who also invented the double-truck railway car which has become all but universal in this century [the nineteenth], only a few years later.

Both of these inventions, with much else that was novel and meritorious, had their origin in the necessities of the earlier years of American railways, which required that the locomotives should be adapted to ready passage over sharp curves and imperfectly surfaced track and road-bed. Both of them are now gradually making their way into England and throughout the world; and both of them, beyond doubt, will eventually become universal, since they are almost equally advantageous on good roads and on poor roads, the only difference being that on poor track they are absolutely indispensable, while on good track they are not indispensable, but merely advantageous. In great part, we owe to them two advantages which experience appears to indicate that the American locomotive possesses: It can (at least it unquestionably does) haul greater loads in proportion to weight on drivers, and it is less readily disorganized, so that it can run in practice (at least it does) a great many more miles in a day and a year. . . . [The] cost per ton hauled is enormously in favor of American engines. . . . [It] remains true, that whenever American locomotives have fairly come in competition with those without their distinctive features, as in Canada, Mexico, South America, and the Australasian colonies (in nearly all of which the right of decision has rested in English officials), they have invariably obtained the preference, with exceptions that prove the rule.[35]

In 1831 the B&O had already been completed to Frederick, though it was operated that far by horse traction. Still, of the 136 miles of American railroad listed as having been completed by the next year, 45 percent were on the pioneer Maryland line. By some measure it was the longest railroad in the world, as long as the Stockton and Darlington and the Liverpool and Manchester combined. Yet the matter of traction had not been fully resolved. The experience with Peter Cooper's *Tom Thumb* encouraged the final adoption of steam traction, a decision that was overdue when the line finally expanded to Point of Rocks on the Potomac, some sixty-nine miles from Baltimore, in April 1832. The decision during the preceding year to abandon, at least temporarily, the use of stone blocks in favor of wooden crossties had speeded up construction, again forcing the issue.

The B&O seems to have come to steam traction not in any grand test of the sort the Liverpool and Manchester staged at Rainhill, though the American line did seek such a contest only to have no applicants. Instead, the company was both pragmatic and lucky. It bought several locally produced locomotives that took on characteristics distinct from those that were lumped together in American terms as typical of the "English engine." The B&O engine was seemingly primitive, powered from a vertical boiler that seemed to suggest George Stephenson's earliest engines built for the Stockton and Darlington. Yet there was a difference: the American engines were clearly much more powerful even in their earliest expression, and they could deal with track that was not vastly expensive to build. From an account written in the mid-1830s by one of the chief engineers of the emergent New York and Erie Railroad, James Seymour, we have a description of early B&O steam that tells us much about this critical phase in the shaping of a distinct and separate American railroad tradition.

On a visit to the Maryland line in 1836 Seymour could particularly compare the British with the American practice. He tells us, "I consider the engines made at Baltimore better than those that are imported from abroad [clearly, only from Britain at this time]. An English engine arrived in Baltimore a few days since which was destined for a Rail Road in Virginia; but upon being tried upon the Baltimore road ran off the track once or twice. The foreign engines appear to be much better calculated for very straight and level roads than those which must be constructed in this country. The State of Pennsylvania has expended $100,000 for English engines, but has recently concluded to abandon the use of them and hereafter to order their engines made in this country."[36] In fairness it should be reported that this engine, the *Tennessee*, intended for the Winchester and Potomac Railroad, ultimately afforded reasonable service on a water-level line, though probably only after some modifications.

The Use of Locomotives on Grades

Far more serious a problem facing the Maryland railroad was a resolution of the question of possible grades opposing operations of the line. Stephenson thought heavy construction or inclined planes operated by stationary winding engines must be employed to reduce grades to less than 1 percent. In laying out the line between Baltimore and Frederick only one serious grade intervened, that between the headwaters of the Patapsco and a tributary of the Potomac, on which Frederick was located. This Parr's Spring Ridge was considered an appropriate location for inclined planes, four of which, two on each slope, were laid out. These ranged between 170 and 264 feet per mile—in other terms, 3.2 and 5.0 percent. While the Baltimore-Frederick line was operated by horse traction, no test of the engines was possible, but with the introduction of the Baltimore-type locomotives it became inevitable. At first locomotive engineers were instructed to go only as far as the eastern slope of Parr's Spring Ridge, but soon they were

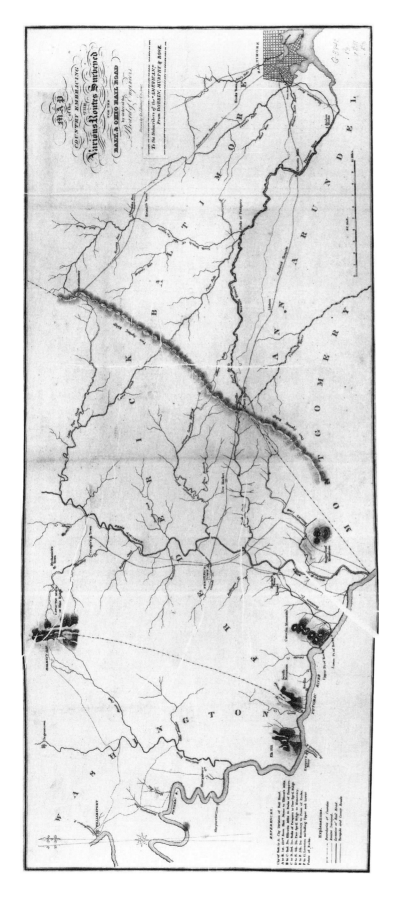

This map shows the countryside of the Maryland Piedmont that was surveyed in establishing the route immediately westward of Baltimore rising up that piedmont to the "Blue Ridge" (Catoctin Mountain). *Source:* Library of Congress map.

attempting to surmount it, which their locomotives proved capable of doing. Seymour gives an account of his run along this line accompanied by president Thomas of the Baltimore road:

The plane is 2150 feet in length—2050 feet of which ascend at the rate of 197 feet per mile [3.7 percent]. . . . From the first plane, the train proceeded to the second, which is 3000 feet in length—2800 feet at 170 feet per mile, 100 feet at the rate of 227, and the 100 feet at the summit at 264 feet to the mile. The engine and its train ascended at the rate of from five to six miles per hour to within thirty feet of the summit of this plane, when, on the grade of 264 feet to the mile, it stopped. The three small cars, weighing 5 tons 1 cwt., were then cast loose, when the engine, starting without assistance on this grade, drew the double car and passengers to the summit with the greatest apparent ease. The steam escaped from the safety valve as well when the engine reached the summit of the plane as when it left the foot.[37]

On this experience the future course of the railroad to the Ohio seems to have been assured. As Seymour tells us,

With such results as the above it is unnecessary to add . . . that [the Erie Railroad] committee are equally gratified and surprised; and from what they themselves witnessed, they have no hesitation in expressing their conviction that the engines of the Baltimore and Ohio Railroad are capable of drawing, with ease, at least fifty passengers up ascents of any length, of from 200 to 220 feet per mile [3.7 to 4.1 percent]. It is now a matter of common parlance to assert that the Alleghenies can be passed by locomotive engines by the Potomac route without the use of stationary power. . . . Excepting the engines manufactured [in Baltimore], there is probably not one in the United States, although some of the best ever made in England have been imported, which is capable of ascending the grades and passing the curves . . . which must occur among the mountains. . . . While nature has done much to facilitate the intercourse of Baltimore from the West, the Baltimore and Ohio Railroad company has not done less.[38]

These Baltimore engines, which shortly became generally characteristic of the United States with the adoption of the horizontal boiler in the B&O's shops, led to the spread of B&O practices to American locomotive building, ranging from Lowell and Taunton in Massachusetts to Paterson (New Jersey), Philadelphia, Virginia, and the Carolinas. The two characteristics of those locomotives that made them distinctive and a great force in shaping the geographical pattern of railroad building in the United States were already present in this early crossing of Parr's Spring Ridge: the swivelling "leading" truck, largely developed by Ross Winans on the B&O, and the access to considerable power to draw heavy loads over steep grades. The heavy curvature that became characteristic of American lines required the leading truck, whereas it was the shortage of capital for heavy engineering of the line that brought the massive power into operation. With those two abilities that the English engines sorely lacked, the American railroad could become a very different thing from its distant English cousin. It seems to me accurate to think in terms of the diffusion of railroad technology in the growth of the American system, but it should be fully appreciated that it was from Baltimore, not Newcastle or Liverpool, that that diffusion took place.

B&O Construction Gains Speed

Once the elements of this American system of railroad construction had been worked out so as to facilitate the building of lines rapidly and reasonably cheaply,

The B&O railroad bridge at Harper's Ferry, West Virginia. *Source:* B&O Railroad photo.

The Queen City Hotel was constructed at the station of the first major western city to be reached by the B&O Railroad, Cumberland, Maryland. It stood until the 1970s, when an effort to preserve it as a historical building failed. *Source:* B&O Museum photo.

considerable undertakings fell within the competence of the rapidly expanding republic. From Harper's Ferry for the ninety-seven miles westward to Cumberland, where the Allegheny Front, the edge of the Appalachian Plateau, was encountered, the B&O made use of the Potomac, which cut in a sinuous course through the repeating ridges of the Folded Appalachians. The main problems encountered were the requirement set by the commonwealth of Virginia, when it gave financial support to the railroad, that its line must cling to the right or Virginia bank of the river in passing between the two preexisting towns, and the sinuosity of the river, which would have made the line excessively long save for three tunnels that cut through the necks of entrenched meanders. The graded slope of the Potomac meant that the line could have easy grades, none above forty feet per mile (0.7 percent). Through the use of tunnels and 3,690 feet of bridging, mostly iron truss in form, good alignment could be maintained to the extent that no curve, save directly at Harper's Ferry, was less than a thousand feet in radius. By 1842 this line was opened using "bridge" or H-rail laid on wooden stringers supported by wooden crossties. At fifty-one pounds per yard this was light rail, only eighty tons per mile, but still costly, as it had to be imported from England, the last remaining "contribution" England was required to make to the initiation of American railroad building.[39]

Once at Cumberland the final stretch of the self-evident course for the B&O had been set, with considerable doubt remaining as to where the line should reach the Ohio River. Some called for projecting the line northwestward to Pittsburgh at the forks of the Ohio; others urged Wheeling in Virginia or the mouths of almost all the left-bank tributaries of the Ohio as far south as the Kanawha, the point Virginia set for the southern limit for the Ohio terminus when it authorized the continuation of the Maryland line within the Old Dominion. These western continuations encountered political as well as terrain obstacles. To reach to Pittsburgh, or even by a direct route to Wheeling from Cumberland, passage through Pennsylvania was necessary, as the Mason-Dixon line lay only six miles north of Cumberland. At first Pennsylvania seemed to encourage such a connection, but rapidly the force of urban mercantilism began to assert itself so that the grant of a charter for such a line was made highly conditional on the failure of a Pennsylvania Railroad that would be a linear replacement for the ill-starred Mainline Canal System. But the Pennsylvania was created in 1846 to continue the rail line that had already been completed between Philadelphia and Columbia on the Susquehanna in 1834 and was extended to Harrisburg by 1838.[40] Thus, the charter for the B&O extension in Pennsylvania was not issued until much later. In that situation the company had to come to terms with Virginia, which required that the moral commitment to Wheeling be honored. A line was carried first directly to the potential crossing place of the Allegheny Front at Piedmont, twenty-eight miles west of Cumberland. In doing so the company entered the most productive coal field in western Maryland and began for the first time to earn the handsome loadings of the bituminous coal that was to make it rich. Still, at that time no such earnings could pay for a line up onto and across the plateau, so the construction of this section was typically "American" in experiencing a shortage of capital. Matters eased a bit only when Baring Brothers in London agreed to provide funds in return for control of the state bonds the company was receiving.

A bituminous coal train reaches the crest of the Allegheny Front at Altamont, Maryland, establishing the ruling grade for the first trans-Appalachian railroad at 2.2 percent. As it turned out, this became the widely adopted grade cap set for Canadian as well as American rail lines. *Source:* B&O Museum photo.

The Bellaire-Benwood Bridge, a through-truss structure, was needed to carry the B&O across the Ohio River when that stream was reached at Wheeling, Virginia, in 1852. *Source:* B&O Museum photo.

The B&O was actually the third trans-Appalachian line to be built; the New York and Erie Railroad was being constructed across the deeply trenched Appalachian Plateau of southern upstate New York at this time, and the Pennsylvania Railroad was progressing on its extension of the older line from Philadelphia to Harrisburg westward to Pittsburgh. The route the B&O adopted westward from Piedmont at the foot of the Allegheny Front commenced with a long ascent, seventeen miles long, bringing the railroad in a single pull to its highest point (2,626 feet) on the summit of the ridge that divides the watershed of the Potomac (the Atlantic) from that of the Ohio (the Gulf of Mexico). At first it would seem to have been simple enough to build the railroad down the valley of the nearest stream that led to the Ohio, but such a route would have taken many more miles. Even more, it would have forced the line to pass northward into Pennsylvania along that first Ohio tributary, the Youghiogheny, but the Quaker commonwealth was not likely to authorize that. Instead, a route had to be carried directly across the plateau, for nearly 175 miles, where the drainage was mostly transverse to the alignment adopted. The result was some very expensive construction, with heavy bridges across the streams and long and prospectively difficult grades up from and down to those crossings. But by dint of ingenious surveying, considerable side-hill excavation, and the building of the first long tunnels on American lines—the longest, at Kirkwood, being 4,100 feet and that at Board Tree 2,350 feet—a reasonable alignment and grade were secured. As completed, the Cumberland-Wheeling line had no grade steeper than 116 feet per mile, which incidentally became the "standard ruling grade" on North American railroads. It was adopted in a number of cases by the national government when it gave financial assistance to railroads, most notably on the Union Pacific in the United States; and later, when adopted by the Dominion government in the authorization for the Canadian Pacific, it became a widely accepted upper limit of grade in Canada. On Christmas Day, 1852, construction was completed, and the B&O then reached 393 miles from tidewater at Baltimore to river level on the Ohio at Wheeling. The first great American railroad had been completed between its initial termini. Of course, Wheeling was not the ultimate objective of the company whose sights had lengthened as it became accepted that urban mercantilism could work over a greater reach than that merely across the Appalachians. But in order to examine how that particularly urban force came to be expressed elsewhere on the Atlantic seaboard, it is best here to stop and return to the projects undertaken by Baltimore's rivals. Later we may return to how that interurban competition came to be expressed geographically west of the mountains.[41]

Pennsylvania Accepts Responsibility

While Baltimore was evolving its Ohio Road and the American practice of railroad building, other coastal entrepôts were examining their own mercantile geography. Pennsylvania responded relatively early, as we have seen, but in a rather equivocal manner. The rail link in the Mainline Canal System, that between Philadelphia and Columbia on the Susquehanna, was authorized by the commonwealth in 1828 and completed over its rolling eighty-two mile length in 1834. As constructed, operation was to be by locomotives between the tops of two inclined planes, one at either end. This, the "first railroad undertaken in any part of the world by a government,"[42] stood at first as an expression not so much of urban mercantilism as of state competition in gaining access across the Appalachians to open up the Middle West. "When the Columbia [Rail] Road was open for use the prevailing opinion regarding its method of operation was that farmers and other citizens along the line should use the railroad as they used the turnpike[s], *i.e.,* purchase suitable wagons to be hauled by animal power and pay a certain toll to the State for the use of the roadway. This method of operation was put into practice for a time." Once it was realized—before the line was completed—that steam engines were likely to be employed, several were ordered from England, as now the "State supplied the locomotive engines for the transportation of goods and passengers, while the cars were owned by individuals or companies."[43] This endeavor proved impractical in two ways: as we have seen, the English engines were unsatisfactory and had to be replaced by ones of American manufacture, and the use of the line for private cars was incompatible with a medium whose vehicles had to be operated in trains. Much had to be transformed about this Columbia Railroad because it was so early in opening. The inclined plane at Columbia was already under sentence when, in 1836, a 6.5-mile relocation of the railroad to gain adhesion working was begun, to be completed in 1840. The Schuylkill plane in Philadelphia, some 2,805 feet in length and 187 feet in height (6.6 percent), could not effectively be worked as it was built, so a line between Ardmore Station and the west end of the Market Street Bridge was finished in 1851, in time to be in use when the Pennsylvania Railroad was completed to Pittsburgh the next year.[44]

Massachusetts Demonstrates a Contrast

Farther to the north in New England the parallel with Baltimore was much more direct: Boston, like Baltimore, could not practically hope to be served by any canal scheme, even a partial one, in reaching to the West. Thus, by 1830, after considerable investigation, Massachusetts was ready to accept the railroad as its ordained medium for mercantile competition. Nearby, Gridley Bryant's Granite Railway was proving efficient in reducing the cost of transporting low-value, bulky goods, and the word from England was that the Liverpool and Manchester was equally successful in encouraging and profiting from the increased movement of passengers. In that climate there were many proposals for the chartering of railroads, and the first to be issued was for one from Boston to Lowell, a distance of twenty-six miles already the route of the Middlesex Canal. In this seeming paradox—that the first railroad charter issued in Massachusetts was for the one pairing of cities within the commonwealth actually possessed of a canal—we have a historical-geographical situation that needs some examination.

The paradox is also typical of the earliest English lines; these were built not into little-developed country but rather as supplemental connections where trade was already vigorous. The Middlesex Canal had been built in the first decade of the nineteenth century to turn the flow of country trade away from the port at the mouth of the Merrimack River, Newburyport, toward Boston, the larger entrepôt. But in 1823 cotton spinning and weaving had begun on a grand scale at the new town of Lowell laid out just downstream from the Merrimack end of the Middlesex Canal, where the impressive Pawtucket Falls interrupted the river's flow on a scale to permit a true city of hydraulic power to be set in motion. The canal could reach Lowell, but the trade that the rapid growth of such a wondrous city generated soon overtaxed it, while that waterway with its five-month closure for ice in winter even more tried the indulgence of the new class of "manufacturers" who were interested in continuous access to markets. Thus, it is not surprising that when railroads became a major topic of interest in Boston, the capitalists who had provided the considerable sums necessary to build Lowell's earlier mills also saw in the railroad a necessary adjunct to further development of their properties.

In a sense this was using the railroad for development, but that sense should be seen to be quite restricted. The group of Boston capitalists realized that, with a dependence for power on falling water, factories would have to be dispersed into the immediate hinterland of their city, even farther afield as those adjacent sites had their waterpower taken up. To make this system work, however, Boston remained the entrepôt where the "Boston Associates" and their cotton and woolen merchants assembled the staples for onward shipment to the mill towns, and to which the product of those mills returned for dispatch to the geographically enlarging market necessary for such a revolution in the scale of textile production. In this waterpower phase of New England textile development, lines of the sort that brought the railroad revolution to Britain had to be undertaken. Just as the Stockton and Darlington and the Liverpool and Manchester were adjuncts to, before ultimately replacing, the system of waterborne trade, the Boston and Lowell Railroad organized by Patrick Tracy Jackson and other members of the Boston Associates was at first a supplement to the Middlesex Canal. In all these cases a short line, twenty-five to thirty-five miles long, was projected inward from a port—respectively Stockton, Liverpool, and Boston—to make it economical to engage in production in the interior away from the coast. With such an easily demonstrable market and access to considerable capital from the mercantile activities of the Darlington Quakers, the Liverpool Party, and the Boston Associates and their colleagues, it was not difficult to envision pioneering in railroad construction and doing so on a generous scale. As Edward Kirkland saw it, in America this led to what might be termed the "Massachusetts-English" school of railroad engineering, wherein heavy construction became possible and building in full scale at the beginning might be undertaken.

The Boston and Lowell: A British Railroad in America

The Boston and Lowell Railroad was first bruited on January 18, 1830, when Patrick Tracy Jackson requested of the agent for the Proprietors of the Locks and Canals at the Pawtucket Falls of the Merrimack River (Lowell) that he call his directors together for a meeting to consider building a railroad between that burgeoning textile city and Boston. On January 27 those proprietors decided to seek a charter for such an undertaking, which was passed by the General Court in time to be signed by the president of the House of Representatives on June 5, 1830, becoming the first such charter in the commonwealth.[45] Given the wealthy paternity of the line, it is not surprising that the best possible structure was sought. To begin with, the projectors rejected the small change of on-line support, seeking instead to build directly to Lowell to gain dollars, and disregarding the intermediate towns to the extent that the line as constructed passed through few settlements, despite the rather high density of population in eastern Massachusetts even in the 1830s. The rationale seems to have been to keep down land-acquisition costs, even though the company was given powers of condemnation of right-of-way. Further, the company publicly expressed interest in the carriage of passengers as well as the staples of the cotton trade. The proprietors of the Middlesex Canal, in remonstrating to the General Court in February, held that "no *mere substitute* for the established accommodation should be allowed without an obvious necessity." Certainly it must be

believed that no safer or cheaper mode of conveyance can ever be established [than the canal], nor any so well adapted for bulky articles. To establish therefore, a *substitute* for the canal alongside of it, and for the whole distance, and in many places within a few rods of it, and to do that which the canal was made to do, seems to be a measure not called for by any exigency. . . . With regard, then, to transportation of tonnage goods, the means exist for all but the winter months as effectually as any that can be provided. There is a supposed source of revenue to a Rail-Road *from carrying passengers.* As to this, the remonstrants venture no opinion, except to say that passengers are now carried at all hours, as rapidly and safely as they are anywhere else in the world; and if the usual time consumed in passing from one place to another be three hours—there seems not to be any such exigency to make that space of time half what it now is, as to justify the establishment of a rail-road for that purpose merely. . . . To this, the remonstrants would add, that the use of a rail-road for passengers only has been tested by experience, nowhere, hitherto; and that it remains to be known whether this is a mode which will command general confidence and approbation.[46]

Confidence the railroad promoters had, both in the growing shipment of commodities throughout the year and in the potential for passenger movement, sufficient to cause them to plan a double-track line, though in the beginning only one set of rails was to be laid on the double embankment. Because of the much greater level of ground frost to be found in New England than in England, it was decided to use granite crossties supported under the rails by continuous walls of rubble-stone sunk some three to four feet into the ground. Fish-belly rail of thirty-five pounds to the yard was to be supported on this enduring and unyielding substructure. In direct reflection of English practice, the Boston and Lowell was authorized to raise or lower the grade of all crossing roads so as to permit the over- or underpasses necessary to a separated grade. Using such expedients in all but three cases—and those became running sores in the history of the line—the Boston and Lowell stood out from almost all other American lines in avoiding conflict with other movements.

The financing of the line was simple by comparison with most others in the New World. Shares were set at $500 par, the only such instruments of participation above $100 to be found in American railroading. The $1.2 million capital was raised rather quickly, and construction was carried rapidly to completion in May 1835. Two incidents during that building jarred the general confidence of the promoters. The first concerned the laying of the single track, which was begun on the right side starting from each end. Needless to say, in the middle it was discovered that a reverse curve was necessary to join the two.[47] The second incident grew out of the overbuilding of the substructure of the line. The light cast-iron rail soon began to fail as the pounding of the locomotives' driving wheels on the anvil-like granite blocks smashed the brittle castings. This failure of British practice came as a particular disappointment, as the machine shop of the Locks and Canal Company had seen to it that all joints were absolutely smooth, even to the extent of filing down any difference in level equal to the thickness of a sheet of paper. More general, of course, was the misfortune that the line was first equipped with a Stephenson engine, which arrived in 1832, early determining that the Stephenson gauge would rule in most of New England. Soon (now) Major George Whistler, who became superintendent of the Locks and Canals shops in 1834 after leaving the Baltimore and Ohio, was building his own version of these Stephenson engines, and they were improved and strengthened for American use, but the gauge had been fixed. Alvin Harlow believes that "had Whistler come to the Lowell Road earlier, he might have succeeded in averting that folly of building the track on a stone foundation. As it was, he made its shops the first locomotive building plant in New England."[48]

As completed, the Boston and Lowell was an impressive example of a British railroad in America. In length and structure more impressive than the Stockton and Darlington and in years only five after the Liverpool and Manchester, it made available for emulation and observation on American shores such a "British" line. That it was little copied, even within Boston, should make it clear that it was not lack of knowledge that led to a separate American tradition of railroad construction. We knew enough and had enough technical competence to copy the British practice if we had wished to do so. The Boston and Lowell demonstrates that. What we also had was sufficient ingenuity and ability to transform that basic knowledge into an improved structure, not merely for American conditions but also even for reexport to Britain and Europe. The much more flexible American substructure totally replaced earlier British practice in much of the world, as did the T-rail that Robert L. Stevens had devised in 1830. American locomotives crossed the Atlantic with much greater frequency after 1830 than those from Newcastle or Newton-le-Willows came westward. Ultimately, the four-wheel truck was widely adopted on the Continent, though very slowly in Britain.

To understand why there was so little American use made of British practice, we need look no farther than the building of the other two "trunk lines" opened out of Boston in 1835, making that city the world's first "railroad junction." In 1830 proponents of rail building came together in proposals to build from the Hub westward to Albany and the Hudson and southward toward the reentrants of the waters connecting with New York via Long Island Sound. Within Massachusetts the closest navigable water opening west of Cape Cod, with its dangerous fogs and shoals, was Mount Hope Bay and its tidal river to Taunton, a city that in 1829 sought a charter for a rail line. Others in Boston believed that Providence at the head of the more easily traversed Narragansett Bay was a better choice for this rail crossing of one of Gallatin's "Four Necks of Land." Finally, proponents of the western line and their supporters in Worcester envisioned solving this problem of easier access to the Long Island Sound steamers by constructing a line from the Western Road at Worcester southward to the head of Connecticut's lone fjord, the lower Thames at Norwich. In the end each of these lines was constructed, but in the beginning only that to Providence.

Thus, we next must look briefly at the lines west and south out of Boston that were constructed between 1831 and 1835.

The Laying Out of the Boston and Providence

Later we shall consider in some detail the laying out of the first transcontinental railroad, the Union Pacific, as an example of the American developmental line in its most fully evolved form. Partly to provide a contrast to that evolved form and partly to examine how the Massachusetts-English engineering practice had to be adapted even in the earliest years of construction, it is useful to examine the laying out of the Boston and Providence Railroad as proposed in 1832.[49] This line is particularly interesting on several scores. It was surveyed and laid out by one of the great pioneers of American railroad design, William Gibbs McNeill, whom we have already encountered while he was working in what some have called the "University of the Baltimore and Ohio"; the Boston and Providence represented the first stage in the evolution of the American railroad system in a region where the initial inclination was to copy slavishly what turned out to be an inappropriate English prototype; and this line could be assured of heavy use virtually upon opening because it supplied the critical shortcut on a water route between two of the most important cities. The transitional nature of the line is well attested by the fact that again we encounter Patrick Tracy Jackson as one of the five directors, no doubt as much because of his experience as the prime promoter of the Boston and Lowell as for his high standing in the Boston mercantile community.[50]

McNeill begins his report thus:

The character of the country between Boston and Providence is such as rather to require the exercise of judgement in the selection of one from among numerous very feasible routes for a Rail-Road, than even [to call for] the ordinary research to determine that such a work is easily practicable between those points. For although to the base of the dividing ridge, which separates the waters flowing northward into Massachusetts Bay, from those descending southward into Narragansett Bay—and which as a consequence must be crossed by any route from Boston to Providence—it is soon apparent that but two general routes can be suggested . . . yet the summit of this ridge may be attained at various points by a gradual approach to it through the valleys of the several branches of the Neponsett, which unite near its base; and we find that from the more level character of the country south of the summit, the preference due to either route must be very much dependent on the comparative facility with which we surmount the Dividing Ridge.[51]

From this statement it is clear that three *fundamental geographical features* were most determinative in laying out this, or any, line: the two established termini of the undertaking and the minimum irreducible summit on the line. With these determined, then *fundamental derivative features* would influence any location decision. These would include securing (1) a practicable "working grade" for the efficient and economical utilization of steam locomotives, (2) a reasonable curvature on the line, and (3) possible access to desirable intermediate settlements. In a special category was the holding of redundant grade to the minimum— in other words, avoiding any secondary "summits" wherever possible. But as always in practical problems, there had to be a system of trade-offs between redundant grade and circuitous routing. Time and fuel consumption, as well as additional track construction and maintenance, ultimately meant that the level

48

THE NORTH
AMERICAN
RAILROAD

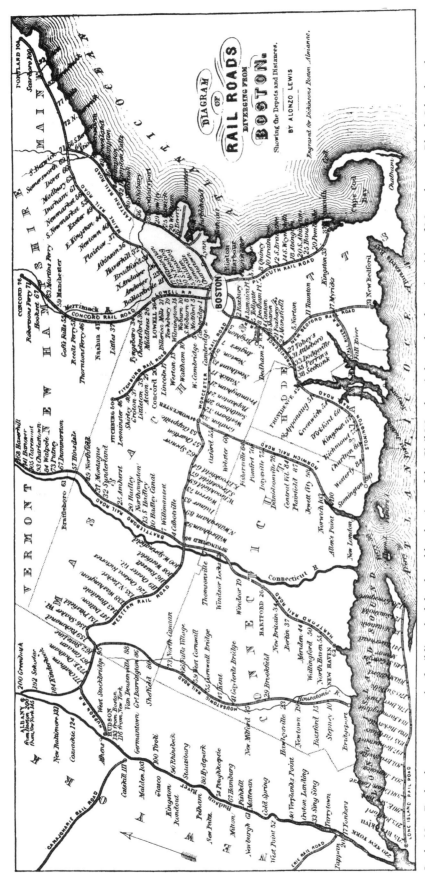

In the New England states a network of rail lines had developed by the time of the Civil War that tied together the major cities of Massachusetts, Rhode Island, and Connecticut, and reached outward to Albany and the lines stretching across upstate New York, to the Hudson Valley alignment of railroads, and to Montreal and the Grand Trunk of Canada. *Source:* S. N. Dickinson, *Boston Almanac for the Year 1846.*

but wandering route would quite likely prove to be a poor choice. In Britain, with Stephenson's rigidities, the solution of the redundant grade–circuitous mileage problem was almost always found in tunneling or heavy viaduct work. But in America, with its scarcity of capital, the solution is usually still evident on the ground: an initial compromise—some redundant grade or some circuity, or most likely some of each—that would, given heavier use and earnings, lead to subsequent reconstructions of the line. Few Europeans, or Americans for that matter, appreciate how much reconstruction has been characteristic of American railroads. And one of the factors contributing to the relatively low technical competence of those lines today is the failure during the last fifty years to continue that necessary but increasingly costly reconstruction process. The line Isambard Kingdom Brunel built between Bristol and London in the 1830s was so overconstructed that it has, with little reconstruction, handled the introduction of the "125 Trains" (in fact those high-speed vehicles themselves have stood up less well than the original Great Western line on which they operate). But the original Shore Line between Boston and New York has had to be reconstructed several times, including the present effort being undertaken by its new owner, Amtrak, to permit even a more modest speed than 125 miles per hour. In that effort, though, the Boston and Providence has held up better than some of its subsequent extensions, because it was a transitional fabric between British and American when first laid out.

McNeill expressed well the control of route alignment by a few critical features: "The extent and elevation of the range of Blue Hills, it will readily be seen, prevent their passage by any route intermediate [between the coast] and the valley of the Neponsett River: and . . . it may be said that it is this range, *that* immediately south of Boston, and the height of the Dividing Range in its several depressions, which together constitute the controlling features of the country."[52] The crest of the Dividing Range, hardly more than a gentle interlude on the worn-down surface of hard-rock New England, was notched in eight places over a latitudinal distance of some fourteen miles, so that ridge was more an elevational than an alignment control. The choice among these eight possible notches had then to be made on the basis of the two characteristics we have already noted: redundant grade and circuity. McNeill in his report examines each route in turn, giving details as to engineering cost—from embankments, cuts, and bridging—with attention to total grade and total length of line. In such ways were the possible routes that could be taken across a rolling erosional plane between two cities some forty miles apart compared and a location decision determined. In the eleven separate routes studied, the height of the summit of the Dividing Ridge varied only modestly (from 140 to 267 feet) and the distances similarly (from 40.75 to 49.51 miles). The shortest route involved an inclined plane, a solution not, by the early 1830s, to be seriously considered:

In order to estimate the relative lengths of the foregoing routes, it now becomes necessary to take into account the combined effect of friction and gravity, which together, may be said to constitute the sole impediment to locomotion on a Rail-Way: . . . the relative resistances of different inclinations, compared with a level, must depend on a ratio affixed to friction compared with gravity; and as a consequence, as the friction of carriages can be reduced, so will the advantages of a level route predominate.[53]

Clearly, a level route would be most economical to operate, but with a longer distance, as might be required to gain such a grade, many of the economies would be lost. Perhaps the best economic measure of "levelness" is not so much the true average gradient, for few lines are actually level, as it is the redundant grade. It is appropriate to note here that the geographical concept of redundant grade needs some economic modification. Returning to our original statement of fundamental geographical features—the termini and the irreducible height of the main dividing ridge—any ascent greater than that directly from each terminus to the divide is redundant. But railroads need not necessarily serve only the termini; it is entirely possible—as on a commuter line, for example—that the series of stops may introduce considerable amounts of both circuity and redundant grade, neither of which qualities is in that case inappropriate to the economic purposes of the line. Because then "circuity" and "redundancy of grade" are conditional qualities, not absolutes, it becomes necessary in planning any route that a decision be made as to the overriding *purpose for the line* so as to judge the bearing of "circuity" and "redundancy of grade" on the alignment to be chosen.

McNeill stated this principle very directly to his directors:

The facts, as developed by the surveys, and the results of the calculations having now been stated, it remains to the Directors to decide, under all the circumstances, which must be considered, [which] is the preferable route for the projected Rail-Road from Boston to Providence. If the object be, facility of intercourse between those places, without regard to the collateral trade of intermediate towns, it would seem clearly deducible from what has been already stated, that this would be best effected by one of the *Sharon routes;* which, inasmuch as they merely differ in the choice presented of either ascending the dividing ridge by an inclined plane, requiring stationary power, or more gradually at an expense of one mile in distance, may be regarded as the same, and no discussion of *their* comparative merits would at this time seem necessary. Indeed, if objections to an inclination, which would not permit the use of locomotive engines, throughout the route, be paramount to considerations of cost of construction, it may prove practicable within a sum which would still leave the direct route in advantageous contrast with the others, to employ an assistant locomotive engine (instead of the stationary) to surmount the elevation from the marshes [along the Neponsett River, directly] to the Summit of the Dividing Ridge. In either case, however, I consider it rather as a favorable feature than otherwise, that instead of a gradual ascent from its commencement, the road may be constructed *on almost one level for nearly 15 miles from Boston,* throughout which the maximum effect of the motive power would be attainable; when nearly the total elevation may be at once surmounted in a limited distance, within which an adequate power may be resorted to, to maintain uninterruptedly the desired speed.[54]

In this argument for concentrating the grade, rather as Thomas Telford had come to do in canal building, McNeill turns to British support, quoting Robert Stevenson of Edinburgh to the effect "that every line of rail-way on which goods are reciprocally carried both ways, should be formed on one level, or laid out in a succession of level compartments."[55] In such argumentation McNeill tended to accept the limitations of the British engines, seeking to construct his line in accordance. As American experience and practice would demonstrate, engines could be greatly improved and the concentration of difficulty in a short stretch was less necessary, and certainly less desirable. With strong engines, trains were

The North
American Railroad
Rises in the East

The original granite viaduct built to carry the Boston and Providence Railroad across Canton Vale, site of Paul Revere's copper works, still serves Amtrak's Boston–New York main line. *Source:* Author's photo.

able to surmount most obstacles and to run at reasonable speeds even on ascending track.

Although William McNeill did not make an outright recommendation to the directors of the Boston and Providence, he guided them toward the route that was finally adopted, that through Sharon, which seems to have been chosen because it was in fact the most direct and possessed the greatest concentration of grade into a single summit without the redundancy found in most of the others. The redundant grade on the eleven routes ranged between an astonishing 6.90 feet and 122.50 feet, with the line selected standing at 16.50 feet; at the same time, it was the second shortest, 53.28 miles, in a range that extended from 52.82 to 63.75 miles. A double-width embankment was to be constructed, but only one track was to be laid. Wooden crossties were proposed instead of the stone blocks that the Boston and Lowell had copied from the Stockton and Darlington.

American Track

It seems appropriate at this point to look briefly at the substitution of T-rail for its fish-bellied ancestor. When iron rail was introduced in Britain in the middle of the eighteenth century, it was for the most part cast rather than rolled—wrought, if you will. Given the substructure that was adopted—stone blocks placed at each junction of short three- or four-foot rails—there were at first no other components of the track beyond pins or bolts; the blocks served as a sort of clamp to hold the rails end to end. These fish-belly rails normally had a widened top, or "head," on which the flanged wheels ran, resting mostly on a very narrow "edge" (accordingly, these came to be called edge rails). Below the top piece was a vertical plate, or "web," that gave the rail strength and kept it from sagging between the blocks. This web was usually fairly thin, less than an inch thick. The bottom of the rail might take one of two forms. The web might rest on a base similar to the top piece, so that in cross-section the rail was shaped like a

THE NORTH
AMERICAN
RAILROAD

recumbent H; or the lower edge of the web might simply be supported every three feet or so by a bracket, or "chair," to attach it to the blocks and hold it vertical, resulting in an inverted-T cross-section. One of the earliest British patents for rail was granted to William Jessop, a mining engineer at Loughborough in Leicestershire, for a rail having an H cross-section, though with the fish-belly that was basically essential to cast-iron track. As produced in the 1780s, this became something of a British standard. But there were a number of attempted variations: hexagonal bars; tram rails with a flange to keep the smooth tires of carts in place; and the Losh and Stephenson patent of 1816—an edge rail with a fish-belly but no bottom member, so that it had to be supported by chairs—that became the standard of the early steam lines.[56]

When Americans began to consider building rail lines, this English track seemed inappropriate for two reasons: it used a large amount of iron per linear foot of line, and it demanded considerable precision in assembly because bolts were used to hold the system together, either in chairs or with joiner plates. Such bolts were expensive to buy or difficult to produce in America. Thus, when the Camden and Amboy Railroad in New Jersey was proposed in the early 1830s, there was interest in trying to reduce the cost of the track, and the president and chief engineer, John Stevens's son Robert, was asked to look into ways to solve the problem. Watkins explains the nature of that problem:

The British railway projectors had the advantage of being able to call into their service a trained force of civil engineers . . . many [of whom] were familiar with what had been done for years on the coal tramroads; men on whose judgement the wealthy capitalist was willing to supply the money for the proposed improvement. England also had numerous machine-shops fairly well equipped with tools and stationary engines, and many coal mines and iron foundries in operation, which made it possible to obtain without difficulty the material for laying the tracks with heavy iron rails firmly attached by strong chairs to the sleepers that were imbedded in stone ballast.

 With the exception of making the rail heavier, and using steel instead of iron, and substituting an iron for a wooden cross-tie, and strengthening the splice chair, there has been no great change in the English system of track laying in the last fifty years [1838–88].[57]

By contrast, many "of the civil engineers who were first called into the service of the American railroads were connected with the Army Engineer Corps, having obtained their training at West Point, the only institution in the United States where engineering was taught during the first quarter of the [nineteenth] century. In many cases these officers were detailed for a term of years to be on the 'Board for Internal Improvements' to make surveys for various projected [rail]roads and canals. The preliminary surveys for the Camden and Amboy, the Pennsylvania, and the Baltimore and Ohio Railroads were made with the assistance of officers of this Corps." In such a capital-poor situation, "on the railroads then built the curves and gradients were frequently sharp and steep, as few cuts or fills were made, and these cheap roads were quickly extended, through a rapidly growing country, with a view to connect the navigable water courses, and to unite with the steam-boat companies in forming 'through line.' By the aid of these roads the Western and Southern States rapidly increased in population and commercial prosperity."[58]

Such developmental line could not possibly afford the high cost of the iron that would have to be imported in considerable quantities if the rail-and-chair track of the English lines were adopted. Instead, a lighter track structure, and particularly one that might be more easily assembled by unskilled labor working in the wilderness, was needed. While sailing to England to investigate construction techniques and to order iron for the Camden and Amboy, Robert Stevens envisioned a solution. He had left in the fall of 1830, instructed by his directors to purchase "all iron rail," not the rolled strap to be attached to wooden stringers first used on the Baltimore and Ohio and the South Carolina Railroad. "Mr. Stevens sailed a few days later, and it was during this voyage that he designed the first rail ever rolled with a base, whittling several model sections out of wood, which he obtained from the ship's carpenter." He was familiar with the T-shaped rail patented by Birkenshaw, but he sought to dispense with the expensive chairs on which it rested. "He added the base to the T-rail, dispensing with the chair. He also designed the 'hook headed' spike, which is substantially the railroad spike of today, and the 'iron tongue,' which has been developed into the fish-bar, and the rivets, which have been replaced by the bolt and nut, to complete the joint."[59] The first Camden and Amboy rail, as it came to be known, was rolled at thirty-six pounds per yard and was laid down on that line before it opened in 1832. Initially, stone blocks were used—almost too appropriately produced in Sing Sing prison— in which the iron spikes were embedded, but the failure to secure sufficient numbers of these blocks led to the substitution of wooden crossties, into which the spikes were driven rather than inserted in drill holes as with the blocks. Ashbel Welch, in his presidential address to the Society of Civil Engineers, summed up the result with concision if not total accuracy: "American engineers have often shown that *poverty* is the mother of invention. For example, they used wooden cross-ties as a temporary substitute, being too poor to buy stone blocks, and so made good roads because they were not rich enough to make bad ones."[60]

The T-rail was not immediately adopted even in America, as it remained too expensive for all but the most sanguine of potential markets. Where there was building over great distance and to an only partially molded market, the strap rail continued to be employed. The problem continued—that iron had mainly to be imported, often with considerable tariff—so the capital-poor lines could not even avail themselves of Robert Stevens's logical and desirable compromise. As earnings increased, imported rail might be substituted for the original iron-plated wooden stringers, but in 1842 Congress passed a high tariff law, which almost immediately led to the establishment of American rolling mills. The first iron rail rolled in the United States was produced at Mount Savage in the iron district of western Maryland in 1844 and was laid on the Baltimore and Ohio between Mount Savage and Cumberland. Camden and Amboy T-rail was rolled at the Montour Rolling Mill at Danville, Pennsylvania, in 1845 and rather rapidly came into widespread employment, though some British-type rail continued in use for many years thereafter.[61]

The Boston and Worcester and Its Extension:
A Reappraisal of Urban Mercantilism

A third line was projected outward from Boston in the early 1830s, the route to the west that had been the greatest concern of the Boston merchants as they saw the wealth that began to flow to the port of New York when the Erie Canal

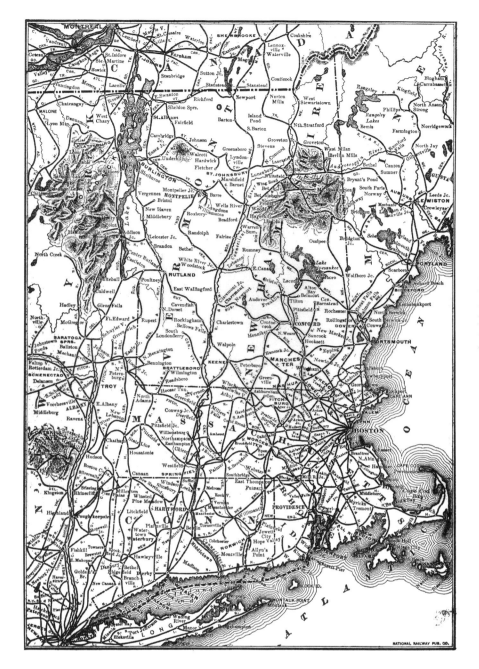

New England was one of the first areas in the world to gain an actual system of railroads, beginning with seven railroad lines radiating from Boston, making the Hub the world's oldest "junction city." The opportunity to use the East River, the Hell Gate, and Long Island Sound gave a chance to five southern New England ports to serve as the isthmian departure point for New York.
Source: Library of Congress map.

opened in 1825. Throughout the years after the authorization of the New York canal in 1817, there had been surveys of possible canal routes across the commonwealth, but they all foundered on the terrain of Massachusetts. This terrain posed a problem far more difficult than that encountered in traversing the Appalachians via the fjorded Hudson Valley and then traveling to the north of that range along its Mohawk tributary, which flowed behind those mountains and south of the great Archean Age Canadian Shield that extended southward in the Adirondacks. In Massachusetts there were two summits to cross, one of over nine hundred feet between Massachusetts Bay and the Connecticut Valley, and a second of nearly fifteen hundred feet between that valley and the Hudson. Proposals were made for a tunnel under the western ridge, the Berkshire Hills,

The North
American Railroad
Rises in the East

but construction of such a tunnel lay far beyond the engineering abilities of the time and place. Ultimately, with the success of the English railroads and the beginnings of the Baltimore and Ohio, the merchant group in Boston settled upon a rail line instead of a canal, but even then the summits were formidable indeed, in a time when the highest English line rose little more than a hundred feet above sea level, and then only at the expense of inclined planes. So challenging were the uplands of Massachusetts that it was deemed wise to undertake in the beginning only the eastern end of the route to the interior, that section of some forty-five miles from Worcester to Boston.

In several reports on the subject the chief engineer of the Boston and Worcester and the company's directors referred repeatedly to the high level of the existing traffic between the inland town and the great Massachusetts port. They were particularly heartened to report in 1833 that during the previous year the B&O had carried forty-one thousand tons of freight and almost nine thousand passengers.[62] The promoters of the Worcester road were unusual in their belief that passenger traffic would be a significant support for the company, and they set out to care for it—first with what were little more than excursions of the curious-minded, but ultimately with a passenger service that early turned the towns west of Boston into true suburbs of that emerging metropolis.[63] It seems that wage levels in America were sufficiently high, and fares sufficient low, to permit the rise of daily commuting by train as early as the 1840s. For the blue-collar workers this was perhaps the earliest rail commuting to be found anywhere (London's burgeoning flow took place only among middle-class professionals and managers in these early years).

The reason for the separation of the western line from Boston into two segments, the Boston and Worcester and what came to be known as the Western Railroad of Massachusetts, was that this route saw an early appearance of those sharp contrasts in purpose that began to emerge with the first decade of rail building in America. From Worcester eastward the line was serving a developed countryside; in fact the directors of that company drew a sharp contrast with the B&O in its eastern stretch: "The country through which the Baltimore and Ohio Rail-road runs, is not as populous, as that between [Boston] and Worcester, Frederick [Maryland] is about as large as Worcester."[64] Given this well-settled area, it was possible to envision serving an existing developed market with the favorable influence such an economic geography would have on the investing group. Still, the B&W had a much harder time raising money than did the Boston and Lowell with its captive capitalists whose mills would benefit directly and immediately from the construction of the railroad. But west of Worcester the potential for a rail route was far less clear. The central upland of Massachusetts was a hardscrabble countryside of often steep slopes and coarse gravel soils. The settlement thinned, and industry had yet to reach its full spread toward the waterpower sites there available. Under the circumstances, the prospective Western Railroad had to be perceived as a developmental line. Before we consider it, however, we should return briefly to look at the laying out of the Boston and Worcester, which stands as the archetype of the more favorably endowed of the lines that were to follow.

The Boston and Worcester faced country more trying than that encountered by any of its American predecessors. There was no master stream, such as the Patapsco for the B&O, to carry the alignment up the eroded Piedmont; instead, the Massachusetts line had to attempt to find a reasonable traverse across the grain of the drainage. Even though the summits were low east of Worcester, they were repeated as the line crossed from Boston harbor drainage (the Charles) to that of the Merrimack (Concord River) and ultimately Narragansett Bay (Blackstone River). In such a situation principles of location had to be applied that were to guide many subsequent undertakings. No single "summit ridge" as on the Providence line could be crossed; instead, a compromise had to be shaped that would keep redundant grade to a minimum and curvature to a reasonable figure. As laid out,

the length of the route . . . , from the depot in Boston to the center of town in Worcester, is about 43½ miles. This is about equal to the distance between the two towns, measured on the public road now most travelled [the Boston and Worcester Turnpike]. It is shown by the levels taken, that Worcester is situated at an elevation of 456 feet above the level of Western Avenue, in Boston. The highest summit over which the road passes, has an elevation of 491 feet. The greatest inclination of the surface of the Rail Road, as it is located, is at the rate of 30 feet in a mile. The whole amount of ascent in proceeding from Boston to Worcester is 556 feet; the amount of descent, which is divided between three different portions of the route, is about 100 feet, and the amount of ascent and descent taken together, is 656 feet. Of the whole distance, 16 miles are level, 14 miles ascend or descend at the rate of 30 feet per mile, and the remaining 13½ miles incline at different rates from 13 to 27 feet.[65]

With a ruling grade of only 0.56 percent, this was a reasonably graded line but one far more rolling than those laid out in England. Fortunately, "the greatest part of the line is straight, and the shortest curves have a radius of not less than 1150 feet." The directors go on: "The road will therefore be adapted to travelling with locomotive engines, and will admit of the most rapid speed which can safely be allowed on any rail road. For grading the road upon this line of location, no very expensive excavation or embankment will be necessary."[66]

From this information it is apparent that a good survey had been run, gaining a reasonable compromise between excessive cost of construction and continuing cost of operation. The curves and grades were gentle by what were to become American standards in somewhat rolling country, and the redundant grade was remarkably small for a route crossing three divides—some one hundred feet in 43.5 miles. The main failure was in the actual construction; a rather narrow subgrade was adopted, twenty-four feet, and only a single line was laid down, though it was doubled by 1838. Iron rail on wooden crossties was adopted after observations on the Lowell road and the B&O showed the failings of a stone substructure.

One aspect of route location that the Boston and Worcester allows us to examine in particular detail is that of finding a station site in a large city. Later in American experience the railroads often came before the town, or at least came while the town's structure was still open to easy change. In Boston, however, the railroads had to deal with the question of an appropriate location for a station, and also whether one station could serve all entering lines. The choices ranged from the one largely followed in Britain and Europe, and in America in Charleston, of placing the "depots" at the edge of the built-up city at the time the companies began operating, and that characteristic of many other American cities, Syracuse for example, of carrying the line directly through the center of an existing town along an established street. In Boston that latter course was hardly practical, and the former was hardly acceptable. Instead, the company examined a number of options. The one selected carried the line from Brighton farther south, to cross a part of the Mill Basin (Back Bay) to enter Boston somewhat along the alignment of Boston Neck, the sand spit that had always tied the peninsular city to the mainland. The line would then proceed across land to be reclaimed from tidal marshes by the South Cove Corporation "to a depot to be established on navigable waters, near the Free Bridge [to South Boston]; and thence it is proposed to carry it to another depot, near Essex Street, at the southerly termination of Lincoln Street [near the present South Station]. The advantages of this route are, that the termination near Lincoln Street is more central than either of the others proposed [adjacent to the present North Station on Charles Street], for the reception and discharge of passengers, and the depot near the Free Bridge will border on deep navigable water, and will be accessible from the ocean by passing one draw, situated not more than 300 feet from it."[67]

The site of the Boston and Worcester station in Boston was eminently successful for the purposes of passenger access, perhaps because the Worcester Company evinced more interest in passengers than had either of the other Boston companies. In selecting the south-side site the directors were making first use of what came to be a very common geographical device to gain access to the heart of an existing city—that is, to carry the line on new fill that extended outward the shoreline of a city located on navigable water. Chicago, Oakland, San Francisco, Seattle, and some smaller places were all to use variants of the Boston solution. But none proved quite so successful, because at the very pinnacle of rail commuting, 1917, South Station in Boston became the busiest passenger station the Occidental world ever knew, outdistancing Grand Central and Penn stations in New York, Waterloo in London, or the Gare St. Lazare in Paris, the other giants of the time. The success of South Station was that it was very close to the cove on which the colonial city focused; thus, no great reshaping of the city was necessary as was the case in New York, when the midtown terminals broke that city's business district into two distinct sections. South Station amply demonstrated the value of a terminal having as central a location as possible. This truth was further borne out when late in the century the New York, New Haven, and Hartford Railroad, successor to the Providence line, among others, joined with the Boston and Albany, successor to the Boston and Worcester, to build the partially surviving but wonderfully restored South Station that became such a magnet for rail commuters.

Passengers and freight both began to support the Boston and Worcester as soon as it was opened in 1835. To appraise the business we should look at what is today called an "operating ratio"—that is, the amount of total income that can be carried over to net income. Today this seldom runs over a small percentage of the total, with the very best lines earning maybe 5 percent. In 1837 the Boston and Worcester had an operating ratio of 47 percent, a net income of $102,281.83 on $215,045.32 of receipts and carried-over surplus, which unfortunately we cannot isolate from the total.[68] In comparison, the net operating ratio of Belgian railroads in 1837–38 was "little more than a half per cent per annum income."[69] No doubt much of the difference stemmed from (1) the relatively low cost of con-

Perspective drawing of the preserved section of South Station in Boston as redeveloped in the late 1980s by the Beacon Company. As suggested in this drawing, the terminal is used for Amtrak trains in Northeast Corridor service and for local commuter trains serving metropolitan Boston. *Source:* Beacon Company drawing, used by permission.

Elaborate neoclassical frieze used in original design of South Station, Boston, when constructed in 1898. *Source:* Beacon Company photo.

The reconstruction of Boston's South Station in the late 1980s emphasized the terminal nature of Amtrak's edifice. *Source:* Beacon Company photo.

struction under the American system, as opposed to the English one employed in Belgium, and (2) the somewhat higher fares available in Massachusetts, though these were lower than in England. It was important that these pioneering American lines did have fairly favorable operating ratios, for their experience encouraged the use of the railroad as a truly developmental device. Yet as might be expected, it proved necessary further to cheapen the cost of construction—particularly to substitute continuing higher operating costs for high initial investments in the road, which were largely impossible to secure because of the scarcity of capital in America—if the true developmental function of the iron road was to be realized.

The Western Railroad of Massachusetts: Toward a Developmental Line

The first promoters of a railroad west out of Boston had seen the natural objective of that line as Albany, on the Hudson, where juncture could be made with the Erie Canal. The caution that tended to characterize New England investment at first led to the building of a line only as far as Worcester. The early financial success of that undertaking immediately suggested the idea of completing a railroad along the natural alignment that Boston needed to undertake to assert its own urban mercantilism in the growing American West. When the line was finally completed in December 1841, the editor of the Utica *Daily News* apostrophized, "Yankee travel and notions will pass through our city for western New York and for westward of New York. Boston may now double her importations and her manufacture of wooden nutmegs and basswood cucumber seeds and all other knickknacks that render life agreeable. Bring them on, gentlemen, bring them on. Here is a western world now, open to Yankees, which all your ingenuity and industry cannot fill."[70] But before that happy day could be celebrated, six difficult years intervened, because not only was this the longest railroad ever built in America by a single company, it also had the highest summit yet reached by an iron road anywhere in the world.

The initial difficulty came in the matter of funds for construction. The three early lines, from Boston to Lowell, Providence, and Worcester, had raised their money with moderate ease because the Hub's merchant capitalists could clearly envision a rapid return; but west of Worcester the horizon was hidden in doubt. The normal flow of trade had been southward toward Hartford and the Connecticut ports, or farther west, down the Hudson to New York. What Boston was attempting might be no more rewarding than were the wooden nutmegs in their puddings, so efforts at selling stock were massively unsuccessful. In separation from the Boston lines the directors of the Western Railroad turned to the one source of capital where profit was not the main appeal, to the treasury of the state. In successive appeals, first in 1836 when the General Court of Massachusetts subscribed a million dollars to the stock of the Western Corporation, the state was to refill the corporation's treasury as abandonment of construction seemed imminent.[71] In this way the Western was following practices already established by most other pioneer American lines, but mainly avoided by the more English-style routes from Boston to the three nearby cities. In the end the state loaned $4 million to the corporation, as well as making its original million-dollar investment in stock. To all intents and purposes the Western Railroad of Massachusetts was a state undertaking, even to the extent that four of the directors were nominated by the state, but legally it remained a private corporation.

The Western Railroad of Massachusetts was the first American line actually to cross the Appalachians, so in its construction the great purpose of the initial stage of national railroad development was first accomplished. That it was only partially successful from an economic viewpoint in gaining for Boston an opening to the West was not the fault of the engineers who accomplished the not inconsiderable feat of crossing two major divides of that Appalachian system; the rub came in the political geography of the eastern United States. In the case of New York State and Pennsylvania, and only in a precise sense less so for Maryland, the trans-Appalachian crossing could be accomplished within the jurisdiction of the state whose metropolis sought through rail building to gain a line of mercantile advance into the interior. But for Boston and Massachusetts, no such easy course was open. Once across the Appalachians, the engineers still had to face the fact that there is no way out of New England within the United States save through New York State. To gain the development objective of the West there had to be cooperation from the state legislature of New York, and that body showed little inclination to render such aid. It was one thing to authorize the extension of the Massachusetts rail line for the ten miles that intervened between the commonwealth's western boundary and the Hudson River, another to en-

61

The North
American Railroad
Rises in the East

courage the extension of Boston interests all the way across the Empire State.

If New York City had sat idly by while such an undertaking was entered into, which was unlikely and did not happen, the interests of the state would have obviated such a course. The state, having invested millions in the building of the Erie Canal, sought to guard that facility, and its tolls, against railroad competition. Even those short lines that had been proposed to connect pairs of cities in upstate New York along the alignment of the canal were forbidden to carry freight that might have gone on the canal save in the winter months when it was frozen. We should not be misled by the fact that one of the earliest railroads in America, the Mohawk and Hudson that was opened between Schenectady and Albany in 1831, seemed to parallel the course of the eastern end of the Erie Canal. The purpose of this line was to avoid the considerable delay engendered by the last thirty miles of the canal, between Schenectady and Albany, where twenty-seven locks intervened; the railroad route was less than sixteen miles and was encumbered by no more than an inclined plane at each end. Those planes, and the trouble of unloading from barge to freight car in Schenectady and reversing the procedure in Albany, meant that the line became mainly a passenger route, saving a day's run on the canal by little more than an hour on the train. The freight stayed on board and could pass without transference all the way to dockside in New York City.[72]

As constructed, the Western Railroad was a true Appalachian line:

The hills certainly determined the road's character. The Boston and Worcester had seventeen miles of level track, the Western only seven; the maximum was 83 feet and there were one hundred and seven miles that had grades in excess of any on the Boston and Worcester. The Western was a road of deep cuts, great embankments, sharp curves, and great costs. The summit section at Washington [Massachusetts], 1,456 feet above sea level, was 1.8 miles long and cost $241,311. As late as the [mid-1860s] the most powerful engines were carrying over the road trains of only eight to ten cars averaging ten tons to a car fully loaded.[73]

The grades were in fact slightly steeper—eighty-seven feet per mile, or 1.5 percent—because at the time of construction it was found necessary to carry the grade somewhat higher above the turbulent streams than had been anticipated.[74] In crossing the eastern summit the company had to choose between directness and gentle grades. Many routes were examined in the "highlands which divide the waters of the Blackstone River, upon which the village of Worcester stands, and those of the Chickopee [flowing into the Connecticut], extended from north to south across the state. They are broken into numerous ridges and ravines; and to surmount these at any reasonable grades, resort must be had to a succession of cuttings and embankments, or a constant series of curves. The declivity on each side of this summit, is too great to admit of passing it from the Blackstone to the Chickopee valley, directly on the proper course of the route without resort to inclined planes. [The engineers were] therefore compelled to conform partially to the direction of the ridges, and take a circuitous course" along their axis so as to lengthen the line and reduce the pitch of the grade. The most southerly of the lines examined passed over the divide 13.82 miles from Worcester and 452.41 feet above the terminus there of the Boston and Worcester Railroad. This, the "Ryan line," seemed rather too circuitous, though its maximum grade was only forty feet per mile (0.75 percent), so other routes were tested. The next summit north, Morey's, was 472.76 feet above the Boston and Worcester but 13.31 miles from it. With a grade of fifty-seven feet per mile (1.0 percent), this alternative route was still within the limits of acceptability for steam operation.[75] By combining parts of these two alignments a reasonable compromise among distance and grades and curves was secured. A cut at the summit reduced the elevation over the Worcester terminus to 430 feet, the highest grade to 49 feet per mile, and the sharpest curve to a radius of 1,146 feet.

Westerly of this eastern summit various tributaries of the Chicopee (as it is now spelled) could be followed down to Springfield and the opening of the line thence from Worcester in 1839. From Worcester to the Connecticut River was about fifty-four miles, over which a "route might have been adopted with a maximum grade of 45 feet, but the distance would have been much increased and the line less direct." The directors of the Western Corporation go on: "And considering the past, and relying upon prospective improvements in locomotive engines, and their power to surmount higher grades than those formerly in use, the directors feel assured, that, so far as the route is decided upon, they have consulted the permanent interests of the corporation and the convenience of the public, by the selection of the one thus far adopted" between Worcester and Springfield.[76]

West of the Connecticut the country became even higher and more broken in the last (western) chain of the Appalachians, the Berkshire Hills. Use was made of the Westfield tributary of the main stream, carrying the line in rocky defiles to a summit at Washington, which was to be reduced by a sixty-foot cutting in hard rock to secure better approach grades. Thence the alignment descended to the limestone Berkshire Valley and the town of Pittsfield, before passing through the convenient Canaan Gap in the Taconic Range to reach the low plateau structures west of the main Appalachians. Progress was slow on this section because construction costs were high and money scarce. In 1839 the corporation, in return for state loans, agreed to try to expedite the work, particularly to undertake construction of the section west of the Connecticut River simultaneously with that section to the east. In this we find one of the most potent weapons railroad companies might wield in seeking governmental assistance: the impatience of those often fairly sparsely settled populations for rail access to potential markets. A committee of the directors journeyed west to Albany in 1840 to view the work and to negotiate with the state of New York and Albany officials for a subsidy on the construction of the Western Railroad in New York State (the Albany and West Stockbridge Railroad). The committee included nine directors, among whom were George Bliss, the president of the corporation, and Elias Hasket Derby, perhaps the richest merchant in America, who had recently taken an interest in the Western for its potential impact on Boston, where his concerns had progressively turned as the Salem shipmasters of his youth yielded dominance to the Boston merchants whose wealth came as well from eastern New England's rise as the "seat of American industry." Successfully negotiating their grant of $650,000 as a loan from Albany and a charter from New York State, the Western directors were also waited upon by delegations from the West. They reported that the people of the West, from St. Louis to Albany, are looking with intense interest to the completion of our Western road, and many of them waited upon your Delegation at Albany. They informed us that so *prolific* was the soil, and so bountiful had been recent harvests at the West, that their granaries were overflowing, and they look to Boston, not merely as the seat of literature and the arts, not merely as a seaport, where capital, in which they are deficient, has accumulated to a large amount, but as the best market in America for the produce of the West, and the Great Centre and depot of American manufactures. . . . And your Delegation concluded, from all which they saw and heard, that the patronage our rail-road will eventually enjoy, if administered in a liberal spirit, will exceed the anticipation of its most sanguine friends.[77]

Diverging Views on Pricing

Greatly under the influence of Derby, who viewed railroad development from a merchant's perspective, the Albany delegation noted first that it would be necessary to work some changes in the mercantile pattern in America. "In the ordinary course of things, it requires time to change habits and to turn business into new channels; but after a revulsion like that which has recently protracted the enterprise of the country [the Panic of 1837 and its aftermath], new arrangements and new connections will of course be formed, and the revival of our manufactures, and the opening of our steam communication with Europe [via the Cunard Line established that year], must direct the eyes of the whole country towards Boston."[78] Then the delegation added, "They have found no system more conducive to a large and increasing income than a moderate scale of charges for freight and passage, giving, as they almost invariably do, a large accession of business with a comparatively small increase in expense, and promoting, as they do, at the same time, the success of the road and the convenience and welfare of the community."[79] Derby, chairman of the delegation, advanced this creed with such great force that the Western Railroad entered into a twenty-year conflict with its eastern connection, the Worcester road, which adopted English-style practices in more than simply creating its superstructure. "The Worcester sought constantly to keep its fares and rates high, so as to maximize its earnings as it saw fit, while the Western adopted a much more directly development technique of seeking to encourage growth, and thereby ultimately the greater prosperity of the Company." The confidence that these Boston merchants showed was well expressed in a report of a committee of the Western road in 1843: "Nobody has ever proposed, we think, to put the fares high, *positively,* nor is anyone so perverse in theory as to propose, *positively,* to put them low; since in either case the effect must be, to diminish the net income of the road. The true principle, all must admit, is to obtain the largest *net* income. . . . The circumstance to govern a sagacious director, will not so much be looked for in Belgium, or France, or Austria, as much as nearer home." Not only did those Western directors fault their eastern connection; they also criticized the string of short lines stitched together between Albany and Buffalo for trying to maintain fares too high, to the detriment of the true regional development for which Derby and his peers envisioned rail transportation to be essential.[80]

This was to become a classic argument in the historical geography of transportation: Was the purpose of transportation to respond to demonstrated needs, or to build for those that might be anticipated? Corollary to the resolution of that question was the choice that must be made between "high-cost" trans-

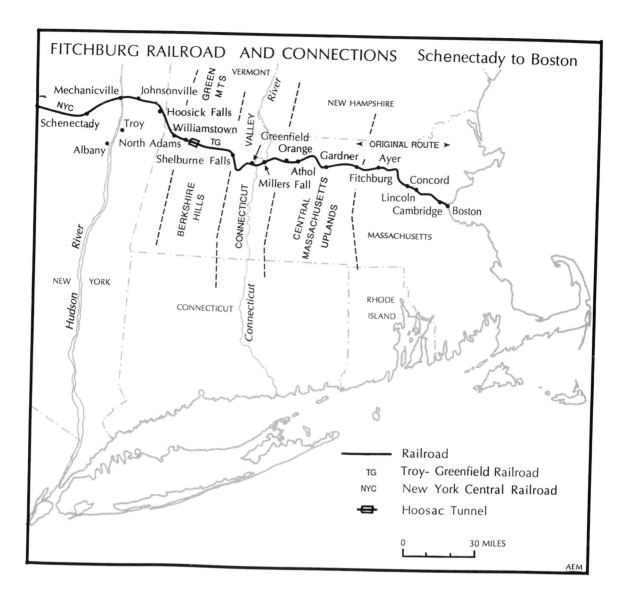

FITCHBURG RAILROAD AND CONNECTIONS   Schenectady to Boston

VERMONT

Mechanicville   Johnsonville   GREEN MTS
NYC
Schenectady   Troy   Hoosick Falls   NEW HAMPSHIRE
        Williamstown   VALLEY
Albany   North Adams   TG   ◄ ORIGINAL ROUTE ►
        Shelburne Falls   Greenfield
                Orange   Gardner   Ayer
            Millers Fall   Athol   Fitchburg   Concord
                        Lincoln
    BERKSHIRE HILLS   CONNECTICUT   CENTRAL MASSACHUSETTS UPLANDS   Cambridge   Boston

River   Hudson   MASSACHUSETTS

NEW   YORK   Connecticut

    CONNECTICUT   RHODE
            ISLAND

━━━━━ Railroad
TG   Troy- Greenfield Railroad
NYC   New York Central Railroad
⊟   Hoosac Tunnel

0   30 MILES

AEM

portation (a result either of overbuilding for the market or of the subsequent failure of a mass market to develop) and "low-cost" transportation (a result either of marginal construction or of the easy development of a mass market). We shall see that this decision has had to be faced repeatedly, not merely in railroad construction but also in the creation of intra-urban rail transport, road transportation, and commercial air service. Although there are some exceptions, in general there has been a transatlantic dichotomy as to "national" approach: Europeans, including the British, have rather consistently shown greater concern for the perfection of high-cost transport (from the earliest rail lines, as John Kellett has shown,[81] to the Concorde supersonic aircraft), whereas Americans have been the great champions of the low-cost, often marginally constructed, transport that could be used quickly to develop a mass market (from the earliest American railroads to the Boeing 747).

This dichotomy has had a particular geographical expression. In Europe the rail systems responded to established market forces: the shipment of coal and the movement of middle-class passengers in England, France, and the Low

Countries; the unification of the state in Italy and Germany, and the military growth of the latter. In America the main "market" that rail-building responded to was the strongly felt need to expand the oecumene of the nation. Similar goals affected rail building in Canada, Australia, South Africa, and Russia. But it was in the United States that the basic design for such developmental railroading was worked out, strongly in contrast both technically and socially to the situation in western Europe. The Western Railroad of Massachusetts, goaded by Elias Hasket Derby, was the first to show what railroading must become in America. Nathan Hale, president of the Worcester road, enunciated the opposing, contemporary English, view: "We directors have a perfect right to establish any rate of fare, not exceeding the rates of stage-coach and wagon transportation charged heretofore, which will afford the greatest amount of income." Derby argued instead, "I do not hesitate to take the ground that the present charges are too high, both for the interests of the stockholders and the public. It is a general principle, recognized by all intelligent statesmen, that the demand for luxuries increases more rapidly than the cost declines, when the reduction of price occurs. . . . Who are the proprietors of the road? They are the enterprising merchants, manufacturers and artisans of Massachusetts; they took their shares not with a view to profit, but the advancement of commerce, and the development of the resources of the state."[82]

From this belief in the seemingly infinite benefit of low fares and rates grew one of the distinctive geographical features of American railroading: the multi-plication of lines serving the same distant termini. In Britain there was ulti-mately a similar competition, in the area delimited by Nottingham, Derby, Manchester, Liverpool, and Exeter and London, but it grew not from Board of Trade (parliamentary) policy but rather from what I have termed the *striving for ubiquity* by the various companies. In Massachusetts and the United States in general there was often a deliberate encouragement of duplicate building, as in the three lines constructed between Boston and New York, the two to Albany from the Hub, and even the three to Montréal. When the Lowell road was chartered it requested and was given a monopoly of that route by the legislature, but this provision proved so unpopular that no subsequent line was so enfran-chised. Instead, both the General Court of Massachusetts and the legislatures of other states showed great abandon in authorizing lines almost whenever and wherever requested. From that proclivity stems much of the current "railroad problem" in the northeastern United States, a problem that has brought about a regionally based nationalization under Conrail.

Unfortunately, the opening of the Western Railroad to Albany in 1841 did not bring the masses of freight the directors had hoped to secure. The failure was Boston's, not theirs. The "rise of the port of New York" was too strong a force to overcome, particularly as New York City had both a shorter route, by fifty miles, and one without the troublesome hills that made strong engines necessary throughout the life of steam and made the Western climb and descend 3,767 feet. As Kirkland notes, in 1811 the foreign trade of Massachusetts and New York were essentially equal, but in 1859 Boston's exports were only $16 million whereas New York City's were $41 million. "Judged by value of product, New York exported in 1859 five times as much pork, eight times as much lard, ten times as much beef, and thirteen times as much bacon and ham; of flour, New York exported nearly

66

THE NORTH
AMERICAN
RAILROAD

six and a half times as much as Boston; of wheat she sent abroad 1,390,828 bushels, but Boston—not a bushel!"[83]

Low fares, then, were not the key to success. As Charles Francis Adams, Jr., pointed out in 1868, "Men buy where they can buy cheapest. They can buy cheapest where goods can be most conveniently laid down, and at centers where transportation is cheapest and best." In the competition with New York, Bostonians finally learned to their chagrin "the fallacy that steam could run up hill cheaper than water could run down."[84] The experience with this line served to show the limits of urban mercantilism within a strongly competitive frame; just as competition among railroad companies became a canon of American practice, so resistance to urban hierarchical domination in trade was the national inclination. But in the case of New England merchants, New York could exercise a legal restraint on their efforts to win the interior. Philadelphia and Baltimore, whose more favorable political geography gave them uncontested access to the Ohio Valley, continued to compete with New York with far greater success than Boston enjoyed.

Having been shut out of direct control of access to the interior, the Boston merchant-capitalists adopted a rational, if odd, course: just as their support for railroads had been earlier and more vigorous than New York City's, they more deliberately turned their attention to the Middle West, where there was a great want of capital. The effort started in Michigan. John Murray Forbes—another evolved China merchant like Derby—and his Boston associates began to gain control of the state-funded Michigan Central Railroad, extending it to Chicago in 1854. By 1859 this group had joined in the financing of the westernmost extension of the expanding American rail net, the Hannibal and St. Joseph Railroad that carried Boston influence to the edge of the Great Plains. After the Civil War the Nickerson group from Boston took on the emerging Atchison, Topeka, and Santa Fe Railway, while the Ames brothers from Easton just south of Boston played the dominant role in the financing and construction of the Union Pacific and a critical role in completing the Central Pacific. It would be getting ahead of our story to detail that picture at this point, but I do wish to bring out the fact that Boston, and New England in general, played an unusually active role in American railroading, and certainly a more constructive one than that played by New York City's representatives—Cornelius Vanderbilt, Jay Gould, and Daniel Drew—in the next stage of railroad development. The Bostonians were far from altruistic in their efforts, but they did combine a striving for national development with some restraint in their expectations for profit from their investments. The capital they poured into American railroad development was all out of proportion to the size of the city or the regional economy. In the years following the completion of the Western Railroad some $90 million of Boston capital was invested in this western development, though there never was to be a Boston line that could cross the Hudson itself.

The Practice of Urban Mercantilism: New England Seeks a Northwest Passage

When we turn to look at the use of railroads as instruments of development in general and of urban mercantilism in particular, we may divide the East Coast of the United States into four sectors, each having a rather distinctive geographical

The Hoosac Tunnel through the main range of the Appalachians in Massachusetts, the Berkshire Hills (locally Hoosac Mountain), at over four miles' length posed a totally new scale of engineering work. Construction took almost a quarter of a century and was finished only after nitroglycerin was introduced as an explosive by Alfred Nobel in 1863. This long tunnel gave the Fitchburg Railroad the lowest and easiest crossing of the Appalachians, but too late to have any serious influence on the geography of that crossing. Top photo shows the west portal, bottom photo the east portal. *Source:* Museum of New Mexico photo.

pattern of construction. Taking these in geographical order, from north to south, so as to tie later efforts by Boston in with those earlier strivings for the Western Railroad, we may look first at the search for a way around New York City's area of political, and legal, domination. That search generated interest in another opening through the Appalachians that is often overlooked, the passage by way of the Champlain–St. Lawrence lowland.

The Appalachians are both higher and wider in northern New England than they are farther south in that region, but they are also more severely glaciated, as the ice was moving outward and southward from the center of accumulation over the Shield north of the St. Lawrence, and thus was thicker and more erosive farther north. The result is rather paradoxical from the viewpoint of the geography of transportation. Although the mountains are higher, rising to over four thousand feet in Vermont and to over six thousand in New Hampshire, they are also breached by deep valleys that normally afford through routings that are less barriers than were the Berkshires of western Massachusetts. When the Bostonians looked northwestward, the Boston and Lowell Railroad was the way out of town, the connection from Boston harbor to the master stream of northern-central New England, the Merrimack. The Lowell road was rather slowly extended along the river to Concord, New Hampshire, which was reached in 1842, because at first the New Hampshire legislature was unfriendly toward railroads.[85] As Caroline MacGill saw it, "Railroads in New Hampshire, as in other New England States, were mainly developments of the Boston system, built with reference to that system."[86] Thus, it was only when natives of the cautious commonwealths to the north could be convinced that the interests of Boston merchants were not inimical to their own that this "end run" could be undertaken in earnest.

While the Lowell road was being extended to the Vermont boundary by end-to-end connections of small railroads, other interests were seeking to support the general advance of Boston's trading boundary. As the Worcester and Western roads had passed basically across the southern tier of Massachusetts, there was interest in a similar line across the northern tier, particularly from Fitchburg to Boston, a distance of some forty-five miles. Chartered in 1842, the Fitchburg Railroad was completed to its namesake in 1845, and was rather quickly extended to Greenfield on the Connecticut in 1850. Thence westward the terrain was tantalizing. The Deerfield River rises on the western crest of the Berkshire Hills and cuts, for New England, a very deep valley, some two thousand feet at the extreme, which descends to join the Connecticut just south of Greenfield. Thus, from that town westward the Deerfield River offered an easy, though tortuous, route across the high hills. But near their western edge an uneroded section of the Appalachian chain, Hoosac Mountain, remained uncut by streams. Yet to the west of it only five miles away lay the open Berkshire Valley on its limestones. If only Hoosac Mountain could be tunneled, a far easier route across Massachusetts than the Western Railroad's could be obtained. The appeal of this work was that the Fitchburg Railroad was particularly a freight route, and an extremely profitable one paying in some years 10 percent on capital, so the economic advantages of a less graded route were easily perceived.[87]

It is clearly established that even in the launching of the fifty-mile Fitchburg Railroad there was the expectation that this would merely be the

69

The North
American Railroad
Rises in the East

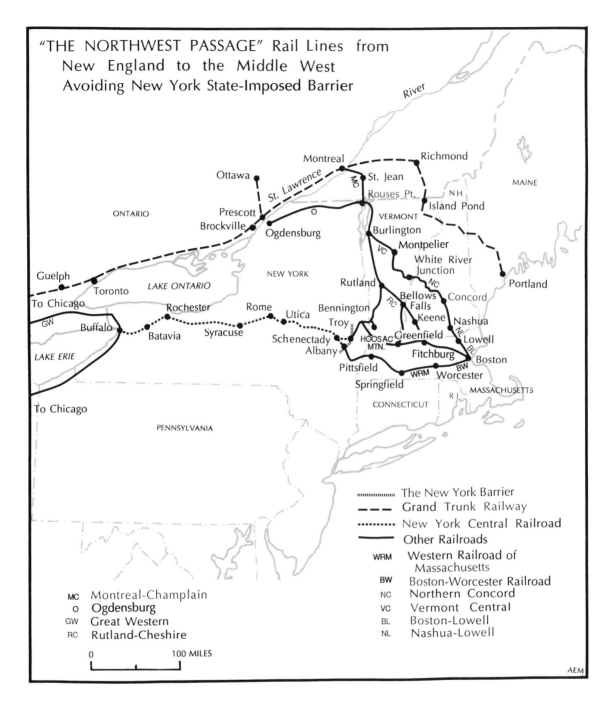

"THE NORTHWEST PASSAGE" Rail Lines from New England to the Middle West Avoiding New York State-Imposed Barrier

	The New York Barrier
	Grand Trunk Railway
	New York Central Railroad
	Other Railroads
WRM	Western Railroad of Massachusetts
BW	Boston-Worcester Railroad
NC	Northern Concord
VC	Vermont Central
BL	Boston-Lowell
NL	Nashua-Lowell

MC	Montreal-Champlain
O	Ogdensburg
GW	Great Western
RC	Rutland-Cheshire

0   100 MILES

AEM

beginning of a transsectional line to extend the mercantile system of Boston. The convention that called for the construction of the Fitchburg line in 1842 held it "resolved, That this route, almost precisely intermediate between [the] Lowell and Worcester roads, is the consummation of the routes essentially necessary for the northern country and Boston—the direct route, when finished, for the travel from our Atlantic steamers to Montreal; and that this first section to Fitchburg is a germ which will ultimate in such fruition."[88] This line was remarkable for being financed entirely through the sale of stock, and that mostly to those living along its route or in Fitchburg, the Boston contribution being extremely minor. Through a linear extension, the Vermont and Massachusetts

THE NORTH
AMERICAN
RAILROAD

Railroad ultimately leased by the Fitchburg in 1874, this route to the "northern country" reached Brattleboro, Vermont, in 1849. From this line it was possible to envision two onward routes, one from Greenfield through the Deerfield Valley to Hoosac Mountain, and the other from Brattleboro north and northwestward toward Canada and the lakes.

Taking up the Deerfield River route first, the interests behind the Fitchburg attempted successfully—though greatly against the opposition of the Western Railroad (which sought to justify a monopoly of western travel from Boston), by noting that it was currently laying a second track to Albany to provide greater capacity—to build a line from Greenfield to Troy on the Hudson. It was obvious from the route laid out in the charter in 1848 that the Troy and Greenfield would have to tunnel Hoosac Mountain, and a capital of $2 million was considered adequate for the total undertaking; such was the confidence that this group of small-town capitalists had gained from their successful and largely debt-free development of the Fitchburg Railroad, certainly as businesslike an undertaking as was then to be found in America. But by 1851 the Troy and Greenfield directors had been greatly sobered on receiving the engineers' location report, and they turned to the state asking for a loan of $2 million. In the legislative hearings on that application it was argued by the railroad that there was already a tunnel four miles long in France, and that it "had been constructed on an average cost of less than five dollars per cubic yard of excavation, including the expense of erecting the required masonry; hence it was supposed that the 350,000 cubic yards of excavation requisite to bore through Hoosac Mountain would at a maximum not exceed $1,750,000."[89] That supposition was based on the assumption that boring could progress at the rate of ten feet a day, with completion of the tunnel in one thousand to fifteen hundred working days. The state granted the loan so that construction could begin. Contracts were let in 1855 and 1856, and before work was suspended in 1861 because of arguments over the contracts, some 2,400 feet had been bored from the east end, and an intermediate shaft had been driven 356 feet to grade to provide two more working faces, and 56 feet tunneled from its base; and at the west end some 610 feet had been cut into the mountain.[90]

In 1863 the state finally took over the whole property of the Troy and Greenfield and began to drill the tunnel directly on its own account. The line from Greenfield up to the east working portal was leased to the Vermont and Massachusetts, and thereby to the Fitchburg, thus assuring their ultimate control of the railroad when the tunnel might at last be completed. That completion was, however, long delayed. Progress on the headings was painfully slow, though somewhat advanced by the adoption of compressed-air drilling. That technology was pioneered on the Mont Cenis Tunnel project then under way in France and Italy, though the equipment used on the Hoosac was invented and manufactured in Fitchburg. The year it took to perfect this Burleigh drill delayed the tunnel construction and led to the allegation that Alvah Crocker, promoter of the Fitchburg and in 1856 the state appointee in charge of the tunnel project, was financially interested in this machinery.[91] In 1866 another innovation, the substitution of nitroglycerine for black powder in blasting, further improved progress. Still, much remained to be done, and the earlier work was found to be shoddy. The railroad line from Greenfield to the east portal had been so cheaply constructed that bridges collapsed and the curvature was excessive. In the end,

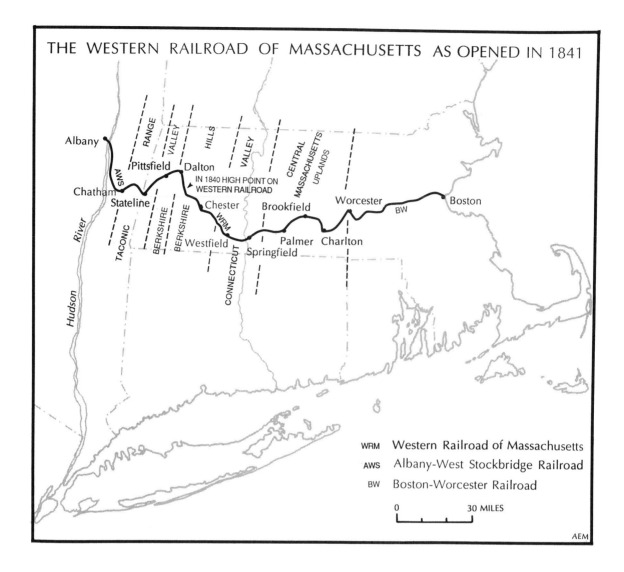

THE WESTERN RAILROAD OF MASSACHUSETTS AS OPENED IN 1841

WRM Western Railroad of Massachusetts
AWS Albany-West Stockbridge Railroad
BW Boston-Worcester Railroad

0   30 MILES

two-thirds of the alignment had to be relocated to gain the efficient and cheaply operable line that all the work sought to secure. The earlier tunnel cross-section, only 14 feet wide and 18 feet high with vertical side walls, failed to meet the state's original specifications—22 feet wide at the base rising in an elliptical cross-section to a maximum width of 24 feet before closing in an arch—as well as making for an unstable opening likely to collapse. In the western part of the tunnel very bad rock and large amounts of water were encountered, which further delayed completion. On November 27, 1873, juncture of the two adits was finally made, only nine-sixteenths of an inch off their headings. Only in 1875 was the tunnel completed, twenty-four years after the first contracts were let. Still, at 25,081 feet, some four and three-quarter miles, this bore was of a magnitude completely new to America. At the portals the tunnel was only some 760 feet above sea level, thus cutting 700 feet from the summit elevation in the Massachusetts crossing of the Appalachians and affording what was for the time, and remains even today, a remarkably efficient freight line across that barrier.

Even though the Hoosac Tunnel route was physically superior to that over the Washington summit used by the Western Railroad, and it remains superior

72

THE NORTH
AMERICAN
RAILROAD

to Conrail's trackage over that same height today, this more northerly line has never proved to be the attraction it might seem. There are several components of the explanation, but the most important was undoubtedly the existence of a functional barrier at Troy, where the Hudson demarcated Boston's sphere of influence as permitted by New York City and its influence on the state legislature that controlled much about operation. Thus, even a better route, one that permitted cheaper operation over a line six miles shorter than the Boston-Worcester-Albany route, could not breach that political barrier. In all of this there was a rather *ex post facto* quality, because the delay in the completion of the Hoosac Tunnel meant that other ways around New York City's barrier had been brought into operation before this last frontal attack was launched.

New England's search for a Northwest Passage essentially guided the piecing together of short lines, which had come into existence in northern New England to meet local needs, into fewer and more profitable systems, normally possessed of one or two main lines and a series of now secondary branches. Although the New Hampshire and Vermont short lines were often independent of Boston, though seldom unattached to that financial market, as time passed it was the metropolitan railroads of the first stage of building that tended to take over and realign the rural railroads of that same first stage. The Fitchburg Railroad was instrumental in creating not only the Hoosac Tunnel route, which it ultimately came to control directly, but also the company that became the Rutland road, leading northwest across the Green Mountains to Lake Champlain and onward to the foot of the Great Lakes navigation at Ogdensburg, New York. Once the tunnel was opened in 1875, the Fitchburg lost much of its interest in the Rutland, and that company fell first to the Vermont Central, then to the Delaware and Hudson, and finally to the Vanderbilt interests of the New York Central.

The Boston and Lowell, though slow in moving outside its native country, did play an ever-increasing role in the development of lines from Boston to White River Junction and Wells River, Vermont. The final force influencing the ultimate geography of railroads in northern New England was Montréal. Anticipating our story, it may be noted that the Grand Trunk Railroad, an English promotion of somewhat checkered history, exercised a considerable influence in New England.

The Grand Trunk in New England was successor to the first railroad to be built across the Canadian border, the Atlantic and St. Lawrence, organized in Portland (Maine) in 1845, and its Canadian ally, the St. Lawrence and Atlantic, that was to build to junction at the U.S. border. This line, as completed in 1853, was yet another trans-Appalachian route, though this time it was built as much to advance Canadian as American interests. Portland was then seen as two days closer to Europe by steamship than was New York, even half a day closer than Boston. And it seemed to offer the ideal winter port for ice-bound Montréal and Québec. The geographical position of this line was conceived in sweeping terms: it was to serve as the year-round door to Canada opened via British shipping docked at Portland. In this case urban mercantilism took on a particularly parochial coloration. The Atlantic and St. Lawrence and the St. Lawrence and Atlantic adopted a distinctive gauge, 5 feet 6 inches, to keep their traffic safe from diversion to the growing Boston network of lines built to the standard (Ste-

73

The North
American Railroad
Rises in the East

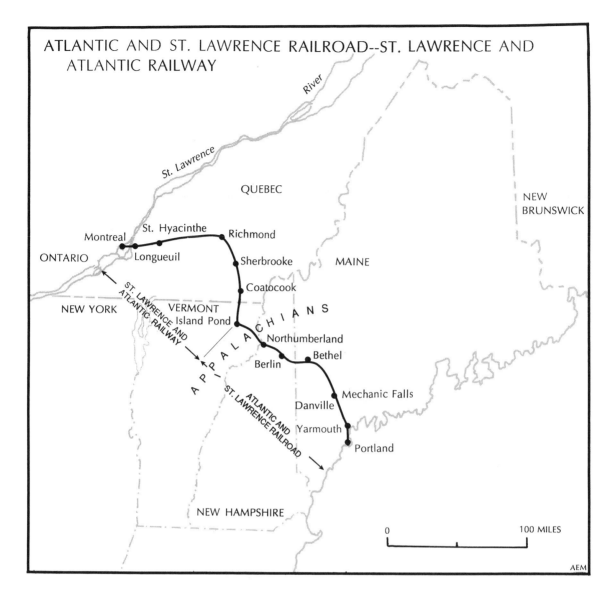

ATLANTIC AND ST. LAWRENCE RAILROAD--ST. LAWRENCE AND ATLANTIC RAILWAY

phenson) gauge. In crossing the Appalachians, the Portland-Montréal line made use of the Androscoggin River valley to reach the eastern slope of the White Mountains at Milan, New Hampshire, where the range was changing into mere hills. After crossing the range with grades no stiffer than sixty feet per mile (just over 1 percent) for about five miles, the line descended a tributary to the Connecticut; and thence, over the generally planed surface lying to the north of the main chain of the Appalachians, itself not very elevated in this latitude, juncture was made with the Canadian line at the border, 149 miles from Portland. When opened in 1853, this 292-mile line became Canada's route to the sea. A new company, the Grand Trunk Railway, was organized to take over a lease on the Portland-Montréal line, as was done in 1856, and to extend it toward Upper Canada, and ultimately Chicago. This was certainly a Northwest Passage, but not one that was of much use to Boston.[92] Once the Grand Trunk was changed to standard gauge in 1874, it began to extend its connections in New England, serving particularly to bail out the Vermont Central between the Canadian border and White River Junction as it foundered under its lease of the Rutland.

THE NORTH
AMERICAN
RAILROAD

By 1885 the Grand Trunk held half the stock in the line, a figure increased to two-thirds by 1898, when the Canadian-British line took over effective control. With it went a second line to warm water, that from Montréal to New London, Connecticut, thus turning New England's Northwest Passage more into a Canadian than a Boston interest.[93]

Boston had lost interest because its routes to the lakes had proved to be of relatively little practical importance. For a short time after 1854, when the United States had a reciprocity treaty with Canada that allowed easy passage of Canadian grain through American ports, the flow of goods to Boston's docks was greatly enhanced, from $21,715 in 1847 to $5,178,911 in 1854.[94] The Western Railroad of Massachusetts, or the Tunnel Route after it opened, always carried far more than did these avowed routes to the lakes. The Welland Canal was still small in prism, so Lake Ontario was not fully part of a continuous Great Lakes navigation. As a result, by 1860 the flour receipts at Boston by the so-called Great Northern Route to Canada and Lake Ontario were only a fifth of those coming via the Western Railroad of Massachusetts, and even less than flour received via the Boston and Providence through Long Island Sound ships from New York, or by ship from the Grand Trunk terminus in Portland.[95] Any expectation that this Northwest Passage was free of New York City's influence left New Englanders disappointed:

Theirs was a delusion. Though it arose from perhaps accurate enough examination of the map, it ignored political and commercial realities. Trade had worn its channels to New York. . . . Similar fanatics of the map and of foreign trade saw that Boston was a day nearer to Liverpool than was New York. They did not realize that, owing to the immense commerce of New York, grain sent thither had "the advantage to the last moment of sale for consumption in the Eastern States, and was sure, in any case, of carriage to Liverpool at so low a rate as nearly to counterbalance the higher charge for inland transportation." Bostonians knew these things at the end of the fifties; they would have saved money if they had realized them a decade earlier.[96]

But also they would not have played the role in American railroading that such persistent effort to expand mercantile frontiers gave to Boston and its investors. Much as the Northwest Passage came ultimately to be controlled by the Canadians, because they were the main beneficiaries of its existence, so did the American Middle and Far West gain from Boston's efforts to jump over the New York barrier and shape a railroad empire for itself in the great interior. But that story must wait for its proper place.

State Mercantilism in the Middle Atlantic States

If we summarize the rail developments of New England as the effort of the Boston mercantile community to spread its direct ties, and influence, over that region, and to extend beyond it if possible, we may turn to the next of the four attacks on the Appalachian barrier, those in the states of New York and Pennsylvania, and view them as a contest between the mercantile interests of those two states. Reference has already been made to the efforts of Pennsylvania to shape a policy of internal improvements. Despite William Strickland's favorable report on railroads, the commonwealth opted in favor of the Mainline Canal System itself (partially a railroad between Philadelphia and Columbia). But the failure

75

The North
American Railroad
Rises in the East

of that overly complex transportation system finally turned attention toward a railroad as a more efficient and practical solution. Because that turn away from waterways was to come only in the 1840s, it is appropriate first to consider New York's adoption of railroads as it occurred in the 1830s, while Pennsylvania was still struggling to make the Mainline Canal System work.

The Erie Railroad: A Test of Developmental Ability

New York's interest in railroads was certainly equivocal. With the construction of the Erie Canal and its opening in 1825, there could be no question which side of the water-rail contest had won the Empire State. There also could be no favorable prognosis for a trunk-line railroad through the Mohawk depression and parallel with the canal, even though that was where the main clusters of upstate population were to be found. The legislature had expressed itself clearly on that matter:

In 1825, that state had completed at great expense, the Erie Canal, one of the great enterprises of the first half of the nineteenth century and was carrying a debt incurred in the work, which it hoped to meet from the use of the canal through the charging of tolls upon the freight conveyed thereon. Accordingly there was . . . a prohibition, total or partial, upon the carrying of freight by these roads in competition with the canal, which was not wholly removed until 1847, and from 1844 until December 1, 1851, a large portion of the freight they did carry was compelled to pay in addition to the charges of the railroads, such sum in tolls to the state as it would have paid if carried upon the canal.[97]

As we shall see, local lines were built between the pairs of towns strung along the canal, but there was no effective integration of the system until 1853, even after Pennsylvania secured a trans-Appalachian route.

The first effort to project a rail line across New York State came as a direct result of the opening of the Erie Canal. When in 1817 that waterway was proposed for state construction, it was necessary to the passage of the enabling legislation that the so-called Southern Tier of counties, those within the Catskills and the Appalachian Plateau lying south of the canal route, vote in its favor. Thus, when the canal proved to be a great success, there was a sense of deprivation in the Southern Tier that had to be dealt with as a political reality. In part that response came through the projection of branch canals into the plateau, but these were roundabout and slow in completion, so the pressure mounted for some alternative solution to the Southern Tier's isolation from markets. The drainage of the area tended to flow either northward through the glacial grooves of the Finger Lakes or southward in the headwaters of the Susquehanna River, which could reach the sea only on the Chesapeake Bay. If the Southern Tier was to be integrated into the New York market as its merchants sought, a railroad was the only practicable instrument of that policy.

There is no need here to go into the details of gaining legislative support; suffice it to say that both the charter and some modest funds for surveys were called forth as a payment for the past support of the canal. From those surveys it became clear that it was possible, though it would be difficult, to build a line through the Southern Tier. Any such line would stand as the epitome of the mercantilist route, though in this instance on a state rather than a municipal basis. As authorized and supported by the New York legislature, the railroad company was required to construct its line entirely within that state, to seek to avoid interchange of traffic outside the state, and specifically to make certain that there was no such loss to New Jersey, Pennsylvania, or Ohio. The myopia implicit in such a policy—the deliberate cutting off of inflow from outside along with the "protection" of internal trade—is hard for us to imagine, but such was the single-minded concern for the rise of New York City at that time. The company even went beyond the requirements of the charter by consciously choosing a track gauge different from the Stephenson gauge that had been most widely adopted by the early lines in the Northeast. The Erie was to be built at six feet— argued intelligently by the engineers as being a better choice, but also by Eleazar Lord and other promoters as assuring the inviolate quality of the company's and the Empire State's trade.

With that requirement to restrict its activities to New York, the incipient New York and Erie Railroad was forced to seek a route not where nature might lead, or even where the market was likely to be greatest, but rather north of the arbitrary geometrical boundary of New Jersey and Pennsylvania with New York. This was not a traditional route, though one of the earlier calls upon the infant republic in 1779 was for constructing a national "Appian Way" westward across the Southern Tier of New York. Nothing came of this proposal by General James Clinton and General John Sullivan, whose interest was aroused by their campaign against the Indians in the area.[98] A number of proposals were made in succeeding years to construct such a road, but none was carried out until the dawn of the railroad era. In 1829 William C. Redfield of New York published a *Sketch of the Geographical Rout[e] of a Great Railway by Which It Is Proposed to Connect the Canals and Navigable Waters of New York, Pennsylvania, Ohio, Indiana, Illinois, Michigan, Missouri, and the Adjacent States and Territories, Opening thereby a Great Communication at All Seasons of the Year between the Atlantic States and the Great Valleys of the Mississippi.*[99] "This route commences on the Hudson River in the vicinity of the city of New York, at a point accessible at all seasons to steam ferryboats, and from thence proceeds through a favorable and productive country to the valley of the Delaware River," and then along the Delaware to a point closest to the Susquehanna, thence along that stream to a divide with the Genesee, and finally to Lake Erie. Thus, Redfield was first to propose such a rail solution to the Southern Tier transportation problem. Soon thereafter Colonel De Witt Clinton, son of the governor who built the Erie Canal and himself a member of the United States Army Engineer Corps, was asked to carry out a survey, and his conclusion was that a railroad over Redfield's basic route was practicable.[100] Chance then entered the history of this venture when in 1831 Henry Pierson of Ramapo, New York—brother-in-law of Eleazar Lord, who was destined to become the first president of the New York and Erie Railroad— was married and went to Charleston on his honeymoon. While he was there, on January 15, 1831, the South Carolina Railroad was opened for a few miles west of the Carolina port and was fitted with a locomotive engine, the *Best Friend of Charleston,* designed at the West Point Foundry in New York City by Horatio Allen, himself later to become a president of the Erie road. The success of that South Carolina Railroad so impressed Pierson that when he returned to his home he conveyed great enthusiasm for this form of traction to his brother-in-law. In due course Lord was to express that confidence in his early statements as

The North
American Railroad
Rises in the East

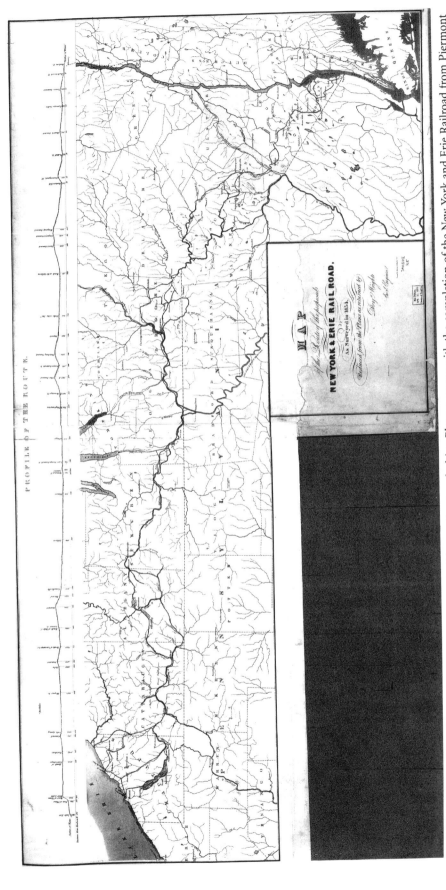

New York State's initial rail crossing of the Appalachians, in this case the Appalachian Plateau, came with the completion of the New York and Erie Railroad from Piermont (just north of the point where the right bank of the Hudson became part of the Empire State) to Dunkirk on Lake Erie. Early seen as America's Appian Way, this six-foot-gauge line was intended to operate solely within New York State—thus its unusual gauge and somewhat obscure termini. *Source:* Library of Congress map.

to the efficacy of locomotives on the line for which he was the most ardent and effective promoter.[101]

The first charter for the New York and Erie Railroad was issued in 1832, but its provisions were so unfavorable that no investments were forthcoming. That charter did not specify the route in any detail: "It is to begin at the City of New York, or at such point in its vicinity as shall be most eligible and convenient therefor, and continue through the Southern Tier of counties, by way of Owego in Tioga County, to the shore of Lake Erie, at some eligible point between the Cattaraugus Creek and the Pennsylvania line." And the railroad was restricted from making juncture with any railroad in New Jersey or Pennsylvania without the legislature's permission.[102] At first the federal government agreed to provide the survey carried out, this time in more detail, by the same Colonel De Witt Clinton who had made the preliminary judgment of the Redfield route. But after authorizing the undertaking President Jackson abruptly ordered it canceled on July 4, 1832. When pressed by the Erie's incorporators, he said he had changed his mind, ostensibly because of constitutional questions but actually because he had been urged by a prominent Democratic politician in New York to do so: "The gentleman tells me that the building of this railroad would make a thoroughfare that would be a rival of the Erie Canal, the effect of whose political patronage would be likely to be neutralized by the patronage of the railroad, the latter not being under state control, thus making it impossible to manage the politics of the State, so well as they are managed now; and, surely, as the gentleman says, that is of far more importance than the railroad to a State already amply provided with means of commercial transportation by its own canal."[103] That "gentleman" is commonly identified as the eternally crafty Martin Van Buren.

In such a pass, probably more typical of American railroad promotion than not, progress was slow. But eventually gaining small investments from on-line counties, some assistance from the Corps of Engineers in the use of Colonel Clinton, and a great reduction in the necessary subscribed capital of the line—down to $1 million from $10 million—to earn state financial support, the company came into active existence on August 9, 1833.[104] In due course Benjamin Wright, famous for his engineering work on the Erie Canal, was asked to carry out the survey, and it is from the report he submitted to New York's secretary of state in January 1835 that we may reconstruct the geographical analysis that lay behind the choice of the actual line constructed.

To begin with, it should be made clear that the requirement that the Erie Railroad be built entirely within New York State forced it to have its eastern terminus on the west bank of the Hudson some miles north of New York City, as in that latitude the right bank is still part of New Jersey. It was not without significance that the first usable valley through the cliffs of the Palisades north of New Jersey was the one in which Eleazar Lord had his large country estate. But now we may profitably turn to Benjamin Wright's own words:

That, in undertaking the important and responsible duty of surveying the route of a railway communication from the Hudson River, near the city of New York, to Lake Erie, I deemed it essential to keep in view the great public objects sought to be obtained by the proposed work. It was obvious that the road was to be constructed not only for the accommodation of the inhabitants of the district immediately adjacent to the route, but also in order to furnish the means of a regular, rapid, and uninterrupted

The North
American Railroad
Rises in the East

intercourse at nearly all seasons of the year, between the city of New York and the extensive and populous communities upon the western lakes and waters. . . . Keeping, therefore, steadily in mind these general considerations, I deemed it an incumbent duty, in selecting the line of location for the proposed road, to obtain a route, which, as far as should be practicable, might combine: (1) Reasonable economy in its construction; (2) Rapidity and regularity of communication for passengers, light merchandise of value, and the public mail; (3) Cheapness of transportation for bulky commodities; (4) Facilities of connection with lateral branches; (5) The general accommodation of inhabitants, and the development of the resources of the country along the route. And I considered it also necessary to take into view not only the present, but the prospective advantages of the route; and to arrange the graduation of the whole work in the reference to such further additions and improvements as might hereafter become necessary, in order to accommodate a great increase in trade and communication.

The great object of securing rapidity and regularity of communication between the city of New York and the lake, being one of paramount importance, I have studiously sought to avoid the use of stationary steam power in inclined planes, as being productive of delay, danger, expense and difficulty and in this respect have been so successful that, with the exception of one single plane, near Lake Erie [which was never built], I have brought the whole line within the power of locomotive engines, drawing passenger cars, light merchandise, and the public mail. The steepest acclivity encountered on the whole line, with the exception before mentioned [in the plane at Lake Erie], will be only 100 feet per mile [1.8 percent]. And having been furnished with satisfactory evidence, that by recent improvements in the locomotive steam engines on the Baltimore and Ohio Railroad, they have been enabled to ascend the acclivity of 176 feet to the mile [at Parr's Spring Ridge], drawing between five and ten tons weight, . . . locomotive steam engines may be advantageously used on the whole of the proposed route[;] . . . they will be able to pass its steepest grades, drawing at least seventy to eighty passengers with their baggage, while upon at least nine-tenths of the whole route they will be able to propel very great burdens at a very great rate of speed. In order, however, to obtain these easy grades of acclivity, I have been compelled to pursue by a serpentine line, the valleys of streams, and thereby lengthen very considerably the linear extent of the route.[105]

Reality thus intruded in the location of this, the route that was given more than local importance, though perhaps not quite the central role the Appian Way played for the Romans. "The route, instead of passing directly over, goes around the hills, and it has not been necessary to surmount any considerable acclivities except in three or four instances, in which the line crosses the natural boundaries of the great valleys, into which the route is topographically divided." As a result of the grand scale of the relief in the Appalachians, and their plateaus to the west, the "natural boundaries of the valleys" that are pursued by the route will serve to subdivide it into six grand divisions, to wit:

The first or Hudson River Division, extending seventy-three and a half miles from a point on the Hudson River [Piermont] twenty-four miles north of the City Hall of New York, to a point in the Deer Park Gap of the Shawangunk Mountains, dividing the waters flowing into the Hudson from those flowing into the Delaware.

The second or Delaware Division, extending from the point last mentioned through the valley of the Delaware and its tributaries, 115 miles to a summit twelve miles northwest of the village of Deposit, in Delaware County, dividing the waters of the Delaware from those of the Susquehanna.

The third or Susquehanna Division, extending from the point last mentioned through the valley of the Susquehanna and its tributaries, 163½ miles to a summit thirteen miles southwest of the village of Hornellsville, in the county of Steuben, dividing the waters of the Susquehanna from those of the Genesee.

The fourth or Genesee Division, extending from the point last mentioned across the valley of the Genesee, thirty-seven miles to a summit three miles east of the village of Cuba, in Allegany County.

The fifth or Allegany Division, extending along the valley of the Alleghany and its tributaries eighty-three miles to the head of the [possible] inclined plane, distant four or five miles from Lake Erie on a straight line.

The sixth or Lake Erie Division, embracing the short and rapid descent to the lake, including the inclined plane and the two branches, one to Portland, nine miles, and one to Dunkirk, eight and a half miles.

In this surveyed alignment the controlling vector was that of staying within the Southern Tier of New York State, but the detail of the route was that of the hydrography of the state's Appalachian Plateau. As is common with such features, the rivers had cut deep and sometimes fairly narrow valleys, though in places they had been enlarged by glacial action, but those defiles still have good grades if too frequently bad curves.

The accordance between hydrography and railroad routing in the United States (and later Canada) is very much a feature of the developmental nature of rail construction in North America. Curves do cost more to operate around than does straight (tangent) track, but in general curves do not tax the motive power so heavily, so even in the first years the locomotives might propel "very great burdens" even though not always at "a great rate of speed." Curvature slows down operation, but it does not burn half so much coal as does a stiff climb out of one minor valley into the next, where the height gained may be quickly lost. Passing over 450 miles across the Appalachians, save for the short distance from the bottom of the prospective inclined plane to Dunkirk, with only five opposing summits was no mean accomplishment, when it is appreciated that no sizable tunnel was bored and only limited viaducts constructed, with one major exception to be noted.

The Erie Railroad proves to be of great interest to historical geographers because of its quintessential qualities as the well-constructed American line. The Baltimore and Ohio shared some of those qualities but not the same level of political constraint, which forced the peculiarly difficult terrain upon the locating engineers, though west of Cumberland somewhat the same conditions were introduced by having to stay south of the Mason-Dixon line. It is remarkable that Benjamin Wright was able to find a trial alignment that was as reasonable as it was:

The only points where the rates of ascent exceeded sixty feet per mile, will be found on the summits above specified, as forming the boundaries of the six grand divisions of the route. The acclivities in passing these summits are respectively as follows: One grade of 100 feet to the mile in passing from the Hudson River Division, down the west side of Shawangunk mountain, into the Delaware Division; one of seventy feet and one of sixty-one feet to the mile, in passing from the Delaware Division to the Susquehanna Division; one of seventy feet and one of sixty-five feet to the mile, on crossing the ridge between the Susquehanna and its tributary, the Chenango River [necessitated by having to remain within New York State rather than following the Proper Valley, which enters Pennsylvania]; and one of seventy-two feet to the mile in passing from the Susquehanna Division to the Genesee Division.

Wright argued that each of these could be operated by locomotives, as the Parr's Spring Ridge crossing on the B&O was so powered despite its grade of 253 feet per mile (4.7 percent). That such a grade was economically impracticable even if physically surmountable was not yet fully appreciated.

Given the riparian nature of great stretches of the Erie road, it is remarkable that Wright could find a line on which the tightest curve was about five hundred feet in radius, which he thought might be increased to six hundred feet by more careful surveying. That following of river valleys, though it lengthened the line to 445 miles, did add one very desirable quality to the property as an economic undertaking: it made it highly conformal to the settlement pattern that already existed when the line was under construction. In this the Erie was typical of American railroads; those undertakings normally conformed to one of two geographical features, preferably to both in coincidental location, if possible. The first conformality was to the settlement pattern where towns were obviously preexisting and important. The first phase of American railroad building, though soon distinguishable from the initial English construction by the lesser engineering scale of the undertaking, was like the European precedent in being mostly an effort to connect large towns somewhat independent of the intervening terrain. That intervening terrain was not always unfavorable, for most American settlement at the time of the rise of railroads was the result of the potamic pattern of earlier transportation. A navigable stream was a gently graded one, so its valley could serve well as the alignment for a railroad. It was mainly when political requirements or aggressive urban mercantilism intervened that a railroad had to be built in defiance of the terrain, as in the case of the Western Railroad of Massachusetts or the Erie road. If the first phase of American railroad construction reflected English practice with respect to settlement, it differed in that settlement in the United States was largely lowland and riparian, so the very first lines encountered few problems with terrain, as in the Lowell, Worcester, and Providence roads out of Boston; the Camden and Amboy line that interconnected New York Harbor and Philadelphia across the coastal plain of New Jersey; the New Castle and Frenchtown in Delaware; and even the South Carolina Railroad, which was on the easily graded coastal plain of that state.

The second conformality of American rail construction was, as already noted, to rivers in the interior. The Baltimore and Ohio had used the Potomac as far west as it reached; the Erie could start with little but the short and more turbulent Ramapo River to gain elevation to the low upland that lay between the Ramapo and Shawangunk mountains, but still it made use of that stream; and the Erie again was to make masterful use of the interdigitated headwaters of the Delaware, Susquehanna, Genesee, and Allegheny to move from east to west in an area where the streams flow generally north-south. By using these streams, the preexisting river towns, usually the largest in the region, gained an additional dimension to their transportation, just as the railroad secured extension of its early line through the "flourishing village of Owego, where it will become connected with the steamboat line now [in 1835] in preparation for navigating the Susquehanna, and also with the Owego and Ithaca railroad, which will connect the main line with the important and fertile section of [New York] state adjacent to Cayuga and Seneca Lakes." The coincidence of settlement and practicably-graded routes along rivers was one of the great aids to the construction of developmental rail lines in the United States and Canada.

The Erie may serve as an example not of all such developmental construction, because it lay in the more settled and economically integrated part of that country, entirely within one of the original thirteen states, and in the richest. The instrument it represented in such a reasonably affluent landscape came to be far more pared down to its minimal essential when the true frontier was breached, as we shall see in the case of the Union Pacific. Even so, the Erie demonstrated how very little actual support for a line there was in the very beginning, quite in contrast to the situation in the parts of Europe that were then receiving rail service. The line had been chosen to serve an area where the largest towns were self-confident but hardly very imposing. Looking at Elmira, the guidebook published three years after the line was opened noted, "This is the queen city along the New York and Erie Rail-road, and is a good specimen of the towns that seems to *exhale* from the American soil. Rapid as has been the growth of Binghamton and Owego, theirs has been as a snail's pace compared with [Elmira]. . . . The traveler, as he skirts along its suburbs to its busy station in the west end, and then passes to his hotel through those compact streets crowded with business and intersected by a canal, can hardly believe that Elmira, 20 years ago, was a little obscure village, though its settlement goes much farther back. It was settled in 1788 . . . [and at] that time it was on the only pathway from Wilkes Barre to Canada."[106] Populations for Elmira are not available until 1870, but even then, twenty years after the coming of the railroad, it was a city of only 15,863; Binghamton first shows up in the census in 1860, nearly fifteen years after the trains arrived, with a population of 8,325.

The deliberate creation of a railroad to serve an area rather than an existing or projected routeway of trade, though there was always the vaguely defined notion that the West would fill the cars of the Erie, created the first reasonably structured test of the development ability of the railroad operating in emergent parts of the oecumene. The Erie became the arena for some of the more extreme stock manipulations witnessed in an era that seems buccaneering in even its more probitous operations—pitting Daniel Drew, Jim Fisk, Jay Gould, and Cornelius Vanderbilt in manipulative competition—and so much of the financial experience of the Erie Railroad is useless for an evaluation of its developmental accomplishments. But turning to its gross earnings and traffic, a picture of solid accomplishment emerges (Table 1). These figures are particularly revealing because they represent, after the opening in 1851, the growth of traffic on basically the same line. Extensions were made, to Buffalo in 1852; to Dayton (Ohio) via the Atlantic and Great Western Railroad, from Salamanca (New York) in June 1864, adding 369 miles to the broad-gauge system; and to Cleveland in 1863. Meanwhile, the Atlantic and Great Western was leased by the Erie in 1871 and was extended from Marion (Ohio) to Chicago, 250 miles, in 1880.[107] Thus, the area directly tributary to the broad-gauge system expanded but the original line remained an entity for which data were collected, so we can see how its use expanded over a forty-year period, from the opening of the original 445-mile section to Dunkirk in 1851. Passenger movements did not expand

83

The North
American Railroad
Rises in the East

TABLE 1 Erie Railroad Traffic and Gross Earnings

	Passengers Carried	Tons of Freight	Passenger Earnings	Freight Earnings	Length of Main Line
1841	11,627	5,779	$15,165	$14,523	46 mi.
1851	688,789	250,096	$1,186,034	$1,091,388	445 mi.
1861	842,049	1,253,419	$1,136,046	$4,351,464	446 mi.
1871	3,598,988	5,564,274	$3,972,065	$2,862,000	459 mi.
1881	6,144,158	11,086,823	$4,041,267	$5,979,568	460 mi.
1891	11,677,902	17,339,140	$5,855,445	$22,162,403	459 mi.

Source: Edward Harold Mott, *Between the Ocean and the Lakes: The Story of Erie* (New York: John S. Collins, 1900), pp. 483–84.

greatly until the extensions were well completed, and even then passengers were not the Erie's road to prosperity. Commuters were significant in suburban New Jersey and adjacent New York. The railroad actively recruited such migrants from the central city, and fashionable New York made particular use of the line in gaining access to its most exclusive reservation at Tuxedo Park, some six thousand acres of romantic country that had originally been the Pierre Lorillard estate, which he opened to his chosen friends so that he could have company in the country.[108] The fact that the railroad could pass between New York (Jersey City) and Chicago, 985 miles, with the largest city on the route in 1890 being Youngstown (33,220), is some indication of the lack of conformality to settlement of this particular line. In freight movements the picture was far different, particularly after the mid-1870s when the Erie was changed to standard gauge. Interchanges became possible, and the line to Chicago had access to the great emporium of freight forwarding, where the Erie could compete on equal terms with the Vanderbilt, Forbes, and Pennsylvania lines. Finally, the Erie had found a useful role, particularly as its original broad gauge had meant that the residual loading gauge of the line was considerably more ample than that of its competitors. Not the same benefit accrued from the million dollars spent on driving piles as a substructure for the first several years of construction, but we shall see how fashionable that practice was when we shortly take up the South Carolina Railroad.

The Creation of the New York Central Railroad

The Erie was not the only trans-Appalachian line in the Middle Atlantic states. The others we may consider briefly, and under a different dynamic, one wherein the fundamental purpose of the line was to serve shorter-distance objectives or a partially developed market; in this they were an integral part of the earliest phase of railroad construction. Two routes deserve at least some mention. The first of these, the one that became the "Water-Level Route" across New York State, running generally parallel to the Erie Canal from Albany to Buffalo, was not a predetermined connection; instead, it was seemingly quite adventitious as a major regional route, being an 1850s end-to-end connection of a string of lines that had been built for the much more typical undertaking of the time—the tying together by rail of a pair of fairly closely located small cities. If we examine the string from Albany to Buffalo, not chronologically but geographically, it is clear that construction did not continue from east to west, or vice versa, but independently by segments:

Albany to Schenectady, Mohawk and Hudson R. R., opened 1831, Schenectady to Utica, Utica and Schenectady R. R., opened 1836, Utica to Syracuse, Syracuse and Utica R. R., opened 1839, Syracuse to Auburn, Auburn and Syracuse R. R., opened 1839, Auburn to Rochester, Auburn and Rochester R. R., opened 1841, Rochester to Attica, Tonawanda R. R., opened 1837, Attica to Buffalo, Attica and Buffalo R. R., opened 1842, Lockport to Niagara Falls, Lockport and Niagara Falls, opened 1838, Rochester to Niagara Falls, Rochester, Lockport and Niagara Falls, opened 1852, Troy to Schenectady, Schenectady and Troy R. R., opened 1842.[109]

The Mohawk and Hudson has already been referred to as one of the earliest lines to open in the United States and as a route built to bypass the heavy lockage encountered on the Erie Canal east of Schenectady. Its promoters were not local men but rather New York City merchant-investors, among them John Jacob Astor, who could see the critical relief such a line could offer. The absence of much thought about a through route is shown graphically by the construction of the road with an inclined plane at each end, not to be removed until 1844 when engines had improved and the line could be partially relocated so as to do away with the direct 185-foot rise at Albany and the 105-foot descent at Schenectady. Only then was the sixteen-mile railroad ripe for extension, which was to come with the amalgamation of all the railroads listed above in 1853.[110]

The Albany and Schenectady Railroad, as it came to be known, led to the Utica and Schenectady, a seventy-eight-mile link between those two cities, with populations, respectively, of 10,183 and 6,272 in 1835 when the connection was under construction. Even Albany that year could count no more than 28,109 inhabitants, so all these links were between places of rather modest scale. When opened in 1839 the Utica and Schenectady, though not the Mohawk and Hudson to the east, was forbidden to carry freight during the open season for canal navigation, unless it paid the toll that would have been charged had the goods moved by barge.[111]

The sections between Syracuse and Rochester, and that city and Buffalo, which completed the set of original links that would eventually be assembled into a regional chain, were initially poorly matched. When assembled, straightening by the New York Central consolidation was carried out because the fundamental purpose of the newly merged railroad line was changed from that of its predecessors (to tie adjacent cities together); the new objective was to share a transsectional line to connect New York City with Chicago, which was accomplished only a year later. A forty-six-mile link between Utica and Syracuse cut six miles off the previous, locally oriented connection, and was undertaken by the Utica and Syracuse interests. Further advance toward this long-distance purpose came with the improvement of the track by the several companies. Having started with little more than wooden stringers with a thin running strip of iron no more than an inch thick attached, companies adopted iron rail as their treasuries gained substance. By 1849 the Utica and Schenectady had laid sixty-five-pound rail, and the Syracuse and Utica followed suit. By 1847 the state made

The North
American Railroad
Rises in the East

it essentially obligatory to replace strap rail on any road using steam power.[112] All subsequent construction had to be built with edge rail of at least fifty-six pounds per yard. By 1849 all of the eventual Water-Level Route between Albany and Buffalo was laid with rail over fifty-eight pounds, most of it with rail between sixty and seventy pounds.

The slow evolution of what had been a set of locally oriented lines capable of end-to-end consolidation more by virtue of their linking of pairs of cities ranged along a previous transportation route, the Erie Canal, than by any design in the minds of their promoters was such by 1843 that a convention was held to establish through trains between the Hudson and Lake Erie at Buffalo. The convention decided that two trains a day should be run, one in the morning and one in the evening, to complete the 326-mile journey within twenty-five hours. Eastbound the train was to leave Buffalo at seven in the morning, reaching Syracuse so that the passengers might spend the night there before going on to Albany. Westbound the train would leave Albany at nine, and Auburn would be the stopping place for the night. As it worked out the times were somewhat different, but the basic practices took hold in February 1843, establishing what was in all truth—that is, outside Massachusetts—the first trans-Appalachian rail line, more than eight years before the railroad with that avowed initial purpose was completed.[113]

The consolidation of the seven companies between Albany and Buffalo, with additional trackage from Schenectady to Troy and from Rochester to Niagara Falls, took place in 1853 when the New York Central Railroad was organized. By then the line from Greenbush, opposite Albany, to Boston was under a single administration, and the Hudson River Railroad from Albany to New York City had opened in 1851. On the west end, the Buffalo and State Line Railroad was under construction to the Pennsylvania line along the lake shore, and the Great Western of Canada was being built between Niagara Falls—where a suspension bridge was soon undertaken—and Windsor, on the Detroit River opposite Detroit. In this way the maintenance of the original short links in upstate New York was impractical, particularly as a through road over this 326-mile route could be both shorter and easier to operate, through judicious relocations of line, which only a consolidated company could effectuate. With the Erie opened to Dunkirk in 1851, the Pennsylvania to Pittsburgh in 1852, and the Baltimore and Ohio to Wheeling the same year as the consolidation, there obviously was going to be heavy reassertion of the pattern of competitive urban mercantilism that had characterized the canal phase of American transportation. To gain the western connection that would determine the next advance of the urban-mercantilist frontier, a line of similar scale to the B&O, the Pennsylvania, and the Erie would be needed. In the 1830s that scale of undertaking had not come about on the Water-Level Route, probably because long-distance transport in the region was still conceived of as being the role of the canal, because the lines were restricted from, or levied a toll on, freight movements, and because most of the capital used for the construction of these short links was obtained locally, secured from those still mainly interested in fairly parochial concerns.

With the clearer focus available in 1853 as to what the eventual railroad geography of the United States was likely to be, the best natural route could not be left in such a poorly organized state. If it was to compete for access to, and

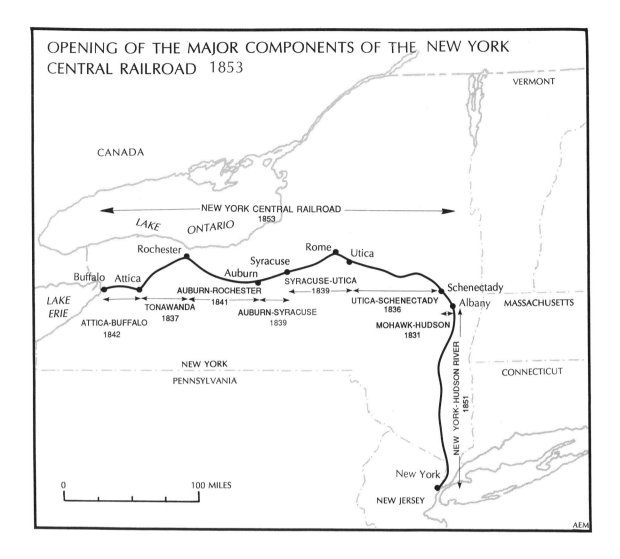

OPENING OF THE MAJOR COMPONENTS OF THE NEW YORK
CENTRAL RAILROAD 1853

VERMONT

CANADA

NEW YORK CENTRAL RAILROAD
1853

LAKE ONTARIO

Rochester
Rome
Utica
Syracuse
Auburn
Buffalo Attica
AUBURN-ROCHESTER
SYRACUSE-UTICA
Schenectady
LAKE
ERIE
TONAWANDA
1841
1839
UTICA-SCHENECTADY
Albany
MASSACHUSETTS
1837
AUBURN-SYRACUSE
1836
ATTICA-BUFFALO
1839
MOHAWK-HUDSON
1842
1831

NEW YORK
PENNSYLVANIA

CONNECTICUT

NEW YORK-HUDSON RIVER
1851

0   100 MILES

New York

NEW JERSEY

AEM

conquests in, the Middle West, it would have to take on a transsectional rather than a strictly regional character. To assume that role the New York Central almost immediately arranged for the Buffalo and Rochester to build a direct line between Batavia and Buffalo, dropping Attica and its less direct route from the main line and the Rochester and Syracuse, which built an entirely new route between the two, relegating the two original-company lines via Auburn, Cayuga, Geneva, and Canandaigua to branch status. In this way the main line was shortened to 297.75 miles, a 10 percent reduction over the pieced-together line.

Once the New York Central was in existence it quickly gained control, partly through taking over stock interests held by its predecessor companies, in the line that was being built westward around the great southern sweep of Lake Erie. The Buffalo and State Line Railroad of New York and the (city of) Erie and North Eastern Railroad of Pennsylvania were controlled sufficiently that they were encouraged to adjust their track to the Ohio gauge of 4 feet 10 inches— usually operable by locomotives built for standard gauge—and to work in concert to make possible a through line to Cleveland and beyond.[114] In this way was begun the westward push that was to conclude the effective transformation of the local to the transsectional railroad, and we may for the time being leave the

87

The North
American Railroad
Rises in the East

When railroads began to encounter wide and deep valleys, as first in the Cumberland Plateau of Kentucky, but soon more extremely in the Niagara Gorge, the cantilever bridge came into use. Although John Roebling had first spanned the gorge with a suspension bridge, the fundamental weakness of such structures for railroad construction soon called for long cantilevers (up to the eighteen-hundred-foot span of the Québec Bridge of 1917 on the National Transcontinental Railway of Canada). *Source:* Library of Congress picture.

Water-Level Route in its completed trans-Appalachian state, reserving until later consideration of its drive to Chicago and the shaping in the third phase of the historical geography of American railroads.

The Delayed Birth of the Pennsylvania Railroad

The other Middle Atlantic line that must be considered is the one built with peculiar hesitation across the commonwealth of Pennsylvania. Again this was not a deliberate undertaking in its earlier years, but rather an adjunct of Pennsylvania's decision in 1826 to pursue internal improvement by water rather than by land. But as already noted, that decision led, strangely, to the conclusion that it was best to provide the eastern leg of the Pennsylvania Mainline Canal System through the building of a railroad from Philadelphia to the Susquehanna River at Columbia, completed in 1834. This original "Pennsylvania Railroad" was

THE NORTH
AMERICAN
RAILROAD

extended to Harrisburg by the Harrisburg, Portsmouth, Mount Joy, and Lancaster Railroad, so that any trans-Appalachian rail line in the commonwealth, which waited upon the confirmed failure of the Mainline Canal System, would in essence be a Harrisburg-Pittsburgh route.

In 1846 there were two competing plans to provide such a connection across the Allegheny Front—one by the Baltimore and Ohio to build northwestward from Cumberland, Maryland, to the forks of the Ohio, the other by Pennsylvania interests to build in some fashion from Harrisburg to that same point. In April of that year the Pennsylvania legislature passed two bills that would allow both such connections, though giving precedence to the Pennsylvania plan such that were a company to be organized successfully, and to put under contract at least fifteen miles of line by July 30, 1847, it would find its charter operative and that of the B&O denied.[115] In this way the state mercantilism of Pennsylvania was fully acknowledged and successfully implemented without literal refusal to outsiders. This truth New York interests discovered when they sought to secure a connection for their line westward from Buffalo on the Lake Erie shore across the narrow corridor of Pennsylvania leading to the city of Erie. The legislature of the commonwealth resisted such an intrusion, as they viewed it, and sought to forfend it by specifying that the Erie and North Eastern must be built at the Ohio rather than the New York gauge. As we have already seen, the New York Central interests controlling this eastern chain of seemingly independent companies outwitted the legislature by accepting the gauge for the line all the way east to Buffalo.

Once the Pennsylvania Railroad Company was organized in 1847, it was given discretion as to the location of its line between its determined termini. Its main restraint was similar to that of the links in the Water-Level Route: it had to pay a toll of 5 mills per mile for each ton of freight transported by rail more than twenty miles between March and December, the "season" for the Mainline Canal.[116] A number of routes were examined across the Appalachians, here comprised of a set of parallel Folded Appalachian ridges in the east, the first of which lay just west of Harrisburg, and the broad Appalachian Plateau stretching west of the Allegheny Front, into which the Ohio and its tributaries had been cut in deep valleys, one of which would be used to reach Pittsburgh, itself in a deep valley still well within the plateau. The chief engineer of the Pennsylvania finally settled on the typical alignment of usually trending rivers to cut across these two physiographic components (as far as might be practicable). The rivers in the east, the Susquehanna and its tributaries, are famous for their water gaps, which cut a relatively graded course through these potential obstacles. The first ridge was encountered just north of Harrisburg as Blue Mountain (also seen as Catoctin Mountain on the B&O and as South Mountain on the Erie just east of Port Jervis). It was easily passed on the Pennsylvania Railroad, as the Susquehanna cuts through it in a wide water gap, which the railroad alignment passed on the left bank. Once north of the gap, the mouth of the Juniata River was encountered as a right-bank tributary, and the Pennsylvania railroad route continued up that stream, alongside the Mainline Canal, passing along water gaps through Tuscarora and Shad mountains before reaching Lewisburg, where the alignment turned south to pass along the broad stretch between Shad and Jackson mountains. At Mount Union, following the Juniata, the rail route turned west through

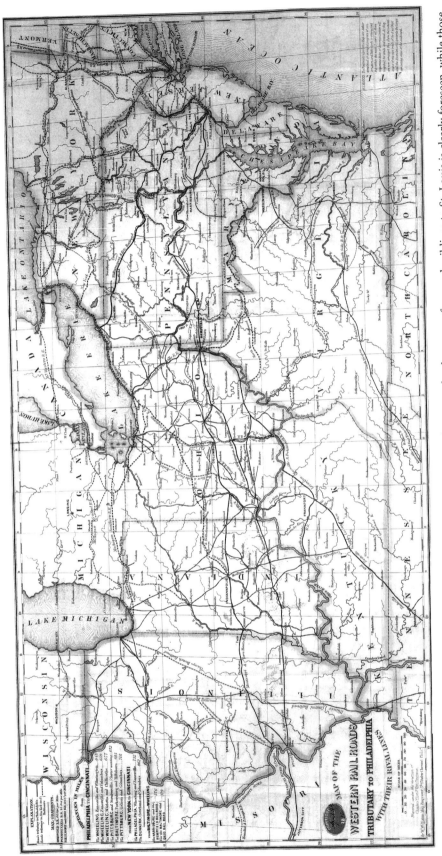

Map of the rail lines seen as tributaries to Philadelphia, mainly via Cincinnati. The subsequent development of onward rail lines to St. Louis is clearly foreseen, while those to Chicago remain quite conjectural because of the doubtful future of that basically canal port. *Source:* Library of Congress map.

a gap in Jackson Mountain and on through Huntington to the mouth of the Little Juniata, which kept the westering better than the main stream, to pass along water gaps through Russey and Brush mountains to reach the longitudinal valley lying along the east side of the Allegheny Front at Tyrone. Following this southwesterly trending valley for 15 miles to a point 132 miles from Harrisburg, subsequently developed as a railroad town to be called Altoona, it was decided there to make the direct assault on the Allegheny Front.

At Altoona the Folded Appalachians had been crossed with no actual summits and only gentle grades, rising from 310 feet elevation at Harrisburg to nearly 900 feet higher at the new railroad town (1,174 feet). But in the next twelve miles, to Gallitzin, the railroad had to rise nearly a thousand feet (984 feet). Such a grade would not have been greater than some already built on other lines—the B&O had a grade of 116 feet (2.2 percent) for 11.5 miles in its crossing of the Allegheny Front—but because this Pennsylvania route was clearly perceived as one that would be used for heavy traffic, it was desirable to hold that grade as low as possible. Passing west out of Altoona, the line ascended at a steady rate of 91.3 feet per mile (1.72 percent), entering the valley cut into the front by Burgoon Run. Carrying up its north slope to the place where an intermediate ridge was encountered at Kittanning Point, the grade dropped to 1.45 percent, and the line made a great sweeping curve with a radius of just over 600 feet—a complex curve with a radius of 637 feet on the north and 609 feet on the south)—to turn eastward on a side-hill bench cut into the south slope of the Burgoon Run Valley. Approaching the outermost front again, the line turned first south and then west up the next valley that cuts into the front along Sugar Run. Passing on a continuous 91.3-feet-per-mile grade to the summit, where a 3,570-foot tunnel reduced the elevation at Sugar Gap, the Pennsylvania had finally surmounted the edge of the Appalachian Plateau, here termed the Allegheny Front. The economic cost would remain high even as traffic increased and further refinements of engineering could be bought. The irreducible grade for the twelve miles remained at 1.72 percent, a very stiff climb indeed for the two million passengers who passed over this line at the height of the Pennsylvania Railroad's prosperity in 1952.[117]

Once on the plateau,

careful thought and study were given to the most feasible of the several routes surveyed from the crossing of the mountain to Pittsburgh, and it was finally determined that the route should descend along the valley of the Conemaugh River to Johnstown, the chief obstacle to overcome being the building of a tunnel 600 feet in length through Pringle's Point, a short distance below Jefferson, but as the route crossed the Allegheny Portage Railroad (part of the State Works of Pennsylvania) five times by bridges and once upon a level, it possessed the advantage of being able to connect with it, bringing each portion of the line into profitable use as fast as it was completed.[118]

Continuing down the Conemaugh for twenty-five miles from Johnstown to just short of Blairsville, the rail alignment then passed over the rolling plateau surface to the head of Brush Creek just west of Greensburg. Thence passing down the creek, it gained the Monongahela branch of the Ohio some ten miles east of Pittsburgh at Braddock. At Johnstown the line had returned to the elevation of Altoona (Johnstown is at 1,184 feet). This thirty-eight miles was the only very heavily graded part of the Pennsylvania Railroad Main Line. The next fifty-one miles to the summit west of Greensburg (1,091 feet) ranged only within a couple of hundred feet and produced fairly easy grades. Using a tunnel through the divide leading to Brush Creek, the line dropped steadily to the Monongahela and then on to Pittsburgh at an elevation of 748 feet. On the line chosen, the distance between Harrisburg and Pittsburgh was 249 miles and the main summit was 2,158 feet.

The completion of the Main Line of the Pennsylvania to Pittsburgh in 1852 assured that at least four companies would, after 1853, be seeking to expand the practice of urban mercantilism in the rich flatlands to the west of the Appalachian Plateau. From north to south these were the New York Central, amalgamated in 1853 but in actual fact a chain of interconnected links after 1842; the New York and Erie, opened from Jersey City to Dunkirk, New York, in 1851; the Pennsylvania, completed in 1852; and the Baltimore and Ohio Railroad, completed to Wheeling in 1852. Branches of these railroads subsequently made additional crossings of the great mountain chain, but no other companies gained a sufficient foothold to enter the trans-Appalachian competition north of Virginia, New England's Northwest Passage having in the end failed to open; and it was in the Northeast that the real traffic lay in the carriage of passengers and high-value freight, the sorts of trade that could be used to produce the funds necessary for the next phase of the American railroad expansion campaign: the forging of ties between eastern entrepôts and the actual production areas of agricultural and manufactured products in the Middle West. But before looking at that phase we must again turn to look at the southern attempts to capture mercantile hinterlands, particularly the efforts in South Carolina and Georgia, but with brief note of the activities in Virginia.

Efforts to Develop Traditional Hinterlands in the South

We must return in time to the earlier period of American railroad promotion to take up the story in the South. It often surprises even those well informed about the transportation development of nineteenth-century America that the first long line, and one of the earliest railroads to open, came not in the North with its quickening pace of industrialization and urbanization, but rather in a South that seems to epitomize the traditional rural economy, with elements of feudalism and certainly the geographical constraint on the movement of labor that we associate with that medieval system. Yet it was in the plantation South in 1833 that the longest railroad in the world up to that time opened, and for a purpose with which we are entirely familiar.

The South Carolina Opening to the West

To understand this development we may reflect on the report of Alexander Black, chairman of a Charleston city council committee, given in March 1828: "The trade of Charleston is supported by about 200,000 bales of cotton and 100,000 bales of clean and rough rice annually. . . . Charleston has for several years past retrograded with a rapidity unprecedented. Her landed estate has, within eight years, depreciated in value one-half. Industry and business talent, driven by necessity, have sought employment elsewhere. Many of her houses are tenantless, and the grass grows uninterrupted in some of her chief business streets."[119] Charleston had no industry for export of products outside the region, and any diminution of the flow of cotton and rice—particularly the former, as the latter was declining in importance—would mean that the grass would grow both more continuously and more lush. It was in this period that the cultivation of cotton was spreading from the inner sandy coastal plain to the potentially more fertile Piedmont lying above the Fall Line. The South Carolina part of the Piedmont was hard to approach from Charleston. Its trade would flow naturally down the rivers that drained it: the Santee system in South Carolina, and the headwaters of the Savannah River in the western part of that state and in Georgia. At the beginning of the nineteenth century the Charlestonian merchants sought to divert their cotton along the lower Santee River toward Charleston, through the construction of the Santee Canal. With the expansion of cotton culture to the Piedmont, the original purpose of this canal—bringing foodstuffs from the Piedmont general-farming areas to the rice staple-producing coastal plain—could be converted to the movement of the great staple export of South Carolina to its main port. But the parts of the Piedmont drained by the Savannah River system were effectively shut off from the great Carolina colonial port, though clearly available to Georgia's burgeoning entrepôt, Savannah. Georgia wished to improve the Savannah River, a boundary stream, but South Carolina did not so desire, for obvious mercantile reasons. The result was no action, save below Savannah, where federal responsibility lay and action could be taken without the acquiescence of the South Carolina legislature. It was in this situation that the frightened merchants of Charleston began to promote a railroad, having given up the notion of another canal, this time to the Savannah River at Hamburg across the falls from Augusta, Georgia. The situation in South Carolina was very similar to that in Massachusetts; it was obvious to the merchant class that for the city to prosper better connections with the interior were required, but preliminary surveys had made canal construction seem impracticable. In that event railroads were accepted more rapidly as a solution than was the case in New York, Pennsylvania, or Virginia, where canals were actively under construction or in operation. In 1827 Alexander Black, as the state representative from Charleston, submitted a bill to incorporate a railroad to build from Charleston to Hamburg, and to Camden and Columbia as well. It passed quickly, and the promoters were faced with the need to decide upon their strategy in this simple and classic campaign of urban mercantile competition.

Almost immediately it was decided, given the presence of the Santee Canal, that the best strategy was to undertake the line to Hamburg and Augusta, for that would divert new trade to the Carolina entrepôt. A preliminary survey showed "that the summit between the two places was 375 feet above Hamburg and 545 feet above Charleston Neck at the Lines [the city boundary]. This summit was 123 miles from Charleston by public road and 17 miles from Hamburg. Obviously, the grade on the Hamburg side presented serious difficulties. However, [the surveyor] Colonel Blanding thought this could be overcome in several ways, depending upon the type of power adopted. In case the locomotive was used, an inclined plane with a stationary engine would be necessary; in case of horse power, those could be dispensed with."[120] Since steam was chosen for power early in the construction of the line, the inclined plane became a requirement in the minds of the promoters.

In planning the route several surveys were conducted, but as the country was about as conducive to railroad construction as might be imagined, there is no need for us to go into great detail. The country to be crossed was described as "alluvial and almost entirely sand on the surface, except in the river bottoms, where the soil consists of a rich loam." The route beginning at the Lines was to continue up the neck of land between the Ashley and Cooper rivers, then via Summerville to the Edisto River thirty miles above Givhan's Ferry. Thence it ran over very favorable ground to a summit 510 feet above tidewater and 119 miles from Charleston. No grade was over thirty feet per mile (0.56 percent), and most were very much less. But between the summit and Hamburg, sixteen miles away, there were difficult problems that were finally met by creating a 3,800-foot long inclined plane, dropping 180 feet, just beyond the summit, and then a moderate grade down to Augusta Bridge with no section over 18 feet per mile (0.3 percent).[121]

The fabric of the line was as experimental as that of most railroads of this time. Following the practice on the Delaware and Hudson Canal Company railroad in eastern Pennsylvania—probably because the appointed chief engineer, Horatio Allen, had come from that road—the superstructure was carried on piles rather than grading. Part of the justification for this peculiar practice was that it would permit the small streams that must be crossed in the generally level-and-straight run between the two termini to be taken without any change in fabric. Soon, however, the truth that should have been evident from the bad experience with wooden structures on the Santee Canal was brought home, and during the first decade of the railroad's existence much of the effort and earnings went into replacing these pile-supported stretches of the line. The other decision Allen made was to adopt a five-foot gauge for the line, rejecting one of four and a half feet. This decision established what came to be the characteristic "Southern gauge," which persisted until massive changes were wrought in a short period in the 1880s. The line was laid with wooden stringers on which was spiked a strap of iron two and a half inches wide and half an inch thick. Allen had wished to use an L-shaped strap, the one-inch flange to point down over the edge of the stringer to protect it from wear by the wheel flanges of the cars, but because of its higher cost, this "track" was used only on the very short length of curving track found on this level, straight line.[122] It was Allen's view that the system of piling was desirable for its solidity, uniformity of level, and accuracy of direction. In addition, it was cheaper to build in an area such as the Carolina coastal plain where pine forests, and some hardwoods, were plentiful and available essentially at trackside. A further advantage was found in "that in passing through cultivated fields such fencing may be saved by digging a wide deep ditch under the rails where they enter and pass out the field in a transverse direction and running the common fence through it."[123] The main objections were that decay of the wooden structure might be rapid and the pile structure might cant outward, leaving a dangerous spread in the track gauge. A further possible objection was presented by the still unresolved question of the motive power to be used. If horses were to be employed, the drawing would be awkward because it would have to be done from outside the tracks, and a friction wheel bearing would have to be used on the inside of the track to counteract the sidewise pull of the towrope.[124]

The South Carolina Canal and Railroad Company was fortunate in the chance occurrence that one of its directors, E. L. Miller, had been present at the opening of the Liverpool and Manchester Railway, there witnessing the operation of the Stephenson engine. He offered to produce an engine from his own design, to be built at the West Point Foundry in New York City. This was done, and the engine for which such high hopes were entertained was called the *Best Friend of Charleston,* the first practicable American locomotive.[125] It was left to Horatio Allen to resolve the question of the tractive power to be used, and we should in that regard not forget that it was Allen who had volunteered to take charge of the *Stourbridge Lion,* the first locomotive ever run on American tracks on August 9, 1829, and had succeeded in running it for three miles.[126] The next month Allen arrived in Charleston to take up his duties as chief engineer for the Charleston and Hamburg, certainly with the experience of the trials at Honesdale, Pennsylvania, on the Delaware and Hudson fresh in his mind. He explained his recommendation for steam power made soon thereafter to the directors of his company: "The basis of that official act [the first adoption of steam for traction on any American railroad] was not the simple estimate resting on the facts as they existed on the Stockton and Darlington Railway, but, as was stated in the report, on the broad ground that in the future there was no reason to expect any material improvement in the breed of horse, while in my judgement the man was not living who knew what the breed of locomotives was to place at command."[127] As Allen continued in his later account of this portentous event, with all the directors present it was voted unanimously to adopt locomotive traction. "The resolution then passed, and placed on record, was the first act by any corporate body in the world to adopt the locomotive as the tractive power on a railroad for general passenger and freight transportation." And it should not be overlooked that the South Carolina Railroad, as it came to be known, used American-designed and -built engines from the beginning. So much for the too casually assumed diffusion of steam traction from a British hearth.

The railroad was built fairly rapidly, no doubt because of its particularly favorable terrain, such that once off the Charleston peninsula the line was straight, nearly level, and located on a continuous gentle dividing ridge south of the Edisto River that avoided both transverse valleys and extensive bridging for the ninety-odd miles to the summit, sixteen miles from Hamburg. Only in the inclined plane did the builders encounter much difficulty. Samuel Dierrick notes that the problems were not so very severe but, "as a matter of fact, the whole work had been executed by apprentices who only began to be skilled when the work was completed."[128] But almost immediately the actual operation of the inclined plane proved costly because of there being several separate slopes in the three-thousand-foot section. In 1835 the plane was shortened to twenty-seven hundred feet and made one single slope; later in the 1830s the operation was further improved by replacing the stationary steam engine, so costly to keep in fire, with a locomotive that passed up and down the slope as a counterweight to the train, to which it was connected by a cable passing around a drum at the top of the plane. This seemed to improve the situation, and the plane remained in use for many years.[129]

When the South Carolina Railroad opened in 1833, it proved to be only a moderate success. Maintenance and operating costs were greater than had been anticipated and revenues were less, partly because there was no through connection at Augusta, even though Georgia interests had begun the construction of the Georgia Railroad between that city and, ultimately, what became Atlanta. In response to local drayage operators and hotelkeepers, the city authorities did not allow a connection between the two lines, so transfer through the city streets was required. And as U. B. Phillips points out, once on a dray it was as easy to reload the cotton bags onto a boat on the Savannah River as onto a car of the South Carolina Railroad.[130] The other problem was that better access to the South Carolina Piedmont was needed. In 1835 the company began to think of a sixty-eight-mile branch, appropriately from what came to be known as Branchville on the Charleston and Hamburg line, to Columbia at the falls of the Congaree. This line opened in 1842, again to be branched at Kingsville for thirty-seven miles to Camden, at the falls of the Wateree. In this way the edge of the Piedmont could be tapped at three places.

Still, there was the strong desire, as expressed in the speech of the company's president on opening the original line, that the natural objective of this Charlestonian search for a hinterland lay well beyond the Piedmont, even beyond the Appalachians, in the food-growing areas of the Middle West. From that desire grew the proposal, taken up as well at the opposite terminus, for a railroad from Charleston to Cincinnati. In 1836 the South Carolina legislature appropriated money to have a survey conducted to discover the practicability of a route across the southern Appalachians. The funds were too small to support more than a reconnaissance survey outside the mountains, but within them an instrumental survey was undertaken. The findings, reported in July 1836, were that the two mountain barriers across the general line between Charleston and Cincinnati—the Blue Ridge, as it was called on the North and South Carolina boundary, and the Cumberland Mountains on the Virginia, Tennessee, and Kentucky boundary—could be passed by a rail line. The western slope of the Blue Ridge, which today we tend to denominate as the Great Smokies, could be passed with relative ease using the valley of the French Broad River from the open valley around Asheville, North Carolina, through the defiles of the Smokies to the Tennessee Valley east of Knoxville. And the Cumberland Mountains could be traversed at Cumberland Gap, where only a narrow ridge less than a mile across separated the relatively open valleys of the headwaters of the Tennessee from those of the Cumberland.

But the real problem arose in surmounting the Blue Ridge, the eastern escarpment of the Appalachians facing upon the Carolina Piedmont in this latitude. As Phillips reports,

The eastern face of the range was so abrupt as to afford a possible railroad crossing from the Saluda valley, in which the proposed road must lie, only in two places; and in these instances inclined planes and stationary power would very probably have to be used. . . . The summit of each of these passes lay nearly on a level with the table-land of Buncombe County [in which Asheville lies], gently drained within by the French Broad. The route to either of these passes must needs overcome rather steep ascents; in the one case 1,344 feet in 11 miles; in the other, 1,102 feet in 18½ miles. The former, the Reedy Patch Creek route, would probably require the institution of three or four inclined planes; in the latter—Saluda Hill—it might possibly be found that it could be overcome without such resort.[131]

Having investigated the eastern front of the Blue Ridge, the survey turned west to discover that the drop from Asheville down to the French Broad could be secured "with an average descent of 13 feet, and a maximum of 45 feet to the mile. The river is often winding, with steep rocky banks, and construction will be costly because of the probable necessity of several tunnels and of deep rock cuts and fills in the bed of the river. The route in Tennessee may run *via* Knoxville, or in a straighter line, around the foot of Clinch Mountain, 18 miles north of Knoxville, and reach the Cumberland Range at Cumberland Gap . . . [where] the mountain is compressed within a breadth of not more than 5000 feet, with a rise on the eastern face of 362 feet and on the western face of 504 feet."[132]

But 1836 was too early in the evolution of the economy and of the rail net of the South for such an ambitious undertaking. Any route from South Carolina across the Appalachians would have to wait till after the Civil War. In the 1870s there was a revival of interest in the Saluda (Blue Ridge) route, so that ultimately the Asheville and Spartanburg Railroad was organized and built the critical part of this line, crossing the eastern face of the Blue Ridge between the two cities of its name. As opened in the 1880s, this line included a section famous to rail-roaders, Saluda Hill, the steepest section of main-line railroad in the United States. We have already seen the conditions that led to the construction of such a line. From Spartanburg near the western edge of the Piedmont this route passed via the South and then the North Branch of the Pacolet River to the eastern face of the Blue Ridge at Tryon, North Carolina, where Saluda Mountain rose abruptly to the west. From 875 feet at Spartanburg the line rose gently to 1,000 feet in twenty-seven miles to reach Tryon. Then the climb began in earnest, continuing steadily for another six miles to Melrose at fifteen hundred feet, at a grade of about 1.5 percent. Saluda, 3.1 miles to the west, lay at the top of a grade that could not be reduced below 243 feet per mile (4.7 percent), so the builders faced the task of directly constructing a shelf along the hill slope above the headwaters of the North Pacolet River to reach Saluda in a crease in the edge of the upland that extends for some thirty-five miles northwestward to Asheville at a general elevation of 2,200 to 2,300 feet.[133] No inclined plane was used at this late date, just massive power. Under steam this 3.1-mile grade was handled even by 2-8-8-2 locomotives of 96,000 pounds' tractive effort for each 550 tons of drag. With modern diesels, helper engines were needed to attain the summit. Runaways still took place, requiring safety tracks. Saluda Hill was a hard place for a railroad to attempt to run a main-line business, so in the early 1990s this steepest main-line track in America was abandoned.

Thus was the South Carolina opening to the West initially secured, but only a generation after the lines in the Northeast and the Middle Atlantic states had gained access, and far later than the railroads of Georgia.

Georgia Adopts the Railroad

The Charleston merchants' adoption of the railroad as an instrument of regional development must have seemed foolhardy indeed to the English visitors who frequented the plantation South during the first half of the nineteenth century. In Britain the iron highway was still something called into existence by a strong and clearly expressed need for frequent or heavy transport. The fact that in the 136 miles between Charleston and Hamburg on the Savannah River there were no real towns, as the English conceived that term, would seem to suggest that the South Carolina Railroad, longer than Stephenson's London and Birmingham, was the ultimate expression of the pioneering American railroad. Yet when it was extended, as was starting to be done in 1835, the country opened by that further pioneering was nearly wilderness for much of the way and only recently settled where any villages or small towns were encountered. It was in Georgia that the first classic expression of the developmental American railroad was laid out and completed. In the 1830s, when the railroad fever swept Georgia, that southernmost of the original states was comprised of a few ports, with only Savannah standing as a real town, and a few inland towns, usually to be found near the Fall Line at the head of navigation on the broad and slow-moving rivers of the coastal plain. Augusta has already been mentioned as the head of navigation on the Savannah River—Macon was the head on the Ocmulgee branch of the Altamaha and Milledgeville on its Oconee branch, and Columbus on the Apalachicola-Chattahoochee stood in the same relative position—at the contact between the coastal plain and the Piedmont, the point where the seaward edge of the eastern Cotton Belt was encountered. Because the most important and valuable commodity that moved on the railroads of the South was cotton bagged, later baled, for export, there was a strong desire among those seeking to develop the Georgia Piedmont that railroads be carried into its broad, rolling hills to bring the cotton thence to the ports whence it would be sent on to England or New England. Thus, the first railroad system of the South was merely an extension of the initial potamic transportation system that had allowed the European settlers to move somewhat away from the coast even in the early years of the Republic. The South Carolina Railroad and, as we shall see shortly, the Central Railroad of Georgia were more a part of that nonrail potamic system than of a rail net, in that each sought to divert the natural flow of cotton, down the streams from the Fall Line to the ports at river mouths, from one of those ports to its more powerful neighbor; from the Savannah River to Charleston rather than to the port of Savannah; and from the several branches of the Altamaha to the port of Savannah rather than to the smaller Darien.

The Central Railroad of Georgia, built from Savannah to Macon with interception of the river traffic from Milledgeville on the Oconee branch of the Altamaha, was, as might be anticipated, the work of the Savannah merchants and investors. In the mid-1830s when Georgia was gripped by a railroad boom brought on by the completion of the Charleston and Hamburg, three projects were promoted essentially in concert: the extension of the South Carolina Railroad within the Georgia Piedmont, initially as a rail line to be built from Augusta to Athens, site of the state university and of two burgeoning cotton mills; the creation of a diverting line from the Altamaha Valley to Savannah; and the continuation of that line from its proposed terminus at Macon to a point farther inland toward the mountain margin of the Piedmont. At the same time a fourth project was broached, for a line across the now merely hilly Appalachians to the Great Valley lying behind them to the north, here drained by the Tennessee River. As the discussion became practically oriented, it was accepted that this fourth project was so wildly developmental that no private investor could be found to risk his capital in its support. In his place must come the state as a direct agency of development, as had been the case in the earlier canals and the original Pennsylvania Railroad from Philadelphia to Columbia.

The Central Railroad of Georgia, normally designated the Central of Georgia, was mostly a coastal-plain line, benefiting from the gently rolling terrain to the point that for the first hundred miles west of Savannah the steepest "grade" was only ten feet per mile, so flat that it could not be perceived as a slope by the naked eye. Even toward the edge of the Piedmont, where the line had to climb over watersheds dividing the various rivers, grades could easily be held to no more than twenty-five feet per mile, well under 0.5 percent. In turn, the curves were gentle, so more economical conditions for construction could hardly have been found. Costs were further kept down by using a rather stingy strap rail, 1½ by ⅝ inches, laid on mud sills of pine cut from the vast pineries of the area. Begun in 1836, the line of 190.5 miles reached Macon in 1843, held up—as were most American railroads—more by a shortage of capital than by any difficulty of construction. To attempt to overcome that shortage, the state of Georgia granted a bank charter to the Central of Georgia as well as to the other two lines under discussion, the Georgia Railroad and the Monroe Railroad. It often turned out that the promoters were more interested in the immediate profits to be made from a banking charter than the problematic ultimate earnings from rail transportation.[134]

In part such hesitation can be well understood when we reflect on the fact that the "city" of Macon had been in existence only some twelve years when the line was proposed and less than a quarter-century when it was finished. The notion of building a line longer than that from London to York through only partially settled country to an only then emerging agricultural area could be advanced only because the construction could be very cheap. The city of Savannah donated five acres for a terminal in that city; its transformed structure still stands as perhaps the finest early-nineteenth-century station remaining in America today, Gridley Bryant's romantic through station in Salem, Massachusetts, having been shamelessly destroyed in the 1950s. The line to Macon cost $13,000 per mile, only about half the American average, because of the level ground over which it passed, the lightness of the rail, and sound administration by a company short on capital. Including equipment, the Central of Georgia cost only about $2.5 million, a low sum indeed for a line 190 miles long.[135]

The Georgia Railroad built westward from Augusta—as a logical extension of the South Carolina Railroad, though built by a different company and physically separated from the older line for a number of years by the resistance of Augusta to any connection—did not have the same role as the Charleston and Hamburg and the Savannah and Macon lines. Instead, it actually moved out onto the Piedmont to supplement, rather than supplant, the navigable rivers of the coastal plain. Chartered in 1833, just as the South Carolina Railroad was reaching Augusta, the company was authorized to build a line westward from that city and to carry branches to Athens, Madison, and Eatonton on the Piedmont. The Athens branch might be extended to the Tennessee River in that state if the company so desired. The company did not have sufficient funds to entertain such notions, but it did gain support from the burgeoning towns of the Piedmont, whence came most of its capital.

The North
American Railroad
Rises in the East

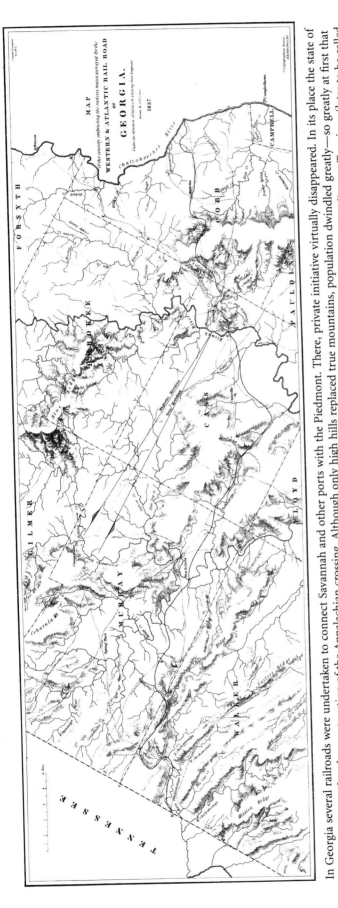

MAP
of the country embracing the various routes surveyed for the
WESTERN & ATLANTIC RAIL ROAD
of
GEORGIA.
Under the direction of Lieut. Col. S.H. Long Chief Engineer
Drawn by J.F. Cooper
1837

In Georgia several railroads were undertaken to connect Savannah and other ports with the Piedmont. There, private initiative virtually disappeared. In its place the state of Georgia had to undertake construction of the Appalachian crossing. Although only high hills replaced true mountains, population dwindled greatly—so greatly at first that only the state treasury could provide construction funds, as it did for the Western and Atlantic Railroad from the junction of the private lines at Terminus (later to be called Atlanta) to and across the Tennessee boundary to Chattanooga, which was reached in 1852. *Source:* Library of Congress map.

As laid out the line was quite favorable, following a gently rolling watershed ridge for 105 miles from Augusta to Athens, save for the rise out of the Savannah Valley at the former place and the descent into the Oconee Valley at the latter, though neither required an inclined plane like that earlier employed on the South Carolina side of the boundary stream. Construction began in 1835, and the line was completed to Athens in 1841. There the further extension was abandoned because as early as 1836 the state of Georgia had begun actively to promote a line from a point to be selected in north-central Georgia to the Tennessee River. When that terminus was selected, and so named for a short time, the Georgia Railroad undertook instead to continue its Madison branch westward along the slope of the Piedmont to Terminus. Construction was still fairly easy, save adjacent to that great exfoliation dome that rises above the piedmont surface at Stone Mountain, just east of the western terminus. The 170-mile main line from Augusta to the junction with the state railroad was completed in September 1845, a month before the Central of Georgia, via its extension from Macon that had begun as the Monroe Railroad in 1836, completed its 103-mile line to Terminus.[136]

These were locally conceived and constructed lines, and it is surprising that they remained independent for nearly 150 years. They proved to be prudent and productive investments, rapidly coming into heavy use for the transport of cotton to Savannah and Charleston and, after the state railroad was completed, significant distributors of food brought from the Middle West to the plantation areas of the Piedmont. Few more successful developmental lines were ever constructed in America.

The strategy of the Central of Georgia was clearly expressed when the state turned its attention to the transmontane route. A railroad convention was held at Macon in November 1836, and from its deliberations came the recommendation that the state undertake to build a railroad, not over 130 miles long, from some point within 8 miles of the Chattahoochee, and in De Kalb County, to Ross's Landing on the Tennessee River at the northern foot of Lookout Mountain.[137] In 1838 the legislature adopted a bill calling for a state commission of three persons to supervise construction of the line, to be paid for by the public treasury. Construction was begun immediately on what turned out to be a 138-mile line to Ross's Landing, soon to become the site of the city of Chattanooga, Tennessee. The country was relatively easy, even though technically it was the southern extension of the Appalachians. A quarter-mile tunnel was required under Tunnel Hill west of Dalton, but otherwise the alignment was remarkably simple, given the numerous north-northeast/south-southwest-trending ridges crossing its path. The Western and Atlantic Railroad, as the state line came to be known, used the Allatoona Pass at under a thousand feet to cross the low southern extension of the Blue Ridge, avoiding the severe grades found in that range only two hundred miles to the north at Saluda Hill. Once northwest of that chain of hills that stood as the southern extension of the Great Smokies, the characteristic Folded Appalachians lying behind the Blue Ridge—here much less definite ridges than in Pennsylvania and Maryland—could easily be crossed at watergaps between Dalton and Chattanooga, save at Tunnel Hill with its short bore, accomplished in 1849. In May 1851 the whole line was opened and the first train between Terminus (now renamed Atlanta) and Chattanooga was run.[138]

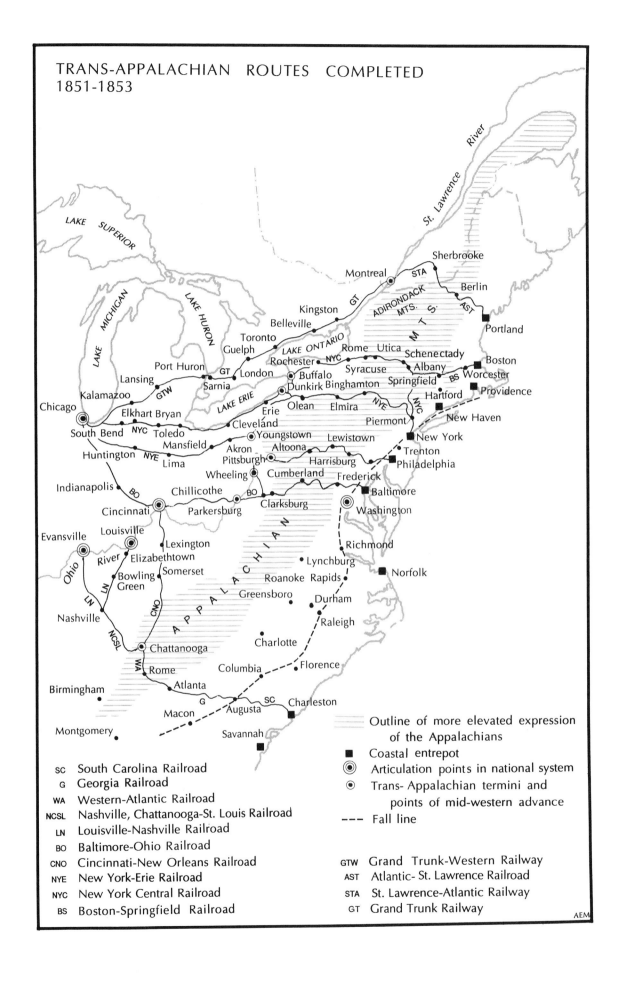

TRANS-APPALACHIAN ROUTES COMPLETED
1851-1853

SC   South Carolina Railroad
G   Georgia Railroad
WA   Western-Atlantic Railroad
NCSL   Nashville, Chattanooga-St. Louis Railroad
LN   Louisville-Nashville Railroad
BO   Baltimore-Ohio Railroad
CNO   Cincinnati-New Orleans Railroad
NYE   New York-Erie Railroad
NYC   New York Central Railroad
BS   Boston-Springfield Railroad

▦   Outline of more elevated expression of the Appalachians
■   Coastal entrepot
◉   Articulation points in national system
⊙   Trans- Appalachian termini and points of mid-western advance
---   Fall line

GTW   Grand Trunk-Western Railway
AST   Atlantic- St. Lawrence Railroad
STA   St. Lawrence-Atlantic Railway
GT   Grand Trunk Railway

AEM

With that construction the five-foot gauge of South Carolina and Georgia was carried west of the mountains, and the South gained its first access to the expanding settlement in the Mississippi Valley. With one exception—a line running from Lynchburg in Virginia through the Blue Ridge to the Great Valley lying to the west of that range, and then southwestward along that depression all the way to the point, at Ross's Landing, where the Tennessee River breaks westward across the Cumberland Mountains, ultimately to join the Ohio at Paducah in Kentucky—the Western and Atlantic remained the only trans-Appalachian route in the South even during the Civil War. That Great Valley line falls more logically with the longitudinal railroads built on the Atlantic coastal plain and adjacent piedmont than with true transmontane railroads.

The Trans-Appalachian Crossings

At this point we may briefly summarize the outcome of the great contest of urban mercantilism that shaped so much of the American rail system. Ports, the entrepôts of a mercantilist settlement system, had already been established during the colonial era from Portland (Maine) to Savannah (Georgia). With independence many of these had gained even greater control of their commercial destiny through the establishment of basic American sovereignty in the original states. These states came to think it important to encourage the growth of their ports, and to secure this the various legislatures sought to expand the hinterlands of these entrepôts, first with canals. These efforts were limited both by the high cost of those facilities and by the barriers the terrain interposed to their extension. In the case of the Appalachians that barrier was generally absolute, with only the New York State efforts proving completely successful in gaining a waterway from the Atlantic to the inland lakes and rivers. Thus, other states came to look more urgently at railroads as the instrument of state mercantile policy. Massachusetts was the first commonwealth to gain a crossing of the Appalachian barrier—but to little avail, since all that was earned was access to the Hudson-Mohawk depression clearly reserved to the benefit of the port of New York.

In a period of some sixteen or seventeen years, seven projects to cross the mountain barrier were advanced and brought to completion, six in the border and northern states and only one in the South, the Western and Atlantic just discussed. It is surprising that these seven lines were all completed to the West within a period of less than two years, between 1851 and 1853. In that first year the "Northwest Passage" that Boston sought around New York City's established monopoly of the Hudson-Mohawk route—actually opened as a rail route in 1842, but hardly as a continuous system across upstate New York—was welded together by the completion of the Rutland Railroad–Northern Railroad of New York route between Boston and Ogdensburg at the foot of the Great Lakes. That same year New York State's own railroad crossing of the Appalachians in the Southern Tier of counties, the Erie Railroad, was finished to Dunkirk on Lake Erie. These two northern openings were matched by the completion of the South Carolina Railroad–Georgia Railroad–Central of Georgia–Western and Atlantic system extending from Charleston and Savannah on the Atlantic to Chattanooga on the Tennessee tributary of the Ohio-Mississippi. In 1852 the first attempted transmontane railroad, the Baltimore and Ohio, reached the Ohio River at Wheeling on the western boundary of Virginia. Pennsylvania's late but vigorous effort at rail construction, the second Pennsylvania Railroad, was finished to Pittsburgh that same year. In the North the first of the international railroads to cross the Canadian border was completed as the Atlantic and St. Lawrence and the St. Lawrence and Atlantic between Portland and Montréal during the same year. This route was immediately taken over by the Grand Trunk Railway of Canada, which as a result was constructed on the broad gauge, 5 feet 6 inches, that this Maine promotion had adopted to protect itself from the stronger Boston system of railroads. In 1853 the New York Central Railroad was created by the corporate merger of the short links of rail between the cities that had grown up along the Erie Canal. That company immediately set about gaining access to New York City in a fashion more direct than by transshipment on the Hudson from Albany to the mouth of that river.

With such an array of railroads ready to turn their urban mercantilist intentions to work on creating through lines not merely to the Middle West but fully within its burgeoning economy, we meet what stands as the third phase of American railroad geography—following on the first, potamic diversion phase and the second, trans-Appalachian era—the projection of the various urban mercantile systems into the great agricultural areas of the North American interior. But before we take up that third phase we should complete our discussion of the development of railroads on the East Coast, even though that tale requires that we return in time to the earlier decades of railroad building and then carry the story beyond the early 1850s. In historical geography one must observe either a chronological or a geographical integrity. Here we use the latter.

The Development of Longitudinal Lines on the East Coast: The Search for Ubiquity

It is impossible here to consider in the same detail we have used for the trans-Appalachian lines the development of the lines that came to replace coastal navigation in the integration of the American transportation system. In the 1830s Americans looked upon railroads as a supplement to nature, extending the navigation system beyond its functional head at the Fall Line. Access from some entrepôts to the interior was all by rail—Portland, Boston, New Haven, Philadelphia, Baltimore, and Charleston all had rail lines from their ocean docks because the rivers on which they were sited were short and disappointing or else flowed from the wrong vector. And even the most useful streams, the Hudson, the Connecticut, the Susquehanna, the Potomac, and the James, were unnavigable above the Fall Line without major lock works and could not be extended across the higher parts of the Appalachians. For these reasons the first railroad efforts were basically perpendicular to the coast, seeking to tie as large parts of the interior as possible to the individual coastal entrepôts.

As the railroads were built across the coastal plain and piedmont to, and through, the mountains, a new process came into operation in shaping the American rail network. That force had already been at work in Europe. We may call it the *search for ubiquity*—the effort to interconnect the greatest number of individual places by a single medium of transportation; subsequently the effort by individual corporations to interconnect by their own operations as many places as possible. The effort toward ubiquity began in the United States in the proposals for rail lines parallel to the Atlantic coast, which would directly replace coastal shipping by rail service. It continued as the effort to adopt a uniform gauge for all American lines.

Some of the longitudinal lines on the East Coast were built during the earliest phase of railroad construction. These first efforts reflected the proposals in Albert Gallatin's 1808 report in which, as secretary of the treasury, he called for the piercing by waterways of the "four necks of land" that interrupted coastal navigation between Maine and the Carolinas. In 1830 railroad charters were issued for rail lines across two of the necks, though in this case interconnecting the major cities on each embayment rather than merely those water bodies as had been proposed for canals. The Camden and Amboy Railroad was chartered in New Jersey to build from the Jersey bank of the Delaware opposite Philadelphia to the lower reaches of New York Harbor at Perth Amboy. Completed in 1833, this line proved extremely profitable, not merely reducing coastal shipping between New York and Philadelphia but also restricting the navigation on the parallel Delaware and Raritan Canal to such an extent as to make it necessary for the railroad to take over the company that had constructed the cut. The other railroad transit of one of the necks chartered in 1830 was furnished by the Boston and Providence. Opened in 1835, this was also a highly profitable line that considerably reduced the employment of coastal shipping. In 1831 railroads were chartered in Pennsylvania and Maryland, and the subsequent year in Delaware, which when linked provided a rail route across the third of the necks, that between the Delaware and Chesapeake bays, by furnishing a line from Philadelphia to Baltimore.[139] In 1838 these three railroads were joined as the Philadelphia, Wilmington, and Baltimore and opened to through service. When linked by ferry with the Camden and Amboy and by city connection to the Baltimore and Ohio branch from Baltimore to Washington, which had been completed and opened in 1835, a reasonable through route was available from New York Harbor to Washington.

North of New York a coastal route was harder to shape, because of both political geography and terrain. Between Boston and New York four states were involved in such a rail line, and several broad estuaries crossed the logical alignment. It was these river crossings—the Thames at New London, the Connecticut at Saybrook, the Hudson at New York, the Delaware at Camden, and the Susquehanna at Perryville, Maryland—that were the last impediments to a through rail line from Boston to New York and Washington, with the bridges being completed in some cases well after the Civil War. On the Boston–New York alignment the Boston and Providence, already noted, was the first limited solution to such a connection, providing a crossing of the northernmost neck of land between Boston Harbor and Narragansett Bay. From Providence boats were run via that bay and Long Island Sound to New York. Three years after the completion of the Boston and Providence, a line that extended it to the old whaling port in eastern Connecticut was opened as the Stonington Railroad. Almost immediately the New York–Providence boats began stopping there, and before long an intense rivalry was established. The Providence (and later the Fall River Line) argued that by using its boats, passengers from New York to Boston would not have to rouse themselves before dawn to debark and board the train, while the Stonington (and later the Norwich line) advanced the claim that its boat-rail connections allowed travelers to avoid passage of what Alvin Harlow called New England's "Cape Hatteras"—Point Judith, Rhode Island, with its ocean swells in the largely unprotected Block Island Sound.[140]

The original competition between the Narragansett and the Connecticut ports became more intense in 1835, when merchants in Norwich, Connecticut, located some 20 miles from the sea at the head of the fjorded Thames River, set about promoting a railroad 58.9 miles long in Connecticut and 18.0 miles in Massachusetts to tap the Boston and Worcester, at the latter city, to provide yet another route between the Hudson and the Charles.[141] Officially opened in 1840, a steamboat service to New York was immediately established from Norwich, but during its first winter a new problem was clearly demonstrated: the Thames was broad and generally navigable, but it was filled with basically fresh water. Ice choked its surface, making navigation from the sound to Norwich impossible. Eventually the company found that at Allyns Point, farther down the Thames, ice was little problem and water in summer was adequate, so the railroad was opened to that dockside in 1843, creating what was for many years the "Quickest Route" between Boston and New York.[142]

Massachusetts interests also wished to join this competition, and they were enabled to do so by the fact that the commonwealth had one port on the Mount Hope Bay arm of Narragansett Bay—Fall River. In 1845 the Fall River Railroad was completed between Boston and Fall River, to be extended as a through route to New York two years later when the leading mercantile family of the city, the Bordens, started the famous Fall River Line of steamboats, which operated between that city and New York for some ninety years until just before the Second World War.[143]

It is surprising to some, but really quite logical, that this heavily traveled route between two of America's largest cities was not provided with a full rail connection until the year Chicago was linked to both New York and Boston. The cheapness and favorable reaction to the boat-rail ties between the two cities seems to have delayed application of the principle of ubiquity to this route. By 1838 Boston and Stonington had a rail connection, and by 1848 New York and New Haven had been tied by rail. Between lay unserved country that only then began to appear as the missing link in a logical and important through route. Chartered in 1848, the New Haven and New London was finished to the Thames port in 1852. All that remained was the eleven-mile stretch to Stonington covered by rail shortly thereafter, leaving only the Thames at New London and the Connecticut at Saybrook as breaks in continuous rails between Boston and New York. For many years these gaps remained, much to Charles Dickens's aggravation during his second visit to America in 1867: "Two rivers have to be crossed, and each time the whole train is banged aboard a big steamer. The steamer rises and falls with the river, which the railroad don't do; and the train is either banged up hill or banged down hill. In coming off the steamer at one of these crossings yesterday, we were banged up such a height that the rope broke, and our carriage [coach] rushed back with a run down hill into the boat again. I whacked out in a moment, and two or three others after me, but nobody else seemed to care about it."[144] No doubt such sterner fiber was the outgrowth of long experience with the

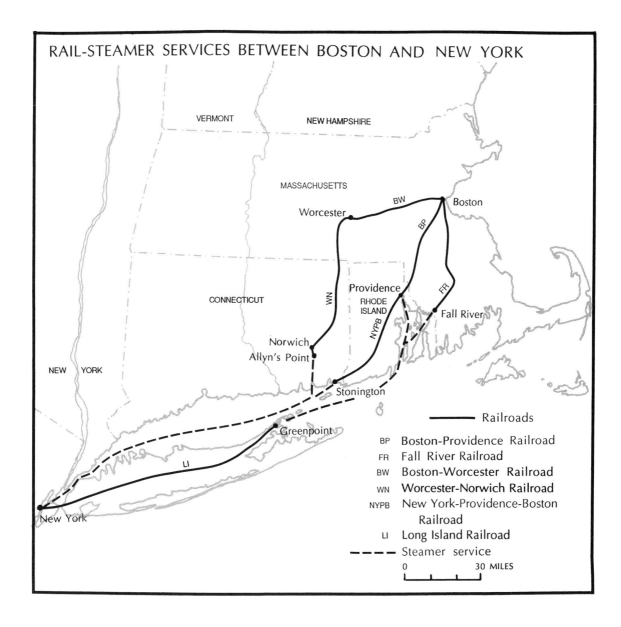

RAIL-STEAMER SERVICES BETWEEN BOSTON AND NEW YORK

VERMONT   NEW HAMPSHIRE

MASSACHUSETTS

Worcester   BW   Boston

BP

WN   Providence
RHODE   FR
ISLAND
NYPB   Fall River

CONNECTICUT

Norwich
Allyn's Point

Stonington

NEW   YORK

Greenpoint

LI

New York

—————— Railroads

BP   Boston-Providence Railroad
FR   Fall River Railroad
BW   Boston-Worcester Railroad
WN   Worcester-Norwich Railroad
NYPB   New York-Providence-Boston
         Railroad
LI   Long Island Railroad
— — — — Steamer service

0   30 MILES

demands of a developmental rail system. When trains averaged little more than fifteen to twenty-five miles an hour, the Long Island Sound steamboat offered a comfort and ease that might easily compete with these early land services. It was left to the hardy to take to the rails. South of Washington similar restraints on rail construction were to be found. Steamboats could easily ply between Baltimore and Norfolk, or even Richmond, as the absolute need for rail lines was less urgent. Yet rather quickly the view took hold that any respectable civilized area must have its trains, and lines were created even paralleling the easily traversed coastal waters, such as the Chesapeake Bay. As *DeBow's Register* noted in 1844, the United States had in fifteen years created the world's largest rail system, some 3,688 miles, to Britain's 2,069, Germany's 1,997, France's 552, and Belgium's 343 miles. Only twenty-five years after the first extensive chartering of lines in 1830, the United States had more railroads than the rest of the world put together, by a surplus of 2,712 miles. At the outbreak of the Civil War the figure reached 30,626

107

The North
American Railroad
Rises in the East

Because of the small capital available for railroad construction in the United States, lines reached the centers of cities using established streets as rights-of-way. Starting with New York City in 1832, certain bylaws forbade steam operation on the innermost parts of the line, leading to the substitution of horse traction. Ultimately a separate medium of transport, the horsecar, grew up, but some railroad trains had to substitute horse traction in parts of certain cities. *Source: Library of Congress picture.*

miles, and even then only the most obvious of lines had been constructed.[145] In the next sixty years, to the eve of the First World War, by which time virtually all American rail development had come to an end, the mileage at Lincoln's inauguration was to be multiplied more than eightfold to just over a quarter of a million miles of railroad in the United States.

With such a search for ubiquity, for a system that might interconnect all parts of a vast nation and secure mobility for those moving in the city as well as in the countryside, the existence of reasonable alternative transportation systems was no bar to rail construction. The fact that the coastal shipping lines in eastern America (and in the West as well) survived until the American entrance into the Second World War, when the ships were withdrawn for war transport uses, was a measure more of the desire for diversity, and perhaps the survival of Dickensian timidity among some of our citizens, than of the absence of railroads. And in the late nineteenth century those railroads rather quickly managed to add a level of luxury unmatched outside the United States. The Parlor Car by its name harks back to a society that Henry Ward Beecher and General Grant knew. With the addition of a *u* it was introduced on the Great Western, the London and Brighton, and other British and continental railroads where Pullman Parlour Cars became the standard of luxury.[146] In yet another instance of the duality of railroad development, with separate British and American lines of descent, Great Britain turned to American experience when it sought the ultimate in railroad service and luxury. As the chairman of Britain's Pullman Car Company noted in 1962, "'Pullman' has always meant 'super—the best.' It is individual, personal—as its American founder, George Pullman, intended it to be."[147]

At first the developments south of the Potomac were neither luxurious nor particularly well integrated with the northern system. That integration had to wait until the twentieth century, when two events had transpired: (1) the completion of the great bridges across the Thames and the Connecticut north of New York, and across the Susquehanna and the Potomac to the south, and the opening in 1910 of the Hell Gate Bridge and the East and Hudson River tunnels in New York City, which permitted the crossing of New York City by rail; and

(2) the creation of a uniform track gauge for main-line railroads. The rail system of the South had several gauges, largely because it had a quite separate origin and evolution from that in the North. The South Carolina Railroad had adopted a five-foot gauge, so that became the most common gauge in the South, though hardly the universal one.

A second component of the postbellum rail development in the South was the further integration of what had begun as short links between adjacent cities into concerted systems for north-south movement. By the early 1890s the Richmond and Danville system had been paralleled by a second line toward the eastern edge of the Piedmont—the Seaboard Air Line, extending from Richmond to Weldon in northern North Carolina and then southwestward along or above the Fall Line to Atlanta. The part of this route between Richmond and Weldon was furnished by the Atlantic Coast Line, which was truly a coastal-plain route southward through either Fayetteville or Wilmington (North Carolina) to Florence and Charleston (South Carolina), with further connections to Savannah and northern Florida. As Florida shifted from a virtual wilderness to an agricultural and resort area at the turn of the century, further amalgamations occurred that carried both the Seaboard and the Atlantic Coast Line all the way between Richmond and northern Florida, even as far as Miami for the first of those.

This transformation of southern rail traffic, from the direct export of agricultural and forest products from the interior via the closest port to an integration with the broader American rail system—essentially a shift toward north-south rail movements—was enhanced by the metamorphosis of the Richmond and Danville into the Southern Railway System under the eye of J. P. Morgan. In the financial upheaval of 1893 some thirty railroads operating under the mantle of the Richmond, Danville, and Southern were threatened with bankruptcy. Morgan—who had just perfected the voting trust in his effort to create the New York, New Haven, and Hartford Railroad out of the tangled situation among the railroads between Boston and New York and their steamboat connections and competitors—went to work in the South. The Southern Railway emerged on July 1, 1894, when twenty-five of the railroads were foreclosed in court proceedings and a new consolidation with far simpler financing and a far more comprehensive geographical extent resulted. In six years this initial consolidation was increased from around 2,000 miles to 7,717 miles of track.[148] Now ties to the northern markets and the middle-western sources of food took precedence over the radial lines to the coast that had been the genesis of railroading in the South.

In similar vein the Louisville and Nashville Railroad, opened for traffic in 1859, was expanded by consolidation, again with a considerable input by Morgan, to include not merely extensions to New Orleans from Nashville but also lines to Georgia and financial control of both the Seaboard and the Atlantic Coast Line, thus creating the other major consolidation that left the South as the field of action of no more than two major consolidations: the so-called Family Lines of the Louisville and Nashville, with routes throughout the South and connections to Chicago; and the Southern Railway, with lines more concentrated in the coastal states but through routes to Cincinnati, Louisville, St. Louis, and, recently, Chicago. Neither of these consolidations invaded "the North"

The North
American Railroad
Rises in the East

beyond the Potomac and the Ohio (with the exception of rather limited main-line extensions from Louisville to St. Louis and Chicago).[149]

The third geographical component of southern railroads to emerge in the postbellum years was the establishment of long-distance ties in the western former Confederacy, ties with the Middle West and with the trans-Mississippi area. Maury Klein has given us a picture of the antebellum southern railroad and the three basic goals sought by its leaders:

First, they hoped to make the road a profitable long-term investment in itself. Secondly, they wished to localize traffic and thereby commercial activity, at the principal terminus [which had often provided much of the original capital that saw the line built]. Finally, they saw their road as the essential tool for developing the economic resources of the region tributary to the road. In one sense, the latter two points melded together, for extension of the road both opened adjacent areas to the marketplace and prevented rival lines from tapping the areas's resources for some other terminal city. . . . From this localized perspective emerged two closely related concepts, labeled for our purposes territorial and developmental, that guided southern railroad policy making prior to the Civil War. . . . It assumed that the road existed mainly to service its key terminus and tributary region. The welfare of the city, territory, and company alike required that all concerned recognize their mutually dependent relationship and the need to perpetuate it. That meant, among other things, keeping the company out of the hands of "outsiders," whose economic interests were not directly related to the road's territory. "Foreign" investors and bondholders could be tolerated, even cultivated, so long as they acquiesced in a policy of localizing traffic at the chief terminus. But outside parties with interests in competing lines or cities were anathema.[150]

It is not hard to see in this context why southern railroading had been so parochial and so plagued by the gauge problem up to the war.

After 1865 the South was forced to abandon this cellular approach to railroad operation. Speaking of the general pattern in the United States, Julius Grodinsky shows how change came about:

An exclusively controlled local territory was a valuable asset, as long as it lasted. A monopoly of this kind was perhaps the most important strategic advantage of a railroad, provided, of course, the monopolized area either originated valuable traffic or served as a market for goods produced in other areas. Territory thus controlled was looked upon as "natural" territory. It belonged to the road that first reached the area. The construction of a line by a competitor was an "invasion." Such a construction, even by a business friend of the "possessing" road, was considered an unfriendly act. The former business friend became an enemy.[151]

In part the enemies were within the former Confederacy; they were the Danville and Western, the Louisville and Nashville, the Mobile and Ohio, each of which sought to bring together—as the South Carolina Railroad had done earlier with the Georgia Railroad and the Western and Atlantic—a "through route" over what was commonly a natural *geographical routeway.* The southernmost crossing of the Appalachians, from Savannah or Charleston to Chattanooga, and the "Piedmont Air-Line" from Washington to Atlanta were such routeways. In addition to the internal southern force, there was the general effort among American railroads to shift from the second to the third phase of railroad development—from a focus on trans-Appalachian crossings to a focus on subcontinental systems. In the North this shift led to the concerted effort during the 1850s and 1860s to create routes from the western slope of the Appalachians to

Chicago and St. Louis. In the South the shift led from the amalgamation of the lines along a major southern routeway—in the fashion of the South Carolina and the Danville and Western—to the projection of external ties from the South to the North. With Morgan's hammering together of the Southern Railway, the power of the northern lines kept the juncture to the Potomac, just as northern railroads were prevented from crossing that line in a southerly direction. But west of the Appalachians no such clear boundaries of zones of activity were determined. Again Morgan was instrumental in shaping the Louisville and Nashville in its more modern guise, but now that consolidation had direct access to Chicago and St. Louis. Similarly, as we shall see presently, the Illinois Central carried its corporate route from Chicago to Cairo and, eventually, all the way to New Orleans.

The third phase, the complete integration of a routeway under a single corporate ownership, was not always fully accomplished. The establishment of the Potomac barrier demonstrates this, and a similar barrier grew up along the Mississippi. At New Orleans no company effectively crossed the river, and trains had to ferry it until 1935, when the Huey P. Long Bridge was completed. Four and four-tenths miles long, including its approaches, the Long Bridge is one of the world's great railroad structures, including a 790-foot cantilevered channel span.[152] Eventually the St. Louis and San Francisco Railway, with its strangely transformed network of lines extending from small railroad junctions in central Kansas and Oklahoma and the Texas Panhandle to Birmingham and Pensacola, crossed the great river at Memphis, as did the Illinois Central in its takeover of the line from Meridian (Mississippi) to Shreveport that had begun under the wing of the Richmond and Danville. At Baton Rouge, Vicksburg, and Helena (Arkansas), the Missouri Pacific Railroad, as successor to earlier short lines, did have crossings of the Mississippi, but not significant trackage on its east bank, save for a MoPac line on the left bank between Baton Rouge and New Orleans. Above Cairo, Illinois, as far north as St. Louis there were several additional bridges, but they served mostly to facilitate interconnections between east-bank and west-bank lines rather than linking long lines on both banks operated by the same company.

The reason for this barrier seems to have been similar to the reason for those on the Potomac and upper Ohio: that the third phase of railroad evolution in the United States was concerned with the completion of what might be called the "natural routeways," long alignments of previously independent companies whose amalgamation reflected a maturing awareness of what the lineaments of American transportation were, or were likely to become. The North and Middle West had become one railroad territory bounded by the Atlantic, the Canadian border, the Ohio, and Chicago and St. Louis; the South, bordered by the Potomac, the upper Ohio, the Mississippi, and the Atlantic, constituted a second territory; and the rest of the United States, west of Chicago, St. Louis, and the Mississippi south of that city, had become a third, the western territory. It seemed that railroads could no longer hope to dominate individual cities, as they had earlier both south and north, but there was a subcontinental (also subnational) limit to linear extension. The New York Central, the Pennsylvania, and the Baltimore and Ohio could cover most of the northeastern territory, though only the NYC entered New England; the Southern and the Louisville and Nashville were nearly coextensive with the South, though the L&N did not reach its northeastern portion. But beyond those territorial boundaries corporate control tended to be very limited. No automatic explanation of these consistencies is available. In the beginning, the highly mercantilist nature of railroad promotion easily explains the initial thrusting of lines from specific entrepôt ports toward their "natural hinterlands." It is not hard to see that once such germinal lines were built, the corporations owning them would think in terms of taking the "next step" toward an Appalachian crossing and access to the vast potential hinterlands of the interior of the continent—in the south-central and middle-western states. But why that next step led not to an ultimate step toward a railroad of national extent is not certain. Possibly it was because the administrative and accounting practices of the time were too weak to deal with such a geographical extent; or it might have been that the gauge problem stymied expansion into the South, or from the South. That latter explanation can be seen to deal with a practical problem that existed until the 1880s, but it does not account for the fact that Chicago became a corporate barrier even where there was no actual gauge differentiation.

One is forced to conclude that there was at work in the United States a tendency to shape routeways of less than national extent. As will be shown at the conclusion of our discussion of American railroads, such interregional but not transcontinental consolidations grew from the rationalization of the originally diverse American railroad network. Corporations sought extensive but subnational mergers, leaving to the creation of national technical standards the role of implementing a truly continental integration. Technical details of gauge, car couplings, braking mechanisms, wheel specifications, and the like were standardized to a high degree, but any sort of integration beyond the scale of the routeway was left more to operating agreements than to corporate control. Stock ownership by the powerful eastern railroads of shares in their western or southern connections tended to assure the maintenance of such extracorporate traffic agreements. This practice had been pioneered by the Boston capitalists detached from the national system by New York's moat. John Murray Forbes and his associates began their efforts to shape a rail system more extensive than New England permitted by investing heavily in the Michigan Central Railroad. That interest then was extended to the Burlington Railroad, which finally reached to the gates of the Rockies and the Gulf of Mexico. Other Boston investors followed suit, as we shall see. It is only in the last twenty years that many of these stock interests have been asserted more directly, with the creation of the Burlington Northern Railroad, or the "Family Lines" system of the Louisville and Nashville, the Seaboard, and the Atlantic Coast Line. In 1887 the Interstate Commerce Commission was created with the responsibility of, among other things, maintaining competition in the American railroad industry. From that time until the 1960s, few mergers were approved because of the effect on competition. Only with a rise to power equal to that of railroads by the airline and trucking industry did intra-rail competition seem less necessary. But even before the creation of the ICC the constraint of the rail consolidation to the demonstrable geographical extent of a routeway was observable. The regulatory agency merely assured that that practice was maintained for the next three-quarters of a century.

The Standardization of Gauge

Reference has been made to a number of different gauges adopted during the earlier years of American railroad development. Far more than in Britain, it was possible to assume in the first years that railroads would remain so isolated one from another that different viewpoints as to gauge, on strictly engineering grounds, might be allowed. Yet even in those early years there were several clear instances of deliberate gauge differentiation used to advance the geographically competitive ends of urban mercantilism: the Erie Railroad chose its 6-foot gauge with competition as at least a partial justification, as evidenced by its effort to avoid any interchange traffic; and with the Wilmington and Raleigh, the first railroad in North Carolina, the promoters sought to shield traffic in that state from Virginia and South Carolina competition by adopting not the "southern gauge" of 5 feet but the "standard gauge," found mostly in the North, of 4 feet 8½ inches. Railroads in the Southwest of Arkansas, Louisiana, Texas, and Missouri used the 5-foot 6-inch gauge found in Canada and in Maine but not generally elsewhere in the United States (adopted in the original instance to shield the Portland-Montréal line from a Boston "takeover").[153]

A further problem was that even where gauges might be the same on the several lines reaching a city, there was quite likely to be no physical connection among them. This situation was particularly true of the South, with its view that the local railroad's first loyalty was to the city that had spawned it. Only junction points, such as the Terminus that had become Atlanta or Charlotte in the North Carolina Piedmont, which had grown because of interconnection among rail lines, allowed the free practice of that aspect of transportation. In Virginia both Petersburg and Richmond forbade such ties, and only the Civil War forced their establishment, in the case of the Confederate capital, and then only for "military traffic," not for civilian purposes.[154] And the South was physically isolated from the other parts of the country. At the outbreak of the war there were no bridges across the Ohio, Mississippi, or Potomac (below Harper's Ferry) and no through rail routes by land.

By the time of the Civil War the pressures for integration of the American rail system had become clear. George R. Taylor cites three forces that increased the pace of such an effort: the war itself, the decision of Congress to adopt the standard gauge for the forthcoming transcontinental railroad, and the growth of the western grain trade, which was aimed mostly at the industrial regions of the East Coast or intended for shipment from those ports to western Europe.[155] The war finally closed the gaps in the eastern seaboard trunk line in both the North and the South, at Philadelphia in the former and at Petersburg and Richmond in the latter. The "broad-gauge" route from Jersey City via the Erie was joined to the Dayton, Hamilton, and Cincinnati at Dayton through the completion in 1864 of the Atlantic and Great Western. At Cincinnati the broad gauge was joined to the six-foot Ohio and Mississippi Railroad, which brought the route to the edge of the West in East St. Louis, Illinois. This effort at integration was, however, not sufficient, because the standard-gauge lines predominated in the North, where the decisions as to the nature of the transcontinental railroad were being made now that the southern senators had been removed from Congress by the secession. Taylor shows that Congress did not determine the gauge of the trans-

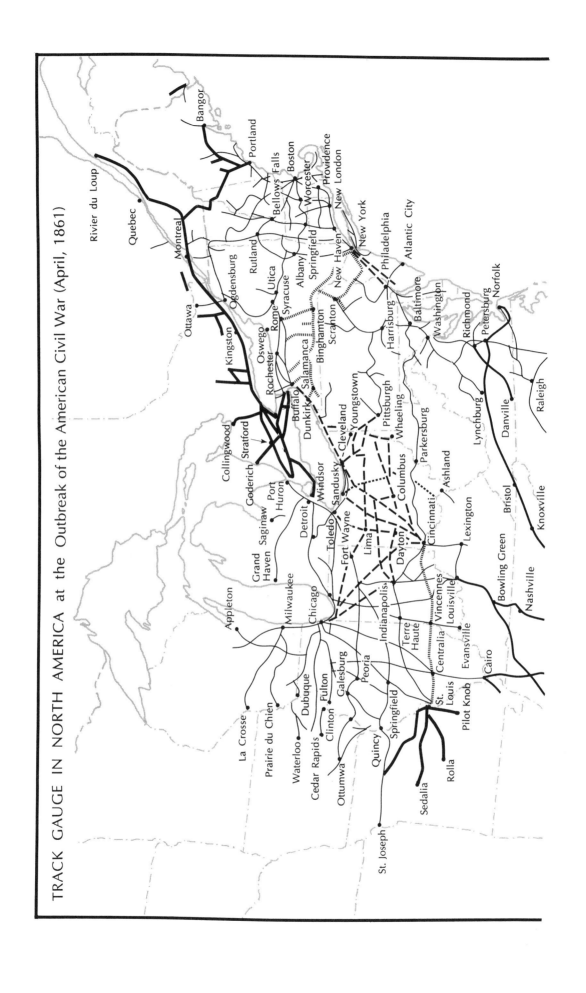

TRACK GAUGE IN NORTH AMERICA at the Outbreak of the American Civil War (April, 1861)

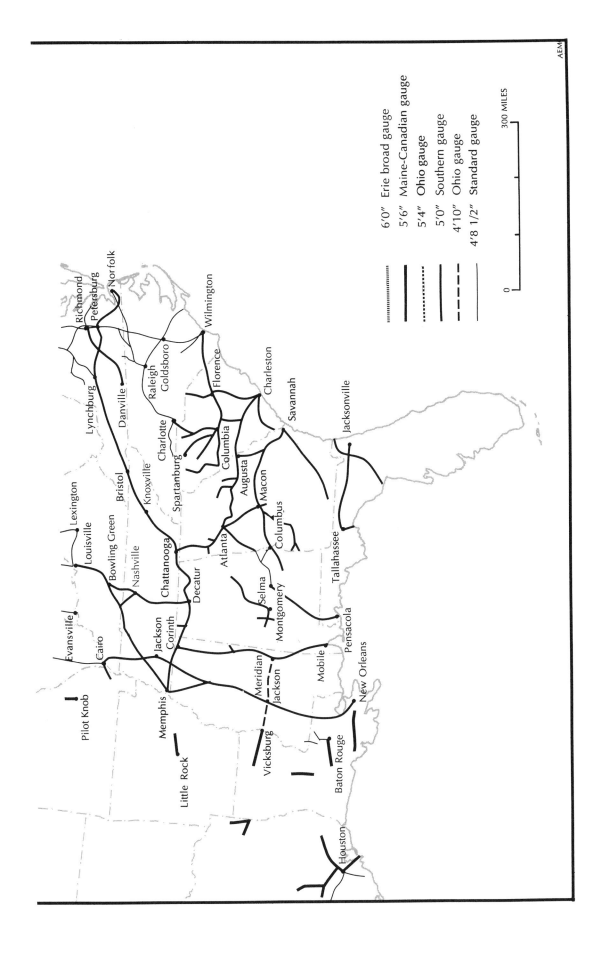

6'0"	Erie broad gauge
5'6"	Maine-Canadian gauge
5'4"	Ohio gauge
5'0"	Southern gauge
4'10"	Ohio gauge
4'8 1/2"	Standard gauge

0   300 MILES

AEM

Richmond
Petersburg
Norfolk
Wilmington
Lynchburg
Danville
Raleigh
Goldsboro
Florence
Charleston
Charlotte
Columbia
Savannah
Spartanburg
Augusta
Macon
Jacksonville
Lexington
Louisville
Bristol
Knoxville
Bowling Green
Nashville
Chattanooga
Atlanta
Columbus
Evansville
Decatur
Selma
Montgomery
Tallahassee
Cairo
Jackson
Corinth
Meridian
Pensacola
Pilot Knob
Memphis
Jackson
Mobile
New Orleans
Little Rock
Vicksburg
Baton Rouge
Houston

continental railroad; the predominant structure of the northern rail network in 1861 did. Then there were 20,567 miles of standard gauge to 1,199 miles of other gauge in the North and the Middle West.[156] Investment was even more one-sided, $849 million to $60 million. It was mostly the senators from the Far West, Oregon and California, who fought the standard gauge for this epic route, perhaps because the Golden State's only line, between Sacramento and Folsom, had been built to the southern gauge.

Although the grain trade in the early 1860s was still dominated by river and canal transport, the railroads were beginning to see that the situation might change. In the winter, when ice clogged the waterways, trains were already carrying increasing tonnages of grain. It also seems to have crossed the minds of the railroad managers that the subhumid regions in the Great Plains, once under the plow, would have to be served by rail rather than waterways. With the loss of the southern market for northern grain during the war, the railroads gained a definite operational edge. The great problem became both capacity for transport and the passage of the Appalachian barrier, for which the rails were far better suited. The loss of the plantation as a customer was more than compensated for by the needs of an increasing industrial proletariat in the Northeast and Europe. For such a west-to-east flow, particularly from areas well removed from the Great Lakes or the Ohio River, transportation entirely by train had considerable advantages. But to enjoy them a physical integration of the line was necessary, requiring both the standardization of gauge and the closing of any gaps in the line.

To overcome the gauge problem, the railroads at first employed sliding wheels, adjustable on their axles, hoists to change the trucks from one gauge to another, and double-gauged lines with three or even four rails. By the end of 1865 the Great Western Railway of Canada had laid a third rail to permit it to serve as a "bridge route" connecting the New York Central at Niagara Falls with the Michigan Central at the Detroit River.[157] During the next twenty years a number of broad-gauge lines adopted the practice, not merely to allow interchange of cars with standard-gauge companies but also to provide a transitional route on which standard-gauge cars and locomotives might be introduced to their own plant without the excessive capital demands of a rapid transformation to the standard track. "The laying of a third rail was more often than not but an intermediate step in the changing of a road's gauge to standard."[158] In some cases, the Canada Great Western for example, trains with cars of both axle widths were operated, at least with no immediate disaster. Thus, by 1880 there were about twenty-eight hundred miles of double-gauge track in the United States, with only about four hundred miles of it intermeshing standard- and narrow-gauge systems.[159]

"During the 1870s, rapid progress toward the adoption of the standard gauge was made all over America except in that part of the South east of the Mississippi River."[160] The Grand Trunk Railway, from Portland to the Detroit River, had accomplished the shift by 1874, the 6-foot Delaware, Lackawanna, and Western by 1876, and most of the 4-foot 10-inch lines of New Jersey and Ohio by 1880. Only the 5-foot lines of the South, some 11.4 percent of the total, remained as the block not integrating with the bulk of American railroads, the 5-foot 6-inch lines of the Southwest having been changed. In North Carolina the

THE NORTH
AMERICAN
RAILROAD

change came in the opposite direction, from standard to southern, such that the five-foot gauge actually increased, from 7,267 miles in 1860 to 12,137 miles in 1880. [161]

In such a situation two systems had emerged: what might be called a national one prevailed everywhere from Atlantic to Pacific save south of the Potomac and the Ohio and east of the Mississippi. There the southern system seemed to have become entrenched when Horatio Allen chose five feet as the track gauge of the South Carolina Railroad some fifty years earlier. The interchange problem became real when the first railroad bridge across the Ohio was completed at Cincinnati in 1870. As others followed, the Illinois Central brought its lines south of the Ohio in conformity with the standard-gauge northern section in 1884, forcing the Mobile and Ohio to do likewise in 1885. This completion of through standard-gauge lines from the lower Mississippi to the eastern ports left the southern competitors—the Richmond and Danville, the Louisville and Nashville, the Cincinnati Southern, and others—at a sufficient disadvantage to lead them to a conference at Atlanta in early February 1886. In a display of the amazing technical courage and confidence that those in Western civilization displayed during the second half of the nineteenth century, it was decided that more than thirteen thousand miles of southern-gauge line would be shifted to standard in a four-month period, with the actual narrowing of lines taking place on no more than two days, May 31 and June 1, 1886. Because even the northern gauge was not quite standard—the Pennsylvania, for example, used 4 feet 9 inches instead of 4 feet 8½ inches—the southern lines had to decide which of the several closely measured "standards" would be used. As their greatest interchange was with the Pennsylvania Railroad, they chose that as their standard, a full inch wider than the one Stephenson had adopted more than sixty years before. But ultimately, by a decision in 1896, all American railroads opted to conform to the English import, just about the only really significant matter British rail practice did establish in America, and that undoubtedly to our ultimate detriment. No one now knows at what precise moment the standard became truly standard, because the half-inch shift was accomplished where necessary only as new rail was laid, though it was certainly well within the twentieth century.[162]

Having established the nature of the problem in the integration of American railroads, the full benefit of the act must be held for later consideration, after we have had a chance to see how the rail system in the Middle West and Far West grew upon the roots planted in what had begun to be considered the "Trunk-Line Territory" out of which the gauge that was to be standard spread. But before viewing that areal extension, it is necessary to look briefly at a parenthesis in the general spread of American railroads—the creation of the coal-carrying railroads of the northeastern United States.

The Coal Roads: Specialization within a Developmental System, and in Bankruptcy

British railroads began mostly as coal carriers, as did many lines on the Continent. But in the United States that history was not truly repeated. A few short and very early lines, notably the Delaware and Hudson Canal and Railroad

Company, were from the very beginning built to transport coal and other heavy commodities. Most lines, however, were undertaken for the purpose of regional development in the sense of opening up an expanded tributary area for a coastal entrepôt or for an inland point of articulation in the evolving rail network. Only subsequently did the coal routes come into existence, as a result of growth in the urban markets that brought the anthracite roads into operation or as a result of the trans-Appalachian roads entering and crossing the great bituminous coal fields of western Pennsylvania, West Virginia, western Virginia, and eastern Kentucky. Later, the opening of the southern Illinois coal field added a further dimension to this transport of heavy mineral products by rail companies originally promoted for more typically American developmental purposes.

Two parts of the northeastern coal fields developed distinctive mineral-hauling lines: the anthracite basins of northeastern Pennsylvania and the bituminous coal fields of West Virginia, western Virginia, and Kentucky. It was only in 1825 that two Philadelphia merchants, Maurice and William Wurts, made an attempt to market anthracite beyond the local sales in eastern Pennsylvania. At that time the United States gained a considerable part of what relatively small amount of coal it used—bituminous coal for the most part, but some anthracite—by sea from Britain. The Wurts envisaged building a canal through the northernmost end of the Great Valley from the middle course of the Delaware to Kingston, on the Hudson. This followed upon their success three years earlier in hauling, on sleds in the winter, anthracite from mines in Wayne County, Pennsylvania, over Moosic Mountain to the Lackawaxen tributary of the Delaware and then down the main stream to Philadelphia. But the nearer Lehigh Valley mines had seemed to saturate that market, so the Wurts looked toward New York City, then beyond the economic market for Pennsylvania hard coal. In 1823 the Delaware and Hudson Canal was authorized by the Pennsylvania and New York legislatures, and in 1825 work was begun under the supervision of John B. Jervis. We should note that the Delaware and Hudson Canal was built at the beginning of the nineteenth century to carry anthracite from the Wyoming Basin of the Susquehanna River in northeastern Pennsylvania through the middle Delaware River valley and Great Valley to the Hudson at Kingston, for final shipment downstream to New York. A gravity railway was used to lift the coal up out of the Wyoming Basin, over Moosic Mountain to the Lackawaxen tributary of the Delaware River. The Delaware and Hudson Canal Company thus became a very early railroad and remains so even today, carrying passengers between Albany and Montréal. Here it is sufficient to reiterate that in crossing Moosic Mountain to reach the Lackawaxen, where the canal might begin, between the Carbondale mines and Honesdale on the Lackawaxen, a gravity railroad was constructed, which went into operation on October 8, 1829.[163] An attempt was made to use a locomotive on this rail section during its first year of operation, but the weakness of the infrastructure was such that the engine, the *Stourbridge Lion*, rocked crazily as Horatio Allen—whom we should recall from his appointment in 1830 as chief engineer of the South Carolina Railroad—drove it along some three miles of track on August 8, 1829. Allen's bravery was widely remarked upon, but this first running of a locomotive in the Western Hemisphere was recorded but not immediately repeated. In 1830 there were only twenty-three miles of rail line open in the United States, of which the Delaware

THE NORTH
AMERICAN
RAILROAD

and Hudson gravity railroad made up sixteen miles. But strangely for the company that ran the first locomotive in America, even if only briefly, the D&H remained a canal operation beyond its gravity section until 1860. The Civil War changed that, as the demand for coal during the hostilities was such that the company decided to turn its attention to rail connections, and several were established with the Erie and other railroads. In 1867 the canal company, which was always one of the more important anthracite mining operations, settled upon the notion of having its own route to Albany and the upper Hudson Valley. Heavy investments in the Albany and Susquehanna Railroad were made, and that line was completed between Albany and Binghamton in 1869.[164] From this beginning the D&H became both a canal and a railroad company, as well as a mining operation, and over the next several decades it expanded its railroads in such a way as to provide routes to prospective urban markets, particularly to Montréal.

Other railroads entered this anthracite trade. In 1868 what was to become the first major American railroad ever to be totally abandoned as scrap, the ultimate New York, Ontario, and Western, was commenced as a road from Weehawken opposite New York in a fairly direct line to Oswego on Lake Ontario, whence lake boats could reach the important Ontario cities—Kingston, Toronto, and Hamilton—on the lake's north shore. The greatest barrier to this construction was again, as on the Erie, the passage of the Shawangunk Mountains, now by a 3,850-foot tunnel at Bloomingburg, New York.[165] Completed in 1871, this bore permitted the commencement of operations in January 1872. The New York Oswego Midland Railroad, as it was then called, provided a link with northern cities that could be expected to be good customers for the "black diamonds" of Pennsylvania, so the railroad company made investments in important coal mines. Given its truly "cross-lots" routing, the O&W intercepted a number of coal-carrying lines—the D&H (Albany and Susquehanna) at Sidney Plains, the Erie at Middletown, the Delaware, Lackawanna, and Western at Norwich—and made connections to the north both with the lake boats at Oswego and lines entering Canada. So long as coal flowed, such a peculiar line could survive, even gaining the attention of and sometimes control by J. P. Morgan's New Haven Railroad, when it began to have visions of a most eccentric New England routing to the lakes and the West. In 1890 almost half a million tons of coal were carried, and an interchange with the New Haven was put into effect at Campbell Hall, connected with New England by a bridge across the Hudson at Poughkeepsie, the lowest crossing of that stream until the Pennsylvania Railroad North River Tunnels opened in 1910.[166] In this way the O&W combined its coal-carrying function, now extended to New England, with a bridge-route function to tie that great northeastern industrial area to its markets in the rest of the country. So important was this coal line, with its own track into the coal fields at Scranton, that the New Haven Railroad bought control in 1904. "Although no changes in O. & W. management resulted, the New Haven was primarily interested in the lucrative coal business. Unofficially, at least, the old [Oswego] Midland changed from a convenient corridor for upstate [agricultural] products and became a busy coal carrier."[167]

The New York, Ontario, and Western assumes more than incidental importance in our discussion of American railroads for the fate that befell it. The line was based on coal, the running of milk trains from upstate New York to the city, and a massive flow of summer visitors from the city to the Catskill resorts along its route, but by the 1920s that support had begun to erode surprisingly quickly. The use of automobiles cut passenger loads dramatically, and trucks began handling milk shipments. But in 1930 the coal movements remained, and the O&W could operate from such revenues. In 1932 coal shipments earned $5.8 million, but passenger receipts had dropped from over $2.5 million to only about $0.5 million.[168] Before that decade of general trial was over, the Ontario road had suffered fatal blows even in the coal trade. By 1957 the operation had become hopeless, and on March 29 freight service was abandoned, passenger service having gone in 1952. In July the 544-mile railroad, the longest ever junked, was sold for scrap, earning about $10 million for its various parts.[169] So much had the seemingly automatic prosperity of coal haulage declined that no economic use could be found for the Old and Weary, as it was then popularly termed; it was quietly abandoned. As the first, it was a natural bellwether for an unusually large segment of railroading in the Northeast, where coal had called many railroads into existence, only to abandon them in the years after 1945.

The network of coal-related railroads is far too extensive and complex for detailing in this short summary. From the anthracite mines of the Lackawanna and other basins of northeastern and east-central Pennsylvania dozens of lines radiated to Philadelphia, Baltimore, Washington, New York, eastern Canada, and New England. The Philadelphia and Reading Railroad, the Delaware, Lackawanna, and Western, the Central of New Jersey, the Erie, the Delaware and Hudson, the Lehigh Valley, the Lehigh and New England, the New York, Susquehanna, and Western, the New York, Ontario, and Western, and several shorter lines were heavily involved in the anthracite trade, and essentially they failed as it collapsed. In addition, the New Haven, Boston and Maine and the Rutland lost a very major part of their freight traffic with the decline of anthracite shipments. Even the Baltimore and Ohio, the New York Central, and the Pennsylvania, each with lines from the anthracite basins to New York, Lake Ontario, and the West, suffered markedly from the loss of the trade.

In western Pennsylvania, West Virginia, western Virginia, and eastern Kentucky a different set of coal roads came into existence, one based on the huge bituminous coal deposits of the Appalachian Plateau. The Baltimore and Ohio was the first railroad to tap these, in the late 1840s when its line was built westward from Cumberland, Maryland, but as the other trans-Appalachian routes were opened they also joined the trade. In the early 1850s the Pennsylvania Railroad crossed the richest part of the fields so that branches in great number were carried north and south of the Main Line, and the second Pennsylvania Railroad line up over the Allegheny Front was opened not merely to gain a lower summit for freight transport but also to serve as a further trunk along which coal from the more northerly stretches of the plateau in Pennsylvania might flow. The Pennsylvania and the B&O eventually built lines to Lake Ontario, as did the Reading from the anthracite fields, to send the fuel to then energy-poor eastern Canada. To gain access to the fuel the New York Central projected its lines southward from central New York (Lyons), Erie, Pennsylvania, and several places in Ohio, gaining a network that reached up the branches of the Monongahela even into northern West Virginia, and up the Kanawha into the central part of that state.

To the south the existence of coal fields in the western part of the Old Dominion, and its subsequently detached section in West Virginia, was instrumental in encouraging further trans-Appalachian lines. The early short links among cities in the Piedmont were joined together and extended to the port of Norfolk to create the Norfolk and Western Railroad, which with branches to Hagerstown (Maryland), Washington (D.C.), and Columbus (Ohio), and a collecting network of lines in the coal fields of western Virginia and eastern Kentucky, became the archetype of the bituminous coal road. Others in that specialized category were the Chesapeake and Ohio, built in the 1880s between ports at Newport News and Alexandria, through the West Virginia coal fields to Cincinnati and Louisville; the Western Maryland, between Baltimore and the fields in the western part of the state; and the Virginian Railway, constructed in the first decade of the twentieth century from central West Virginia to the docks at Norfolk.

At this point it may be noted that the general prosperity of the bituminous coal–hauler railroads has held up to the present. Although these lines suffered some in the 1930s, with the general decline in American economic activity, and again in the late 1950s and the 1960s, when coal was somewhat in a slump, they have had decades of profitable operation. Particularly as mineral carriers they have avoided the great overbuilding that characterized the northeastern roads when they sought to provide rail service to any town of modest size. What branches were constructed by the coal roads came to tap mines that loaded a great number of hopper cars throughout the year, avoiding the generally modest freight movements of the average small-town and rural area. If mines closed, there was no difficulty in abandoning the branch, unlike the situation found with respect to the ever-confident but seldom-accomplished hopes of the average small town, which would fight rail abandonment even if it seldom used its facilities. While a line like the Boston and Maine or the Erie was being crushed under the weight of maintenance charges on lightly used track, these coal roads tended to be crushed by business itself.

Thus, as the American rail system came under extreme competition from trucking, buses, and airlines in the years after the Second World War, the one group of lines almost proof against that competition was the coal roads. The result was that when mergers began to be bruited as the "salvation" of the railroad, it was the bituminous coal roads that were courted. The Norfolk and Western–Virginian merger of two soft-coal carriers in 1959 was virtually the first in the East, and its profitable outcome encouraged other consolidations, some of which showed a misunderstanding of the geographical conditions that made the expanded Norfolk and Western so relatively prosperous—that is, the absence of excessive branch-line operations and the preservation of its freight base because that support was from coal shipments. In the next decade, the Chesapeake and Ohio and the Baltimore and Ohio were merged, along with the strictly coal-hauling Western Maryland, to create another strong system with a coal base. The innate strength of the coal roads came to be a strangely unsettling force among eastern railroads when the enlarged N&W and the Chessie System shaped of the

The North American Railroad Rises in the East

C&O-B&O merger became realities. The New York Central had already become very restive in the late 1950s when the N&W, then about one-third owned by the Pennsylvania Railroad, sought a merger with the Virginian. The Central and the Virginian had been particularly close, with an interchange at Deepwater, West Virginia; thus, the tying of the coal road to the Pennsylvania—itself competitive in a number of markets with the Central—even though only by merger with a line in which the Pennsylvania had a major interest, left the Central uneasy. When the Chessie System was then proposed, the officials on Park Avenue could see Vanderbilt's great empire surrounded by larger and more prosperous lines, so they began talking in earnest with Pennsylvania Railroad officials, picking up from rather casual merger discussions carried out in the late 1950s. Alfred Perlman, president of the New York Central, broke off those talks because he believed

that the huge Pennsy system coupled with the growing N&W network plus the Central would unbalance the Eastern rail network. He conceded that adding the N&W-Virginian combine to the [possible] Penn Central "would have made it [the merger] more financially acceptable to us, actually." But he argued against this lineup on grounds that it would have "precluded balanced Eastern systems." If the PRR were to stick with the N&W, he preferred to see the Central join the C&O or the B&O, or both. And in an interview in August 1969, before the Penn Central merger began to fly apart, Perlman said he still would have favored linking the Central to the C&O-B&O, leaving the PRR to join the N&W and its satellites. "I think that would have given us a better balance geographically, physically, and trafficwise."[170]

Ultimately, of course, the balance was struck by joining the two largest railroads in the United States, though neither was a true coal road and both had a surfeit of branch lines as well as a bureaucracy worthy of an aspiring state government. The desired balancing came by shaping three potentially large systems in the Northeast: the Penn Central merged lines; the Chessie System and the Norfolk and Western, considerably expanded by taking over direct control of the Wabash, in which the Pennsylvania had a 99.8 percent interest; and the Nickel Plate Line, a railroad that the New York Central had previously controlled by stock interest but had had to relinquish under antitrust pressure from the Department of Justice. With the N&W thus enlarged and the Pennsylvania pulling the strings, it is no wonder that the New York Central—which was probably a sounder line on the whole, as it had trimmed its operation more effectively than had the Pennsylvania—became worried. In the end the Central rushed into an ill-advised marriage with a middle-aged wastrel, now headed by a slick Virginia lawyer, Stuart Saunders, who had begun all this dashing for protection by his pushing of the N&W-Virginian merger while president of the N&W.

The eastern mergers showed a very contrasting outcome. The coal-based roads—the Chessie System and the Norfolk and Western—proved to be effective amalgamations, continuing to operate in the black and providing the base for further enlargement. The lines either without significant coal support (the Boston and Maine, Rutland, and New Haven) or with an anthracite base that had largely disappeared (the Delaware and Hudson, Erie, Lackawanna, Jersey Central, and Reading), as well as the Penn Central merger with its much weaker coal base and plethora of branch lines, all collapsed in the late 1960s and 1970s. The New Haven had been included in the 1968 merger of the Penn Central. The

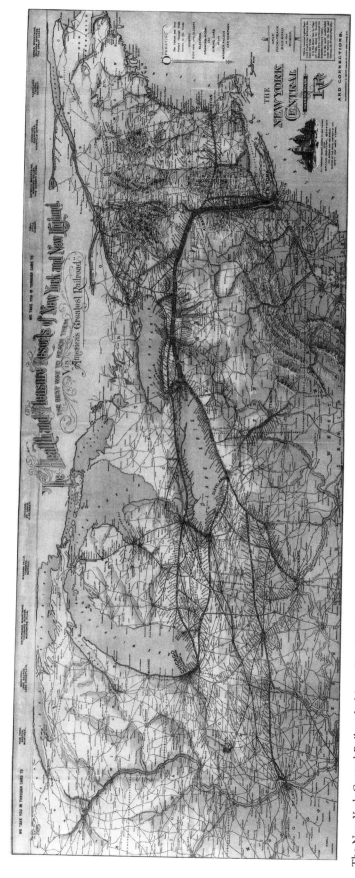

The New York Central Railroad ultimately gained control of main lines both south and north of Lake Erie and reached to the emerging junction of the American interior, Chicago, which as the quintessential railroad metropolis came to symbolize the nineteenth-century city. *Source:* Library of Congress map.

Norfolk and Western holdings of the Pennsylvania had specifically been excluded from that marriage by an agreement between the then presidents of the New York Central and the Pennsylvania. Symes for the Pennsylvania would sell that line's interest in the Norfolk and Western, while Perlman for the Central would sell that line's 20 percent interest in the Baltimore and Ohio.[171] This was done to guard against any antitrust opposition to the Penn Central merger, but such action signaled the end of what had become the established method of constraining excessive competition and assuring end-to-end cooperation among railroad companies in the East. The Pennsylvania and the N&W complemented each other geographically, just as the Central and B&O did, and the coal haulers added needed revenue to lines overblown from past efforts to provide effective rail transportation in a densely settled region.

124

THE NORTH
AMERICAN
RAILROAD

CHAPTER TWO

The Drive for Ubiquity

The Middle-Western Railroad

The attention given to the railroads of the Northeast and South is fully justified in any genetic account of the evolution of the North American railroad. It was not only that the rails on this continent began in the East and the basic features of the American system were worked out there, but also that the private corporations, and the investor groups that shaped them, came into existence east of the Appalachians in the United States and in the St. Lawrence River drainage of Canada. Thus, to understand the pattern of lines west of those barriers, both in the Middle West and in the trans-Mississippi area of the transcontinental railroad, it is necessary to build heavily on such an eastern foundation. In doing so we shall examine the evidence and the geographical patterns in terms of the drive from the western side of the Appalachians to the settlement frontier on and beyond the Mississippi, and the building thence to the Pacific of the transcontinental railroad.

From Local Links to Subcontinental Systems

In the Middle West there was an initial phase of railroad development that was as localized as that stage along the East Coast. Pairs of cities often sought to secure a connecting rail line largely without reference to any long-distance objective. The multiplicity of possible connections in the extensive and largely flat Middle West was such that it is totally impractical to attempt here to give any overall view of the early geography of such localized undertakings, beyond noting a couple of characteristic examples. "In the early period of railroads the passenger business was of greater relative importance than freight, in Ohio as well as on the Atlantic coast. Passenger routes were more flexible, and, moreover, the roads were not built substantially enough to transport large amounts of merchandise. The long use of the water routes to New Orleans formed a powerful factor in retarding the developing of freight traffic, while the novelty and rapidity of travel by railroad as compared with other modes quickly attracted many passengers."[1] Although the transfer from one train to another in a string of short lines was inconvenient for passengers, it was not so completely disruptive as it would have been for freight movements. Focusing on Ohio, the first strivings for rail development were expressed in terms of the internal transportation system of that, the first of the states in the Old Northwest. The three centers of interest—Columbus, Cincinnati, and Sandusky—fostered several early proposals, all of which were basically north-south in their orientation; that is, they were intended to serve as logical supplements to the water transport of the region on the Ohio River and Lake Erie. Such was the extent of local aspirations. Only among easterners did there seem to be broader geographical interest in the Buckeye State. We have taken note of the Baltimore and Ohio, which in the late 1820s already held vague notions of moving beyond its stated western terminus at Wheeling. In 1829 De Witt Clinton saw as the logical supplement to the waterway system of his Erie Canal a railroad across the Southern Tier of New York State, the Erie Railroad, which would probably be extended westward through northern Ohio, Indiana, and Illinois to his conjectured western terminus—not at Chicago, yet to be founded, but instead at the mouth of the Rock River flowing into the Mississippi, where Rock Island grew up. The distance was 1,050 miles from the Hudson to the Mississippi, and it was confidently assumed that such a major national railroad could be built for $15,000 per mile.[2] Ultimately the routeway was occupied, but not at first by any such Great Western Railway as was at first proposed. Instead, much more localized projects paved the way that led to eventual consolidation.

In 1853 there were twenty-two railroads operating in Ohio, the longest of which extended 234 miles from Cleveland to Cincinnati and 216 miles from Cincinnati through Dayton to Sandusky on Lake Erie. The early railroad patterns of Michigan and Indiana were similar, with initial short links between cities eventually elongated to produce long radials from a few major nodes—of which Indianapolis and Detroit were the dominant ones within these states, with Toledo, Cincinnati, and Louisville serving this function near their borders. As construction got under way, Chicago began to serve such a function just to the west of the two initial middle-western states. In 1837 the state of Michigan became impatient with the slow rate of construction that private rail promoters obtained—by then only a line from Toledo to Adrian, Michigan, had been completed, so the state legislature authorized the construction on the state's account of three lines across the Lower Peninsula: the Michigan Southern from Adrian westward toward Lake Michigan, the Michigan Central from Detroit to St. Joseph on Lake Michigan, and a third across the northern reaches of the peninsula that was not to be of much importance.

By 1843 Michigan had so taxed its credit that state construction began to slow. The Michigan Central reached Jackson in 1843 and Kalamazoo in 1846. It was clear that this was to be the short route to the West, and through service by rail, stage, and lake boat from Detroit to Chicago had already been established by 1843. As the rail line was pushed westward, the time of the journey was reduced, from thirty-nine hours in 1843 to less than a day the next year. But the state could not finance the line's completion, so in 1846 the Michigan Central was sold to eastern investors, particularly John Murray Forbes and his associates from Boston. The Michigan Southern was similarly disposed of, and each became the basis for an east-west main line across the Middle West. Such routes came to dominate the geography of middle-western railroading, each serving to tie a western terminus of a trans-Appalachian railroad to the two points of articulation that developed with respect to the Mississippi River and further westward advance—that is, St. Louis and Chicago. In the spring of 1852 both the Michigan Central and the Michigan Southern opened track to Chicago. As yet there was no connection eastward from Detroit, or Toledo, but in 1855 a route was opened between Maumee Bay at Toledo and Cleveland. In this way was established the first rail connection from Boston and New York to Chicago.[3] It used the New York Central to Buffalo, its connections to the Pennsylvania border, a string of short lines to Cleveland, the Lake Shore Railroad to Toledo, and the Michigan Southern and its connections to Chicago. Detroit was tied to the east via a branch to Toledo owned by the Michigan Southern.

The Michigan Central was in this period a Boston railroad, having its corporate headquarters in that city. Thus, it owners sought to secure a direct connection with the East by passing across the southern peninsula of Ontario, something that was accomplished by the Great Western Railway of Canada extending from the New York Central at Suspension Bridge on the Niagara River through Hamilton and London to Windsor on the Detroit River, where it was joined by ferry to the Michigan Central in Detroit.[4] An even more direct route was subsequently secured from Fort Erie via the Canada Southern Railway through St. Thomas to Windsor 228 miles to the west, completed in 1872.[5] This line had been promoted by the Michigan Central and was formally leased by it in 1882.

Subaqueous Ties between Canada and the Middle West

In 1871 James Joy, the president of the Michigan Central, sought in conjunction with the Canada Southern to organize a tunnel company to build what would have been the first important subaqueous rail tunnel, under the Detroit River; but the project was ahead of its time and had to wait until the New York Central had absorbed the Michigan Central and discovered the problems of ferrying across the river in the winter. Between 1906 and 1910 a new technology was invented for use on this 1.2-mile tunnel, almost half of which was under water: the steel sections of the two single tunnels were prefabricated on shore and taken to the alignment of the tube, where they were sunk and then bolted together in a previously dredged trench. Earlier the Grand Trunk, which had been completed to Sarnia on the St. Clair River in 1859, had hoped to operate ferries across that more swiftly flowing connection of the Great Lakes, but ice did form even there. So in 1891 the Grand Trunk opened the first subaqueous tunnel in North America between Sarnia and Port Huron, Michigan, over a distance of 6,027 feet. In this way were the east-west routes across Michigan reshaped from local links into subcontinental systems.

The Grand Trunk Railway

From Montréal the Grand Trunk Railway was originally envisioned as tying together Upper and Lower Canada; hence its pretentious name. But its English proprietors thought constantly of the larger market to be found in the American Middle West, particularly after the signing of the United States–Canada Reciprocity Treaty of 1854, which permitted the export of middle-western grain

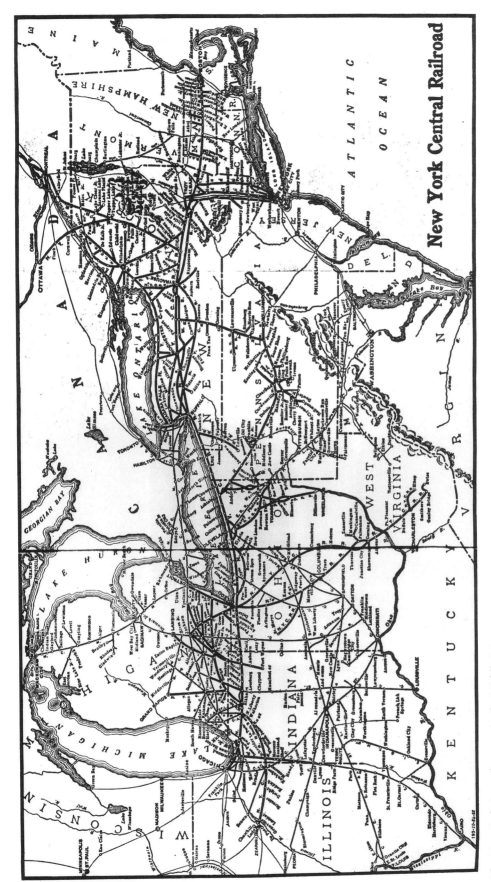

New York Central Railroad

The New York Central system in the Middle West. *Source:* Library of Congress map.

through the St. Lawrence river ports. To tap that market the Grand Trunk was extended to Sarnia and Windsor, where junction was effected with the Michigan Central Railroad bringing grain from farther west. Once that Michigan line was taken over by the New York Central in 1877, however, the Grand Trunk's owners felt it likely that the Vanderbilt line would divert traffic from the Montréal route. Well they might have worried, for they themselves had done the same: when the New York Central's interchange point with the Michigan Central was at the Niagara frontier, traffic had been diverted over the Ontario line of the Grand Trunk. The Canadian carrier's response was to consolidate five middle-western short lines between Port Huron and the Indiana-Illinois boundary, and to build a thirty-four-mile extension of the line to reach Chicago in 1880.

The Ogdensburg Gateway, as it was termed, which the Fitchburg and the Rutland worked as an end run around the New York Central's monopoly of the Mohawk route across the Empire State, used this Grand Trunk–Vanderbilt rivalry to its advantage, making common cause with the Canadian line to reach Chicago over basically friendly tracks, in contrast to those of the New York Central. While the Canadians might also have held back traffic from the Vermont company, the Rutland might during the Great Lakes navigation season carry its route farther west via the Rutland steamship line to Milwaukee and Chicago (and direct junction with the western lines that eventually focused on the latter).

The New York Central Railroad

From the industrial Northeast the New York Central was to become one of the two giants among American railroads. Starting with the route across upstate New York, consolidated in 1853, the company came, under Vanderbilt control after the late 1860s, to shape a proper subcontinental line. Gaining control of the Hudson River Railroad in 1864, Cornelius Vanderbilt soon saw that his western connection via the New York Central was uncertain, so he manipulated events to assure that in 1867 he was invited to take over control of the Central. Once in his hands—and probably more important, in the hands of his son, William H. Vanderbilt—the Central moved quickly to shape its own subcontinental line. Within ten years the New York company had gained control of the Michigan Central, the Lakeshore Railroad, and the Michigan Southern to secure an effective route from New York City to Buffalo, and thence on either side of Lake Erie to Toledo and Detroit respectively, for the approach to Chicago over the Michigan Central rails or the heavily reconstructed Michigan Southern route. At Cleveland a line to the other middle-western point of articulation was secured through consolidation that ultimately took the New York Central lines to St. Louis. That entree was gained by the effective takeover of the Big Four, the Cleveland, Cincinnati, Chicago, and St. Louis Railroad, which had been shaped of many short lines in the Middle West. Starting as little more than short links, the Cleveland, Columbus, Cincinnati, and Indianapolis Railroad had come into existence by the years after the Civil War, and in 1870 it gained its own controlled line to St. Louis. During the next twenty years other lines were added, transforming this Bee Line, as it was first called, into the Big Four with a north-south route from Chicago to Cairo, Illinois, and a set of six lines radiating from Indianapolis.

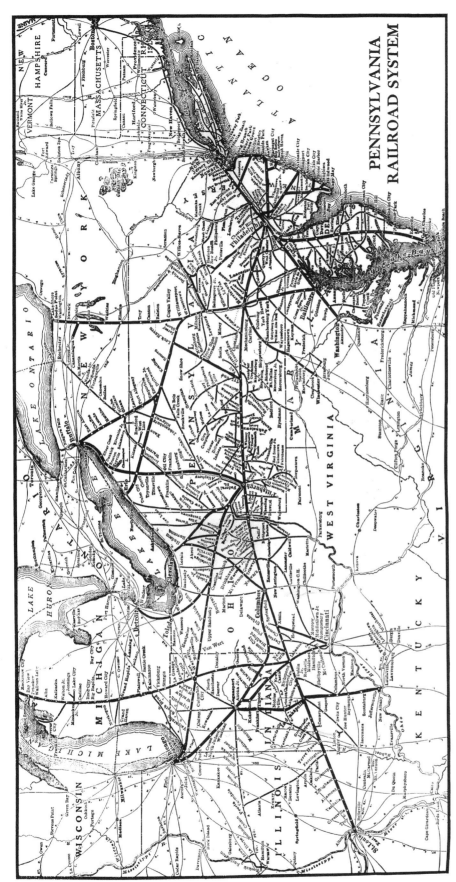

Pennsylvania Railroad system in the Middle West. *Source: Report of the Joint New England Railroad Committee to the Governors of the New England States, June, 1923.*

At St. Louis, Peoria, and Chicago it gained interconnection with the developing western railroads, so the New York Central was glad to take over control in 1891.[6]

The Erie Railroad

The Erie Railroad was hardly an equal in financial power to the Vanderbilt road, but it entertained the same notion that while a trans-Appalachian line might have sufficed in ambition during the first and second phase of American railroad development, it could no longer do so after the Civil War. The original western terminus of the Erie at Dunkirk on Lake Erie was one of those peculiar geographical abstractions in which the United States abounded during the nineteenth century. Once there, the proprietors of the railroad appreciated that a better goal was needed. First, they undertook a continuation of their line to Buffalo, which with its canal was the main eastern port in the American Great Lakes system. Even more distant goals loomed on the western horizon, along lines to the two points of articulation with a western network that were arising. From Salamanca, New York, an extension was projected that became the Atlantic and Great Western in Pennsylvania and Ohio, reaching as far as Dayton with the broad gauge. Thence the broad gauge was carried to Cincinnati, and from there the Ohio and Mississippi Railroad was constructed to that specification to the right bank of the Mississippi opposite St. Louis; however, this latter line fell ultimately to the Baltimore and Ohio and was subsequently reduced to standard gauge, becoming that company's road to St. Louis. The Erie thus never reached what seemed its first western objective, but in the years after the Civil War its efforts were turned, after unsuccessful alliances with middle-western lines, to gaining its own route to Chicago. This was accomplished in 1880, when the Chicago and Erie was completed over the 250 miles from Marion, Ohio, on the Dayton line to Hammond in western Indiana. Thence a terminal road, the Chicago and Western Indiana, carried it to Dearborn Station in the great junction city.[7] This opening coincided with the final shift of the Erie to standard gauge, which was completed on Sunday, June 22, 1880.

The Pennsylvania beyond the Mountains

From Pittsburgh the extension of the Pennsylvania Railroad contrasted strongly with all these lines to the north. Even before the company that was to call itself the Standard Railroad of the World was finished to its first destination, it was thinking of moving beyond the Appalachians. The Pennsylvania had encouraged the chartering—and modestly participated in the financing—of lines to extend the Main Line into the Middle West. The Ohio and Pennsylvania Railroad (linking Pittsburgh with Crestline, Ohio, finished in 1853) moved outward on an alignment picked up by the Ohio and Indiana Railroad (chartered to construct a line thence to Fort Wayne, Indiana, reached in November 1854). The Pennsylvania had given partial support to both, and it continued that practice when the Fort Wayne and Chicago was organized to complete the route to what was then distinguished as the Garden City of the World. In 1856 these three lines were merged, and their 468-mile route to Chicago was opened on Christmas Day, 1858.[8] From that time through service was possible from Philadelphia to the Great Junction of Chicago, but actual control of the merged western line, the

Pittsburgh, Fort Wayne, and Chicago, remained separate, a situation that continued until 1870, when the Pennsylvania Railroad secured a 999-year lease on the line. This was done because the PFW&C began to evince interest in building its own road east of Pittsburgh, or else in joining the interests of Jay Gould in the Erie Railroad. A thousand-year lease seemed adequate to attach its western connection firmly to the Pennsylvania, as it clearly proved when the Standard Railroad of the World disappeared into government control as Conrail just a century later.

The lease of the Pittsburgh, Fort Wayne, and Chicago indirectly involved the Pennsylvania in the creation of a route to St. Louis as well. This came through a half ownership of the Indianapolis and St. Louis Railroad extending from Indianapolis to Terre Haute, whence that company held under lease the St. Louis, Alton, and Terre Haute connecting to St. Louis. The Pennsylvania—which, like most of the trans-Appalachian lines, was in an expansive phase after the Civil War—had already gained control of the St. Louis, Vandalia, and Terre Haute Railroad, a newer and shorter line between its terminal cities, so in 1870 it found itself the possessor of two roads into St. Louis. That clear miscalculation of a merger strategy was resolved by selling the Alton route to the Big Four, which in turn became part of the New York Central, furnishing that rival line its entrance to St. Louis.[9] In this rash of consolidations in the decade after the Civil War both the Pennsylvania and the New York Central gained not merely routes to the two important points of articulation with the western roads, but also lines, or at least the beginnings of such, to the two important points of articulation with the southern railroads—Cincinnati and Louisville.

The B&O West of Wheeling

We have now come to the point where we may logically examine the extension of American's first trunk railroad into the Middle West. The Baltimore and Ohio had reached Wheeling on Christmas Day, 1852, in a rather exhausted state. For a time, boat connections on the Ohio seemed to serve the company's ambitions, but as the other trans-Appalachian railroads began to stake out or buy up routes to the West, the B&O looked that way as well. Wheeling became merely a jumping-off place for an effort to reach the other great waterway of the interior, the Great Lakes. But bridging the Ohio there was very difficult, so the junction point was moved four miles downriver to Benwood-Bellaire, where ultimately a bridge was built to connect to the Central Ohio Railroad running thence to Newark, Ohio. Another junction there tied the B&O to the first railroad to be built in Ohio, the Mad River line constructed southward out of the port of Sandusky on Lake Erie. Thus, by the mid-1850s it was at last possible for Baltimore to serve as the Atlantic port not merely for the Ohio Valley but also for the Great Lakes, for which it was in fact generally the closest tidewater. But the route to Sandusky, then tied only by a loose linkage of independent lines, was less appealing than two other vectors of advance, one from Cumberland (Maryland) to Pittsburgh, and the other from Grafton (Virginia) to Parkersburg on the Ohio River and thence to Cincinnati, and ultimately to St. Louis. The line to Pittsburgh was slow in coming, despite its shorter length, being completed only in 1871.[10] But this was from the beginning an integral part of the B&O. The line to St. Louis came, as most of the longer lines in the Middle West did, from the

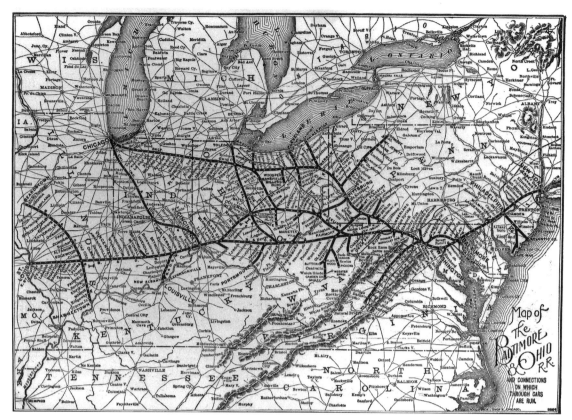

consolidation of earlier companies. From Marietta, close to Parkersburg, an early line had been projected to Cincinnati; it was even heavily financed by the Pennsylvania in its first and largely unsuccessful years. Here in the Appalachian Plateau, as in that range where the Appalachians are called the Green Mountains, no line could be built with ease; so the line to Cincinnati was slow in its construction but finished by the time its western connection, the broad-gauge Ohio and Mississippi Railway, was completed to East St. Louis in 1857. With such an alignment the B&O had its frontier on the Mississippi, and it was only a matter of time until it took over control of its western allies, placing under single ownership what had come to be known as the American Central Route.[11]

The culmination of the B&O's efforts to gain at least a reasonable access to the great interior market came with its drive to Chicago. This was mounted from Chicago Junction, eighty-eight miles north, on the line it had absorbed that ran from Newark (Ohio) to Sandusky. Thence it was only 263 miles to the outskirts of Chicago, where at Baltimore Junction the pioneer railroad gained access to the city over the tracks of the Illinois Central. This arrangement was changed in the 1890s, when the B&O built its own terminus at Grand Central Station, gaining thereby the jocular distinction of being the only railroad to the East Coast that took more than an hour to reach the city limits. The line to Chicago was opened in November 1874, gaining for the original trunk line its own access to the great interior junctions where contact was made with the rather separate system that was to develop to the West. In gaining routes to the western articulation points the B&O, like the Pennsylvania and the New York Central, also secured lines to those with the South, at Cincinnati and Louisville.[12]

The B&O Railroad ultimately was extended to reach the four major articulation points delimiting the Official Territory. *Source: B&O Railroad, Official Guide of the Railways, 1893.*

133

The Drive for Ubiquity

The southern articulation points that emerged were different in nature from those that lay on the western slope of the Appalachians at Montréal, Buffalo, Pittsburgh, and Wheeling-Parkersburg. Chattanooga fulfilled that role with respect to the lines from Savannah and Charleston, but it still lay a long way from the Middle West, to which rail lines were projected to bring southward the food staples necessary to supplement the insufficient local produce. A gap intervened in through routing between the southern limits of the middle-western system—which lay on the Ohio River at Portsmouth, Cincinnati, Jeffersonville (Louisville), Evansville, and Cairo—and the northern termini of the railroads of the South. Of these southern articulation points, Cincinnati and Louisville were far the more dominant, drawing to themselves the Pennsylvania, the New York Central, and the Baltimore and Ohio, as well as several discretely middle-western lines such as the Monon (Chicago, Indianapolis, and Louisville Railway). To create an integrated network it was necessary to project lines southward across Kentucky and Tennessee to junction with the railroads developing in the Deep South.

Beginning to feel strongly the need for a north-south line to fill that gap, the cities and counties of Kentucky and Tennessee took the leading role in organizing and financing such a route, even to the extent that the sitting governor of Kentucky, John L. Helm, served as the president of the resulting Louisville and Nashville Railroad Company from 1854 to 1860. Based mainly on government subscriptions to the company's stock, construction began in 1853 at Louisville, and work progressed sporadically southward. Muldraugh's Hill—a five-hundred-foot limestone cliff marking the edge of the interior low plateau of western Kentucky, where it drops off toward the Ohio Valley—presented the worst engineering obstacle the line was to meet. It was pierced by a 1,986-foot tunnel passing 135 feet below the crest.[13] In knobby karstic terrain the line continued southward toward the deeply incised Green River, where the longest iron bridge in the United States built up to that time was thrown across the stream over a length of eighteen hundred feet. This plateau country interposed still another escarpment, at the Tennessee Ridge on the watershed between the Darren and Cumberland rivers, which was traversed in two tunnels; but construction was merely heavy rather than frightening, so the line was completed to the north bank of the Cumberland opposite Nashville in 1860, when the Muldraugh's Hill Tunnel was opened.[14]

The Louisville and Nashville was a beginning toward bridging the gap between the southern and middle-western systems. When completed to Nashville in 1860, it provided a through route to the Southeast via the Nashville and Chattanooga (constructed to connect those two cities between 1848 and 1854) and the Georgia Railroad (opened to Chattanooga in 1851).[15] A Memphis branch of the L&N was completed in 1861, but many links between the southern ports and the Ohio River had to wait until after the Civil War. The L&N managed to maintain its monopoly on connections through the two river cities until 1872, when the city of Cincinnati, directly on its own account, secured from the Kentucky legislature a charter for the Cincinnati Southern Railroad, the only municipally owned trunk line to be built in the United States. With further legislation in Tennessee this line of 338 miles was undertaken, and before it was completed in 1880 its crossing of the Appalachian Plateau had required 27

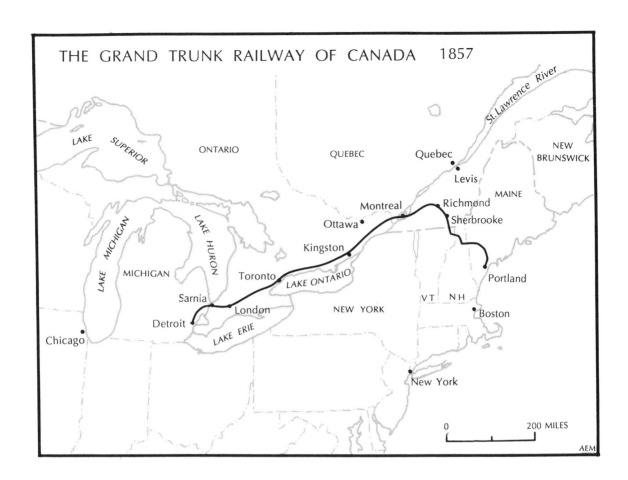

THE GRAND TRUNK RAILWAY OF CANADA 1857

LAKE SUPERIOR

ONTARIO

QUEBEC

St. Lawrence River

Quebec

NEW BRUNSWICK

Levis

MAINE

Montreal

Richmond

Sherbrooke

LAKE HURON

Ottawa

LAKE MICHIGAN

Kingston

MICHIGAN

Toronto

LAKE ONTARIO

Portland

Sarnia

London

NEW YORK

VT NH

Detroit

LAKE ERIE

Boston

Chicago

New York

0   200 MILES

AEM

One of the lesser articulation points delimiting the B&O's Official Territory was on the Ohio River at Louisville. There, a high-level truss bridge carried the connecting railroad well above the height demanded by the steamboats navigating the Ohio River. *Source:* Library of Congress picture.

tunnels and 105 bridges.[16] When subsequently leased to the Southern Railway, the line that had begun grandly with the sobriquet the Queen and Crescent Route had more graphically become the Rathole Division. Still, it provided a direct route from the Queen City to Atlanta and New Orleans, which was why the thrifty burghers of Cincinnati had it built, and why they have continued to hang on to it.

The Pioneering Illinois Central

The other connection between the Ohio River articulation and the Gulf Coast came as part of one of the great undertakings in nineteenth-century American railroading, the construction of a line from northern Illinois to the Gulf. The project began merely as a rail line from the northern to the southern part of the state of Illinois. In 1850, to secure investment in such a frontier venture as a line from Chicago to Cairo—when the former, though the largest town in the state, still had no more than thirty thousand inhabitants—some attraction was needed in addition to the confident hope that the future would be bright. This attraction was furnished by a bill submitted to Congress by Senator Stephen A. Douglas of Illinois calling for a land grant to the state of Illinois, to be passed on to the railroad company, conferring alternate square-mile sections for six miles on either side of the line. The alternate sections left in the public domain were to be doubled in price, from the standard $1.25 an acre, so that the loss to the federal treasury would be nil and the aid to the railroad considerable. In addition, the railroad companies were forever to carry federal goods as well as persons on federal business free of charge. To gain political support for the Illinois-Gulf land grant, it was found expedient to enlist the interests of the states of the Deep South, particularly Alabama and Mississippi. This was done by extending this first of the railroad land grants to cover the route in Kentucky, Tennessee, and Alabama, a line organized separately a year earlier and called the Mobile and Ohio Railroad. When the Douglas bill was passed by Congress and signed by the president in 1850, construction was begun at both ends by two separate companies: the Mobile and Ohio in Alabama, and the Illinois Central in Illinois. The IC was chartered to build what came to be known as the "charter lines," a railroad extending from Chicago southward to Centralia in south-central Illinois, where it was joined by a line from Dunleith (East Dubuque) tapping the northwestern part of the state. At Centralia a single road was carried southward to Cairo at the confluence of the Ohio and Mississippi rivers. As constructed, the Illinois Central was the longest railroad ever undertaken by a private company up to that time, 705 miles, and was completed within a very short period, by 1853. The Mobile and Ohio pushed northward from the Alabama port at a more deliberate pace, reaching Columbus, Kentucky, only in the spring of 1861 just as the Civil War was breaking out. Even then there was a gap of some twenty miles separating Cairo, the southern terminus of the Illinois Central, and Columbus, the northern terminus of the Mobile and Ohio. Until after the war a steamer on the Mississippi provided the only end-to-end connection on this route, and even then it was plagued by a change from standard gauge on the IC to the southern five-foot gauge on the M&O.[17]

While the land-grant route was thus being shaped, more local interests were creating relatively short linkages that ultimately came to form a second

THE NORTH
AMERICAN
RAILROAD

through route from New Orleans northward in competition with the Mobile road. The New Orleans, Jackson, and Great Northern Railroad was completed over the distance of 206 miles from New Orleans to Canton, Mississippi, in 1858.[18] The Mississippi Central carried this alignment farther north to Jackson, Tennessee, where in 1860 junction was made with the Mobile and Ohio, furnishing through service to Columbus, Kentucky, and the steamer connection to Cairo.[19] Thus things stood until 1873, when the now consolidated line from New Orleans to Jackson was continued northward to East Cairo, Kentucky, as the New Orleans, St. Louis, and Chicago Railroad. Large train ferries were introduced across the Ohio between Cairo and East Cairo, which ran until a bridge was finally constructed there in 1889. But the southern line was financially very weak, and by 1877 it was in receivership. This offered the Illinois Central the opportunity to buy in at a bargain price, which it did, and in 1882 it secured control of the line now titled the Central Mississippi Railroad through a four-hundred-year lease. Many years later, in the 1970s, the Gulf, Mobile, and Ohio, the original land-grant line from the Gulf to the Ohio, was added to this Chicago–New Orleans trunk line.

The geographical pattern of rail lines in the Middle West was in the end shaped mainly by connections between important external entrepôts and the two great points of articulation at the western edge of that portion of the American interior that was occupied when railroad lines crossed the Appalachians, just after 1850. Either Chicago or St. Louis tended to become the ultimate objective of lines projected inland from entrepôts as widely separated as Montréal and New Orleans. As locally organized and delimited links between two adjacent cities were completed, virtually without exception there was an effort made to move beyond this first phase of rail construction to a second one of consolidation, out of which came first the regionally important rail companies, such as those in New England or the South. The third phase of rail evolution was concerned with the forging of trans-Appalachian crossings. The fourth phase, the crossing of the Middle West and the low plateaus of western Tennessee and Kentucky, was a drive toward articulation points aligned on either the Ohio or the Mississippi. From the Frontenac axis of the Canadian Shield—where that axis crosses the St. Lawrence River near the Québec-Ontario boundary—to western Tennessee, rail lines were pushed outward into the great open plains of the interior of North America. This push was not so much one of construction as one of consolidation. Earlier the Middle West—like parts of peninsular Ontario—had experienced its own first, second, and third phases of development. In essence we may approach the analysis of middle-western railroads in two ways: the actual trackage was first located mainly in response to local or subregional views, as in the East and South, but the ultimate alignments of railroads came out of the desire to continue consolidation until the eleven entrepôts stretching between Montréal and New Orleans were tied to at least one of the points of articulation with the yet-to-emerge western American rail system.

The Drive for
Ubiquity

This allegorical representation of passengers being carried by the Illinois Central Railroad on its trunk line from Chicago to New Orleans was intended to suggest the role the company meant to play in the settling of the American interior on the first of the railroad land grants, which was conferred in 1850.
Source: Library of Congress picture.

Chicago: The Great Junction City

Chicago, the archetype of the railroad city, presents for us the story of the rise of a great railroad junction. Its rise to that role was rapid indeed; the city was not even established until two years after the world's first railroad hub, Boston, had gained that distinction. Yet within twenty years of its founding there was no serious doubt that Chicago would assume the role of the Great Junction in the American system of railroads. Because those railroads were the most extensive anywhere—in 1850 four out of every ten miles of rail on earth were in the United States—the nexus of that American system would obviously become a transportation hub unlike any other in scale. London, Paris, Berlin, Vienna, and Milan all developed important networks of lines, but none could compare with Chicago when the national rail systems were completed, as they were in most advanced countries by the 1930s or even earlier. While the American system ultimately reached over a quarter of a million miles, that in Britain extended to just over twenty thousand miles, that in France to a bit over twenty-six thousand, and that in Germany to about thirty-eight thousand.[20] In 1850 Chicago was still at the geographical margin of the American system, so to explain its ultimate dominance of that network, we must examine why it became the essential point of articulation for a continental pattern of railroads. In the end almost no railroad bypassed Chicago, whether traveling from east to west or from north to south.

The consolidation of regional into subcontinental lines, the third phase in American railroad structuring, stopped when Chicago was reached.

The most likely explanation of that breaking of corporate extension is to be found first at the level of the conception of transportation geography possible in the period 1850–80, the time when most railroad companies reached Chicago. We are told that when Cornelius Vanderbilt gained control of the initial New York Central extending from Albany to Buffalo, he thought his rail system completed, but his son William H. could see that only by controlling its western connections could the trunk line be safe from diversion of trade to a different trans-Appalachian route. The Central therefore gained control of the Lakeshore, Michigan Southern, and Michigan Central railroads to reach to Chicago, and the Big Four to reach to St. Louis. At the outbreak of the Civil War these were the main trading centers at the edge of the undeveloped interior, so they became the objective of most railroad construction in the Middle West. Illinois in the late 1850s witnessed some construction of lines from the hub at Chicago westward toward the river ports that had developed on the Mississippi, whence lumber and some mineral and agricultural products could be collected into that burgeoning city. Further lumber came by lake boat to be distributed by rail outward from a lumber district on the South Branch of the Chicago River to the treeless prairies where the farming frontier was then being advanced. "Soon the area along the river became the largest center for lumber distribution in the world. . . . The city's leadership in the grain trade was no less commanding. With this commodity as with lumber, Chicago owed its supremacy to both its location and its ingenuity."[21] Operating in the most modern and efficient manner—it was here that some of the earliest grain elevators were built— Chicago gained a domination of the trade that was reflected in the paramount role the Chicago Board of Trade came to play in the creation of auction markets for all sorts of agricultural products, most notably wheat. Slaughtering and meat packing also gained a large component of Chicago's attention; given the proximity of the eastern railroads and the emerging use of refrigerator cars, Chicago could hope to tap the eastern market, even ultimately the European, for processed carcasses rather than livestock. (The first refrigerator car had been used on the Michigan Central in 1857 for the carriage of fresh meat eastward, though the Rutland had pioneered the use of iced cars in 1851 in the transport of butter from Ogdensburg to Boston.)

The conception of how far inland the interests of the trans-Appalachian lines required outright ownership of trackage was undoubtedly influenced in considerable measure by this rise of Chicago as a collecting and fabricating point for lumber, grain, animals, and other raw materials beginning to flow from the more westerly parts of the settled interior. The distinction between the collection of wheat, hogs, and cattle and their dispatch to distant markets was enhanced in some cases by the need to process the product, and in almost all cases by the requirement of trade that an auction market be held to set the price. Obviously, that market need not gain physical possession of the product, but in a period when telegraphs were only starting to become available, such possession would very likely give greater confidence to the traders involved. Chicago served well as an ultimate objective for the eastern railroads, and as the city came to be the Great Trader, as well as the Great Junction, it could continue to dominate the

139

The Drive for
Ubiquity

articulation with the eastern systems even well after railroads were extended far to the west of that point.

Chicago's Terminal Problem

As the Great Junction, Chicago faced a terminal problem shared with other hubs of extensive rail networks. Boston had been relatively lucky, initially having only some four or five stations and soon seeing those reduced to two. New York, because of its island nature and the lateness of the arrival of some of its lines—1910 in the case of the Pennsylvania—also managed with two great terminals. But Chicago was not so fortunate. The first railroad to reach the city was actually built from the west as the Galena and Chicago Union Railroad, which established a depot at Canal and Kinzie streets, just west of the confluence of the two branches of the Chicago River, in 1848. In 1852 this line was carried by bridge across the North Branch to a new station on Wells Street—essentially where the Merchandise Mart now stands—which served until the present Chicago North Western Station was opened four blocks to the south and back on the west bank of the South Branch in 1911.[22] Soon the Galena Road became the nucleus for the Chicago and North Western, so we may best use that name, which still barely survives among Chicago railroads.

When the Illinois Central Railroad was chartered in 1850 and began to lay out its line, it sought to enter its northeastern terminal city at a depot adjacent to that of the Chicago and North Western, but the city council opposed clustering the terminals, instead requiring the IC to find its depot site east of the central business district at Randolph Street and Michigan Avenue. This course was taken because it forced the railroad company to carry its line to the mouth of the Chicago River along the then lakeshore of the business district, thus providing an embankment that would guard the downtown from the beating of waves during storms on Lake Michigan. When the Michigan Central reached the vicinity in 1852 and gained access to Chicago via the Illinois Central tracks, it refused to participate in this scheme, which the Bostonians saw as an outright holdup by the city to make a corporation provide what the municipality should have supplied. The first IC station stood between Randolph Street and the Chicago River east of Michigan Avenue, but in 1892 the terminal for long-distance trains was shifted southward to East Eleventh Place and Michigan Avenue, leaving the northern part of the line, and the Randolph Street terminal, for suburban service conducted by electric trains after 1926.[23]

These two pioneering lines became the avenues along which other railroads reached the heart of the city in the 1850s and 1860s. The Chicago, Burlington, and Quincy, which began as the Aurora Branch Railroad, reached Chicago via the North Western tracks starting in 1852. But the Burlington seems to have been ever restive, shifting in 1856 to the Randolph Street depot of the IC and again, in 1880, to the newly constructed Union Station of the Pennsylvania, of which more in a moment.[24]

The next station to be built in Chicago came with the rapid construction of the Chicago and Rock Island Railroad, opened to Joliet in 1852 and Rock Island in 1854. There the line was projected westward over the first railroad bridge across the Mississippi, completed in 1855, becoming the pioneer granger road.[25] The Rock Island sought two things in Chicago: to get as close to the central

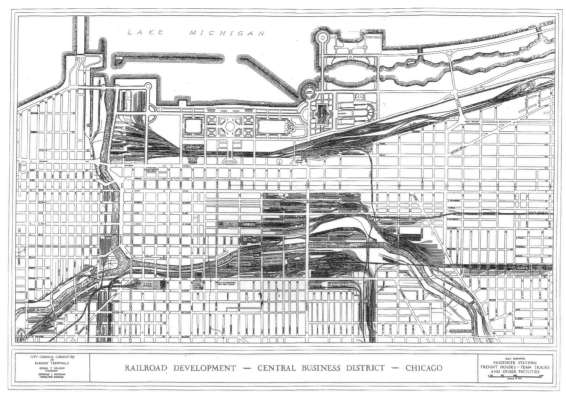

RAILROAD DEVELOPMENT — CENTRAL BUSINESS DISTRICT — CHICAGO

The belt of railroad yards and terminal sites came by the time of the First World War to form a virtual wall around The Loop in Chicago. *Source:* Chicago City Council, *The Railway Passenger Terminal Problem in Chicago* (1933).

business district as possible, and to have its own line thence. At first it was authorized to build directly to the south bank of the Chicago River, but fortunately that plan was stillborn, and a site somewhat to the south, at Van Buren and La Salle streets, was occupied and service reached there in 1854. That same year the other eastern line, the Lakeshore and Northern Indiana—later the Lakeshore and Michigan Southern, and later still the New York Central—found its Chicago depot in the Rock Island's Van Buren Station.[26] Several rebuildings on this site took place, the last in 1903, when the well-remembered La Salle Street Station was opened (a facility that stood until demolished in the early 1980s).

Two other stations came to stand nearby the Rock Island depot on the southern fringes of downtown Chicago. The first was located on Polk Street, opened in 1885 as the Chicago terminal of the Chicago and Western Indiana Railroad, a line constructed mainly to afford to several railroads terminal and freight facilities in the city. That same year the Chicago and Eastern Illinois Railroad, the Grand Trunk Western Railway, the original New Albany and Salem Railroad, the Louisville, New Albany, and Chicago Railway (Monon), the Wabash Railroad, and the Erie started their Chicago service out of Dearborn Station (Polk Street). The Cleveland, Cincinnati, Chicago, and St. Louis Railway (Big Four) joined the others in Dearborn Station in 1886, and the Atchison, Topeka, and Santa Fe Railway began using that depot in 1888, when it completed its line from Kansas City to Chicago. This same practice of using existing stations was adopted by the regional lines that developed internal to the Middle West. The Wabash, the New York, Chicago, and St. Louis Railroad (Nickel Plate), and the Pere Marquette Railway all came into existence fairly late in the second phase of regional consolidation, and they failed to break out of the regional frame of the

141

The Drive for Ubiquity

Middle West. They did, however, all gain access to Chicago. The Nickel Plate was a consolidation hatched first in New York's financial district in 1880 and rather quickly brought to fruition as a railroad extending from Buffalo to St. Louis and Chicago, which it reached at the Randolph Street Station of the Illinois Central in 1882. After ten years the terminus was shifted to La Salle Street, where it remained until passenger service was given up after the Second World War.[27] The Wabash reached the Great Junction in 1885 at Dearborn Station, and the Pere Marquette at the Baltimore and Ohio's terminal in 1903. In 1910 the Chesapeake and Ohio came to Chicago, at the Illinois Central's station, but it gave up service to the city long before the others, in July 1933.[28]

The central business district of Chicago became further isolated on the south when the Baltimore and Ohio, which had entered the city in 1874 using first the Illinois Central's Randolph Street Station, then its own depot on the lakefront at Monroe Street, set about building its impressive terminal, opened in 1890, south of the Loop on the east bank of the Chicago River. To reach that site a very circuitous access line was shaped from bits and pieces in the southern parts of the city, which in the end allowed the B&O to move off IC tracks. Ultimately the B&O was joined at this terminal—perhaps the most elegant of the Chicago stations, and certainly the one most to be regretted in its demolition—by several others: the Pere Marquette, reaching around the southern end of Lake Michigan to serve the Lower Peninsula of Michigan and along its own line across the Ontario peninsula to Buffalo; the Chicago Great Western Railroad, a significant carrier operating a great cross of lines, meeting at Oelwein, Iowa, which interconnected Chicago, Minneapolis, Omaha, and Kansas City; and the Wisconsin Central Railroad, earlier leased by the Northern Pacific Railroad and ultimately consolidated with the Minneapolis, St. Paul, and Sault Ste. Marie Railway (the Soo Line owned by the Canadian Pacific Railway), which extended from Chicago to a junction at Abbotsford, Wisconsin, whence one line departed for Duluth (and ultimate juncture with the Soo Line and the CPR) and another for Minneapolis. The B&O's Grand Central Station (Chicago) survived up to the formation of the government-operated national passenger service Amtrak in 1971, but by then all its former occupants, save the B&O, had given up passenger service. In the mid-1970s the comfortable, almost Craftsman-style Grand Central was wrecked, mainly to save on taxes.[29]

The final station to be built in the Great Junction was that for the Pennsylvania Railroad interests when they reached that far west, starting with the arrival of the Pittsburgh, Fort Wayne, and Chicago in 1857 and growing with the arrival of the Pittsburgh, Cincinnati, Chicago, and St. Louis in 1861. The Fort Wayne road acquired land on the west bank of the South Branch of the Chicago River, extending between Van Buren and Monroe streets, and built its depot facilities there. In 1872 a charter was secured by the Chicago and Milwaukee Railroad to build between those adjacent cities, in a late return of the first phase of railroad organization. By 1880 the Milwaukee road had completed its line and had gained control of the Chicago and Pacific Railroad then building westward from Chicago toward its distant, and belatedly reached, Pacific goal; the Milwaukee therefore needed a Chicago terminal, which it found in the Pennsylvania's depot. That dominating company concluded around 1880 that its prestige required a better facility in the world's greatest railroad town, so it began organizing a

"Union Station." In the late 1860s the Chicago and Alton Railroad, the first Chicago–St. Louis line, had taken up residence in the Fort Wayne road's depot, so with the arrival of the Milwaukee in 1880 the need for a larger facility was clear. In seeking to make it a union facility the Pennsylvania's promoters did persuade the Chicago, Burlington, and Quincy, with its lines radiating into the city's suburbs and to Kansas City, Denver, and Billings (Montana), to become a tenant in such a consolidated facility. The first Union Station was opened shortly after 1880 and soon became overcrowded. Plans for a more commodious terminal were advanced in 1913, the Pennsylvania having completed work on its even greater station in New York only three years before. Between 1913 and 1925 massive construction was carried out in a five-block stretch along the South Branch, leading to the completion of Chicago's only through station, though most of its tracks are actually stubs.

Still, in 1925 there was at last a station in Chicago that was the peer of the great terminals rising at South Station in Boston, at Pennsylvania and Grand Central stations in New York, somewhat later at Thirtieth Street in Philadelphia, at Union Station in Washington, and in Buffalo, Cleveland, Cincinnati, and Kansas City. Chicago's archrival had stolen a considerable march when St. Louis Union Station was opened in 1894, earning a title never exceeded as the world's largest station with some thirty-two tracks under a single train shed, the most extensive ever built.[30] Union Station Chicago came into its own in 1971, when Amtrak was organized, as it was still modern enough and by then plenty large enough to serve all the trains that still reached from a distance to the Great Junction.

The Fixing of Articulation Points

As the American rail net expanded to compass the West, Chicago took on a role that no city before it had assumed. Companies that had restlessly sought to project short intercity links into regional systems, and those in turn into subcontinental lines reaching well across the settled interior to the last cities before the settlement frontier—St. Louis, Chicago, Memphis, and New Orleans—seemed to find first in Chicago, and later in the other three, a natural frontier of their own. Money from the Pennsylvania, the New York Central, and the Baltimore and Ohio did find its way in the support of the western railroads, but there was no sustained effort to push the corporate frontier farther west. Instead, the investment in western lines seems to have come mainly in the interests of exercising a certain leverage on the management of those trans-Mississippi lines to assure that they would interchange traffic with a specific eastern line in an "orderly and established" way.

Only the Bostonians seem to have stood outside this general practice; they had to figure more as investors than as operators in the eastern lines because of the barrier of New York State, so the Hub's base was from the earlier years one of financial control. But financial control creates financial interest, so it was the investors in the Michigan Central who turned, once that railroad reached Chicago in 1852, to assuring its western connections. Boston money flowed into the Chicago, Burlington, and Quincy, and then into the post–Civil War lines—the Union Pacific and the Santa Fe—that gave further control of traffic, as originators thereof, that would pay to those investors dividends on the Burlington or

143

The Drive for
Ubiquity

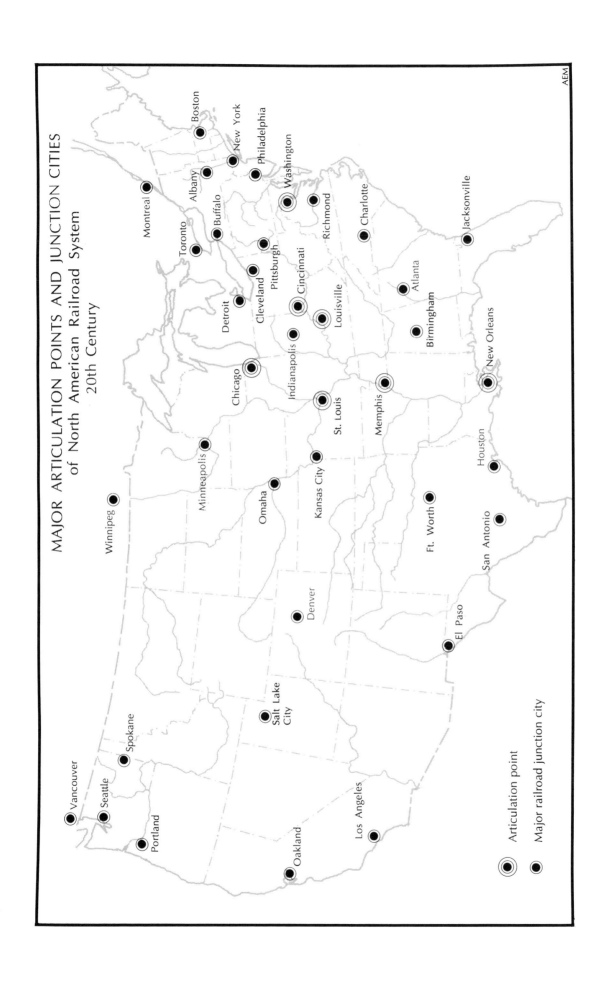

MAJOR ARTICULATION POINTS AND JUNCTION CITIES
of North American Railroad System
20th Century

Boston
New York
Philadelphia
Albany
Washington
Buffalo
Richmond
Charlotte
Jacksonville
Montreal
Toronto
Cincinnati
Cleveland
Pittsburgh
Detroit
Louisville
Atlanta
Birmingham
New Orleans
Chicago
Indianapolis
St. Louis
Memphis
Houston
Minneapolis
Omaha
Kansas City
Ft. Worth
San Antonio
Winnipeg
El Paso
Denver
Salt Lake
City
Vancouver
Spokane
Seattle
Portland
Los Angeles
Oakland

Articulation point

Major railroad junction city

AEM

Michigan Central stock they might hold. Yet even among the Bostonians there was no attempt to amalgamate the eastern and western lines, so with the passage of time the Michigan Central fell into Vanderbilt hands, and the Burlington shares passed from the heirs of the original investors to the corporate coffers of the Northern Lines—the Northern Pacific and the Great Northern Railway. Investment interest proved more ephemeral than operational control; but the eastern railroad frontier extending from Chicago to New Orleans remains even today the most definitive feature of the railroad geography of the United States, even with the mergers of the Norfolk and Western and the Southern; of the Chessie System and the Family Lines; of the Union Pacific and the Missouri Pacific and Western Pacific; and of the Southern Pacific and the St. Louis and San Francisco.

The railroad geography of the Middle West ultimately came down to the shaping of lines to extend from the coastal entrepôts to the four articulation points on or near the Mississippi. Just as there were some systems that never made it westward across the Appalachians (the Boston and Maine, the New Haven, the Delaware and Hudson, the Reading, the Georgia Railroad), there were some incipient middle-western consolidations that never made it eastward across the Appalachians (the Wabash, the Nickel Plate, the Monon, the Pere Marquette) until very late in the day, after the 1930s. Yet all the middle-western lines did eventually become part of the expanding eastern giants. Only New England and Georgia seem to have been excluded from such efforts at consolidation; they have become the last habitat of the regional system. Today all the railroads that made Chicago their Great Junction have disappeared as regional carriers and stand as the arms of distant lines seeking to pass on their traffic there. The Middle West is not a back eddy in American transportation; it seems to have a pace that destroys any eccentric patterns and quickly forces them into flows that are the ultimate ones for American railroads. Here the current phase of American rail development, the spanning of a few very comprehensive subcontinental systems, has clearly shown itself.

The Evolution of the Regional Network beyond Chicago

It is doubtful that the promoters of the trans-Appalachian lines looked upon Chicago and St. Louis as points of articulation in a national system of railroads. Instead, they probably viewed those cities as the ultimate in regional hubs, places from which lines would radiate over only moderate distances to collect the agricultural, mineral, and forest products of their tributary regions for shipment to consumers in the East and in Europe. Earlier American geographical thought held the view that west of the Missouri River lay a Great American Desert, devoid of economic interest, a great ellipsis in the oecumene of the nation, as Walter Prescott Webb phrased it in his many writings on the American frontier. It was thought unlikely that any appreciable use could be made of that stony Arabia for centuries to come, so westward of Chicago and St. Louis the anticipation of rapid development had to be restricted to the band of territory extending only as far west as the Missouri in its north-south course. Within that band regional rather than subcontinental rail systems were envisioned. The Boston interests, for example, promoted the Aurora Branch Railroad—a pair of lines extending from the immediate environs of Chicago to the Mississippi, at Burlington (Iowa) and

Quincy (Illinois), with an extension from the latter place, via a connection with the Hannibal and St. Joseph Railroad (which the Bostonians also invested in heavily) to St. Joseph on the Missouri River. But at St. Joe, reached in 1859, these capitalist venturers confronted Webb's ellipsis. Westward from there it was thought likely that pioneering types of transport would have to serve for decades to come; the Oregon Trail and Pony Express did until a telegraph line was opened to the West, and the staging and hauling companies did for another decade. The rapidity with which rail extension came surprised many, but before we take up that matter we should conclude our consideration of the regional systems projected onward from Chicago and St. Louis.

Prior to looking at those companies whose initial objectives were so clearly regional rather than subcontinental, it is worth emphasizing that their growth came almost entirely westward from the points of articulation, though often north or south of west (but almost never east of Chicago or St. Louis). Before the Civil War the Illinois Central had been carried westward to Waterloo in eastern Iowa. Using trackage rights on the Galena and Chicago Union Railroad, this northwestern branch of the IC gained a fairly direct access to Chicago, pushing that city's tributary region to the edge of active settlement in northeastern Iowa. The Galena road itself reached to Fulton (Illinois), across from Clinton (Iowa), and before the Civil War this spoke in Chicago's rail net was pushed westward to Cedar Rapids from Clinton.

As we have already seen, the Chicago and Rock Island Railroad reached its western terminal in 1856, bridging the great river to Davenport, Iowa, a year later. From that river port the Mississippi and Missouri Railroad was pushed westward into the settled eastern tiers of Iowa, and by the outbreak of the Civil War it had penetrated to Marengo. Also by that time, the Chicago, Burlington, and Quincy Railroad (via a subsidiary) had not only gained St. Joseph, but, from its Burlington terminus, had started a line westward, the Burlington and Missouri River Railroad, that reached to Ottumwa.

Northwestward from Chicago, the Chicago and Milwaukee Railroad had joined those cities and made juncture with the Milwaukee and Minnesota (which carried the rails to the Mississippi at La Crosse) and with the Milwaukee and Prairie du Chien (which reached the river at its western terminus). Also from the Great Junction, the Chicago and North Western Railroad reached into northern Illinois, southern Wisconsin, and junctions with the M&P at Milton and the M&M west of Horicon, finding its prewar terminus at Appleton, Wisconsin.

This summary of the regional system centered on Chicago may be concluded by mentioning the St. Louis, Alton, and Chicago, which tied the two points of western articulation together. Before the war there was no bridge at St. Louis; the Eads Bridge, which stands as one of the most fascinating and significant of the nineteenth century's engineering works, was not opened until July 1874.[31] Thus, the Alton was really a Chicago line reaching to the gates of its rival. The gauge of the Alton—and of all the railroads of Illinois, save for the Erie-gauge Ohio and Mississippi, which tied Cincinnati to East St. Louis, Illinois—was the standard 4 feet 8½ inches. But St. Louis, isolated from all other lines on the right bank of the Mississippi, had strangely adopted the Maine-Canadian gauge (5 feet 6 inches) for the rather limited system radiating from its hub. The

Pacific Railroad of Missouri (which before the war reached to Sedalia, two-thirds
of the way to Kansas City, and to Rolla on the route to Springfield) had adopted
that same gauge, and the St. Louis and Iron Mountain (extending to Pilot Knob
in the iron-mining area) had followed suit. The North Missouri, running northwestward from St. Louis to Macon on the Hannibal and St. Joseph, followed this
Missouri gauge, but the Hannibal road showed its Chicago (and Boston) ties
through its use of the standard gauge. There was, then, at the outbreak of the
Civil War a sharp rivalry between Chicago and St. Louis, expressed in these rival
rail developments even within the state of Missouri. As Wyatt Belcher has
shown, the "superior transportation facilities of Chicago afford the chief explanation of trade statistics . . . showing that city's predominance over St. Louis in
the leading articles of commerce." And that dominance, already obvious at the
close of the Civil War, was made permanent in 1869 when the Pacific railroad was
opened to Chicago through the use of the several standard-gauge regional systems that by then tied the Great Junction to the Missouri River frontier.[32]

Although we are somewhat anticipating the completion of the Pacific
railroad, it is convenient here to cover the next phase in the evolution of Chicago's regional rail network, the extension of the Iowa lines to the Missouri River
frontier. Four companies are fundamentally involved: the Chicago and North
Western, the Rock Island, the Burlington, and the Illinois Central. The North
Western bridged the Mississippi in 1865 and went on rather quickly to cross Iowa
to Council Bluffs in 1867, becoming the first through line from Chicago to the
established eastern terminus of the Pacific railroad. Viewing that success, the
Rock Island—now called the Chicago, Rock Island, and Pacific—quickly extended its line from Marengo through Des Moines to reach Council Bluffs in
1869, in time for the opening of the Pacific railroad. The Burlington, which had
bridged the Mississippi at its namesake town in 1868, was at the same time
continued westward from Ottumwa, reaching Council Bluffs in 1870.[33]

The Drive for
Ubiquity

In 1855 interests in Dubuque, Iowa, had begun to promote a line westward across that state. In 1867 the Dubuque and Sioux City, which grew out of that effort, stalled at Iowa Falls only halfway across the state. But in that year a long lease by the Illinois Central was arranged, and construction of the 184-mile line thence to Sioux City was begun. This line had been proposed before construction of the Pacific railroad began, and its course was much advanced when the initial proposal for the transcontinental line, which foresaw a set of five eastern terminals ranged along the middle Missouri River from Sioux City to St. Joseph, was abandoned in 1864. For twenty-five years the Illinois Central sought to make the best of the situation, but by the mid-1900s it was clear that the IC, as the only one of the four trans-Iowa railroads not at first reaching Council Bluffs, was not profiting like the others. In a great rush in 208 days during 1899 the IC carried out the construction of a 131-mile line between Fort Dodge on its Dubuque–Sioux City main line and Council Bluffs. So successful did this "branch" prove that it usurped the main-line function from the older route so that the effective western terminus of the premier Illinois regional carrier became the eastern end of the first transcontinental road.[34]

The Ultimate Connection: The Pacific Railroad Survey of 1854

Almost as soon as the United States entered the second phase of rail construction, when regional systems began to emerge from the amalgamation of the short links between adjacent cities, there were individuals who envisioned a transcontinental railroad. In 1832 an anonymous writer in the *Emigrant,* a paper published in Ann Arbor, Michigan, proposed that a steam railroad be built from New York City to the Oregon Country by way of the Great Lakes and the Platte Valley. Certainly his prescience was considerable, for at that time there were few stretches of rail line open in the United States, and even fewer Americans had any experience with the joint occupation that was Oregon. Others followed in succeeding years—Hartwell Carver petitioned Congress to construct a line to San Francisco—but none did much more than vaguely propose such a line.[35] It fell to Asa Whitney, a successful New York merchant, to assume the role with respect to the transcontinental railroad that many nineteenth-century protagonists had to play: that of never letting those in power forget their proposals. Whitney's plans, as well as those of practically all transcontinental enthusiasts of the 1840s and 1850s, were based fundamentally on government action. His first proposition was that he be given a sixty-mile strip of land from Lake Michigan to the West Coast, which he would sell as necessary to pay the cost of construction. Any remaining proceeds would constitute his profit. The land involved in this plan would have been somewhat more than is included in the present state of Illinois. Thus, even before the Illinois Central grant was made in 1850, this 1844 proposal by Whitney envisaged using land as a way of raising the capital necessary for the road's construction. Later he was ready to pay 16 cents an acre for the land granted to him, which the House Committee on Roads and Canals reduced to 10 cents an acre, a price they thought more fair. But Congress did not act, perhaps more from sectional jealousies than from timidity about a western railroad.

The route Whitney proposed was similar to that of the correspondent to the *Emigrant*—indeed, there was little choice before 1848, when the close of the

Mexican War brought most of the Southwest into the United States. California was Mexican, so any transcontinental line would have to pass through the Louisiana Purchase to western Wyoming or Montana and then into the joint occupation that was the Oregon Country—in which no one could forbid such a line, even if the United States could hardly assert full sovereignty over the land until the signing of the Oregon Boundary Treaty in 1846. But before any serious undertaking for a transcontinental railroad could come of Whitney's proposals, the treaty of Guadalupe Hidalgo (February 2, 1848) had been signed, bringing most of the Southwest into consideration for railroad location. To make that consideration complete, it was found necessary in 1853 to purchase from Mexico the area south of the Gila River of Arizona and adjacent sections of New Mexico that would ease the construction of a railroad along the 32d parallel. That Gadsden Purchase was the only element of the American political geography determined by the needs of transportation, and it was to play a rather disruptive role in the securing of a solution to the Pacific railroad problem.

Asa Whitney had taken up the question of the transcontinental railroad in response to the signing, in 1844, of the treaty negotiated by Caleb Cushing between China and the United States.[36] This encouraged American commercial interest in the Orient, leading to the signing of a similar treaty with Japan in 1854. As. Mr. Dooley had it, "We didn't go in; they kim out," and for that reason the eastern American merchant group was anxious by 1854 to have a route to the Pacific, regardless of the Great American Desert and the extent of American settlement in the West.

The Mexican War and the Gadsden Purchase greatly complicated the matter, because from the earliest proposals it had been expected that the federal government would heavily subsidize the construction of such a transcontinental line. But involving the government forced the issue upon a Congress nearly paralyzed by sectional conflict. While a line to Oregon was the only possible one, though hardly a practical one, its proponents could agree only on the need for such a line, disregarding hard questions as to its location. The accession of the Southwest improved the practicality of such a line but made its location most trying. In that situation Congress took a course that seemed logical, both politically and in the intellectual context of the nineteenth century: it decided to refer the matter to scientific opinion, to be garnered from an extensive Pacific Railroad Survey carried out by the Corps of Topographical Engineers of the United States Army, then a very active agency engaged in mapping the vast unknown reaches of the American West.

As established in 1854, the Pacific Railroad Survey was to consider the relative merits of various routes from the Mississippi River to the West Coast. These might seem to be myriad, but in fact this was as much a political as a geographical question, so the routes considered were those with strong congressional interest more than anything else. Asa Whitney's "northern route," first located by the needs of American political geography in the 1840s, had its staunch supporters calling for a line from Duluth or Chicago via the northernmost tier of American territory—that is, between the 47th and 49th parallels—to Puget Sound. Senator Stephen Douglas, speaking for Illinois, and Chicago above all, called for a route westward from Chicago to Davenport, Council Bluffs, and South Pass to some rather indeterminate point in the Oregon Coun-

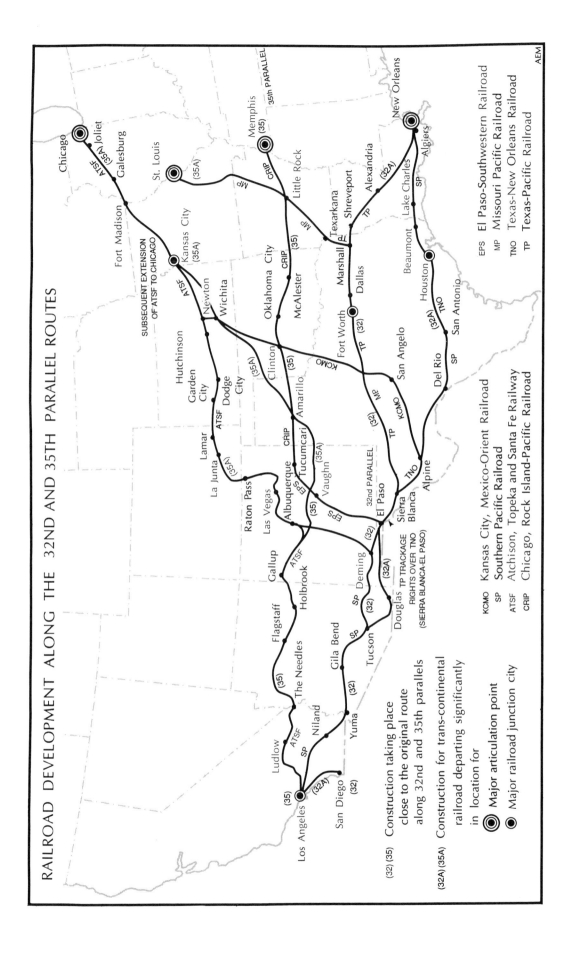

RAILROAD DEVELOPMENT ALONG THE 32ND AND 35TH PARALLEL ROUTES

try. This was a route along the 41st parallel. Missouri interests were stridently advanced by Senator Thomas Hart Benton, who just knew that there was a usable route westward from Missouri to the Rockies and then through those mountains via a mythical Cochetopa Pass near the 39th parallel. Westward from there, it was assumed, a line could be found across the Great Basin and the Sierra Nevada to afford access to California. These were the lines favored by northern groups, though no one of them could be adopted as a compromise even among those in the North. "The Southern interests generally favored three alternatives: (1) a road west from Memphis along the 35th parallel; (2) [a route proposed by Senator William McKendree Gwin of California for a] main trunk along the 35th parallel to Fulton on the Red River, with branches to Kansas City, Council Bluffs, the Gulf of Mexico, and Puget Sound; and (3) a route sponsored by Senator [Thomas Jefferson] Rusk of Texas to run from Vicksburg across Texas and along the 32nd parallel Gila River route." This last route was very much favored by a company recently organized in New York and called inclusively the Atlantic and Pacific Railroad.[37]

As planned, the Pacific Railroad Survey was to consider four latitudinal routes: along the 47th-49th parallel, the 41st parallel, the 35th parallel, and the 32d parallel. In addition, special consideration was to be given to the location of a longitudinal route along the West Coast from San Diego northward to Puget Sound. Ultimate responsibility for the conduct of the survey rested with the then secretary of war, Jefferson Davis, so there was even in the beginning a sense of sectional bias. This was to show up in the assignments of leaders and parties to the various route surveys. The two lines in the north, along the 47th and 49th parallels, were assigned to a single party, and it was led not by a member of the Corps of Topographical Engineers but by the newly appointed governor of the Washington Territory, Isaac Stevens. For the 41st-parallel route it was decided to do without an organized survey, and to use instead the report of Captain Howard Stansbury published the year before, recounting an expedition sent to find not a rail route but a wagon road that might be used by the army in case of a conflict with the Mormons, which at that time seemed quite probable.[38] But as Stansbury's account dealt only incidentally with a possible rail route, the decision to use his report seems a negative prejudging of the results. Stansbury did advance certain views as to the logical alignment of a wagon road, or railroad, to be built from the Missouri frontier adjacent to Westport Landing (Kansas City) to the Great Salt Lake. These are worth some attention in light of subsequent events.

Accepting that the approach to the Rocky Mountains from the east would be likely to follow the Platte Valley, as did the Oregon and Mormon trails, the captain of the Topographical Engineers considered particularly the crossing of the Rockies in that latitude:

It has been ascertained that a practicable route exists through the chain of the Rocky Mountains, at a point sixty miles south of that now generally pursued, and in a course as much more direct as the chord of an arc than is the arc itself. [This line used a left-bank tributary of the South Platte, Lodgepole Creek, to approach directly the Laramie Range of the Rockies rather than passing in the noted arc around their northern end along the North Platte branch.] A glance at the map, and a little attention to the table of latitudes, will show that from the Great Salt Lake to the head of Lodge-pole Creek, a distance of four hundred and eighty-four miles, the difference of latitude is but 35′ 42″; and that while the greatest northing made by the proposed line is but little more than 20′ north of Lodge-pole Creek, the greatest deviation to the south is but little more than three miles; so that the entire route through that whole distance *varies but a trifle from a straight line.* When extended to the junction of Lodge-pole with the South Fork of the Platte, it will appear to be the chord of an arc formed by the present course of emigration [the Oregon Trail]. The distance from Fort Bridger to Fort Laramie, by the present route, is four hundred and eight miles; while the new route from Fort Bridger to the eastern base of the Black Hills [Laramie Range], a point equidistant with [Fort] Laramie from the forks of the Platte, it is but three hundred and forty-seven miles: so that a saving is effected, in the total distance, of just *sixty-one miles* [and] . . . there can be no doubt that even this large saving in distance may be still further increased, by shortening the route wherever [by more careful surveys] it shall be found practicable. The examination of the country proved it to be more favorable than we had at first supposed; for even after so successfully crossing the summit dividing the Pacific from the Atlantic waters, serious fears were still entertained lest some formidable, if not insurmountable obstruction, should be encountered in the character of the Black Hills, intervening as it does between the Laramie Plains on the west and the great slope to the Atlantic which commences at their eastern base. All apprehensions on this head were, however, set entirely at rest by the reconnaissance, which fully demonstrated the existence of a route through these hills, not only practicable, but free from any obstructions involving in their removal great or unusual expenditure.[39]

Thus, using either the Lodgepole or the Crow Creek tributaries of the South Platte, the generally east-west alignment of the Platte and the lower course of its South Platte branch was continued in Crow Creek to the crest of the Laramie Range (Stansbury's Black Hills). This approach was thought basically usable for either a wagon road or a railroad. From the crest down into the Laramie Basin, across that broad elevated plain to its northwestern edge near Elk Mountain, and then down to a crossing of the North Platte—there flowing from south to north on the western side of the eastern and central ranges of the Rockies—Stansbury believed a railroad route was possible. West of the North Platte crossing, a practicable climb carried the alignment to a new pass, Bridger's, found in the eastern rim of the Wyoming Basin where the western range of the Rockies, the Sierra Madre (Stansbury's Park Range), stood as only a range of low hills.

The broken country of the Wyoming Basin seemed practical of transit following the course of Bitter Creek, which joined the Green River at what became the town of Green River, Wyoming. From the Green westward via Fort Bridger, Stansbury's route passed up right-bank tributaries of the Green and across a low divide to the upper Bear River, as it flowed northward from the Uinta Mountains to turn the northern end of the Wasatch Range. To gain a more direct routing, the Topographical Engineers proposed climbing over the low divide between the Bear and the upper parts of Weber Canyon, thus dropping directly westward to the Great Salt Lake. There was some question about this drop down to the lake level, Stansbury proposing turning southward out of the Weber Canyon to pass via Camass Prairie to gain a canyon opening out onto Utah Lake in the southern part of the Wasatch Oasis. West thereof Stansbury had no actual knowledge, but he reported the general local belief that a wagon or rail route was possible via the Humboldt River across northern Nevada to some probable pass across the northern Sierra Nevada.

This was the state of knowledge concerning the 41st-parallel route when

Secretary Davis organized the Pacific Railroad Survey, and he seems to have been willing to make his recommendation on such extremely sparse information. That recommendation would be based on detailed examinations of the 47th- and 49th-parallel routes carried out by Governor Stevens, and of the three more or less southern routes that were explored in 1853. At the insistence of Senator Benton an alignment westward from St. Louis and Independence to the Colorado Rockies, and presumably across that great wall of mountains, was to be tested for a way west. The 35th-parallel route—starting at Memphis, passing through the Arkansas Valley to reach the Great Plains near Fort Smith, and progressing westward to the eastern face of the Rockies and thence across the plateau country to the Colorado River on the California boundary—was to be examined. Finally, a possible route across the southern tier of national territory—starting at Shreveport on the Red River of Louisiana and moving westward across the plains of Texas to enter the new Gadsden Purchase at El Paso, then using that new domain to reach the lower course of the Gila River and its confluence with the Colorado at Yuma on the California boundary—was to be considered as the 32d-parallel route.

The actual survey as organized is hard to explain rationally. As already noted, the 41st-parallel route was not surveyed in any consistent manner. The same fate befell the 32d-parallel route, but for the opposite reason: so much was already known of it, Davis reasoned, that no additional information was required. Senator Benton's Cochetopa Pass opening in the Rockies seemed the most problematic, but because of Old Bullion's political power that 38th-parallel alignment had to be investigated. In simple truth the only coherent and comprehensive surveys were conducted along the 47th-49th parallels and along the 35th parallel. In addition, the part of the 41st-parallel route from Fort Bridger (Wyoming) to Salt Lake City was investigated for a pass across the Wasatch Range, a reconnaissance survey was run from Salt Lake to the Sierra Nevada to extend Stansbury's earlier exploration, and toward the end of the short period of the survey the southernmost route was reexamined from the Red River to El Paso and in the passage from the Continental Divide down to the Gila River. The territorial legislature of Washington also amplified the original organized survey by having Frederick Lander examine a rail route from South Pass in Wyoming to the Oregon Country via the Snake and Columbia rivers. In the end, the investigations did emerge as reasonably comprehensive, but not from the initial organization Secretary Davis bestowed upon it. One is left with the strong impression that Davis sought merely to justify his fairly obvious preference for the 32d-parallel route, but in the end the logic of the geography of the American West seems to have forced an investigation that elicited the necessary understanding to make a reasonable judgment of where the transcontinental railroad should be built.

The 47th- and 49th-Parallel Routes

Turning to the results of the various surveys, we find that Isaac Stevens was the first to begin his investigations, though his account appeared only in the next to the last of the thirteen volumes of the published survey.[40] In his report Stevens sought to address two major doubts about the northerly route: the severity of the winter, and the availability of passes through the Rockies and the Cascade

Mountains. The governor's conclusion was quite sanguine with respect to the winter:

As shown by the accounts of all who have traversed the Rocky Mountains, during almost every winter month the snow there would not present the slightest impediment to the constant passage of railroad trains. And, in regard to temperature, the whole of these mountains between Fort Benton and Bitter Root Valley, a distance in a straight line of 190 miles, have a milder winter climate than Wisconsin or Iowa, or any part of Nebraska east of the 100th meridian. A mean temperature of 20° to 25° must prevail throughout, excepting about five miles of the dividing ridge, which rising 2,500 feet above the Bitter Root valley, and 3,400 feet above Fort Benton, will . . . fall to a mean of 16°; though from its very narrow extent, and the almost constant influence of the west winds, it must usually approach nearer the climate of Bitter Root valley, or have a mean of 19°.5. . . . From the increasing altitude and width of the Rocky mountain plateau, towards the south we find that the length of country, having a climate of similar coldness, must be much greater, as traversed by any line of railroad between [Montana] and . . . the 35th parallel.[41]

This notion of the mildness of the western Montana winter was widely scoffed at when Stevens's report was published, but time has borne out many of his conclusions with respect to the Pacific's moderation of the cold climate of the continental interior. His views on the Great Plains are too favorable, but on the valleys of the western part of the northern Rockies he was closer to subsequent experience than were his critics.

As the Rockies become lower in general, and particularly in the critical heights of the passes offering a traverse of the range, as one moves from Wyoming northward, the openings through the range in Montana were examined more for the possible grades along their approaches than for anything else. From the highest tributaries of the Missouri River at the western margin of the Great Plains several surveys were run through prospective gaps. Using the Sun and Dearborn headwaters of the great river, approach was made to Cadotte's Pass at an estimated elevation of 5,195 feet. A 4.19-mile tunnel would be required to hold to so low a figure, as well as several high bridges, much side-hill embankment, and grades up to sixty feet to the mile (1.13 percent). This was hardly a practicable route for what would have to begin as an essentially developmental line.[42] Other passes were reconnoitered. Lewis and Clark Pass seemed to have heavy grades and would require a 2.13-mile tunnel to keep to a fifty-seven-hundred-foot summit level. Although Stevens presented a sanguine report, from the detail in his volume of the Pacific Railroad Survey it is clear that he failed to discover an economically practicable route through the Montana Rockies, even if a route could have been engineered. It remained for the locating engineers of the Northern Pacific Railway to solve this problem, as they did in the late 1870s.

What Isaac Stevens did accomplish was to discern the basic route from the Minnesota frontier, at St. Paul, westward to the Missouri and then along that stream to its headwaters above the Great Falls. There he failed to find a readily usable pass, but west of the Continental Divide he discovered the alignment of rivers, variously the Big Blackfoot, Hell Gate, Flat Head, and Clark's Fork, that made possible a passage of the repeating ridges of the Rockies westward to an opening onto the Columbia Lava Plateau. Thence following westward to the Columbia, that major stream would be crossed near the mouth of the Yakima, which would be ascended to Snoqualmie Pass, and the line carried to Puget Sound at Seattle. A branch was envisioned to be carried down the Columbia, through its water gap in the Cascades, to Fort Vancouver, where ocean navigation might be reached.[43] This route lay basically along the 47th parallel, leaving the 49th parallel without any specific proposal for a rail line. This was due in some measure to the same reason that Meriwether Lewis had failed to complete his transit of the northern pass at the headwaters of the Marias River: the country of the Blackfeet lay across its eastern entrance, and that band of Indians had the well-deserved reputation of being perhaps the most hostile of any roaming the plains. If a northern rail line was to be built, it would almost certainly come along the 47th rather than the 49th parallel.

The 38th-Parallel Route

To the south, as we have seen, the 41st-parallel route was not directly studied by the Pacific Railroad Survey. The extension of Stansbury's explorations to cover the country west of Salt Lake came as an aftermath of the negative and bloody exploration along the 38th parallel forced upon the survey by Senator Benton. Lieutenant John Gunnison had been placed in command of that reconnaissance, whose main purpose was to see if a railroad route westward out of the San Luis Valley of southern Colorado could be discovered. Leaving Fort Leavenworth on the Missouri River in eastern Kansas in June 1853, Gunnison's party, which included Lieutenant E. O. Beckwith as assistant, passed over the divide from the Kansas River to the Arkansas and up that main stream to the western edge of the Great Plains. Using south-bank tributaries of the Arkansas, first the Apishpa and then the Huerfano, Gunnison discovered that a crossing might be found at or near Sangre de Cristo Pass in the front range of the southern Rockies. "A single grade," he said, "could easily be carried from the summit to the gorge of the Huerfano river; but two, one along Gubbison's creek and one on the river, would probably be preferable." The report of Beckwith adds, "By descending from the summit of [Sangre de Cristo] pass along the side of the mountains on the right of the Sangre de Cristo [stream], a railroad can be constructed throwing a larger portion of the descent upon the lower part, where it should curve around a mass of low hills in a bend of the mountains, to the plain . . . , which subsides gently into the valley of the San Luis in the direction of the Cochetopa Pass. The entire descent from the summit of Sangre de Cristo Pass to our present camp [in the San Luis Valley], is 854 feet in a distance of seventeen miles."[44]

Thus, the first of the two main ranges of the southern Rockies could be, and ultimately was, crossed by a railroad near Sangre de Cristo Pass. But west of the broad San Luis Valley, a second range lay across the proposed route, though it was thought to be breached by the vaunted Cochetopa Pass of Senator Benton. On September 2, 1853, Gunnison's party climbed the eastern slope of what Old Bullion had assured the world was the geographical key to the building of a transcontinental railroad. Beckwith describes that climb:

The width of the pass at the summit does not exceed six hundred yards, but the slopes to the low peaks rising above it are not abrupt. The ascent from the valley of San Luis, by which we reached the summit, was very gradual, increasing with considerable uniformity until we approached it within a short distance, where the ravine of the stream was narrow and thickly timbered; and we left it with the wagons, making an

The nature of the Great Plains was little understood by earlier travelers, it being common to refer to the vast grassland as the Great American Desert. The scale of 1870 trains, the flatness of the terrain, and the low-grass vegetation cover are all suggested by this woodcut from Frank Leslie's *Illustrated Newspaper* for February 19, 1870. *Source:* Library of Congress picture.

THE NORTH
AMERICAN
RAILROAD

abrupt descent to the right to the level of the summit, "which we could have reached by an easier grade," Captain Gunnison says in his notes, "by keeping to the left of our track, where the ravine winds gently round to the summit-level." The approximate elevation above the sea of our camp at the Puerta, as we left the valley of San Luis, was 7,567 feet. To our next camps, twelve miles and twenty-seven hundredths above the Puerta, on the Sahwatch creek, we ascended slightly over thirty-nine feet to the mile; and in the next fifteen miles, to our camp 3.83 miles east of the summit, we ascended 913 feet, or nearly sixty-one feet to the mile; our altitude at this camp being 8,960 feet, while the indicated height of the summit itself is 10,032 feet, giving an ascent of 492 feet in that distance, or, in whole numbers, 370 feet per mile. . . . If, therefore this pass be deemed desirable for a railroad, it will be necessary, after having gained this elevation at [the camp 3.83 miles east of the summit], which will require a tunnel [to reduce the rise to even that heavy grade], including a deep approach from the west, of not less than two miles in length, entering the hill three-fourths of a mile below the summit on the east, and a short distance above our camp 1.33 miles west of the summit— diminishing the elevation to be overcome by 490 feet. Below this camp the natural grade again becomes practicable for a railroad, for a wagon road this pass is already practicable.[45]

Cochetopa Pass was not practicable for a railroad without the considerable effort of drilling a tunnel through its crest. No doubt if the route had otherwise been highly satisfactory this effort might have been made. But the necessity for such a laborious engineering work, the circuitous line of the route, the need to cross both the Sangre de Cristo and the Cochetopa Pass, and the difficult terrain west of the Continental Divide, in the Cochetopa Hills, all argued against the 38th-parallel route as the first choice for a Pacific railroad.

Gunnison's party continued down Pass Creek to Cochetopa Creek, which flows into the Gunnison branch of the Colorado. The Gunnison provided the main alignment to be surveyed, though it posed severe problems where the stream enters the Grand Canyon, with absolutely sheer walls rising two thousand feet straight above the river. The party's wagon had to cross the plateau into which the river cuts, as did the railroad that was built along this route in the latter decades of the nineteenth century. Below the canyon the river valley served more adequately, carrying the survey with ease to the junction with what was then known as the Grand River, today's Grand Junction on the Colorado. Below the junction the Colorado affords a broad valley with a graded slope, and even in crossing the acute angle to the Green River tributary, the country is a rolling desert surface. Westward from the Green River crossing, Gunnison's party sought, and secured, a reasonable transit of the Wasatch to enter the Sevier River valley in mid-October 1853. During that month, while seeking to explore Sevier Lake, Gunnison and seven others were massacred by Utah Indians, leaving Beckwith to conclude the survey to Salt Lake City on November 8. The general conclusion was that a railroad could be built along the 38th-parallel route, but it would be less direct than one along the 41st parallel arriving at the same western terminus (the Great Salt Lake), and it would present considerable engineering problems.

It is important to realize that a railroad can be carried over very heavy grades, up to 4.5 percent, but operation over such a line imposes such severe operating costs that it becomes economically infeasible. Governor Stevens had found that a railroad could be carried along the 47th-parallel route, but both in the Montana front range (the Lewis Range) and in the Cascades in Washington he failed to find a pass through which a rail line might be carried without tunneling. Gunnison's survey had been similarly confronted, and for the three lines of investigation—the 49th, 47th, and 38th parallels—the results had to be considered rather equivocal. In the context of western railroad construction, any considerable engineering had to be avoided because of the cost and long delay it might impose, thus limiting the line's ability to begin earning income to help in an undercapitalized operation.

Filling Out the Survey of the 41st-Parallel Route

Out of each of these surveys, Stevens and Gunnison-Beckwith, there came almost immediate efforts to find a proper developmental-railroad route where the initial survey had been seen as a failure for not finding one even before Secretary Davis had made his decision and conveyed it to Congress. One of the participants in the west-end operations of the Stevens survey, Frederick Lander, was so dissatisfied with its results that he undertook, at his own expense, to make a reconnaissance survey of a route from Puget Sound to South Pass on the Oregon Trail in Wyoming, where he assumed the 41st-parallel survey would have its northernmost point. This branching alignment Lander proposed would be superior to that along the 47th parallel. Similarly, when Lieutenant Beckwith reached the Great Salt Lake he sought permission from the War Department to continue his efforts by looking at certain parts of the 41st-parallel route that seemed inadequately covered in Stansbury's earlier, and nonrailroad, exploration of the way through the Wyoming Basin. In particular, Beckwith wished to reexamine the crossing of the Wasatch Mountains east of Salt Lake and to extend the reconnaissance to include the possible alignment from Salt Lake westward to the Sacramento Valley of California. Lander was encouraged in his efforts by a unanimous resolution of the Washington Territorial Legislative Assembly, while Beckwith received the permission he sought to continue his explorations along the 41st-parallel route. Lander's reconnaissance is reported as part of the Pacific Railroad Survey (as the third item in volume 2 of that survey). In his report he makes an extended analysis of what a developmental railroad should set out to accomplish in an engineering sense. Drawing a sharp contrast between the British and American systems of rail development, he makes the following statement about the nature of a fundamental trunk railroad under each system:

Grand Trunk, or first-class railroad, English.—A (practicably) direct route between termini reduced to a close approximation of level gradients, without attempts at deflection to reduce cost. A line of durable and costly works, drained, sodded, and elaborately prepared in road-bed and permanent way for the rapid passage of weighty trains; thoroughly equipped and furnished, of gauge adapted to traffic and connexions.

Grand Trunk, or first-class railroad, American.—A line adjusted to irregularities of surface between termini, by application of curvature and gradients, regarding obstacles to be overcome and traffic to ensue. A road-bed ditched, sloped, and drained, and made ready for rail by a cheap ballasting of clear gravel. A superstructure adapted to the passage of weighty trains at paying rates of speed. Works erected in apprehension of a division of traffic with competing lines, as avoiding misdirection of capital and the entailment of high rates of fare. In view of improvements in transportation liable to ensue, and contingencies that inevitably occur, omitting as extravagant and unnecessary many of the operations deemed indispensable to foreign first-class construction.[46]

Lander envisioned the Pacific Railroad as a "trunk line" reaching as "the extension of a rough American railway, of weighty superstructure, but of medium equipment, from the extreme western border of eastern civilization to the Pacific."[47] The location of that extremity engaged his attention. Arguing that the selection of a route for the transcontinental railroad was already determined "on constitutional grounds of the cheapest and earliest consummation of the military defence of the Pacific possessions by overland railways," he saw the only rational decision favoring a line commencing on the Missouri River, "near the mouth of the Platte." Lander explained: "As the navigation of the Missouri, as high as this point, is ample for the transportation of rails, equipment, and furnishing, the road—finding its own means of rapid extension—would reach the mountains, over the flat sandy surface offered, at about the same period of time that the local roads of Iowa and Missouri were completed [to the Missouri River], to become its connecting links with eastern lines—say in three, four, or five years. The line (of five hundred . . . miles length) would traverse the edge of a range of low sand hills, skirting a broad and fertile valley, which reaches, without a break in surface, from the mouth of the Platte to the first broken country of the great grazing section of the Black Hills [the Laramie Range of Wyoming]."[48] By 1856, when Lander's comments were published, Captain Stansbury's reconnaissance of the approaches to the Laramie Range from the east along Crow or Lodgepole Creek was already available in print. That earlier survey had found this crossing of the front range of the Rockies practicable, along with the transit of the Laramie Basin and the drop from it down to the North Platte west of the Medicine Bow Range. And west of that river Stansbury's examination of Bridger's Pass had shown that it would serve to carry a rail line up out of the Platte Valley and over the low ridge forming the eastern side of the Great Divide, or Wyoming Basin. Lander seems to have favored the "emigrant route," that is, the Oregon Trail, which lay to the north of Stansbury's proposed alignment from the forks of the Platte (at present-day North Platte, Nebraska) to Fort Bridger in western Wyoming. From South Pass along the Oregon Trail Lander proposed a branch that would continue this transcontinental rail line on to Puget Sound, and it was to that segment that he gave his attention.

The branch that Lander envisioned was to start at Seattle on the authority of Captain George B. McClellan—later to become rather too well known as the Union commander and presidential candidate in 1864—who had been the leader of Stevens's western party. "I have mentioned Seattle as the proper terminus for the road, whether it crosses the mountains by the main Yakima, or by the Columbia-river Pass. This place is situated on Elliot bay, and is by far superior to any [other] harbor on the eastern shore of Puget Sound."[49] Thence the line was to pass over the flat bottom of the structural valley lying to the south of the sound and connecting it with the lower Columbia. Using the Columbia Gorge, the railroad would gain the lava plateau lying to the east of the Cascades without surmounting that crest. To avoid the deep canyons of the Snake River, Lander examined a line passing across the Blue Mountains of eastern Oregon, but with mountain grades somewhat abated through the use of the Grande Ronde Valley to cross their heart and gain the moderate divide between the Grande Ronde and the Powder tributary of the Snake, joining that stream above the impassable stretch of Hell's Canyon. Once back on the lava plateau to the east of the Blue Mountains, the rail alignment would be relatively direct to the low crossing—where Pocatello was later laid out as a railroad town—between the Port Neuf tributary of the Snake and the northern great bend of the Bear River. Once beyond the southern end of the Salt River Range, Lander's route headed generally eastward across the upper Green River Basin to join the Oregon Trail at South Pass, though he admitted that the final choice between the South Pass (Oregon Trail) approach from the east and that more directly across the Laramie Range to Bridger's Pass and the Great Divide Basin would have to wait upon more detailed surveys. It was the engineer's conclusion that the money that could be saved building the 41st-parallel line, as opposed to one farther north, would be sufficient to cover the estimated $26.8 million cost he attached to his branch from South Pass to Puget Sound.[50]

The weight that Lander piled on the scales in favor of the 41st-parallel route was further increased by the reconnaissance conducted by Beckwith in the winter and spring of 1854. When his party reached the Great Salt Lake via the 38th-parallel route, it seemed obvious to the lieutenant that the real road to the West in this latitude was likely to be found farther north, more or less along the alignment that Stansbury had explored from the Missouri frontier to the Mormon capital. Doubt seemed to persist, however, on the question of a railroad approach from the high basins of Wyoming, at elevations of six thousand to seven thousand feet, to the lower basin in which the Great Salt Lake lay, at about four thousand feet. To attempt to find an assuredly practical route, Beckwith set out eastward as far as Fort Bridger in the Green River Basin and reexamined as well the information on the passage across the Green River, Great Divide, and

Laramie basins that separated the Wasatch rising east of Salt Lake City from the front range of the Rockies in Wyoming.

Speaking of the area of the Green River and Great Divide basins, Beckwith noted,

It is more than two hundred miles in extent from east to west, and has a variable width, north and south, from twenty to over a hundred miles. It is enclosed on the east by the Rocky mountains, and on the northeast by the Sweet Water and Wind River mountains—Green river entering it from the north—and on the northwest and west by the Bear River mountains; and on the south by the Uinta mountains; broken by the deep canon by which the Green river continues its course to the south. Its borders are occupied by spurs from the surrounding mountains, and a few detached buttes are seen east of Green river; but its general character is that of an elevated rolling plain or valley, easily traversed in any direction.[51]

The passage of the eastern and western borders of this string of three basins—the Green River, the Great Divide, and the Laramie—became the critical question with respect to a railroad route along the 41st parallel. Beckwith accepted Stansbury's conclusion as far west as Fort Bridger. Where doubt remained was with respect to the crossing of the low Bear River Range (separating the Green River Basin from the valley of the upper Bear River and the main Wasatch Range lying to the west). A ridge separated the upper Bear valley from the lower basin around the Great Salt Lake.

In April 1854 Beckwith's party set out to explore the eastern approaches to the Salt Lake valley. Passing thirty-five miles north of Salt Lake City, they turned eastward, ascending the lower gorge of the Weber River, where despite the precipitous sides of the canyon they found it possible to rise with a slope of just 1 percent, fifty-three feet per mile.[52] For the next twenty miles up the Weber River the ascent moderated to around twenty-eight feet per mile, essentially 0.5 percent, even though there were places where the valley narrowed to little more than a cleft in the mountains. "In constructing a railroad through this defile," Beckwith reported, "it will be necessary to bridge the stream several times, which can be readily done; but for the most part the road would be carried immediately at the base of the mountains, where it can be constructed with facility by cutting along their sides and filling in at their bases."[53] Grades were reasonable farther up the Weber River valley, and near its top the White Creek tributary furnished a relatively easy crossing of the divide and the beginning of the descent into the Bear River valley. Grades did stiffen in passing up the White Clay Creek valley, 10 miles at 84 feet per mile (1.5 percent), 9 miles at 54 feet per mile (1.2 percent), and the last 9 miles at 42 feet per mile (0.9 percent). The pass was reached at an elevation that Beckwith estimated at 7,491 feet, little above the general level of the Bear River valley in this vicinity.[54] Passing across the Bear River flood plain, here several miles wide, the party began to ascend the hills lying to the east, the Bear River Range, to a divide between the Great Basin interior drainage and that flowing by the Green River to the Gulf of California, found here at 8,133 feet. This crest was sharp but narrow, as to the east the route entered the Muddy Creek valley, which connected to the Black's Fork of the Green River, passing by the emigrant trading post at Fort Bridger.

In this section Beckwith advised a slightly revised routing for a railroad carried in a curve to the south from the head of White Clay Creek to Muddy

The Pacific Railroad Survey, begun in 1854, studied parts of six possible routes for a railroad to the Pacific. In his report of 1856 Secretary of War Jefferson Davis presented a map of the routes studied, along with his recommendation for adoption of the 32d-parallel route from Shreveport, Louisiana, to San Diego, California—a recommendation that led to the Gadsden Purchase. *Source:* Library of Congress map.

Creek. That way an ascending grade, eastward, of fifty feet per mile for thirteen miles (0.94 percent) could precede one of forty feet for six miles (0.74 percent), to reach a single crest (for the Wasatch and Bear River ranges there joined) of 8,373 feet.[55] From the crest a uniform descent could be gained to the vicinity of Fort Bridger. Beckwith concluded his survey of the eastern reaches of a 41st-parallel route here near Fort Bridger: "The line eastward from our present camp should be continued directly to where it should cross Green river, near the mouth of Black's fork, and be continued thence eastward by the line followed by Captain Stansbury from Green river, by way of Bridger's Pass, to the Great Plains, as reported by him in his expedition to the Great Salt Lake, and thence descend by the South fork and main Platte, or pass over to the Republican fork of the Kansas, and descend it to connect at a suitable point with eastern lines of commerce."[56] Thus was the crossing of the western rim of the Green River Basin explored and a satisfactory route for a railroad, with a ruling grade of 1.5 percent, discovered.

The 41st-Parallel Route toward the Pacific

Returning to the Great Salt Lake, Beckwith gave his attention to exploring westward along the 41st parallel toward the Pacific. On May 5, 1854, his party left Salt Lake City, moving around the southern extremity of the lake and across several low divides in the basin ranges that protrude from the great salt flats. The main problem encountered came from the infirm surface of parts of these great bolsons rather than from the grades of any potential line. Only to the west, where the Utah-Nevada boundary was subsequently drawn, did the alignment of basin ranges become sufficiently continuous to require trying grades. Beckwith noted that the great lake could be skirted either to the north or the south and that the specific route a railroad might take would have to wait upon the completion of a detailed survey. What he sought was merely to demonstrate that such a line along the general route of the 41st parallel was practicable. That he found to be the case between Salt Lake City and the Humboldt Range in what is now eastern Nevada. There a crossing of the mountain was essential, and he demonstrated that there were several places where a line might be carried over the range to descend into the Humboldt River valley, using that graded route to approach the eastern base of the Sierra Nevada at the western margin of the great interior basin extending from the Bear River Range to the cordillera of California.

The crossing of western mountains became the main objective of the expedition. "In order to discover a practicable railroad pass, if possible," he tells us, "in the Sierra Nevada—this portion of which had never been explored—I determined to examine every opening and depression which could be seen to the east, commencing with the northern, and proceeding toward the south—determining not only the merits of each, but establishing their comparative value."[57] The passes he examined led mostly to the northernmost section of the Sacramento Valley, or to the gorge where that river breaks southward into its great structural depression. As a result, the difficulties of the route were found in dropping down the western slope of the great lava plateau that begins in that latitude rather than in ascending the short slopes to reach the crest from the east. Beckwith's selection of passes to examine seems to have been dictated by several considerations: he envisioned as direct a route westward from the Great Salt Lake as might be found, taking him due west from the point where the Humboldt River turns southward (near present-day Winnemucca, Nevada), thus encountering the Sierra Nevada–Cascades between Mount Lassen and Mount Shasta; he sought to minimize redundant grade, an objective gained by crossing the lava plateau north of Mount Lassen, where the rise from the east was little more than a thousand feet to a crest of about fifty-seven hundred feet;[58] and he obviously thought in terms of minimizing the amount of heavy engineering in construction and heavy hauling in operation, ends facilitated by the adoption of as low a summit as could be secured. The fact that such a northern route would have introduced a more circuitous line to San Francisco Bay than one across the Sierra farther south could be overlooked when it was not certain that the bay was the ultimate goal. Also, the problem of passage through the gorge of the Sacramento River was appreciated only after most of the mountain exploration had been carried out. Further exploration produced a proposed alignment running just north of Mount Lassen and reaching the open Sacramento Valley at its northern end at "Fort Reading." Beckwith concludes his report thus:

It will be seen that the route explored conforms throughout to a remarkably straight line, deviating, west from Fort Bridger, only at Timpanogos canon, if that line be preferred to the Weber, and on the northern portion of the Sacramento river; and then only 3 minutes and 4 minutes [of latitude], respectively, from the line of the 41st parallel of north latitude. The length of this route from the Missouri to the Black Hills [Laramie Range] may be safely estimated not to exceed 647 miles, the distance given by Captain Stansbury from Forth Leavenworth to Fort Laramie (outward journey); and his distance from the Black Hills to Fort Bridger, 347 miles, is given from actual measurement. From Fort Bridger to Fort Reading [by the line explored], the distance is 1,011.71 miles (which hereafter may be diminished by at least 106 miles [through realignment in western Nevada], giving a total length for this [41st-parallel] line of 1,899.71 miles).[59]

The 35th-Parallel Route

Along the 35th parallel a full investigation was ordered and carried out by Lieutenant A. W. Whipple between Fort Smith (Arkansas) and Los Angeles. It was argued that there were already three railroad termini emerging as the points of access to any southern transcontinental rail line: St. Louis, Memphis, and Vicksburg. In proposing a 35th-parallel route it was assumed that branches could be carried from such termini to a main line passing westward along that parallel: from St. Louis via Independence a branch would run to a junction in northern New Mexico, probably Galisteo near Santa Fe; from Memphis via Little Rock and Fort Smith the main line would be constructed; and from Vicksburg a branch would be carried to Shreveport and on to a junction with the main line somewhere along the Canadian River in Oklahoma or the Texas Panhandle.[60] In this way it was assumed that a single transcontinental line might stand as a compromise among the several regional proposals that had counteracted each other's efforts in Congress.

The approach from Memphis to Fort Smith was direct, passing across the bottom lands of the Mississippi Delta to Little Rock and then up the valley of the Arkansas River between the Ozarks and the Washitas to reach the frontier post of Fort Smith on the Indian Territory boundary, where these westernmost extensions of the Appalachian folding sank under the flatter strata of the plains. The serious survey began thus at Fort Smith, using the graded course of the Arkansas River to its junction with the Canadian and then passing up that river's valley nearly to its headwaters in northern New Mexico. As the explorers moved westward, they examined a number of short deviations from the Canadian River route but in the end settled their recommendation upon it. A hundred miles east of Santa Fe their line of exploration passed across the low interfluve between the Canadian and the Pecos, using the upper course of the latter stream to its Canyon Blanco branch and then via that broad valley to its head only a few miles east of Galisteo, located on the tributary of the Rio Grande of the same name that joined the main stem at the pueblo of San Felipe. "By the Canon Blanco there is no difficulty, except at the point of leaving it. There, to diminish the grade, it will be necessary, at considerable expense for cutting and filling, to ascend by the side of the canon. Beyond this point the route is plain, with light grades and gentle

163

The Drive for Ubiquity

curvatures, to a branch of Rio Galisteo east of the Gold mountains. Following its gentle stream through a wide puerto of the Rocky mountains, we pass within twenty miles of Santa Fe, and strike the Rio [Grande] del Norte at Pueblo de San Felipe, where formerly a bridge spanned the river."[61]

In such a reasonable fashion this transcontinental railroad would pass across the Rockies without any considerable engineering works. From Albuquerque thirty miles down the Rio Grande, where the mountains to the west of that stream die out in a high desert plateau, a line of railroad could be conceived passing easily out of the Rio Grande valley using the Rio Puerco and its tributaries to reach the Continental Divide in what is today western New Mexico.

The exploratory expedition passed toward the Pacific via the Zuni pueblo, but it assumed that several routes across the relatively open country of the plateau could be found. More of a problem was encountered in securing a favorable route across the rim of those plateaus and down to the Colorado River on the eastern boundary of California. Moving directly westward, the key to this passage was the discovery of a pass across the southern shoulder of the San Francisco Mountains, a cluster of extinct volcanic cones lying near the edge of the plateau but still on its surface. By staying on the plateau, rather than passing down toward the low Gila Valley in southern Arizona, the grades could be kept moderate. Only by finding a reasonably graded course off the plateau (here at six thousand to seven thousand feet) down to the Colorado River (not much more than five hundred feet above sea level where it would be likely to be crossed) could a railroad be carried along the 35th parallel. An easy way through the Rockies having been found, it was this descent that became the critical question facing Whipple's party. They ran preliminary surveys on a number of the headwater streams of the Bill Williams Fork of the Colorado. Finding "Aztec Pass" near Hope Peak, they gained the Sycamore Creek, which cut a water gap through the Aquarius Range to join the Big Sandy and then the Bill Williams Fork to reach the Colorado along a reasonable, though far from ideal, course. The course was less than desirable, in part because it forced a great southward-bending loop in the direction of march, requiring a passage north up the Colorado once it was reached to regain the general alignment between Albuquerque and the Mojave River that was to carry the party across the deserts, which reach to the Colorado River from the west. But the main disadvantage came from the steep stretches in the general descent from the Chino Plains of the high plateau that lay west of the San Francisco Mountains. This survey suggested that a way through could be found but did not actually discover it.

Once on the Colorado, the crossing of the Mojave Desert became the next concern. Indian guides showed the party an arroyo forty miles above the mouth of the Bill Williams Fork that gave a gradual ascent of the mountains to the west. This reasonable ascent continued for fifty miles until a summit 5,292 feet above the Colorado at the Needles was reached. Nowhere was it found likely that the grade need exceed seventy feet per mile (1.32 percent), an acceptable slope for a developmental railroad.[62] Soon the sink where the eastward-flowing Mojave River disappears was reached, and that stream could be followed to the southwest, growing with each mile as desert streams tend to do. Whipple tells of the upper course of the Mojave River:

THE NORTH
AMERICAN
RAILROAD

Proceeding through groves of yuccas beautiful as coconut and palms of southern climates, and dense thickets of cedars, by a gradual ascent, averaging probably sixty feet to the mile, we reached the summit of Cajon Pass, where the mercury measured 25.4 inches. . . . This pass appears the most truly difficult part of our route. It seemed, however, possible, by winding from the Pacific side around the slope of the mountains, thus increasing the distance, to locate a route on a spur bounding the valley of Cajon creek, to the foot of the crest of drift over which passes the road. Here may commence a tunnel of about four or five miles in length, and eight hundred feet below the surface at the summit; thence becoming gradually less, until it issues upon the prairie slope near the Mojave river [on the north]. [On the south] we descended about twelve hundred and fifty feet in eleven miles from the first point of striking the arroyo at the [southern] foot of the [summit] ridge. As we proceeded, the valley opened finely. . . . The descent became less steep, and the sides of the valley were regular slopes, where a railway might ascend so as to rise above the bed of the creek, and diminish the grade to one hundred feet per mile in the canon above.

This development diminishes the obstacles of Cajon Pass. The work will not be so extremely difficult nor as expensive as at first seemed possible. Our greatest regret is, that is leads not directly to a port as safe and commodious as that of San Francisco.[63]

From that comment it is clear that Cajon Pass was used more for its terrain virtues than for the route it afforded into the Los Angeles Basin; it was thought to be the easiest crossing of the California Coast Ranges, unfortunately leading to an inhospitable coast, a virtually empty desert basin, and a still small Mexican town.

From the foot of Cajon Pass Whipple's party continued across the great alluvial fans that border that parched basin on the north. The road, however, passed through a considerable band of greenery as the streams from the San Gabriel Mountains (then called the Sierra Madre) spread mountain waters on the fans as they disappeared below the surface. No obstacles to rail building were encountered, and the party reached the Los Angeles Valley. "The town had the sombre cast of a Spanish pueblo, relieved, as it were, by innovations of American comforts," Whipple observed. "There was the bustle and activity of a business place. Many new houses were in the process of construction. Everywhere was indicated a thriving population and a land of intrinsic wealth. Los Angeles is said to number five thousand inhabitants."[64] But a small town was not the end of such an important exploration; that lay twenty-four miles to the south, at the small and unsheltered port of San Pedro, which Whipple judged rather harshly: "A city has been laid out, but its success is problematical."

In reviewing the whole route as surveyed, the assistant railroad engineer who accompanied the party concluded that a rail line could be built along the 35th parallel with few grades over 1 percent. In crossing from the Pecos to the Galisteo south of Santa Fe, grades might have to climb to 1.5 percent and a fairly long viaduct might be required. In the descent from the high plateau down to the Colorado River in western Arizona, again a grade of nearly 1.5 percent might be needed. And in crossing Cajon Pass, grades might rise to nearly 2 percent. Otherwise, the 35th-parallel route afforded remarkably easy grades and curves, as it passed for most of its length up the gently graded slope of the Great Plains, then across the high plateaus of New Mexico, Arizona, and eastern California, and finally along the fans of the northern edge of the Los Angeles Basin. But this

The Drive for
Ubiquity

route served few places of importance, the most notable being the small, formerly Mexican towns of the upper Rio Grande valley of New Mexico.[65]

The 32d-Parallel Route

If the 35th-parallel route was advanced as a compromise between the sectional interests of the North and the South, the 32d-parallel route stood as the most rigid expression of that sectionalism. There had already been several government expeditions to examine the country between western Arkansas and Louisiana and El Paso, and between that pass through the basin ranges and the Gila River, which was generally seen as the way to drop from the high to the low desert country in this region. The Gadsden Purchase had been made to facilitate the building of such a 32d-parallel route. What remained were several questions as to the passage of critical terrain in the Guadalupe Mountains of West Texas, the edge of the high desert in eastern Arizona, and a possible crossing of the mountains east of San Diego to gain direct access to that best of southern California ports. It was to answer these questions that several limited explorations were conducted under the general auspices of the Pacific Railroad Survey. From the reports of Lieutenant John G. Parke we have information on the El Paso–Colorado River section, and from those of Captain John Pope work on the section from Preston on the Red River to El Paso.

Taking Pope's account first: The captain divided his survey into three sections, the first of 352 miles from the Red River to the eastern base of the Llano Estacado in the Texas Panhandle, the second of 125 miles crossing that Staked Plain, and the third of 169 miles from the crossing of the Pecos to the Rio Grande at Doña Ana in southern New Mexico. The expedition actually commenced at its western end, at Doña Ana on the Rio Grande on February 12, 1854, reaching the eastern terminus at Preston on the Red River in Texas on May 11. But for purposes of comparison it seems best to describe this route as progressing from the east, as have most of the other descriptions. Preston, some ten miles west of present-day Denison, Texas, was a rather arbitrarily chosen eastern terminus that Pope criticized, favoring instead Fulton in Arkansas, just east of Texarkana, where a railroad was expected to reach the Red River from Memphis, as it soon did. From Preston the line surveyed climbed out of the Red River valley and passed along rolling ground for sixty miles, with a rise of 676 feet to the eastern edge of the Upper Cross Timbers, where some heavy but rather short grades would be encountered in passing through that belt of rough country. Climbing westward along a general slope, there were places where any railroad would have to drop down into the valley of a river, the drainage being basically at right angles to the alignment of the prospective rail line, but those descents and rises fell within the limits of practicability for a developmental rail line. Continuing on a gentle upslope, the route reached the eastern slope of the Llano Estacado 350 miles from the Red River. Pope estimated that this section could be built for $50,000 per mile:[66]

From the Sulphur Springs of the Colorado [in West Texas] the ascent of the Staked Plain is so gentle and uniform as to be barely perceptible, and no bluff nor unusual swell of ground marks its existence. To the summit-level of the plain the ascent is 423.6 feet in a distance of 89.1 miles, or an average ascent to the mile of 4.8 feet. Neither excavation nor embankment would be required in this whole distance, as the ascent is both gradual and uniform, and uninterrupted by hill or ravine. The descent to the Pecos, although more rapid, is in all respects similar; and so well adapted in this section to the construction of a railroad, that, with the exception of transporting the ties, no work is required. The surface line from the summit-level to the Pecos descends at the rate of 18.3 feet to the mile, over a distance of 35 miles.[67]

Because of the simplicity of this construction, Pope figured that this section could be built for $40,000 per mile.

West of the Pecos the alignment surveyed took on a different character: three mountain ranges, the easternmost of the parallel blocks so characteristic of the basin ranges of the west, lay across the route: the Guadalupe, Hueco, and Organ ranges. Of these the Guadalupe posed the greatest barrier. The approach from the east was gentle, 3.5 feet to the mile from the Pecos to the eastern slope of the range, but there rising to 61.8 feet to the mile (1.17 percent) over the Guadalupe Pass, with a three-mile stretch of 2 percent grade dropping to the west. Next in line, the Hueco Range seemed passable, though again with fairly heavy grades. In both cases a diversion from the most direct line somewhat to the south would avoid the ranges entirely, keeping the rail line from the Red River to the Rio Grande at El Paso essentially a plains route. At El Paso the water gap of the Rio Grande, El Paso del Norte, carried the alignment around the south end of the Organ Range and to its western terminus at Doña Ana.[68]

West of Doña Ana earlier explorations had suggested that it would prove easier to reach the Gila River, and thereby the Colorado to the west, south of that stream rather than north of it in what had been American territory since 1848. Thus, the United States sought to purchase nearly thirty thousand square miles south of the Gila, which it succeeded in doing in 1853, adding the Gadsden Purchase through which the survey line, and the railroad built basically along it, ran almost all the way between the Rio Grande and the Colorado. Again, the exploration actually proceeded from west to east, but for comparability it will be described here in the opposite direction. This expedition, led by Lieutenant John G. Parke, was carried out before the legal transfer of title to the purchase, so it was conducted in foreign territory with the permission of the president of Mexico. Its main purpose was to examine the slopes that connected the high plateau of southern New Mexico with the low desert plains south of the Gila in what became Arizona. Exploration parties encountered great difficulty in crossing westward from the Rio Grande, because of the shortage of water in this true desert, but it was assumed that a railroad could secure water by drilling wells. Only in the descent to the low desert to the west was rail technology really challenged. Although no definitively good route was discovered, it was determined that a line could be carried with grades of no more than 2 percent, and probably much less after carefully detailed surveys. Thus, it was reasonable to argue that a successful transcontinental railroad could be built along the 32d parallel.[69]

The main barrier on such a route lay not east of the Colorado but rather in the crossing of the Laguna Range east of San Diego. Try as they might, the explorers could find no practicable pass through that mountain mass north of the Mexican border, so the 32d-parallel line had to be proposed to pass northwestward from the Yuma Crossing of the Colorado River to reach the Pacific via the San Gorgonio Pass, by then well explored, into the Los Angeles Basin.

The Drive for
Ubiquity

The Outcome of the Survey

The Pacific Railroad Survey was published over the last years of the 1850s, making available the most extensive geographical investigation of the American West that had been made up to that time, as well as a very extensive reconnaissance of potential rail routes between the Mississippi and the Pacific coast. The survey had been undertaken in the hope of solving a political problem, the resolution of the sectional conflict over where a transcontinental railroad should be built, and it failed in that objective. In due course the secretary of war, Jefferson Davis of Mississippi, made his recommendation that a rail line be built along the 32d-parallel route because of the favorable terrain encountered there, the ease of construction, and the temperate winters that would facilitate year-round operation of a railroad in that latitude. That recommendation was received in its time as a highly partisan one, perhaps representing financial as well as sectional interests, and subsequent research has not seriously shaken that view. There was little question that a railroad could have been built along any of the latitudinal routes, save Senator Benton's Cochetopa Pass alignment, so any decision as to which to use depended upon other than strictly geographical analysis. As geographical research was conclusive only to the extent that there were several practicable routes to the Pacific Ocean, it failed to solve Congress's problem, and that body proved totally unable to do the job for itself. Thus, the decision had to be put off until events solved much of the political problem, without in any way changing the geographical realities.

The Pacific Railroad Survey is exceptional as an item in the historical geography of transportation, not merely for its extent but also for the conditions under which it was conducted. In most of the locational decisions that had been made with respect to railroads, either in Europe or in North America up to that time, two aspects of reality had had to be considered: the location of the cities that were seen as the potential markets for such transportation improvements, and the characteristics of the terrain, the physical geography, that would guide any routing of rail lines between or among the cities under consideration. As we have seen, most of the earliest railroads were envisaged as lines, rather than as complex networks, to tie two important cities together. If those cities were rather close together, there might be only one logical geographical route between them, but as the termini became more separated in space, there would be a tendency for several possible alignments to be reasonably considered. In the latter eventuality the assignment of a route to the undertaking would be more a matter of physical geography in the initial instance, when one self-evidently superior route might be available, but as time went on there might be a practicable alternative alignment that would serve other intermediate towns or tie into an emerging network based on a somewhat different initial city pairing. In this way the settlement fabric would always play a very important role in any locational decisions for rail development. But at the time of the Pacific Railroad Survey in the early 1850s, settlement west of the Mississippi was so sparse and tentative that the main components that were at all determinative were the emerging ports on the Pacific coast. When one headed west out of Chicago, St. Louis, Memphis, Vicksburg, or New Orleans, the next real objective was seen as San Francisco Bay, the mouth of the Columbia, Puget Sound, or San Diego Bay, and possibly one of the incipient ports being roughly nailed together on their shores. The coast in the Los Angeles Basin was not in the same class, because it was known to lack practicable natural harbors. How one reached San Francisco Bay, Puget Sound, or even San Diego Bay was mainly a matter of physical geography, not of settlement.

The truth was that in a developmental rail line there was a conscious decision to shift the components of transportation costs from capital investment to operating charges. The cheapest developable route with reasonable prospects for a break-even traffic would tend to be favored. Thus, there was not a very reasonable basis for building a line along the northern route to Puget Sound or the southern to San Diego, even though sectional rivalries seemed to many to have made it otherwise. It seems to me that once the Gold Rush had turned the interests in the East and South toward northern California, the only practicable objective on the Pacific coast was that area. Before any transcontinental railroad had been constructed and operated, the question of its utility and economic survival was most genuine—so real, in fact, that I find it improbable that the pioneering line could have been financed save along the best alternative route. Whether or not the 41st-parallel route was the best physically—which it probably was—there could be no doubt that it was by far the shortest between the Missouri frontier and the northern California diggings, and therefore the cheapest to construct. Similarly, when the desire arose to secure a rail route to the Pacific Northwest, it was secured in the cheapest way possible, by extending a branch, as Frederick Lander had proposed, from the environs of Fort Bridger to the lower Columbia. For southern California, branching came even farther west with the opening of the line down the San Joaquin Valley to cross the mountains to Los Angeles in 1876, only seven years after the completion of the transcontinental line and five years before the completion of a direct route from Los Angeles eastward. The cost of operating a longer route could not weigh as heavily as the cost of constructing a totally new and more direct route in terms of settlement fabric.

The Implementation of the Pacific Railroad

The Pacific Railroad Survey did nothing to resolve the political dispute, but in the long run it provided to be an essential pandect for the shaping of the rail network of the United States west of the Missouri frontier. So long as the sectional conflict remained dominant, nothing could be accomplished. But in 1861, when the southern states seceded from the Union, withdrawing their representation in Congress, there was overnight a change in that political conflict, even in the face of actual armed conflict. Congress had a perhaps enhanced interest in advancing the cause of a Pacific railroad, to counteract the efforts of the Confederacy to detach the territories and western states from the Union. Two pieces of legislation that had a major effect on American life, the Pacific Railroad Act and the Morrill Act to offer free land in homesteads, were adopted early in the war in an effort to wage psychological warfare, as we would call it today. The Pacific Railroad Act was an attempt to counteract the efforts of Senator Gwin,

169

The Drive for
Ubiquity

The Missouri River
Bridge between
Council Bluffs and
Omaha. This bridge
was of eleven spans,
each 250 feet in
length, supported 50
feet above the water
on cast-iron col-
umns. The terminus
of the Union Pacific
was deliberately
located on the east
bank of the Mis-
souri so that the
company would be
required to build
the bridge, an
undertaking it
delayed beginning
until February 1869.
Before the bridge's
completion in 1872,
passengers and
goods had to be
ferried across the
river. *Source:* Union
Pacific photo, used by
permission.

THE NORTH
AMERICAN
RAILROAD

himself a promoter of the 35th-parallel rail line, to detach his California from the
Union, and the Morrill Act was an effort to give the urban proletariat, as we
might now term it, a vested interest in a free soil.

On July 1, 1862, President Lincoln signed the Pacific Railroad Act that the
twenty-five-state Union Congress had adopted with resounding majorities. The
prime geographical problem, of the termini of such a Pacific railroad, was dealt
with somewhat more easily than in the 1850s. The western terminus was established, without any serious questioning, as resting at Sacramento in northern
California. But the eastern end of the line still posed a problem, even with the
strictly southern contenders now on the other side of an actual battle line. St.
Louis, the Iowa towns, and St. Paul still contended for the critical juncture
between the integrated eastern rail system and the proposed Pacific road. In a
typical legislative compromise, the eastern-terminus question was only partially
resolved. An "initial point" was to be established between the southern margin
of the valley of the Republican River (in the Kansas Territory) and the northern
margin of the valley of the Platte (in the Nebraska Territory) somewhere along
the 100th meridian of west longitude.[70] Thence eastward, four branch railroads
were to be constructed to the several competing points of attachment to the
eastern network: a branch to Sioux City, one to Omaha, one to Atchison, and

one to Kansas City. The Omaha line was to be constructed by the Union Pacific Railroad, to become its main line to the Missouri River frontier; it was called the Iowa branch because it was to have its official terminus, to be determined by President Lincoln, established on the Iowa side of the Missouri River (requiring that the UP pay for the river bridge). The three other branches were to be assigned to other railroad companies. Only one of these was undertaken during the construction phase of the Pacific road; this was the Leavenworth, Pawnee, and Western Railway Company, later to be called confusingly the Union Pacific Railroad Company Eastern Division, even though it stood as a company fully independent of the main Union Pacific. Constructing westward from Kansas City, the Eastern Division company was originally intended to reach only as far west as the "initial point" on the 100th meridian, but it failed to make that juncture, ultimately building all the way west to Denver as a line parallel to, rather than branching from, the main UP. Neither the Atchison nor the Sioux City branch was built in the fashion originally intended.

The Iowa terminus that President Lincoln determined was at Council Bluffs, across the river from Omaha. In so siting the juncture Lincoln had not merely the bridging problem in mind but also the question of which Iowa railroad to favor with a direct connection. In the mid-1850s Frederick Lander had already suggested the successful solution that Lincoln adopted: setting the eastern terminus sufficiently far beyond existing railheads that the companies seeking to make junction with the Pacific railroad would be able to build to it—in fact, would undertake to construct the several hundred miles of line needed to reach the junction at their own expense, rather than the government's. As we have seen, that activity came quickly.

The Pacific Railroad Act of 1862 had other provisions that were to have great importance in later rail developments. It was originally proposed that separate lines would be built from east and west: respectively, the already organized Central Pacific Railroad of California, which would construct eastward

President Lincoln determined that the eastern terminus of the Pacific railroad would be at Council Bluffs, Iowa (shown in the background east of the Missouri River), requiring the Union Pacific Railroad to construct a major bridge crossing the river. At Omaha the Nebraska Territorial Capitol became a symbol of the anticipated commercial role of the emerging city. *Source:* Library of Congress picture.

The Drive for Ubiquity

from Sacramento, presumably to reach the westward-building railroad near California's eastern boundary; and a company yet to be organized to build from the Iowa terminus, through the finally determined "initial point," to a junction with the Central Pacific. To aid in the construction of the transcontinental line, the federal government, as the sovereign of the territories through which most of the trackage would pass, undertook to loan to the companies government bonds for a thirty-year period and to provide a land grant of five alternate sections on each side of the line for ten miles in either direction. Thus, sixty-four hundred acres in ten square-mile sections were granted for each mile of track. The bonds loaned to the companies were to be at the rate of $16,000 per mile of track between the termini and the foot of the mountains they would first encounter, the Sierra Nevada for the Central Pacific and the Rockies for the Union Pacific. Westward from the eastern base of the Rockies and eastward from the western base of the Sierra, for a distance of 150 miles in each case, the bond subsidy was at a rate of $48,000 per mile. Any remaining mileage, after that 150 miles beyond the base of the mountains, was to be subsidized at the rate of $32,000 per mile. These bonds had to be repaid to the federal treasury, both principal and interest, at the end of thirty years, so the companies faced a large-scale debt retirement in the 1890s. As the Union Pacific was constructed at an average rate of $26,222 per mile, this bond subsidy seems adequate.[71] Still, the companies were to find that their most vexing problem was to raise enough capital to carry out construction. Another provision of the 1862 act required that the Pacific road be constructed with grades not to exceed 116 feet per mile (2.2 percent), with curves of 400-foot radius or larger (14 degrees), and that it use only American-made iron. In 1863 Congress further specified that the line must be at standard gauge (4 feet 8½ inches).[72]

Although somewhat tentative efforts at construction began at each end of the line, the provisions of the 1862 act proved to be inadequate to support actual prosecution of the work. Congress was asked to revise this legislation, which it did in 1864. The 1864 act reduced, from twenty miles to ten, the section length that must be completed before bonds could be loaned, and it changed the security for the repayment of those bonds from a first mortgage on the property to a second. The land grant was doubled, to 12,800 acres per mile (ten alternate sections on each side of the line), and was made absolute, giving mineral as well as surface rights to the company. The meeting of the Central Pacific and the Union Pacific was to be no farther than 150 miles from the eastern boundary of California. The four lines east of the "initial point" on the 100th meridian were reduced to one. And the strange restriction that an individual might own no more than twenty shares of stock in either company was abolished in the face of extremely slow sales of those securities.[73]

Even with those improvements in the government subsidies, only some twenty miles of grade, and no actual track, had been laid by the Union Pacific by the end of 1864. By that time the Central Pacific had finished thirty-one miles of track to Newcastle in the foothills of the Sierra.[74] The problem was that it was virtually impossible to interest enough investors in buying stock in the companies to secure working capital; even the government bonds were selling at a 10 percent discount, and the Union Pacific's land-grant bonds were selling at 70. The prospects for the company, or for the rapid sale of its land grant, were perceived as so poor that stock sales were sluggish indeed. Some device was needed that would raise money more quickly. It was found in the creation of a construction company, with officers drawn from the Union Pacific Company for the most part. A convenient Pennsylvania charter was bought up for the Pennsylvania Fiscal Agency, and its name was changed—at the suggestion of George Francis Train, an American promoter of street railways in London—to Crédit Mobilier of America, mirroring the then powerful French investment firm Crédit Mobilier de France, which was to collapse in 1868.

Even with Crédit Mobilier, little effective construction was carried out on the Union Pacific before the Civil War came to an end in April 1865. Money was scarce and expensive, goods hard to secure, and labor largely tied up in the first really modern war, with its conscription and over four million men under arms. The Central Pacific actually made better progress, probably as much because it was insulated by distance from the "theater of the war" as because it secured government bonds at a particularly rapid rate, since the mountains whose passage earned the maximum subsidy lay so close. However slowly the western line crawled up the Sierra slope, the line westward from Council Bluffs advanced even more sluggishly. On the day Lee surrendered at Appomatox Court House, April 9, 1865, the Union Pacific had not one mile of track and only a rough grade climbing steeply out of the Missouri Valley in the loess hills west of Omaha.

The Union Pacific

The line of the Union Pacific, which was to become the world's finest railroad in the 1920s, was far from that in the 1860s. Then only nature was grand in the operation. General Grenville M. Dodge, who assumed the role of chief engineer of the line in June 1866, fully understood that fact, telling an Omaha audience in 1906,

I wish to say here that while my surveys and my conclusions may have been of great benefit to you, still they were made because there was no question, from an engineering point of view, where the line crossing Iowa and going west from this river, should cross the Missouri River, and it was also my conclusion that it was the commercial line. The Lord had so constructed the country that any engineer who failed to take advantage of the great open road from here west to Salt Lake would not have been fit to belong to the profession; 600 miles of it up a single valley without a grade to exceed fifteen feet; the natural pass over the Rocky Mountains, the lowest in all the range, and the divide of the continent, instead of being a mountain summit, has a basin 500 feet below the general level.[75]

Thus, when Dodge undertook primary responsibility for locating and constructing the line his problems were great, but at least the route was reasonably set for a year's construction. The crossing between the Missouri and the Platte was then established, even if on a poor alignment, and Dodge could follow up the Platte Valley as it cuts a broad, gently ascending swath across present-day Nebraska. Only as the track approached the Rockies was there much question as to how to proceed westward.

On this score Dodge already had a fairly clear personal view, as a result of his own reconnaissance in the Rockies over the period of a decade. This had come about while he was in his twenties and served him well in his responsibilities in the building of the Union Pacific. Born in Danvers, Massachusetts,

Once out of the
Missouri River
valley, the route of
the Union Pacific
Railroad in the
Platte River valley
was level and very
gently graded.
Construction
required little more
than common farm
equipment applied
to a simple grading
of the surface, with
lines of crossties laid
on a most modestly
changed natural
surface. *Source:* Library
of Congress picture.

Dodge as a boy had come to know Frederick Lander, whom we have already met, and who grew up on a nearby farm. Lander had attended Norwich Academy (later University) in Vermont, where one of the earliest engineering training programs in America had been established. On his suggestion Dodge also attended Norwich to pursue an engineering degree. At the time, railroad engineering engaged the attention of the more adventurous boys, my own great-grandfather among them, and when Dodge graduated in 1850, he joined some classmates at Peru, Illinois, working for the Illinois Central Railroad chartered that same year. From the IC in 1852 he went on to become the principal assistant of Peter Dey, the chief engineer of the Mississippi and Missouri Railroad then being built across Iowa. In a report to President Oliver Ames of the Union Pacific, made in 1869, Dodge told of his first visit to the Rockies:

Henry Farnum and [Dr. Thomas] Durant, the then contractors of this road [the Mississippi and Missouri], instructed Dey to investigate the question of the proper point for it to strike the Missouri River to get a good connection with any road that might be built across the continent. I was assigned to the duty, and surveys were accordingly extended to and up the Platte Valley, to ascertain whether any road built on the central or the northern line would, from the formation of the country, follow the Platte and its tributaries over the plains, and thus overcome the Rockies.

Subsequently, under the patronage of [Farnum], I extended the examination west to the eastern Rockies and beyond; examining practicable passes from the Sangre Cristo to the South Pass; made maps of the country, and developed it as thoroughly as could be done without making purely instrumental surveys. The practicability of the route, the singular formation of the country between Long's Peak, the Medicine Bow Mountains, and Bridger's Pass on the south, and Laramie Peak, the Sweetwater, and the Wind River ranges on the north demonstrated to me that through this region the road must eventually be built.[76]

THE NORTH
AMERICAN
RAILROAD

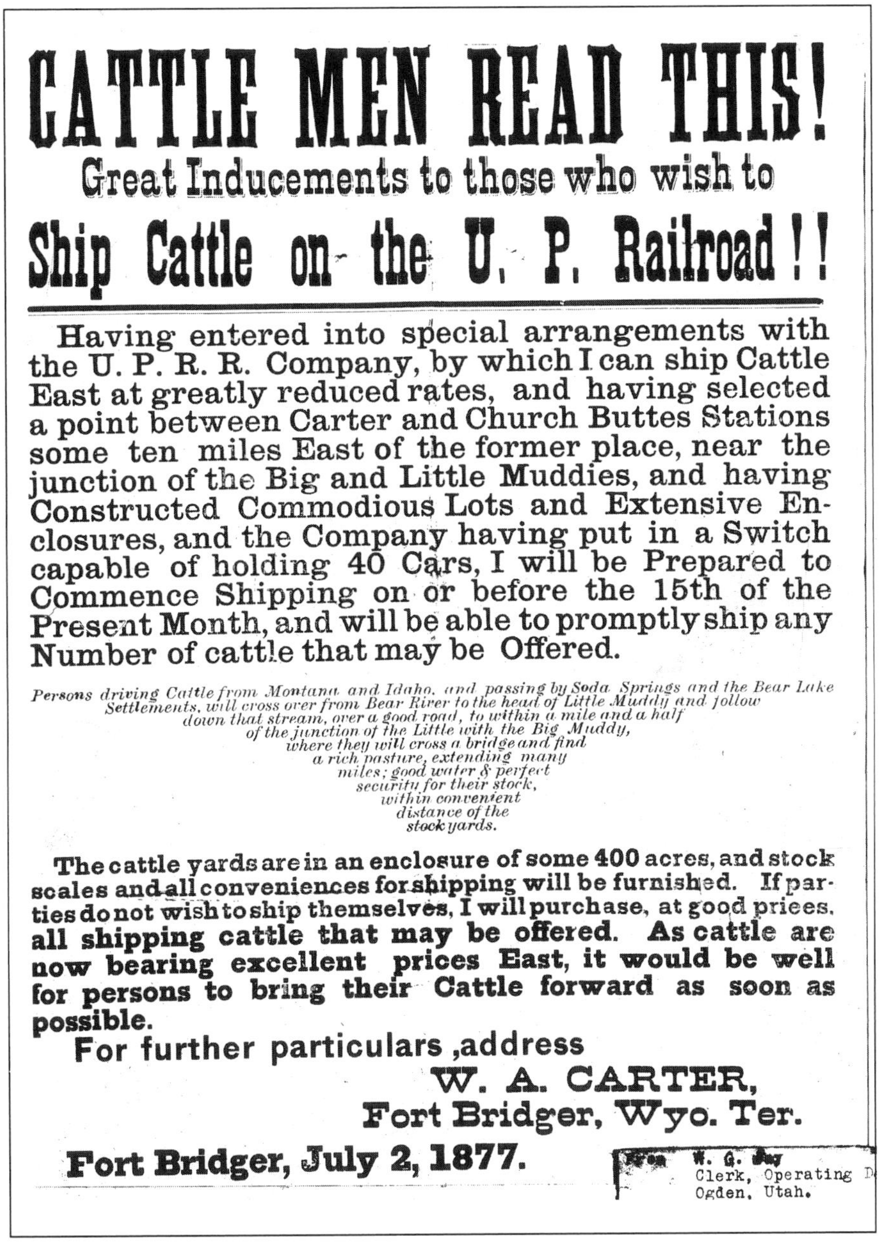

Ad for stock shipments from Fort Bridger. *Source:* Union Pacific photo.

During the Civil War Dodge had had wide experience as a commander of both combat troops and troops engaged in the repair of southern railroads. In 1865, as an army commander in Missouri and much of the Great Plains, he had gone westward to attempt to subdue the Plains Indians, many of whom had attacked and destroyed wagon trains and homestead farms on the plains during the war. He was only partially successful in that operation, but while in Wyoming he had examined in detail the crest of the Black Hills (Laramie Range), looking for an improvement over a pass that James Evans, a surveyor in the employ of the Union Pacific in 1865, had found. Dodge's small exploring party was followed by a band of Crow who seemed to be hostile, and in evading them he passed over a critical piece of ground that was soon to become known as Sherman Pass (and today, with engaging modesty, as Sherman Hill). As Dodge tells it,

175

The Drive for
Ubiquity

In 1865, as I was returning from the Yellowstone country, after finishing the Indian campaigns, I took my command along the east base of the Black Hills, following up the Chug Water, and so on south, leaving my train every day and going on to the summit of the Black Hills with a view of trying to discover some approach from the [plains in the] east that was feasible. When we got down to the crossing of the Lodge Pole, I knew the Indians were following us, but I left the command with a few cavalrymen and guides, with a view of following the country from the Cheyenne Pass south, leaving strict orders with the command if they saw smoke signals they were to come to us immediately. We worked south from Cheyenne Pass and around the head of Crow Creek[;] when I looked down into the valley there was a band of Indians who had worked themselves in between our party and the trains. I knew it meant trouble for us; they were either after us or our stock. I, therefore, immediately dismounted, and giving our horses to a couple of men with instructions to keep on the west side of the ridge out of sight and gun shot as much as possible, we took the ridge between Crow Creek and Lone Tree Creek, keeping upon it and holding the Indians away from us as our arms were so far-reaching that when they came too near our best shots would reach them and they soon saw their danger.

We made signals for our cavalry, but they did not seem to see them. It was getting along in the afternoon as we worked down this ridge, that I began to discover we were on an apparently very fine approach to the Black Hills, and one of the guides has stated that I said: "If we saved our scalps I believed we had found a railroad line over the mountains." About 4 o'clock, the Indians were preparing to take the ridge on our front, the cavalry now saw our signals and soon came to the rescue, and when we reached the valley I was satisfied that the ridge we had followed was one which we could climb with a maximum grade within our charter and with comparatively light work.[77]

In his *Autobiography* Dodge further illuminates that conclusion: "Over the ridge which I came down, the Union Pacific railway was built. When engineers, under my instructions came to examine it, they found a line with a grade not to exceed 90 feet [1.7 percent], and where the sedimentary and granite formation came together instead of dropping off as it usually did, about 500 feet, there was only a depression here in the ridge which as soon as crossed took up its elevation again and kept it gradually falling to the plain."[78]

It was not the ridge between the valleys coursing down the eastern slope of the Black Hills that mattered so much as a physical contact between the highest level of the High Plains strata in this area and the granite core of the Laramie Range. By passing up the highest stratum of the plains to an actual direct contact with the granite core of the range, without the intervening longitudinal valley that borders the Front Range of the Rockies throughout virtually its entire length, the rail line gained a leg up that permitted it to crest the Black Hills with reasonable grades. Granite Canyon, where the contact of the sedimentaries and the granite was encountered, was at an elevation of seven thousand feet, while the crest of Sherman Hill was only about twelve hundred feet higher, on a generally open slope where whatever length of line was necessary to secure a workable grade could be laid out by the locating engineers.

The remarkable qualities of the Union Pacific line as it was laid down between 1866 and 1869 were to be found in the relative ease with which it could be carried over a thousand-mile course that crossed the great cordillera of North America and the watershed between the Atlantic (Gulf of Mexico) and the Pacific (Gulf of California). After the contretemps of gaining the Platte Valley at

The Union Pacific Railroad reached the 100th meridian 247 miles from Omaha—in important symbolic terms, the beginning of the West. *Source:* Library of Congress photo.

Fremont, Nebraska, the course of the Union Pacific was clear to all observers. "Once on the Platte at Fremont . . . a river at grade provided an excellent and gentle rise directly to the mountains in the west. The only considerable obstacles to construction were the crossing of the Loup River, the securing of ties and railroad iron from the Missouri frontier, and the pilferage of goods by Indians. Thus, the 291 miles of rail from Omaha to the forks of the Platte at North Platte was determined by the location of the eastern terminus at Omaha."[79] A comparison was made between the Platte and Republican valleys, and the former was greatly favored for its breadth and the reasonably direct course of the stream, which allowed the rail line to make a great sweep westward without curves in the meanders of the stream, as on the Republican, or bridges across those arcs. On the Platte only the relatively few north-bank tributaries had to be bridged, and the railroad could follow the riverbank virtually all the way to the forks of the river:

At the forks of the Platte, General Grenville Dodge, who had been appointed Chief Engineer of the Union Pacific and was to find the best route across the Rockies, faced several alternatives of nature, and even more proposals. These may be summarized under three general classes: first, a crossing basically along the Oregon Trail; second, a series of crossings of the "Black Hills," or present-day Laramie Mountains, into the center of the Great Divide and Green River basins and thence to a joining with the trail at Fort Bridger; and the third, the use of some pass across the Colorado Rockies westward of Denver. The last suggestion stemmed from the actual existence of a market in the gold workings around Denver developed after 1859. The [engineering survey] reports of the railroad leave little doubt that the alignment would have been diverted through Denver had any practicable pass been found. As an economic route, the railroad was greatly concerned with on-line traffic, but the terrain required that Denver be served by a branch, which was soon built from Julesberg, Colorado[,] up the south fork of the Platte.[80]

177

The Drive for Ubiquity

Although many preliminary or reconnaissance surveys were run by the company engineers across the Laramie and Front ranges, none was ever carried along the Oregon Trail. The reasons for rejecting this route are, however, fully cited. "Impracticable canons," diversion away from the river gradient by narrow and choked valleys (as in the Hartville Uplift of eastern Wyoming), "a much larger amount of valuable timber contiguous" to a more southerly line, "snows [that] are reported much worse on the Sweetwater River than to the south of it," the large deposits of coal found in the Laramie Basin and Bitter Creek Valley of the Green River Basin, and the more direct route to the West found south of the trail—all appear to have weighted the choice in favor of the Wyoming Basin route. Even though the locating engineer, Evans, concluded with respect to the trail route, "I do not mean to be understood that there is anything insurmountable here," he also expressed the view that it was not a good route for a railroad.

The characteristics of the country south of the Oregon Trail that led the engineers to favor building the railroad there may be presented briefly. Most important, at least most often cited, was the greater directness of that route. From the beginning it was stated that the trail route would be seventy miles longer between the forks of the Platte and Salt Lake than the route through the Great Divide Basin. Next, perhaps, was the greater snowfall of the Sweetwater (River)–South Pass line. General Dodge stationed a party at the crest of the Laramie Range in the winter of 1866–67 to report on snow conditions. It was found that if the line were kept to the broad interfluves in the mountains, the snow could be expected to be blown into the valleys, leaving a fairly open track. West of the Laramie Range, in the Laramie and Wyoming basins, the track was deliberately located on the eastern side of valleys, with cuts oriented toward the west or northwest and embankments two to four feet higher than necessary in order to profit from the sweeping action of prevailing winds. Economical travel must be year-round, so the location of the railroad, unlike that of the trail, was influenced by winter conditions.

Throughout the building of the Union Pacific the concern for coal and timber was frequently expressed. Coal was reported as early as 1850, when Stansbury passed through the Wyoming Basin. During the building of the railroad a geologist was employed, and his reports began to delineate the vast coal reserves of the area. Before the railroad was completed, coal mines were opened at Rock Springs in 1868 and at Carbon shortly thereafter. Nearness to the northern spurs of the Colorado Rockies afforded the builders a source of ties. On the trail, railroad timber was available only at South Pass, whereas on the line selected, ties could be cut in the Medicine Bow Range, the Uinta Mountains, and the Wasatch, Wyoming, and Salt River ranges in the west, then floated down short streams to the site of construction:

In water the Great Divide Basin route was inferior to that along the Sweetwater [to South Pass]. Although there was little contrast between the two east of the Wyoming Basin (at Casper on the trail and Rawlins on the railroad), within the Basin severe disadvantages were found. Wells had been drilled along the railroad as it moved west from Laramie to the Green River. These were found to be highly subject to mineral salts. East of Rawlins substitute sources from the Laramie, Rock, Medicine Bow, and North Platte rivers could be secured. Thus, every water crossing became a watering point and Rawlins could receive piped water from the North Platte. West of there,

Skull rocks, semiarid
weathering of red
granite at Sherman
summit on the
Union Pacific in
Wyoming from
Williams's *Pacific
Tourist.*

however, the railroad faced 135 miles of poor water, [a problem that] was not fully solved until the . . . shift from steam to diesel-electric engines. West of the Green River its various right-bank forks rising in the Wyoming and Uinta ranges could provide good boiler water.[81]

In this way was decided the route of the Union Pacific from the forks of the Platte to the Wasatch Mountains bordering the Great Basin, with its interior drainage. Near present-day Evanston, Wyoming—named for the company's chief locating engineer, James Evans—the alignment abandoned the northward-flowing Bear River, instead passing over a low divide to the headwaters of the Weber River, a stream that had been fully explored when Beckwith carried his reconnaissance eastward from Salt Lake to Fort Bridger in 1853. Grades were heavy in Weber Canyon, but it was found that a ruling grade of ninety feet per mile (1.7 percent) could be maintained uninterrupted for the twenty-five hundred feet of drop between the crest of the Wasatch and Ogden.[82]

It is hard to imagine a thousand-mile rail line built under pioneering conditions more favorable than these. The only substantial bridge, other than that crossing the Missouri at the line's eastern terminus, was across Dale Creek near the summit of Sherman Hill. But even that spindly structure could be built of pine timber brought westward as the iron advanced, and be completed with reasonable dispatch so that construction could continue apace. When railroad construction began in earnest in 1866, progress was rapid. On October 6 the track crossed the 100th meridian, then as now seen as the boundary of the arid and mainly unsettled interior. December 3 saw track to the forks of the Platte where a railroad town, North Platte, was laid out. When winter finally stopped construction, the rails had reached O'Fallons Bluffs, 305 miles from Omaha.[83] In 1867 a great deal of trouble with Indian attacks was encountered, but the gentle upslope of the High Plains geologic structure provided an ideal subgrade for a

179

The Drive for
Ubiquity

The Dale Creek Bridge was built of timber to carry the original Union Pacific line at the grade of the peneplained granite upland on the top of Sherman Hill, close to the summit at eight thousand feet. *Source:* Union Pacific photo.

Dale Creek Bridge. In the early 1880s the timber structure was replaced by a light and airy structure of steel built mainly to avoid fire danger from wood-burning engines, such as the leading locomotive shown here (1885–1901). *Source:* Union Pacific photo.

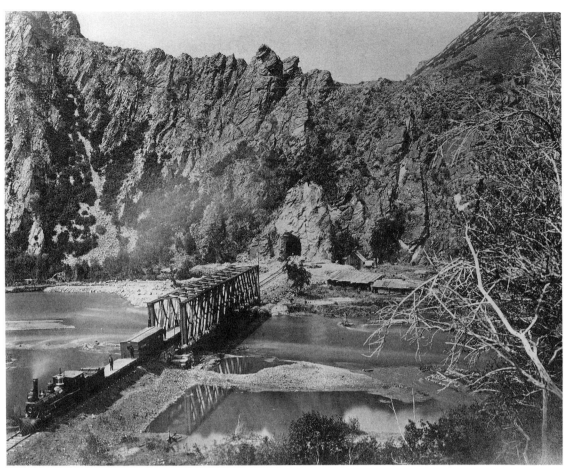

railroad. That year's construction carried the head of track to Granite Canyon on December 31, as building continued even during the winter, adding 233 miles for the year. From Granite Canyon, at 7,298 feet, actual construction required a rise to the Sherman Pass at Sherman (8,242 feet) of less than 1,000 feet, a favorable situation made possible by the use of this minute contact between the sedimentary High Plains structure and the granite at the place where those sedimentaries have their highest elevation.

Between New Year's Day, 1868, and the completion of the whole Union Pacific on May 10 of the next year, construction was continuous. Sherman was reached on April 5, and by the end of the year the iron was finished to Wasatch, at the headwaters of the Weber River just west of the present Wyoming-Utah boundary. Four hundred and forty-six miles had been laid during the calendar year 1868. During the following four and a half months the line was completed down Echo and Weber canyons and then around the head of the Great Salt Lake to the summit of the Promontory Range, one of the basin ranges that extended as a point into the lake from the north. There, 1,108 miles west of Council Bluffs, the tracks were joined on May 10, for a construction in 1869 of 102 miles.[84]

The Central Pacific

The Central Pacific Railroad faced a very different kind of terrain from that along the Union Pacific, and a different kind of supply problem. For the Union

After a long passage of the high basins of Wyoming, the Union Pacific Railroad descended from seven thousand feet to four thousand in the Wasatch Oasis by following the generally reasonably graded course of Weber Canyon to the prospective site of Ogden, Utah. *Source:* Library of Congress photo.

Pacific, ties and iron for the first stretch of line had to be brought from some distance away using the shallow Missouri River at least from St. Joseph, Missouri, the closest railhead when construction began. The transport was difficult but not over much distance beyond the long-established river ports of the Missouri. As early as 1820 steamboats were plying to Westport Landing (Kansas City), and as St. Joseph and other river towns were nailed together on the frontier of settlement, boats could bring thence the goods they distributed to the tiny mining and staging settlements scattered widely but thinly beyond the continuous frontier. Thus, when the Union Pacific began to lay iron on July 10, 1865, it secured the fifty-pound-per-yard wrought-iron rails directly by boat from the mills at Pittsburgh.[85] The Central Pacific, on the other hand, lay twelve thousand miles from its supplies in a journey that took months to accomplish by the sailing ships that were the main haulers of freight to California. Yet these goods could be carried directly to the terminus of the line in Sacramento and be laid down in an area that, though vastly removed from the main settled area of the country, was reasonably populated and quite experienced with heavy earth moving and blasting. Even labor was more available in California when construction began than it was in the eastern Nebraska Territory. California was largely isolated from the manpower demands of the war, and in the Chinese it had a mobile labor force totally detached from the historical events straining the rest of the country. The California railroad was altogether a smaller thing in contemporary estimation; it was entirely privately financed and directed, and it was assigned what was, admittedly, a difficult construction project but one of limited length, perhaps as little as 142 miles between Sacramento and the Nevada boundary. Like the Union Pacific, the Central Pacific had great difficulty in securing construction funds, not being any more able than its eastern partner to sell stock in sufficient quantities. But its project could look forward to a much more rapid receipt of the loaned federal bonds to support its construction because the "foothills" of the mountains, and the mountains themselves, lay close to the point of initial construction.

From a geographical viewpoint the critical problem facing the Central Pacific was the crossing of the Sierra Nevada. It was first thought that this undertaking was so difficult that the Union Pacific, building from the east, might well make the juncture with the Central Pacific on the California-Nevada boundary, 1,553 miles from Omaha and only 139 miles from Sacramento as the line was finally built. The summit of the Sierra was actually more than a thousand feet lower than that of the Rockies at Sherman Pass (Sherman Hill), but the approaches were so different that there was doubt as to how to make the rapid climb from near tidewater at Sacramento to Donner Summit, only a hundred miles away but seven thousand feet above the river port. While answering the general query of whether it was possible to cross the range at all, the Pacific Railroad Survey had not effectively answered the more definite question of where precisely to secure that passage.

Lieutenant Beckwith's party had examined a number of passes and had paid the most attention to the country near Mount Lassen, particularly the canyons of the several left-bank tributaries of the upper Sacramento River. The conclusion was that a line could be carried down from the high Modoc Plateau of northeastern California following one of those tributaries to reach the Sacra-

In the largely unforested country along the Pacific, railroad ties and bridge timbers were transported from a distance by water wherever possible. *Source:* Library of Congress picture.

mento where it was still within its own gorge south of Mount Shasta. The eventual construction of the Pitt River Railroad demonstrated that such a line was in fact practicable, though this would have been an unlikely route for the pioneer line, as it was both tortuous and indirect. The economic heart of California had, by 1860, become the country northeast and southeast of Sacramento, with a westerly extension via the lower Sacramento and San Joaquin rivers to San Francisco Bay and its several trading cities. This concentration of activity in the "Mother Lode" and "Northern Diggings" was further accentuated after 1859, with the opening of the Comstock Lode in Nevada, due east of the Northern Diggings. Economically there was a considerable sharpening of the geographical focus between the time of the Pacific Railroad Survey and the undertaking of construction a decade later.

Also within that period further investigations had been carried out with the specific purpose of railroad location in mind. The leader among these explorers was Theodore D. Judah, the chief engineer of the first railroad to be built on the American West Coast, a twelve-mile line begun as the Sacramento Valley Railroad and carried from Sacramento eastward to Folsom, with an opening in February 1856. The more distant objective of this line was Placerville in the foothills of the Sierra and thence, via some pass in the mountain crest, the Great Basin. The promoters of this route became so strident that the *Alta California,* San Francisco's main newspaper, noted, "We shall next hear that the best way to Heaven is through Placerville."[86] Judah held different geographical views, which led to his departure from the company's employ. His obsession with the building of the Pacific railroad had caused many of his contemporaries to dub him Crazy Judah when he not only wandered the Sierra looking for the way east but actually went there to argue before congressional committees for the provisions he believed essential for the successful prosecution of the under-

183

The Drive for
Ubiquity

taking. Thus, he is credited with improving the financial subvention from the federal treasury and with finding the best rail alignment across the great block of the Sierra Nevada.

The key to that crossing is to be found in an understanding of the basic structure of the mountains. Unlike the Rockies, the Sierra is a simple, though huge, fault block that has been raised to ten thousand feet or more on its eastern face while dipping toward the west to form a ramp some fifty to seventy-five miles wide. The rise from the west is at best long and taxing but, if we take the line as built, there was sufficient distance to keep the grades within a reasonable range so long as redundant grades could be avoided. The Central Pacific had a hundred miles in which to climb seven thousand feet. If a perfect ramp for the distance were available, the climb would have been at a rate of seventy feet per mile, or 1.3 percent—stiff but manageable. Obviously a uniform ramp was not available, so the grades on the line were below that modular figure for part of the distance, and above it for other sections. But with a steadily climbing line the locating engineers could hope to hold the ruling grade to around 2 percent. The critical task was to find a continuous ramp, even if not a uniform one.

It was Theodore Judah who found that steady incline, not along the several routes where wagon roads had been cut through the forest and over the crest of the range, but along a new alignment that came to be known as the Dutch Flat Route, named for the mining camp where access was gained to the interfluvial ridge that lay between the Bear River and South Fork of the Yuba River on the north and the American River on the south. Using the foothills approach to Dutch Flat, that critical ridge could be gained without any intervening valley having to be crossed. Once on the interfluve, a continuous ridge rose all the way to the vicinity of the crest, and in a place where a reasonable crossing could be made. It is coincidental, but not insignificant, that on both the Union Pacific and the Central Pacific the key to a reasonable pioneering line came from avoiding redundant grade—keeping out of any depressions that might lie across potential lines. In the Sierra the deep canyons meant that the grain of the drainage had to be observed and followed to avoid those declines that would make the line either excessively long or curving to prevent unmanageable grades. And a further trap had to be missed, that interposed by the north-south structural valleys that tended to furrow the crest of the block. The Dutch Flat ramp was particularly desirable because its crest, at Donner Pass, dropped away to the east into a glacial valley that in turn drained via the Truckee River across the graben, a structural trough, occupied at its southern end by Lake Tahoe. The part crossed by the rail line, the Sierra Valley, is bordered on the east by the Carson Range, a section of the great Sierra block isolated from the main crest by the graben. Fortunately, the Truckee River, which drains both the Tahoe and Sierra valleys, breaks across the Carson Range in the narrow Truckee Canyon to flow eastward out into the Great Basin, affording a reasonably continuous descent toward the east without any secondary crest. By using the fifty miles between the Truckee Meadows, where the Great Basin was reached (and later Reno was laid out), and the summit, the twenty-five hundred feet of elevation could be handled within reasonable grade limits, similar in magnitude to those encountered on the western slope. Only at the head of the glacial valley, in which Donner Lake was found, did an excessive grade confront a continuous and direct routing. There the locating engineers

The rivalry between the Asian laborers of the Central Pacific Railroad and the American and European construction gangs of the Union Pacific was intense and often violent. *Source:* Library of Congress picture.

resorted to an old trick of their art, passing up an intersecting side valley toward its head and then returning to the main valley along the opposite slope at a much higher level. That extension of the distance and a long tunnel under the actual crest held the grades to within the 2.2 percent the government required in return for its various subventions.

The discovery of the Dutch Flat Route so encouraged those interested in railroad development in California that they sought to organize a company to build on this rather than on the Placerville alignment. Judah attempted to interest San Francisco mercantile and mining capitalists in the scheme, but they shunned him, so he turned to Sacramento where the merchant community was much more enthusiastic. In fact, the Central Pacific Railroad, incorporated under state law in June 1861, was fundamentally a Sacramento creation with its four main backers—Leland Stanford, Charles Crocker, Collis Huntington, and Mark Hopkins—all coming from that river port's mercantile community. But the backers, and Judah, who became their chief engineer, were not absolutely committed to the city, as they demonstrated when the local authorities tried to deny the Central Pacific access to the river front (because the older Sacramento Valley Railroad, whose embanked right-of-way crossed the town, was seen as being responsible for holding the American River's floodwaters within the built-up area, rather than allowing them to flow down the gentle backslope of the stream's natural levee and away from the town). The Central Pacific company did not hesitate to propose an alternate river terminus at Freeport, to be established sixteen miles down the Sacramento. The threat worked, and the citizens of

Sacramento agreed to a line giving the new railroad access to the levee where steamboats could provide the link to the Bay Area towns.[87] Thus, when the Pacific Railroad Act was adopted by Congress a year later, it specified that the Central Pacific was to be the western undertaker of construction and to begin that work "at or near San Francisco, on the navigable waters of the Sacramento river"; the company could use that latitude to ensure sympathetic dealings with the city of Sacramento.[88] That act made the company responsible for utilizing the "most direct, central, and practicable route" across the mountains, which the company's backers believed they had in the line surveyed via Dutch Flat.

Because the Central Pacific had settled on the Sacramento terminus by the time the federal act was adopted, the Big Four who ran the company—Crocker, Hopkins, Stanford, and Huntington—decided not to build a connection to San Francisco Bay under their own aegis, but rather to assign any government subventions attaching to that part of the transcontinental line to a new creation, the Western Pacific Railroad (not to be confused with the line completed in 1910 that later adopted that name). The original WP was the creation of a short-line railroad built as the San Francisco and San Jose Railroad between those two cities in the early 1860s. The WP was to be constructed from San Jose via the Suñol Canyon to the Livermore Valley and over Altamont Pass in the Coast Range to the Central Valley, where it would turn north through Stockton to join the Central Pacific at Sacramento. This was the route taken, save that in the late 1860s it was decided to turn the line northwestward from the mouth of Suñol Canyon to gain an independent terminus opposite the Golden Gate in Oakland. As the Central Pacific was not then directly involved in this western connection, a further tie to San Francisco Bay could be successfully promoted, passing in a more direct fashion from Sacramento via American Canyon in the Coast Range to Vallejo at the northeastern corner of San Francisco (San Pablo) Bay. This California Pacific Railroad, like the original Western Pacific, rather quickly fell under the direct ownership of the Central Pacific.

On January 8, 1863, Leland Stanford, the Sacramento grocer whose fortune became the source of the early money behind the Central Pacific, and who had become its first president in 1861—and the first Republican governor of California shortly thereafter—with a silver spade turned the first sod for the western part of the transcontinental line. Collis Huntington, then a Sacramento hardware dealer but later to become the real force behind both the Central Pacific and its much larger successor, the Southern Pacific Railroad, stayed away, telling his associates, "If you want to jubilee in laying the first spike here, go ahead and do it. I don't. These mountains look too ugly and I see too much work ahead. We may fail, and I want to have as few people know it as we can."[89] By midsummer the first locomotive had arrived, brought by the *Herald of the Morning* around the Horn to San Francisco, and thence on the schooner *Artful Dodger* to the levee in Sacramento. Thus, trains could run on the eighteen miles of track to Grider's Ranch, renamed Roseville, when iron reached there in November, and public service was commenced when the track extended thirty-one miles to Newcastle in the spring of 1864. By then Stanford's funding and other local money was running out, yet the loan of federal bonds could not commence until another nine miles had been finished. In that bind Huntington showed geographical ingenuity, however disingenuous he was in fact. Because the federal subsidy was

186

THE NORTH
AMERICAN
RAILROAD

The high elevations of the terrain between western Nebraska and the western slope of the Sierra Nevada west of Donner Summit, where the elevation never drops below four thousand feet, posed a major problem for rail operation when blizzard conditions struck. *Source:* Library of Congress picture.

based on terrain as well as mileage, he decided that the best thing to do was to move the beginning of the foothills, where the mileage loan increased from $16,000 per mile to $64,000, closer to the initial spike on the line. For reasons that have never been made clear, the terrain being no hillier to the immediate east or west of the point—in fact being so flat that water commonly lay in ponds all around—Huntington selected the seventh milepost east of Sacramento as the "base of the Sierra Nevada."[90] It seems to have been just at this time that the Central Pacific finally gained modest access to the eastern capital market, in the guise of Oakes Ames, who subsequently did the most to finance the Union Pacific. In a letter to the New York *Herald* in 1871 it was stated, "A year or two after the first attempts to raise capital, meeting no encouragement from any source, Mr. Huntington, their energetic Vice President was in Boston . . . and seemed very much discouraged; there he was introduced to Oakes Ames, who loaned them $800,000 to start up the fearful and untried ascent of the lofty Sierra Nevada."[91] For the first time Boston capital entered the California scene, once again showing the desire to move beyond the cramped frame of New England railroad development.

The Drive for Ubiquity

The construction of the Central Pacific is epic but rather simply explained. In passing up the ramp through Dutch Flat to Donner Summit, in what railroaders have ever since called Sacramento Hill, the main problem was to stick to the interfluve between the Bear River and South Fork of the Yuba on the north and the American River on the south.[92] In places, as at Cape Horn near Colfax, the rails had to be carried on a narrow shelf blasted out of the rocky sides of the canyons, here the North Fork of the American. And in time, as the line ascended the natural slope of the ramp, the incline narrowed sufficiently that the line was carried across onto the south slopes of the South Fork of the Yuba, passing through Emigrant Gap, a notch in the crest between the two valleys, and there again lifted upward on a narrow rock shelf.

The work involved in this ascent of Sacramento Hill was prodigious for the time and the available technology. Labor had been scarce until the Central Pacific realized that it might recruit its own workers in China, mostly around Canton. The earlier problem had been that American laborers, or even fairly recent European immigrants, tended to go to the head of the track and then quietly disappear into the forest to hike across the crest to the still-exciting Comstock Lode workings in Nevada. The Chinese, who tended to be excluded from mining areas until only the thin dregs were left, could be kept on the line with greater ease. It was with these gangs of Chinese laborers—armed at first only with black powder, and later with a still unreliable nitroglycerin, to aid their picks, shovels, and small barrows—that the line was built.

The progress was slow. Fairly brisk advance was made as far as Newcastle, which was reached at the end of 1864, thirty-one miles east of and some 940 feet above Sacramento. But there the line encountered granite (granodiorite) and other resistant rocks that required so much hand-drilling and blasting that construction began to lag. Clipper Gap, forty-three miles from Sacramento and 1,750 feet in elevation, was reached in June 1865. The end of the construction season for that year came as a result of increasing elevation, which meant that the ground actually froze in the winter; work stopped at Colfax, fifty-three miles from Sacramento and 2,422 feet above the sea. Service was established over this section: "Passenger rates were 10 cents a mile, freight rates 15 cents a ton per mile, all payable in gold. Gross revenues for 1865 were $405,592; construction expenses $3,200,000."[93] Thus, the Central Pacific began to earn money even well before the line was completed. So important was the route to the supply of the Comstock Lode mines that the company had a wagon road constructed across the Sierra via Dutch Flat soon after actual construction began.

Picking up work in 1866, the really heavy construction became almost continuous. In all, fifteen tunnels had to be dug, the longest under the crest of Donner Summit to allow a reasonable upbound grade from the east. By the summer of 1866 work was rapidly under way, heading up the western slope of the great Sierra Nevada block. At first the northern slope of the ever-deepening American River gorge was used to carry the line higher as it was built eastward. At Emigrant Gap it proved beneficial to cross the narrow interfluve, adopting the southern slope of the North Yuba and Bear River valley as the location of the line. Bare rock became the country rock exposed by the scour of valley glaciers. This section of the line required the Chinese laborers to hang in baskets as they drilled holes in the granodiorite to blast out a shelf in the ledge to carry the track ever

Snow sheds came into heavy use, sometimes extending for tens of miles in mountainous terrain. *Source:* Library of Congress picture.

higher. As the forty-seven-hundred-foot level was approached at Blue Canyon, it began to be necessary to enclose the railroad in snowsheds to deal with winter snows that could accumulate to a depth of twenty feet or more. Thence for more than twenty-five miles to Donner Summit at 7,175 feet the sheds became more frequent, until at the higher parts of Sacramento Hill they became continuous, extending to Strong's Canyon five hundred feet below the summit on the eastern slope of the Sierra Nevada. All told, some sixty-five million board-feet of timber were used in this construction, an unexpected cost of the Pacific railroad.[94]

On December 13, 1867, the track finally crossed the California-Nevada line, and the race to gain territory for the Central Pacific was under way. The summit portions of the line were still not completed. East and west of the summit the CP was carrying freight and passengers and earning revenue, but passengers and cargoes rode the intervening gap in the traditional manner—via stagecoach, freight wagon, saddle horse, and pack mule.[95] By the spring of 1868 Tunnel 6 was open, and continuous working to the head of the track in Nevada could be secured. In moving down the eastern slope of Donner Summit, the engineers used two side valleys to carry horseshoe-shaped loops; by this means the engineers avoided building high viaducts across the mouths of those valleys, and the longer line allowed the 110-foot-per-mile grade (2 percent) to be maintained. Once at the outlet of Donner Lake, which was dammed behind a moraine at the eastern end of the great glacial valley into which the rail line descended, the CP followed down Donner Creek to juncture with the Truckee River, where the railroad town of Truckee was laid out, and then down that major stream until it

189

The Drive for Ubiquity

The Northern Pacific Railroad was given the most generous of land grants—alternate sections for twenty miles on either side of the route. *Source:* Library of Congress map.

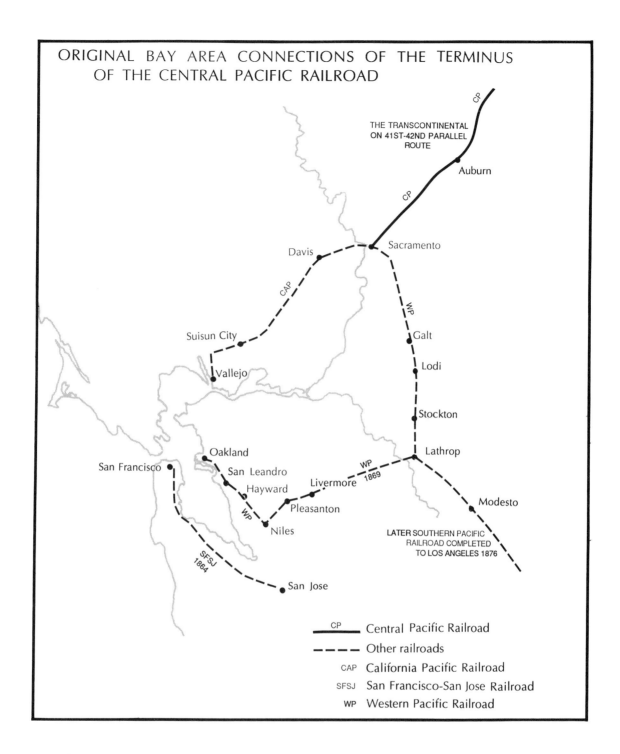

ORIGINAL BAY AREA CONNECTIONS OF THE TERMINUS
OF THE CENTRAL PACIFIC RAILROAD

THE TRANSCONTINENTAL
ON 41ST-42ND PARALLEL
ROUTE

Auburn

Davis   Sacramento

Suisun City   Galt

Vallejo   Lodi

                               Stockton

Oakland   Lathrop
San Francisco   San Leandro
                 Hayward   Livermore   Modesto
                      Pleasanton
                 Niles   LATER SOUTHERN PACIFIC
                               RAILROAD COMPLETED
                               TO LOS ANGELES 1876

San Jose

CP ——— Central Pacific Railroad
– – – – – Other railroads
CAP   California Pacific Railroad
SFSJ San Francisco-San Jose Railroad
WP   Western Pacific Railroad

opened in meadows watered by its spring floods into the bolsons of the Great
Basin.

Eventually the Truckee took a northward course, so the locating engineers
picked their way across a structural opening between the Trinity and Carson
(block-faulted) ranges into the next valley east, that of the Carson River near the
bolson where it disappeared into Carson Sink. That bolson also serves as the
disappearing "sink" into which the Humboldt River from the east empties itself
in times of high flow, though not low. Once there, the route to the east was

The Drive for
Ubiquity

predetermined and proceeded as established by the Pacific Railroad Survey of 1854.

The Humboldt is the only stream in the Great Basin that extends for any great distance east-west. Rising in the mountains just west of the Great Salt Lake, it flows westward for two hundred miles until it reaches Humboldt Lake, or in high water Carson Sink at some thirty-eight hundred feet. Any rail line crossing the northern Great Basin can obviously benefit from a reasonably graded course by following the Humboldt. This the Central Pacific did as it rushed construction across northern Nevada. Only where the river meanders widely was major construction necessary, in short tunnels passing across the loops. As the river moves westward, it cuts the ends of several of the block-faulted basin ranges, and these natural cuts gave the railroad an easy route to follow. Only at its head east of Humboldt Wells (today's Wells, Nevada) did the locating engineers face any real decisions. There they found, with a more detailed reconnaissance than Lieutenant Beckwith had been able to conduct in 1854, a route that kept the crossing of those basin ranges to a minimum. Ten miles east of Humboldt Wells, at 6,166 feet, they crossed an open saddle in the Independence Mountains that was only 500 feet higher than the Wells. Moving east, a line could be laid out along the slope of those mountains to another saddle north of the Pequop Mountains leading to the Toano Range and a final descent into the great bolson floored by the Great Salt Lake. Thence an opening north of the Pilot Range carried the line to Lucin at the northwestern edge of the Great Salt Lake Desert. Passing around the northwestern arm of the lake, the line had to be carried eastward over a saddle in the Promontory Range, whose heights jutted southward as a point in the great lake. It was in that saddle on May 10, 1869, that final junction was made with the Union Pacific and the first transcontinental railroad in North America was completed.

Much remained to be accomplished in the next fifty years, which saw the essential completion of the American railroad network. But on that pleasant May morning when the golden spike was driven at Promontory, Utah, the fully experimental phases of American railroading certainly came to an end. Despite the subsequent construction of seven more American transcontinental lines, and three in Canada, most of the central practices of railroad technology on our continent had by now been determined. Other American transcontinental lines commonly accepted the standards first used on the Union Pacific, as did the Canadian government in determining the standards for the Canadian Pacific Railway when it was effectively begun in the early 1880s. The most basic of all principles was that initial construction should be as cheap as possible, with any improvements in the line to be bought with earnings. In a system of private provision of railroads, this meant that corporate strategy came to prevail over geographical strategy in determining where and when the filling out of the continental rail system would take place.

THE NORTH
AMERICAN
RAILROAD

CHAPTER THREE

The Geography of the North American Railroad Company

The completion of the first Pacific railroad was in several ways anticlimactic. The excitement and heroic endeavors seemed to die with the whistles of the first trains to meet at Promontory. It was decided that the Utah mountain station was a poor place for a continuing junction, so the Union Pacific sold the westernmost fifty-two miles of its construction to the Central Pacific, thereby establishing Ogden as the working junction between the two lines. And within a year both companies were suffering severe financial problems, so great in the case of the Union Pacific that Oakes Ames, who had been its president and its most reliable source of money in times of great stress, was bankrupt. The nature of the financing of the great venture has been exhaustively covered in the general histories of the lines, so there is no need here to do more than take note of the fact that the promoters of both the CP and the UP shared the common view of the time that any money to be made from the floating of railroads was to be made from their actual construction. Once completed, as clearly developmental lines, the financial prospects were so obscure as to be recklessly speculative. It was a common practice for those promoters to try to unload their holdings once construction, with its immediate and considerable profits, had been completed. Most of the UP syndicate got out right after Promontory, but the CP Big Four continued to participate in the operation of their line—not, it seems, out of higher motives, but probably because their efforts to sell their shares were so totally unavailing. The shares market at the time viewed the stock of either company as literally not worth the paper it was printed on, because the financial commitment it might represent was seen as greater than any reasonable antici- 193 pation of return. Thus, the elation about the Pacific railroad passed with the flowers of the spring during which it opened.

The difficulties were several: the line had been constructed literally in a rush, a great deal of the work needed firming up and improvement within a very short time; the very purpose of the road had been symbolic and political more than economic, so the traffic was not massive even in the most sanguine expecta-

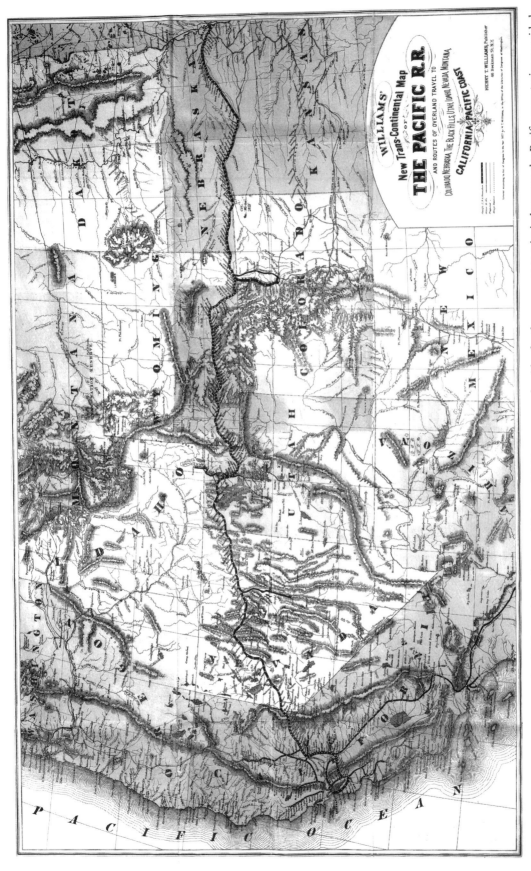

Henry T. Williams was one of several publishers who made a good living publishing maps and guides for the emergent tourist industry to the Pacific once trains provided transportation. Within a few years George Pullman, Wagner, Jerome Marble, and others were furnishing sleeping and dining cars that catered to tourists who sought luxury with their novelty. This map, from Williams's guide of the 1870s, shows the construction of a line from Sacramento to Los Angeles and onward toward Yuma, and ultimately a line to the west bank of the Mississippi at New Orleans. *Source:* Library of Congress map.

tions; the groups who had become involved in the construction of the lines had not by nature been "railroad men" interested in conducting that business, so their operating capabilities were at best untried and at worst nonexistent; and the measures taken to secure money on short-term borrowings, combined with the need to create a sinking fund to repay the federal government for its bonds and the interest thereon, meant that the cash demands on the railroads were extreme. I leave the discussion of the financial matters to others, here merely noting that the experience of these lines was generally not such as to encourage emulation. Yet as we shall see, the next fifteen years witnessed the completion of three additional transcontinental lines and the launching of several additional routes that were either supplements to those or partially completed alternatives.

These facts have always posed economic historians a problem: given the nearly disastrous outcome of the CP-UP construction viewed in economic terms, how can we explain the continued efforts by several groups to secure additional lines? Julius Grodinsky has provided us with a detailed study of the entrepreneurial motives for such construction in his *Transcontinental Railway Strategy, 1869–1893: A Study of Businessmen,*[1] this in keeping with the general historiography that views this as fundamentally a question of the working of nineteenth-century capitalism. Here I wish to argue that in addition to, and somewhat independent of, business strategy there was a specific business geography, a strategy that can be seen in the events and the network of lines that resulted.

The strategy operating in the construction of further transcontinental railroads was exercised within the same framework that had held for the first such line—that is, within the findings of the Pacific Railroad Survey. It is a testimonial to the thoroughness of that reconnaissance, and its resolution of the basic questions as to practicable routes, that essentially all the alignments ever utilized over any great distance were examined in 1854–55. Minor relocations were made, but seldom were they more than shifts from one notch to the next in the crest of a range, or from one side to the other of a valley or basin. What happened once the UP-CP route was opened in 1869 was the effort by one group of capitalist promoters or another to gain an assumed monopoly of one of the half-dozen potential alignments for a transcontinental railroad. Before effective development ceased, with the opening of the Western Pacific Railroad in 1910, eight separate transcontinental railroads were carried across the Rockies, lines that came ultimately to have more ramified connections both east and west of that great cordillera.

The first to follow after the UP-CP connection was the earnest prosecution of the Northern Pacific Railway to tie the head of the Great Lakes at Duluth in Minnesota with the Pacific Northwest at Puget Sound. On this route construction was already under way before Promontory. Soon thereafter two lines being organized on the border of the Great Plains, the Texas and Pacific Railroad in the South and the Atchison and Topeka Railroad on the Middle Border, were pushed outward from the continuous frontier toward the clusters of European settlers to be found in the thinly populated aboriginal realm. The rail objects in the West were in the towns the Americans were establishing or taking over from the Spaniards in New Mexico and southeastern Arizona, in coastal California, or in the Willamette Valley of Oregon and along Puget Sound, in the emerging Mor-

The Geography of
the North American
Railroad Company

mon towns around the edges of the Great Basin, and in dots of settlement at the site of mines for precious metals in the Colorado, Montana, and Idaho Rockies and in the basin ranges of Nevada. Although these were the ostensible goals for the promotion of the Northern Pacific, the Atchison, and the Texas Pacific, as the latter two were then popularly known, we had best look at another aspect of railroad development in the United States to reach an understanding of the historical geography of this activity.

The Natural Territory

As railroad companies grew from short lines linking two adjacent towns on the East Coast into trans-Appalachian routes and then alignments tying the eastern ports with points of articulation along the Mississippi or the western Great Lakes, the theoreticians of this development, though in the background in corporate councils, tended to advance the notion of the *natural territory* of a company. In the area east of the western Great Lakes–Mississippi River, such territories had a fundamentally linear quality; they were connections across the mountains from a specific eastern port to the Middle West and ultimately to its great articulation points—Chicago and St. Louis in the North, Memphis and New Orleans in the South. As we have already seen, the major northern trans-Appalachian routes all sought to reach Chicago and St. Louis, and all save the Erie made it to both. For the South the major trans-Appalachian systems were those of the Southern Railway and the Louisville and Nashville. Again, each reached Memphis and New Orleans, and because the South was as interested in ties with the Middle West as with the Old Southwest, each reached to the articulation points at Cincinnati and Louisville on the Ohio River. In this way the "natural territories" of these penultimate eastern railroad companies had, by the turn of the century, been staked out as extending from the seaboard to the western Great Lakes–Mississippi River in the West and to the Ohio in the South for the northeastern railroads, and from the coast to the Mississippi and the Ohio for the southeastern lines. But within these blocks there tended to be intense competition among companies, so the concept of "natural territory" was one of extent rather than monopoly.

West of the Mississippi River articulation points, projected northward to Chicago, Milwaukee, and Duluth on the lakes, a different theory was advanced —that of a *natural monopoly of territory*. Certainly the notion of extent was implicit in this. The Union Pacific considered not only that its "territory" was the central Great Plains, but also that that tributary region should extend untouched by the lines of other railroads as far west as its line of ultimate accommodation with the Central Pacific, which had been established at Ogden in Utah. West of that "boundary" the Central Pacific became wildly proprietary of a territory that reached to the Pacific and was thought to be absolute within, and coextensive with, California. For the remainder of the nineteenth century Collis Huntington was both vigilant and vigorous in defending California as the fief of the Central Pacific (termed the Southern Pacific after 1884) to the extent that his efforts carried the company's lines northward to Portland, eastward to New Orleans, and, through its St. Louis Southwestern (Cotton Belt) subsidiary, to St. Louis.

Union Station at St. Louis was the ultimate in stations when it opened in time for the 1904 World's Fair, the largest exposition up to then. Combining the terminals of all the railroads converging on St. Louis, with thirty-two tracks it was the largest station ever constructed, though now reduced to only a few actual tracks used by Amtrak service to Chicago, Kansas City, Carbondale (Illinois), and Little Rock. Fortunately, the building survives and has been restored as a major shopping and cultural center. *Source:* Library of Congress picture.

As the Atchison built westward from the Great Bend of the Missouri right after the Civil War, it envisaged such a "territory" for itself, extending to and within the Rockies at least as far as Santa Fe and the mining towns of Colorado's Western Slope. When Pennsylvania Railroad interests, personified by the great Philadelphia company's vice president Thomas Scott, promoted the Texas and Pacific, that newly organized Great Plains line gained grand notions of its ordained "territory," refusing to yield the area west of El Paso to the Southern Pacific line then actively being driven eastward by Huntington (much to the consternation of his three traditional associates, who thought they were already beyond remedy in debt). Both Huntington and Scott had become dogmatists; they believed that their "natural territories" had to reach from sea to sea. Starting on the Gulf, Scott thought he must reach the Pacific at San Diego; starting on San Francisco Bay, Huntington thought he would not develop his company's ordained mission unless he reached the Gulf. In the late 1870s Scott ran out of money and had to give up at El Paso, but Huntington managed to maintain his credit—he never had that much actual money to work with—and carried his line to Houston, and then on to the west bank of the Mississippi at Algiers opposite New Orleans.

These are the more graphic examples of the concept of the "natural territory"; most western railroad development has such an element in its geographi-

By the latter part of the nineteenth century the commanding tower had become the *signum* of the great city station. Worcester, Massachusetts, played the role of the crossroads of New England railroads with lines to Boston, Providence, Norwich (Connecticut), Springfield and Albany, Amherst and Northampton, Gardner, Fitchburg, Montréal, Québec City, Lowell, Portland and Bangor, and the Maritimes. This station with extensive train sheds survived as a Victorian gothic structure until after the Second World War. (It had already been replaced by the more stylish neoclassical structure rendered in architectural terra cotta in the era of the "new" Grand Central in New York and other giant stations in large cities from Boston to Oakland. Note the suburban trolley to Leicester and Spencer departing, as was typical, from the central city union station. *Source:* Photo courtesy of Massachusetts Historical Society.

cal pattern. When blocked at the Royal Gorge of the Arkansas River west of Pueblo in Colorado, the by then renamed Atchison, Topeka, and Santa Fe Railway could not accept that stalemate, so it quickly sent its locating engineers into Raton Pass south of the Arkansas River to gain a new line to the Pacific yet farther to the south, but again along a route examined by the Pacific Railroad Survey in 1854. Subsequently, when confronted by the aggressive defense by the Southern Pacific of its "territory" in California at both the Yuma and the Needles crossings of the Colorado River, the Santa Fe turned again southward, seeking a Pacific port on the Gulf of California in Mexico. By that time Huntington had decided that Sonora in Mexico was also part of the Southern Pacific's fief, so he made a victory out of adversity: because he was short of capital, he sold to the Santa Fe the line nearing completion that the SP had built from Mojave to the Needles in California, in return both gaining money and assuring the abandonment of the other company's line to the Gulf of California. California was simply too bright a prize to be denied permanently to all other railroads, so Huntington settled for the west coast of Mexico, which the Southern Pacific managed to monopolize until its line was expropriated by the Mexican government in 1951.[2]

We shall see the concept of the "natural territory" applied repeatedly in the trans-Mississippi West. For now it is sufficient to note that the other transconti-

THE NORTH
AMERICAN
RAILROAD

The Boston and Albany Railroad was rich and powerful in the late nineteenth century. Its line from Framingham to Boston had virtually no grade crossing and operated with three or four tracks. It had a set of suburban stations of great architectural merit. Some were designed by America's first great architect, H. H. Richardson, certainly by his office if not by him personally. The picture shows the station at Natick, an industrial satellite and emerging suburb possessed of commuter service by the early 1850s. *Source:* Photo courtesy of the Massachusetts Historical Society.

nental routes—the Northern Pacific, the Great Northern, the Milwaukee, and the Rio Grande–Western Pacific—all had considerable elements of asserted geographical destiny in their layout and history. Grodinsky has provided us with an insight into the way the concept gripped the prime actors in railroad development, those men who might determine the corporate control of various routes even if nature and the Pacific Railroad Survey had actually determined and defined the routes. Consider, for example, the activities of Henry Villard, whose role as the guardian of the North American interests of a group of German investors had led to his effort to salvage their earlier investments in steam navigation and railroad short lines in Oregon. Grodinsky tells of Villard's success in amalgamating those disparate enterprises:

Villard has scored another notable success, [after which he] was swept away by the boom psychology. He envisioned dreams of a truly imperialistic character. He looked forward to the creation of a transportation monopoly in the area between Seattle and San Francisco. He would build a railroad from Portland east to a connection with the Northern Pacific in southwestern Washington. He would build another road south and east to join a Union Pacific extension from Salt Lake City. His road would thus serve as the outlet for the Union Pacific and the Northern Pacific to the rapidly growing Northwest. He would make heavy investments in coal, timber, and agricultural resources. He would thereby not only realize profits from their exploitation but also feed his railroad lines with an abundant volume of business. He would also extend the unfinished roads from Portland south to the California boundary. There he would connect with Huntington's Central Pacific.[3]

The Geography of
the North American
Railroad Company

The modern station was created for Amtrak in Union Station, Washington, D.C. *Source:* Amtrak photo.

Such plans could be dreamed up, but the execution was often constrained or diverted by the dreams of other territorial imperialists. In Villard's case Collis Huntington and Jay Gould eyed "territories," for the Southern Pacific and Union Pacific respectively, that did not accord with the incipient domain of the Oregon Railway and Navigation Company that Villard organized. In the end, it was easier for Villard to take over the Northern Pacific Railway, in an American *Drang nach Osten* that carried his interests and those of his investors all the way to St. Paul, but away from the "territories" of the UP and SP. Those companies developed essentially exclusive territories in eastern Oregon, southern Idaho, northern Utah, and Wyoming for the Omaha road and in the Willamette Valley, southern Oregon, and northern California for the Sacramento line. Such a balancing of power had to take place when strong forces sought control of the same "territory." But the result in the American West was, at least for a generation, a fairly clear separation of those "territories" that did evolve from the initial contest. Only in the lowland between Portland and Seattle and in the Los Angeles Basin was there competition from the beginning, and the developments a generation later added modest competition only in the Bay Area and the Central Valley of California. It waited for the early 1980s for the territorial balance finally to be questioned, a full century after it was originally evolved. That balance has been shaken by the effort of the Union Pacific—via its merger with the Missouri Pacific and the Western Pacific—to expand its role in the Pacific Northwest on the relict of the bankrupt Milwaukee road, and to assert a growing pattern of transcontinental service in the face of the Southern Pacific's expansion into the bankrupt domain of the Rock Island road.

The Construction of the Transcontinentals: The United States

It is impossible to cover in as much detail as that given to the first transcontinental the lines that followed. Within less than fifty years nine other transcontinental

200

THE NORTH
AMERICAN
RAILROAD

TABLE 2 Transcontinental Construction

Transcontinental Line	Termini	Date Completed
Southern Pacific	New Orleans/San Francisco	January 1883
Atchison, Topeka, and Santa Fe	Kansas City/Los Angeles	August 1883
Northern Pacific	St. Paul/Portland	September 1883
Canadian Pacific	Montréal/Vancouver	May 1885
Great Northern	St. Paul/Seattle	June 1893
Chicago, Milwaukee, St. Paul, and Pacific	Chicago/Seattle	May 1909
Western Pacific (as completion of Denver and Rio Grande and Missouri Pacific)	Salt Lake City/Oakland (St. Louis/Oakland)	July 1911
Grand Trunk Pacific (as completion of National Transcontinental)	Winnipeg/Prince Rupert (Moncton/Prince Rupert)	February 1914
Canadian Northern	Montréal/Vancouver	January 1915

lines were completed, six more in the United States and three in Canada. Since then, no further line of a transcontinental nature has been undertaken. The pattern of transcontinental construction emerged as shown in Table 2. In addition, several other lines of a semicontinental nature were undertaken in this same period. As early as 1881 a transcontinental route of sorts existed in the use of the completed section of the Southern Pacific Railroad extending as far east as Sierra Blanca, Texas, some eighty miles east of El Paso, where it met the Texas and Pacific Railroad being built westward from Shreveport. As that Gould line was at daggers drawn with Huntington's Southern Pacific, no very effective junction was made, though the T&P did secure running rights over the SP westward into El Paso, where transfers took place with decreasing frequency once the California giant gained its own line to the west bank of the Mississippi at Algiers opposite New Orleans in 1883.

Modifications of this transcontinental pattern came with some regularity in the remainder of the nineteenth century. In 1884 the Oregon Short Line Railroad was completed to a junction with the Oregon Railway and Navigation line that had been projected eastward across the Blue Mountains of Oregon. Although the track was completed in February 1884, a four-foot gap in the Snake River bridge leading to the junction at Huntington, Oregon, delayed the first passenger train over this new line from Omaha to Portland until January 1, 1885.[4] Once opened, the Oregon Short Line not only gave to the Union Pacific the branch that Frederick Lander had seen thirty years before as the desirable route for the first transcontinental; it also opened to that company a field for development in the Pacific Northwest that it has pursued right down to the present with its efforts to take over the "abandoned" relics of the Milwaukee Railroad transcontinental line in Washington.

In the Northwest the line that had been seen as the main route to those parts had entered its empire in a rather equivocal manner. The Northern Pacific Railway had been under construction for some fifteen years when it finally made a connection of its eastern and western sections in Montana in 1883 when Henry Villard drove the last spike. Even then, this continuous route was accomplished by using the track constructed by the Oregon Railway and Navigation Company between Wallula Junction (Washington) and Portland, a distance of 214 miles, a fact that accounts for the intrusion of Villard at this stage into the history of the Northern Pacific. Villard, as we have already seen, became engaged in Oregon railroading as the agent of German investors, and in so doing he came to dominate the Oregon Railway and Navigation Company. To use that company as the conquering army for the first empire he envisioned, he had to assure its eastern connections. Doing so, he gained control of the Northern Pacific and sought to turn its westward course away from its long-assumed terminus at Tacoma to Portland, the capital of the Oregon empire Villard envisioned. In this process Villard downgraded Tacoma to the status of a branch terminal, building a mean wooden station that was not even conveniently central in what was as yet no more than a small town.[5] But Villard's control was short-lived, crashing along with his other speculations in 1884. Once he was off the stage, his successors returned to the traditional route, essentially that along the 47th parallel, and sought to complete the Cascade Division that would see the Northern Pacific across that range directly from eastern Washington to the Puget Lowland at Tacoma. Impatience for the delay already met gripped the company, so it sought an expedient line over Stampede Pass, using steep grades and switchback tracks, to open a route before the tunnel under that notch in the Cascade crest could be bored. The switchback line opened on June 1, 1887, a date that in the matter of the historical mission of the Northern Pacific can be considered its actual completion. The tunnel was completed in May of the next year, affording the city on Commencement Bay a reasonably graded and direct route to St. Paul and the East.[6]

Two other modifications of the simple transcontinental pattern that had first been delineated in the 1854 Pacific Railroad Survey came in the era under the financial control of Edward H. Harriman, when the Southern Pacific was owned and operated in essential concert with the Union Pacific, which was the initial interest that magnate had in western railroading. By constructing a branch northward from El Paso to Tucumcari in eastern New Mexico, junction might be secured with the Rock Island Railroad, which had reached that point in 1902. In this way southern California could be tapped by the Southern Pacific on a line far less indirect than required of the company to serve that growing region via the original transcontinental route as far west as Sacramento. In 1876 the San Joaquin Valley branch was completed over the Tehachapis, at 2,734 feet, to reach the Los Angeles Basin. In any direct competition with the Santa Fe route to Chicago from southern California the Southern Pacific was at a considerable disadvantage, so long as those flows had to pass via Sacramento on the Overland Route shared with the Union Pacific or the Sunset Route via Houston or New Orleans. But with the Rock Island connection at Tucumcari, a new and reasonably direct line, fulsomely named the Golden State Route, was obtained.

Three years later this vast UP-SP system created another articulation in its

THE NORTH
AMERICAN
RAILROAD

network. This came when a line between Los Angeles and Salt Lake City was completed. The route had been pioneered by two of the moguls involved in the very private sport of railroad warfare in late-nineteenth-century America. In the early 1890s a subsidiary of the Union Pacific, the Oregon and Utah Northern, had graded a 290-mile line southwestward from Salt Lake City into the Meadow Valley Wash of southeastern Nevada, only there to abandon the whole project during the Panic of 1893. Soon thereafter William Clark, who had made a fortune in Montana mining, decided to promote a railroad from the San Pedro roadstead of Los Angeles northward to that city and then eastward and across the San Gabriel Mountains, via Cajon Pass, to gain the Great Basin and ultimately Salt Lake City. This ambitious promotion was advanced when he secured running rights over the existing Santa Fe line through Cajon Pass, from San Bernardino to Daggett (just east of Barstow), thus breasting the first terrain barrier in its way. But in passing northward in the plateaus of eastern Nevada and southwestern Utah, Clark's line needed to occupy Meadow Valley Wash, as had the UP's earlier grade. When this became evident Edward Harriman quickly sought to resurrect the Oregon and Utah Northern project so as to protect his "natural territory" from possible invasion by the interests of the Gould railroads (Missouri Pacific, Texas and Pacific, Denver and Rio Grande, and St. Louis Southwestern in the West) making common cause with Clark. In an agreement with the latter, Harriman secured half an interest in his project, in return for yielding Clark half an interest in the Oregon and Utah Northern undertaking, and a guarantee that Gould would be kept from joining this line to his Denver and Rio Grande. This joint ownership persisted for sixteen years after the San Pedro, Los Angeles, and Salt Lake City Railroad opened in 1905, but in 1921 the UP decided to buy out Clark for $29 million so as to control this route to southern California at a time when the Harriman interests were forced to divest themselves of their control of the Southern Pacific.[7]

A Geography of Railroad Competition

In the case of the Los Angeles–Salt Lake City line and the Golden State Route, we encounter a feature that came to play an increasing role in the development of western railroads. This was the substitution of a geography of railroad competition for the more straightforward geography of terrain minimization that had characterized and guided the Pacific Railroad Survey in the 1850s. Thus, we may distinguish two fundamental periods in the expansion of the American rail network into the West: the first, extending between 1862 and 1885, was the time of realization of the lineaments that had been laid down during the Pacific Railroad Survey with companies formed to accomplish that goal (normally along a single route), and the second, extending from 1886 to 1915, was the period of competitive positioning during which companies that had been created to develop a single route undertook to make an aggressive entry into the "natural territory" of one or several other lines. During the first phase the force that guided location was basically physical geography, save for distant termini, as few large settlements existed to guide the alignment away from the physically easiest route considered. The second phase, however, was most critically shaped by the burgeoning settlement geography of the West, and the desire to attach as many potential "markets" to a company's lines as possible.

There was obviously some slight overlap in the two periods, in the mid-1880s, and there was an unusual case with respect to the first transcontinental. Because the first line had been created by an act of Congress and given to two companies to build, those companies initially had less than a full route, less than the logical "natural territory" they might have expected. To compensate for that restriction, both the Union Pacific and the Central Pacific (Southern Pacific) sought almost immediately to develop their own completely transcontinental route. In the case of the Southern Pacific this was extremely obvious: the line pushed southeastward from Oakland toward the Colorado River, occupying the two possible crossings, at the Needles and Yuma, and then forging ahead on the 32d-parallel route without any authorization from the federal government. Originally the company had envisioned using the easiest route from the viewpoint of terrain, passing eastward from the northern base of the San Gabriel Mountains at what became Palmdale and dropping off the Mojave Plateau through Cajon Pass to gain the eastern edge of the Los Angeles Basin at San Bernardino. But by the early 1870s when this route was being advanced, the pueblo of Los Angeles had become a city—still of modest size, but sufficient to offer the payment of $250,000 if the SP would divert its advancing transcontinental route through the San Fernando Valley and the water gap of the Los Angeles River to reach the ever-confident pueblo before heading eastward across the basin to return to the originally projected line at San Bernardino. In this way the increasing attraction of an established market, even when modest, began to show in the location of these lines.

The Union Pacific was in a far shakier financial position during its early years, so what efforts it could make to occupy its "natural territory" came through limiting the competition on its eastern section, between Cheyenne and Omaha. On this section the original legislation had authorized the building of a Kansas feeder, the Kansas Pacific, which soon sought by a branch from Denver to

Cheyenne to intercept the rather modest flow of goods and people passing on the Overland Route of the first transcontinental. As originally organized, the line from Cheyenne to Denver, the Denver Pacific Railroad, was built with considerable UP participation and was operated in concert with the objectives of that company when it was opened in June 1870. But the Kansas Pacific Railroad, which reached Denver in August, stood as a threat to the transcontinental line until it came under UP control in 1880.[8]

Having resolved the intrusion into its "natural territory" in the east, the Omaha company turned its attention to its western connections, viewed with concern once the Central (Southern) Pacific Company began actively to pursue its own transcontinental line via Yuma and El Paso. The first thrust to expand the UP's "natural territory" came, however, in the building of Lander's Oregon branch of the 41st-parallel route. Grenville Dodge saw this route as the easiest to the Pacific coast, and "ere long it will become the great through route from the northwest, and control the trade and traffic of the Indies."[9] Even before the Overland Route was joined at Promontory, the UP had sent an engineering party to find the best route to the Columbia. Dodge clearly expressed the territorial imperative that affected all rail developers in this period: "I shall always think that the mission of the Union Pacific Railroad is not fulfilled until it builds this branch to the Pacific Ocean."[10] But Oliver Ames, the often-maligned president of the railroad, brought such imperial objectives into accurate focus when he argued, "I am satisfied that the Road to Oregon will be a first rate operation when the time comes for doing it. But with the amt. of other work we have the present year on hand and the probability that all aid by gov't. will be refused the lines of Pacific Railroad until those now in progress have been completed leads me to think the Oregon Road will get the go bye this year."[11]

The wait was considerable, until the early 1880s, when the market potential of the Northwest must have seemed a hedge against any diversion of traffic that might result from the Southern Pacific's completion of its Yuma line. The catalytic element was furnished by the activity of Henry Villard in the Oregon Country when, in 1879, he organized the Oregon Railway and Navigation Company to build a rail line up the Columbia, passing along its gorge through the Cascades, toward the mining communities then springing up in eastern Oregon and in Idaho. One branch was projected toward La Grande and Baker in the Blue Mountains in the eastern part of Oregon. Such a thrust clearly came close to the Snake River Plain that the UP, since the late 1860s, had come to consider its own territory, causing that company to take quick action. Sidney Dillon, then president of the line, acted forcefully. He recalled, "I had that Oregon Short Line built. . . . I gave it that name myself at Omaha, and created it and fixed it up at that time, and telegraphed to [company headquarters in] Boston that with their concurrence we would build that road." In part his quick response was with a look over his shoulder at the Southern Pacific, because, as he said, if they "shut down the gate at Ogden, and the traffic goes around the other way, we can [then] stand it."[12]

The original plan had been to build the Oregon Short Line from Kelton on the Central Pacific west of Promontory, but the UP was unable to work out a practical arrangement with the California company, so it started construction of a far better line beginning at Granger west of the Green River in Wyoming.

Thence during 1881 a reasonably graded railroad of fifty miles was completed. The next year the railhead was advanced some 270 miles farther to Shoshone, Idaho, crossing the generally level lava plateau, with the main obstacle being furnished by the bridging of the Snake River at the American Falls. Even with the desire to defend its "territory," the UP still diverted its attention for six months to construct a branch to the Wood River mining district from Hailey on the main line to Ketchum (later Sun Valley) near the diggings. On June 7, 1883, attention returned to the main line west of Shoshone, and in February 1884 the grade was completed to the last crossing of the Snake at Huntington, Oregon, where 542 miles from Granger junction was made with the Oregon Railway and Navigation line.[13] In the almost immediate collapse of Villard's Oregon empire, the UP managed to gain control of the line west of Huntington, thus pushing its northwestern frontier to the Willamette Valley and ultimately to Puget Sound.

By the mid-1880s the territorial objectives of the early western lines had for the most part been gained. The two partners in the original (Overland) route had each contrived to project a line to the other's "coast"—to New Orleans on the Mississippi for the Southern Pacific and to Portland on the Columbia's Willamette tributary for the Union Pacific. In each case the construction was considerably easier than it had been for the original company building on its segment of a transcontinental route. The Southern Pacific encountered some heavy grades in crossing the basin range, Mohawk Mountain, west of Tucson, but generally its course through the low desert was easy, with one five-mile-long curve and a tangent or straight track of forty-seven miles heading east from there. East of Tucson the climb stiffened up through the canyons that form the edge of the plateau that here is the North American cordillera, but these were minor obstacles in comparison with the Sierra Nevada, so the course of construction was rapid. Yuma had been reached in May 1877, only eight months after the first line from San Francisco to Los Angeles had been completed. Just four years after the SP entered Arizona it was completed to El Paso, on May 19, 1881.[14]

But even there the drive for their own transcontinental line led the Big Four to push construction eastward at a feverish pace, now to limit the territorial expansion of Thomas Scott and the Philadelphians backing the Texas and Pacific. The key to the 32d-parallel route was the crossing of the intervening basin range at Sierra Blanca, which the Southern Pacific raced to occupy ahead of the Texas and Pacific. Gaining that ground, the SP was secure in its hold of the Southwest, even forcing the Texas and Pacific to enter El Paso through a trackage agreement over its rails from Sierra Blanca westward and stopping Scott's westward push of empire at that point. From Sierra Blanca eastward the crews faced some deeply trenched rivers, particularly on the Rio Grande and its Pecos tributary, the latter originally crossed at its confluence with the Rio Grande. Only in 1892 was this section of the line improved through the construction of the highest railroad bridge in the United States, the 321-foot-high Pecos River span, which kept the railroad out of the deep valleys and on the gently sloping plateau that drops from West Texas toward the Atlantic.[15] It was at this river crossing, on the original low-level structure, that the last spike of the line from New Orleans (Algiers) to Los Angeles was driven on January 12, 1883.

In order to reduce grades in the high plains of eastern New Mexico and Texas, and again on the plateaus of northern Arizona, spindly steel bridges were built to allow rail lines to cross broadly flat surfaces without having to descend into deeply trenched valleys. *Source:* Museum of New Mexico photo.

The Northern Pacific Railway

It is important to realize that the Northern Pacific Railroad was organized only a short time after the Overland Route, in 1864, but it represented the undertaking of an earlier proposal. This was the route that Asa Whitney advanced in the mid-1840s as the first—at that time the only practicable—transcontinental railroad for the United States. As organized, the project was particularly a child of northern New England. Maine interests—led by Josiah Perham, who had early promoted a People's Pacific Railroad over the northern route—joined with those involved with the Vermont Central to organize the company even before the Civil War ended. Securing money proved difficult until Jay Cooke of the Philadelphia investment firm of that name took up the project in 1869. With funds in hand, construction began on the eastern end in 1870 and advanced fairly rapidly across the rolling glacial till and lake-bed deposits that made up the surface of northwestern Minnesota and the eastern Dakotas. With its original cheap construction, the Northern Pacific managed to reach its crossing place of the Missouri River, which when laid out by the company in 1873 was named Bismarck, partly in recognition of the German investors whose money had paid for some of the 446 miles from St. Paul. In September 1873 the ardent search for further funds by Jay Cooke and Company proved ineffectual, and that firm—probably then the most prominent of American investment houses—closed its doors, precipitating the severe Panic of 1873 and specifically ending construction on the Northern Pacific.

  Only in the late 1870s did the financial climate improve sufficiently to make further bond sales possible and new construction practical. The Northern Pacific was under way again, building westward from Bismarck—actually from Mandan, Dakota Territory, on the west bank of the river—and eastward and west-

The Geography of
the North American
Railroad Company

ward from Glendive, Montana Territory, where construction material could be deposited by riverboats passing up the Missouri and its Yellowstone tributary. In 1879, when the grading entered the Yellowstone Valley at Glendive, at 2,000 feet elevation and 667 miles west of St. Paul, there was a natural route nearly as fine as that along the Platte in Nebraska for the next 341 miles to Livingston, Montana Territory, at an elevation of 4,510 feet. The graded valley of the Yellowstone provided most of the essential rise toward the Rockies, leaving only about a thousand feet to be surmounted before the Continental Divide.

Beyond Livingston the westering line had to turn away from the Yellowstone, which rises in the great lava plateau that is Yellowstone National Park, and attack directly the first of the Rockies' spurs, the Gallatin Range—a significant barrier there at about fifty-five hundred feet. Using a tributary valley to its head and then a steep ramp to climb the 996 feet to the eastern portal of a 3,610-foot tunnel under the crest, grades were held to a maximum of 116 feet to the mile, the magic 2.2 percent.[16] Only later did the company build a 12.2-mile side-hill ramp with a uniform and continuous grade from Livingston to Muir at the eastern portal of the Bozeman Tunnel, thus making the westbound crossing more manageable. On the western slope of Bozeman Pass a heavy grade could not be avoided, as there was a drop of six hundred feet to be taken in about six miles. Once in the Gallatin Valley, however, the terrain became more amenable to railroad building, and a reasonably straight and level line could be carried from Bozeman for thirty miles to Three Forks, where the Jefferson, Gallatin, and Madison rivers come together to form the Missouri. The alignment continued down the confluent river with the loss of only a couple of hundred feet more before turning west along the foot of the main chain of the Rockies, to gain Helena twenty miles to the northwest but at the same thirty-nine-hundred-foot elevation.

It was at Helena that the Northern Pacific encountered its major terrain barrier in the Rockies, the passage of the Continental Divide in the Montana Front Range at Mullan Pass. Between the territorial capital and the eastern portal of the tunnel that was driven under the crest of the pass, a distance of twenty miles, 1,618 feet had to be risen. Grades were kept reasonable by using a winding side-hill line, and a couple of sharp loops could be introduced to lengthen the run. "Originally the road was carried over the summit but on the completion of the tunnel the high line was abandoned. The upgrade continues through the tunnel, which is 3,875 feet long, and reaches the highest point at Blossburg, at the far end. . . . The traveler has now crossed the backbone of the continent."[17] The trip down the Pacific slope repeats the experience to the east, where the locating engineers utilized the graded courses of river valleys as much as possible to avoid excessive grades and redundant rises and falls.

The Pacific slope from the Continental Divide westward is, in this latitude, a jumble of mountains shaped from the Rockies themselves and the Idaho Batholith that lies to the west, as well as the broadest part of the Cascade Range that rims the Columbia Lava Plateau following to the west. It is impossible here to deal in any detail with the separate ranges, so we must settle for a brief summary of the route chosen, based mainly on the river courses on which it is aligned. Passing westward from Mullan Pass, the Northern Pacific used the Little Blackfoot River tributary of the Clark Fork of the Columbia and then that main stream to pass in deep valleys within this jumble of mountains to its west side at the slope of Lake Pend Oreille and onward across the Columbia Lava Plateau for the hundred miles to Spokane. At Spokane the engineers were fifteen hundred miles from St. Paul and finally west of the Rockies. In laying out their line they returned to taking account of the geography of railroads rather than that of nature. While the Northern Pacific was languishing from a shortage of investors, largely German and Dutch interests had gained a wide ownership of transportation in the Pacific Northwest, leading to the arrival of Henry Villard on the scene to look after those interests. By the time the Northern Pacific was approaching this Oregon Country from the east, Villard had become concerned about an intrusion into his empire, so he sought to be assured that the NP would make junction with his Oregon Railway and Navigation rail line at Wallula Junction in Oregon, fourteen miles south of the confluence of the Snake and the Columbia. This the Northern Pacific refused to promise, so to secure his existing traffic Villard sought control of the NP, thus assuring the use of his Oregon line for the 214 miles from Wallula Junction to Portland, while holding the NP main line to the 1,699 miles from St. Paul to Wallula. It was thus that matters were resolved when the line opened in 1883. The crossing of the Columbia Lava Plateau for the 150 miles beyond Spokane was relatively gentle in its descent westward, dropping the line down to 389 feet at Pasco, Washington, where the northern transcontinental finally reached the Columbia.

So long as the Northern Pacific and the Oregon Railway and Navigation line were jointly operated, the transcontinental was formed of those two companies, but in 1884, when Villard lost control of both, the Union Pacific soon gained control of the Oregon company, leaving the NP in what was seen as a vulnerable situation. To obviate that, the new proprietors began the construction of the uncompleted stretch of the 47th-parallel route, that across the Cascades from Pasco on the Columbia to Tacoma, the original terminus of the line. Builders had completed the eastern part of the Cascade Division in 1885, when track reached Yakima ninety miles up the Yakima River, which joins the Columbia just above Pasco. By passing up this reasonably graded valley the engineers gained six hundred feet in their assault on Stampede Pass notched into the crest of the Cascades east of Mount Rainier. Still, some nineteen hundred feet remained in their climb. To gain that component the line continued up the valley of the Yakima, here a deep canyon in the volcanics that make up this range. The next forty miles, to Ellensburg, carried the railroad to 1,500 feet, with the succeeding thirty-seven miles toward the headwaters of the Yakima adding another 600 feet to reach the foot of the mountain grade at Easton, at 2,176 feet. Thence westward the climb was stiff but short, making the use of helper engines effective. Between Easton and the eastern portal of the two-mile tunnel under the crest of Stampede Pass, 676 feet had to be gained in about nine miles. The American standard ruling grade, 116 feet to the mile (2.2 percent), could be kept to on this stretch. Only at the crest, where a temporary "high line" was carried in the open over the ridge during the construction period, would a stiffer grade have been required. On this temporary line a grade of 290 feet to the mile (5.4 percent) was accepted, but no economical working line could have tolerated such grades, so the tunnel was actively advanced to open in July 1888.[18]

Once that tunnel was opened, the trains could move westward within the

2.2 percent limit. On the Pacific slope the drop was sharp indeed, from 2,812 feet in the tunnel down to 1,875 feet at Weston, the helper-engine terminus on the west, in a distance of only some nine miles. Beyond, the descent toward Puget Sound was considerable, about seventeen hundred feet in the fifty miles from Weston to the Puyallup Lowland at Auburn, but still not much over 0.6 percent on the average. This was mountain railroading, but not impossible in its economic costs.

As completed in 1888, the Northern Pacific was 1,940 miles long between St. Paul and Tacoma, crossing the greatest width of the American cordillera with no more than two major crests. In the Cascades the normal American ruling grade could be maintained, but only at the expense of what was then the second longest tunnel in North America (after the Hoosac), drilled for over two miles through the volcanics of the Cascade crest. For such a long line crossing two major mountain ranges, the Northern Pacific was remarkably well engineered. Its "summits" were quite reasonable, fifty-five hundred feet in the Bozeman Tunnel, the same in the Mullan Tunnel, and twenty-eight hundred feet in the Stampede Tunnel. Only later, when a second main line was constructed between Three Forks and Garrison, Montana, to pass through the bonanza copper town of Butte, was a higher crest accepted, that at Homestake Summit (6,345 feet), which was crossed in the open. The relative efficiency of the Northern Pacific Railroad came from a very careful and wise accommodation to the pattern of streams that form the interfingered headwaters of the Missouri and Columbia rivers. In this the NP was the obvious successor to the explorations not merely of Isaac Stevens on the 47th-parallel railroad survey but of Lewis and Clark at the beginning of the nineteenth century.

The human and physical forces that shaped the Overland Route, the Southern Pacific line to the Gulf, the Santa Fe (constructed partially on the 38th- and then on the 35th-parallel route), and the Northern Pacific continued to operate so long as there was any additional plausible route that might be followed or territory that might be claimed. The Pacific Railroad Survey had been essentially accomplished in actual construction by the time the Northern Pacific was completed to Tacoma, save for the 49th-parallel route adjacent to the Canadian border. That this line was undertaken and completed in 1893 should not surprise us; what does startle is that a second railroad line was built along the alignments of the 47th-parallel route and adjacent to the Northern Pacific. These may be considered only briefly.

The Great Northern Railway

The origin of construction along the 49th-parallel route is to be found in the notion of the "natural territory" of railroad companies. In the 1860s, while Minnesota was still under the threat of Indian depredations, several small lines were proposed and undertaken that led to the formation of a grandly ambitious line called the St. Paul and Pacific Railroad. These efforts were poorly conceived geographically, and perhaps even more shaky in their physical structure. But once the Sioux had been driven westward and the Civil War had been concluded, the potential for a regional rail system in Minnesota was greatly improved. At that time James J. Hill, then an important steamboat operator on the Red River of the North, sought with the financial assistance of Donald A. Smith, the governor of the Hudson's Bay Company, and George Stephen, president of the Bank of Montreal, to gain control of the St. Paul and Pacific project with the idea of extending it to the Canadian border at Pembina, there to make juncture with the Canadian Pacific that was being promoted in Canada. The results of the Panic of 1873 finally opened the way, forcing the St. Paul Company to accept the Canadian capitalists' 1878 offer, at about one-fifth the actual worth of the line. As the managing partner in the operation, Hill quickly set about building the line to the border from St. Paul, reaching that point in 1879. The rapid settlement of western Minnesota and the Red River Valley, and the considerable movement of freight westward over this route to be used in the construction of the Canadian Pacific Railway then getting under way in the prairies, made the St. Paul and Pacific—now renamed the St. Paul, Minneapolis, and Manitoba—highly profitable. This base ultimately wrought great things in the prairies; the wealth that Smith and Stephen gained from the venture aided their entrance into the promotion of the Canadian Pacific, while the capital it provided to Hill led him to invest, with vast profit, first in Minnesota iron-ore lands and ultimately in the construction of a transcontinental line to Puget Sound.

Once the Manitoba Road, as it was now called, had reached the border, it turned westward from Grand Forks, Dakota Territory, and started building one of several branches into the prairies in search of grain shipments to support the line. The railhead was pushed westward across Dakota north of the Missouri River, reaching Minot in 1886. From there Hill pushed rapidly westward in 1887, completing 550 miles of grade in the astounding period of only four months.[19] Once iron was laid, this branch to Great Falls on the Missouri River proved quite profitable as Montana coal began moving to the Minnesota market; and with the line connected via the Hill-controlled Montana Central Railroad to Helena and Butte, a new though somewhat circuitous transcontinental route existed between the Manitoba Road to Butte and the Oregon Short Line thence to Pocatello and Portland. But such a sharing of the market was not in Hill's character, so he almost immediately began to think in terms of his own route to the Pacific. Using great care in locating the line—seeking broad curves, the best grades, and the shortest route—he had the line located by 1890. He sought a new way through the Rockies, better in most ways than any that had been found before its time.

Several forces encouraged the extension of the Manitoba Road—soon to be renamed, more encompassingly, the Great Northern Railway—to the Pacific. During the 1880s, while the Manitoba Road was being extended into the northern Great Plains, Hill had shown the two sides of his character that made him probably the greatest of the western railroad builders: he was a genius at developing a market for his company, and he was willing to invest money in the early years to gain greater profits with the passage of time.

Unlike the earlier generation of moguls—Huntington, Gould, Dillon, and the like—Hill seems never to have intended to move in and out of rail ownership simply for speculative gains. All evidence suggests that his motive was to develop the best route he could, built it well, create a supportive market, and then reap his profits as the continuing owner of the line. Certainly he was *sui generis* in his era—as ruthless as any railroad promoter but, like Elias Hasket Derby, con-

The Geography of the North American Railroad Company

vinced that reasonable rates would return much more in the long run than the monopolistic rates of the initial period might gain. Above all others he understood what was required to create, develop, and maintain his perceived "natural territory"; and even in his grandeur he managed to collect the first-rate French Impressionists being painted in his time rather than the third-rate Renaissance paintings and genre pieces that would bring more contempt than regard for connoisseurship to most of the other railroad moguls.

The fact that the Northern Pacific had finally finished its Cascade line to Tacoma in 1888 gave that company a seeming competitive advantage over the Great Northern, while the Union Pacific at Butte—reached by Hill's Montana Central in 1889—proved a rather unwilling partner for any transcontinental route. Hill's experience in selling the St. Paul road's land grant in the Red River Valley, in encouraging homesteading in eastern Montana to pour wheat into the Manitoba Road's boxcars, in promoting and utilizing the Montana Central to carry coal from the mines of the Rocky Mountain foothills and copper from Butte—all these experiences had shown the man who was beginning to be called the Empire Builder the advantages to be secured from "development." As a trunk carrier he realized he must be transcontinental in his aspirations or else he would always be at the mercy of other such potential imperialists. But to become a transcontinental line, the Great Northern had to find a better way through the Rockies than that held by the Northern Pacific. Hill had several times in the 1880s forcefully expressed his view that the Northern Pacific was a poorly laid out line, with bad grades and tight curves, as well as a rather indirect route, all of which made operation expensive. When Hill set his mind on his own route to the Pacific Northwest, he clearly wished it to be a better operating proposition. For that he needed a simple pass through the Rockies, not the two summits the NP had (the one at Bozeman Pass, and the other at Mullan Pass). In addition, it was desirable that the pass be relatively low and reasonably approachable from both sides.

As early as 1806 the possible existence of such a pass had come into American geographical lore. In his expedition to the Pacific Captain Meriwether Lewis had heard from the Indians of a wondrous pass near the headwaters of the Marias River tributary of the Milk and Missouri that offered an easy route across the mountains. But the enmity of the Blackfoot tribe, whose range lay to the east of the mountains, kept him from reaching it. The fur trappers from Montréal had subsequently sought such an opening, but the Blackfeet again very effectively kept them away, forcing the mountains to be crossed several hundred miles to the north at Yellowhead and the other passes near the headwaters of the Athabasca River. Even as late as the time of the Pacific Railroad Survey, efforts were made to find the already-named but actually undiscovered Marias Pass. In 1853 Isaac Stevens had sent an aide, Abiel Tinkham, to try to reach this geographical abstraction from the Indians' blind side, from the headwaters of the Columbia system in the Flathead River. Tinkham did succeed in crossing the range and regaining Fort Benton in central Montana, but in doing so he passed through the cirque country of what became Glacier National Park, finding a pass only at some seventy-six hundred feet, with grades far too steep for any railroad.[20] Again Marias Pass as a usable route eluded discovery.

Even Hill's earliest efforts were without fruit, but he persisted, and in

December 1889 his insistence led to the dispatch of John F. Stevens to try his luck—or more particularly, his perseverance. Though he lacked any formal engineering training, Stevens was an experienced locating engineer who had already worked on finding a route through Tennessee Pass for the Denver and Rio Grande and through Kicking Horse Pass for the Canadian Pacific. Going by train to Havre, Montana, Stevens trekked westward to the base of the range. From a half-breed Flathead he learned basically where the pass must lie and so set forth to find it, even though it was December 11 and snowing hard. Abandoning a drunken assistant, he set out on snowshoes for the pass, reaching it at dark. It seemed to be what everyone had hoped for, but he had to survive the night to return with the news. To do so he beat down a circular path in the deep snow at the open summit and spent the night walking continuously "to survive the bitter forty-below-zero night."[21]

As surveyed in the spring, Marias Pass was indeed found to be the best of all crossings. At 5,215 feet it was, as Stevens recounted, "the lowest railway pass in the United States north of New Mexico."[22] And as Ralph Budd, a later president of the Great Northern, summarized the situation, "The actual location of it was at an altitude of five thousand two hundred feet on a one percent grade Westbound and 1.8 percent Eastbound, and without a summit tunnel. It fully confirmed Stevens' report. At one stroke the discovery of Marias Pass shortened the proposed line to the Coast by over one hundred miles, afforded better alignment, much easier grades, and much less rise and fall."[23] The Great Northern east of Havre was a true Great Plains line, rising gently along the course of well-graded rivers toward the cordillera. Even from Havre to East Glacier, some seventy miles, the new construction was of the same sort. Only in the twelve miles thence to the summit of Marias Pass was a grade as heavy as 1 percent encountered. The concentration of the heavier effort in this short distance was highly efficient, in comparison with the problems encountered on the Northern Pacific. Even dropping westward from the pass the line could be located in the Bear Creek and the Middle Fork of the Flathead River until it debouched into the broad structural depression (the Rocky Mountain Trench) of the Flathead Valley. Some two thousand feet of descent had to be taken in fifty miles, but there was no redundant grade.

Once in the Flathead Valley the complex rift terrain of northwestern Montana offered several graded courses between high ranges affording good grades in the passage of this great mountain block. The Rocky Mountain Trench itself provided a structural valley northwestward toward the Kootenai River at Rexford. In this way the Great Northern passed between the Galton and Flathead mountains until the erosional valley of the Kootenai (southwest of Rexford) gave a crossing between the Flathead and Purcell mountains and between the latter range and the Cabinet Mountains to reach the next structural valley, the Purcell Trench, at Bonners Ferry, Idaho, at an elevation of only 1,773 feet. Using the Purcell rift valley, the engineers could carry the line southward to the northern shore of Lake Pend Oreille, where the same lava-floored plain used by the Northern Pacific could be used to reach to Spokane and the open lava plateau of eastern Washington. Thus, the Great Northern was carried entirely across the Rockies in one of their wider stretches with only a single summit, and that the lowest in the mountains in the United States. It should be added, parenthetically,

The Geography of
the North American
Railroad Company

that starting in 1966 the then second longest tunnel in the Western Hemisphere was drilled through the Flathead Mountains, a distance of over seven miles, to cut off the northern detour via Eureka and Rexford, leading more directly westward from the Rocky Mountain Trench. This was done entirely at government expense as part of the flooding of the Kootenai Valley above Libby Dam, which submerged extensive sections of the Great Northern's original tracks.

West of Spokane the line could be carried across the lava plateau until it reached the Columbia at the confluence of the Wenatchee and then up that right-bank tributary toward the crest of the North Cascade Mountains. In its search for the most direct route to Puget Sound, the Great Northern sought to avoid the southward bend, to Pasco nearly on the Oregon boundary, that the Northern Pacific had accepted during construction (because its first entrance to the western lowland came via a connection to the Oregon Railway and Navigation line at Wallula Junction just south of the Oregon boundary). Even when the NP constructed the Cascade route via Stampede Pass to Tacoma, it began the assault on the western range first at Pasco only some eighteen miles farther north. But the Great Northern built directly westward from Spokane to Wenatchee and then sought to find a pass across the northern Cascades that would continue the direct line as close to Seattle as possible. The pass that was located, again by John Stevens, was almost as low (at 4,061 feet) as Stampede Pass, and it gave a far more direct route. But that route did bring its costs. If constructed in the open without a tunnel, the sixty miles of line from Wenatchee to the crest of Stevens Pass would have to climb some thirty-four hundred feet, more than a thousand of that in the last seven or eight miles, some at severe grades. On the western side the problem was even worse, leading to grades of 4 percent in the last pitch up from Scenic to the pass. As opened in 1893, this line had eight switchbacks where the train had to reverse direction as well as one horseshoe curve partly in a tunnel. The curvature was excessive, the grades brutal, and the snows very deep indeed. Probably no other stretch of railroad in the United States at this time, certainly no other transcontinental, was so taxing in its operation.

Given Hill's desire for a well-engineered line, the original Stevens' Pass section had to be no more than a temporary solution. The snows at the crest, if nothing else, made year-round operation extremely difficult. So soon after the Great Northern opened from St. Paul to Seattle, construction began on a tunnel under the pass, which managed to cut out the switchbacks, though not the horseshoe curve or much of the snow. When opened in 1900 this 2.63-mile tunnel still forced 4 percent ruling grades on the Great Northern. But even worse as an operating problem was the extremely heavy snow that piled up for many months here in the North Cascades. In order to get low enough to reduce the snow problem and the costly upkeep of miles of snowsheds and heavy plows, the company undertook what was then, and remained until late 1988, the longest railroad bore in the Western Hemisphere, the Cascade Tunnel of 41,152 feet or 7.79 miles. With the Cascade Tunnel, opened for service on January 12, 1929, the Great Northern finally gained the properly engineered line that Hill had always had in mind. In the fifty miles of original line over the Cascades between Peshastin and Scenic, all but seven miles was relocated, shortening the route by nearly nine miles as well as removing both the horseshoe curve and the snow-sheds. "Nearly 20,000 feet of tunnels, 40,000 feet of snowsheds and the equivalent of more than five complete circles of curvature were eliminated. The grade was reduced to 1.6 percent."[24] Thus, the ruling grade on the Great Northern was shifted back to the 1.6 percent climb up the Middle Fork of the Flathead River from the Rocky Mountain Trench to Marias Pass.

As built, the Great Northern was the best engineered of all the American transcontinentals, a status it did not lose even when two additional lines were completed in the twentieth century. Nature played its part, for Marias Pass was the truly exceptional opening it had been rumored to be for nearly ninety years. And the great rift valleys of western Montana also made a single-crested crossing of the Rockies possible (remember that the Flathead Tunnel was completed only just in time to be available when Amtrak began running the great *Empire Builder* in 1971, and then for the convenience of power generators rather than rail-roaders). Until the Cascade Tunnel was opened in 1929, the directness of the Great Northern's alignment across the Cascades was desirable, but its grades were not. But as Hill's practice of doing a great deal to encourage business in his "natural territory," his empire, was followed in western Washington, the Great Northern could undertake to bore that Cascade Tunnel on its own account without any government assistance, in the manner its whole line had been constructed.

In many ways it seems to me that the Great Northern was the first modern transcontinental to be built, showing how a railroad should be engineered and run to earn its keep rather than simply speculative profits for its promoters. Having shown the way, Hill's engineering and operating practices were taken up by others, by Harriman on the Union Pacific and Southern Pacific and by several chief operating officers of the Santa Fe. Those railroads were so massively rebuilt between the turn of the century and the Second World War that in many ways they stand as newer lines than the Great Northern, but still as pupils of its effective lesson.

In his effort to secure his empire, Hill expanded his control first to the Northern Pacific and then to his middle–western connection, the Chicago, Burlington, and Quincy. But a stockholders' suit blocked the formal merging of those lines, something that had to wait until the 1960s. It is not surprising that the corporate personification of Hill, the Burlington Northern, came into existence in the early 1980s to be the world's largest private railroad when it added to its own territory that reached by the St. Louis and San Francisco Railway, with which it merged. At that point the Burlington Northern stretched from western Florida to northeastern California, from the Gulf of Mexico at Galveston and Pensacola to the edge of the North in Vancouver, and from Chicago to most of the cities of the Great Plains and Rocky Mountains north of Raton Pass. In this successful merger campaign of the 1970s and 1980s the Burlington Northern became the great western railroad with access to parts of all western states save Nevada, Utah, Arizona, and New Mexico, and to the Middle West as far east as Chicago and the Old Southeast west of the Appalachians. In its takeover of the Frisco, whose ancestor was the Atlantic and Pacific Railroad of 1865, the Burlington Northern came close to being what that grandiose name implied.[25]

When the Atchison, Topeka, and Santa Fe Railway reached the high plains of northeastern New Mexico, as here at Wagon Mound, cattle ranching became the mainstay of the local economy. *Source:* Museum of New Mexico photo.

The Milwaukee Transcontinental

The occupation of a railroad company's "natural territory" led to the building of the third of the northern transcontinentals, the Pacific extension of the Chicago, Milwaukee, and St. Paul. That company, as its title identifies, began as a short line between Milwaukee and Waukesha, Wisconsin, expanding over the years to became the dominant line between Chicago and St. Paul–Minneapolis and perhaps the most prosperous of the granger roads that carried wheat from the northern plains to shipping points on the Great Lakes. Interest in the Milwaukee road was taken up by a number of wealthy eastern capitalists—the Rockefellers, the Harknesses, and E. T. Harriman in particular—whose efforts seemed threatened by the operating association of James J. Hill and J. P. Morgan in the creation of the "Northern Lines," starting with the Great Northern but expanded by control of the Northern Pacific. To contain that expansion Harriman sought to gain control of the Burlington road when its ownership was open to purchase, but he lost out to the Hill-Morgan effort. With the Northern Lines thus having direct access to Chicago, circumventing the Milwaukee, Harriman and William Rockefeller decided that the only defense for the prosperous granger road was a gentleman's agreement with Hill and Morgan. Such was accomplished in the creation of the Northern Securities Company in 1901, combining the two groups under the control of the Northern Pacific, but prosecution under the Sherman Antitrust Act, in 1904, forced a separation of the two groups. In that circumstance it was the conclusion of the directors of the Milwaukee that only their own line to the Pacific would guard their interests as they perceived them.[26] Within a year the company had decided to proceed with such an "extension" to begin from the terminus of its westernmost granger line at Evarts, South Dakota.

Thence a short construction carried the chosen branch to the Missouri River, where work on a large steel bridge was begun, creating the official eastern terminus of the undertaking at appropriately named Mobridge, South Dakota. Early in 1906 construction got under way on the fourteen-hundred-mile extension.

The construction across the Great Plains was notable mostly for the absence of settlement along the line chosen. In seeking new territory to develop, the Milwaukee's locating engineers had certainly found virgin ground. Only later was it realized how sterile much of it would remain. A casual reading of the timetable for this route is an introduction to the thinness of settlement in the northern Great Plains. Names of obscurity follow one another for most of the seven hundred miles to Butte. And those places of common note that are to be found were located in the Yellowstone River valley already served by the Northern Pacific. In terms of construction, the line was similar to the others crossing the plains; there were many small streams to bridge, some shallow canyons cut into the flat strata to thread through, and three major bridges across the Yellowstone to build. The Milwaukee faced the same obstacle as the Northern Pacific: it took a sufficiently southerly route across Montana to require it to climb over the Belt Range there lying in front of the main Rocky Mountain crest, though the original prospectus of the line pointed out that the route would be 150 miles shorter between Chicago and Seattle than the Burlington–Northern Pacific, and would have mountain grades between 1.7 and 1.8 percent in contrast to the NP grades of 2.2 percent.[27] Pipestone Pass was used in crossing the Continental Divide of that main chain of the Rockies east of Butte, but to keep even a 1.8 percent ruling grade a major tunnel had to be bored. Farther west the alignment was set to assault the Bitterroot Range directly west of St. Regis, Montana, where in the St. Paul Pass a tunnel was required to keep the grade reasonable. Beyond that crest the Milwaukee line passed down the St. Joe River valley south of Lake Coeur d'Alene to reach the lava plateau and Spokane. Avoiding the southward bend that history had put in the Northern Pacific, the Milwaukee road passed more directly westward to use the upper Yakima River valley to approach the Snoqualmie Pass across the Cascades, where the 3.62-mile Snoqualmie Tunnel was completed in 1915 to relieve the stiff grades and deep snows of the original "high line" in the open.

It is remarkable that yet a third distinct line between the Upper Midwest and Puget Sound could be found, perhaps even more remarkable that it was constructed. The completion of such a route came at the expense of two fatal flaws: there was extremely thin support along the line, and it faced unusually severe working conditions once opened. In the twenty-two hundred miles from Chicago to Tacoma, the first four-hundred-mile stretch was bordered by a prospering market. This of course was the original main line of the Milwaukee. West of Minneapolis, however, the towns were small. Aberdeen was the only sizable place in all of South Dakota, and Miles City was the largest settlement in Montana east of Butte that the railroad served. Butte itself had to be shared with three other railroads, the first the Union Pacific, then the Great Northern (Montana Central), and then the Butte line of the Northern Pacific. Once beyond the Copper City, the Milwaukee road managed to cross the Bitterroots not into the lead-zinc-silver area around Wallace and Kellogg but into the far less productive

The Geography of
the North American
Railroad Company

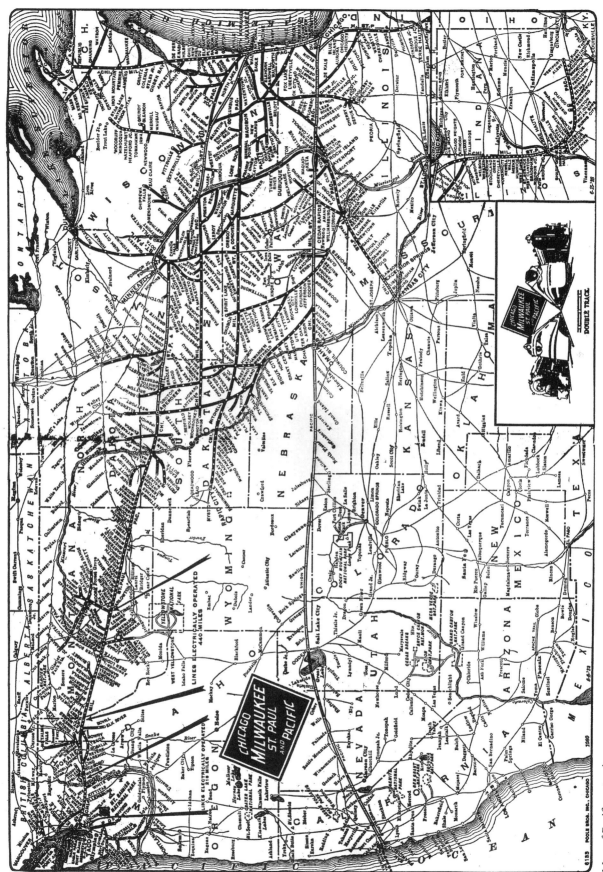

Map of Pacific extension. *Source:* Library of Congress.

St. Joe Valley to the south. Even in the Yakima Valley the Milwaukee tapped the less productive upper stretch. In this way the line managed to cross over eighteen hundred miles of ground between Minneapolis and Seattle-Tacoma with a remarkably small amount of on-line support. And in crossing that country four major mountain summits had to be climbed. The Belt Mountains were crossed at 5,799 feet, only to lose nearly 2,000 feet before climbing to 6,347 in the Pipestone Pass Tunnel east of Butte. Using the river valleys of western Montana, the line still had to climb back some 1,300 feet and pass through an 8,771-foot tunnel at 4,170 feet to transit the Bitterroots. From 541 feet on the Columbia River the Cascade line had to climb back to 2,584 feet in the Snoqualmie Tunnel, which took some 500 feet off the height of the pass as well as avoiding much of the winter snow.

The Milwaukee road extension was a striking case of a misappraisal of the market. The line had no significant on-line support that was not already shared by several other railroads. Only Butte and Spokane were sizable places, and they had become major rail junctions. And the seemingly endless summits on the line introduced so much curvature and grade that it was found difficult to operate with steam engines. The result was that the Milwaukee road became the first main-line railroad to engage in extensive electrification. Between 1914 and 1918 over six hundred miles of line were put under the catenary, with significant savings in energy cost, partly due to regenerative braking that put current back into the line, and operation was much improved. But the four summits remained, and the market along the line never grew very much. The result was that once the railroad industry as a whole was attacked by subsidized truck competition, the Milwaukee—by far the weakest of the transcontinentals—became bankrupt. And in the early 1980s it was decided to abandon the "Pacific extension," selling off bits and pieces to other railroads, notably the Union Pacific.

The Last Transcontinental: The Western Pacific

The last of the transcontinental railroads to be built in the United States came to occupy elements of the Pacific Railroad Survey that had been presented very equivocally in 1854, as impractical or at best unproved as to feasibility. Owing to Thomas Hart Benton's belief that there must be such a route along the 38th parallel, a survey had been run basically along that line seeking the vaunted Cochetopa Pass with its "practicable rail route." This was an effort to pin down an indeterminate, still only partially formed view that the route across the Colorado Rockies must be found toward the south. By survey a crossing of the Sangre de Cristo Range was found, but beyond that easternmost range no route passable by rail leading westward out of the San Luis Basin could be found. When the Union Pacific was undertaken, strenuous efforts were expended on trying to discover a route farther north in Colorado that would carry rails over the summit of the Front Range. All transit of the cordillera in Colorado seemed denied to a railroad. Once the Colorado mining booms began in the area behind the easternmost ranges, the efforts toward discovery of a route were redoubled and some progress was made. At the close of the Civil War, with the undertaking of the first transcontinental, a branch across Kansas, the original Union Pacific, Kansas Branch (later Kansas Pacific), was constructed under the supervision of a former Union general, William Jackson Palmer. It was his ceaseless inquiry as to geographical conditions in the area that led to the first proposal to construct a line southward from Denver, toward first the Arkansas River and then the Rio Grande, which germinated the complex plan that had this Denver and Rio Grande Railroad building a cross of lines. Joined at Pueblo on the Arkansas River just in front of the Rockies, that cross would have carried rails southward through Raton Pass into the high plains of northeastern New Mexico before reaching the Rio Grande valley between Santa Fe and Albuquerque, and a second line westward up the Arkansas into its Grand Canyon, later called more grandly the Royal Gorge, to reach beyond the Front Range into the auriferous areas within the mountain complex. Palmer tried to interest the Kansas Pacific managers in this scheme but they rejected it, so he resigned from their employ and set about promoting the company himself. In this he was successful, interesting capitalists in Philadelphia and elsewhere in the construction of a three-foot-gauge line southward from Denver toward El Paso.[28]

In south-central Colorado there were two geographical features, Raton Pass and the Royal Gorge, that seemed to hold the key to railroad development in the region. Given that fact, and the entrance into this area in the 1870s of two active railroad projects—the Atchison, Topeka, and Santa Fe building westward from the Great Bend of the Missouri River to the northward bend of the Arkansas River and then westward along that stream, and the Denver and Rio Grande pushing its thinner line southward from Denver over the high piedmont at the foot of the Rockies toward the sag where the Arkansas River cut its valley into the plains strata—conflict and a changing of plans were inevitable, unless an accommodation could be worked out. Neither General Palmer nor the Bostonians pushing the Santa Fe were ready for such a timid course, so confront forcefully they did. In the first "battle" the Santa Fe's locating engineers reached Raton Pass with their surveyor's stakes ahead of the Rio Grande, forcing that line for the time to abandon its eponymous objective. Determined not to lose the second geographical key, the Rio Grande's engineers and their henchmen managed to occupy the Royal Gorge just ahead of the Atchison's crew, and in greater force. Ultimately the matter had to be decided in proceedings in the United States Supreme Court, in which the Rio Grande became the victor, so that company was transformed from a north-south project in Colorado to one more dominantly east-west.

The Royal Gorge was not Cochetopa Pass, nor was South Park the San Luis Valley, but the vector of construction was the same and the latitude similar. At first, of course, the Rio Grande was merely constructing the line with the easiest grades between Denver and the gold fields of South Park. But ultimately, under the push and with use of the pocketbook of the Union Pacific, a second, more direct, railroad from Denver to Leadville—the Denver, South Park, and Pacific —was built, restricting the control the Rio Grande could exercise over this territory into which it had turned for support when New Mexico was denied it. Without here going into detail, we should note that the Rio Grande did manage to carve out a very significant territory for itself in southern Colorado and northern New Mexico, even reaching the Rio Grande there by building from the San Luis Valley southward to Santa Fe. But with a good line through the Royal Gorge—where the great groove in the mountain allows the railroad to pass on a

In rising southward out of the Purgatoire River valley (tributary of the Arkansas River of Colorado), the Santa Fe Railway was forced by too steep grades to resort to a tunnel under the crest ridge, the highest point on the transcontinental line. This Raton Tunnel became a favorite spot for photographing the locomotives of the time. This picture shows the north portal of the Raton Tunnel in the era of wood-burning locomotives. *Source:* Museum of New Mexico photo.

grade of about fifty feet per mile, in a valley up to eleven hundred feet deep and in some places little more than fifty feet wide at the bottom, with walls actually overhanging the river—the Rio Grande had an economically practicable route. By following the Arkansas River toward its headwaters the railroad could be kept within reasonable bounds for steam operation, through the climb was steady and not inconsiderable. Between Canyon City at the mouth of the Royal Gorge and Pleasanton, a distance of thirty-one miles, the railroad ran in a series of narrow canyons cut into an elevated plateau, with the line rising 997 feet in that distance. Beyond Pleasanton the alignment turned from southwest to northwest and began to follow the reasonably broad structural valley in which the river was flowing. At Salida (7,050 feet and fifty miles from Canyon City) a branch was

221

The Geography of the North American Railroad Company

subsequently constructed westward over Marshall Pass (at 10,846 feet), rising 3,000 feet in thirty miles and then dropping into the head valley of the Gunnison River just north of the Cochetopa Hills. The Marshall Pass route always remained narrow gauge but did in its odd way provide the sought-for Cochetopa Pass transcontinental, for it connected at Montrose with a standard-gauge branch leading to Grand Junction, and ultimately Salt Lake City. Lieutenant Gunnison's crossing of the Sangre de Cristo, La Veta Pass, was also used by a Rio Grande line connecting from Walsenburg in the eastern foothills to Alamosa in the San Luis Valley.

Returning to the main line to Leadville, it continued up the Arkansas Valley rising steadily, to eight thousand feet in the twenty-eight miles to Wild Horse, a second thousand feet in the next seventeen miles to Waco, and another eleven hundred feet in the further seventeen miles to Leadville. At 10,200 feet, Leadville was the highest railroad station in the world when it was reached in August 1880.[29] By then, however, the Rio Grande had been forced to conclude a peace with the Santa Fe and the Union Pacific. In what came to be known as the Treaty of Boston—for the location of the corporate headquarters of the other two lines—the Rio Grande agreed in early 1880 to abandon its drive toward El Paso, among other things stopping any construction along the Rio Grande thirty-one miles north of Santa Fe at Espanola, New Mexico, and any notion of building the eastward arm of the cross from Pueblo toward St. Louis along the Arkansas Valley of the plains. This cession, for which the Rio Grande gained freedom to build to Leadville and westward therefrom without Santa Fe competition, made a line to Salt Lake City seem imperative.

From Malta Junction just outside Leadville it was a fairly easy construction job to carry the line twenty miles up the Arkansas for a rise of only another 1,000 feet to pass over the rather stiff summit grades at Tennessee Pass, 10,500 feet above sea level and the highest stretch of mainline railroad in the United States. The original narrow-gauge line crossed this crest in the clear, but later, when the main line of the Rio Grande was made standard gauge, a tunnel 2,572 feet long was bored to remove the last, and steepest, pitch on this stretch, by reducing the summit elevation by some 250 feet.[30] "The heaviest grade on the main line on the east side of the Continental Divide is 1.42 percent, or 75 feet to the mile. This grade extends with few interruptions from Buena Vista to Tennessee Pass, a distance of 41 miles. The heaviest grade on the west side is 3.3 percent on the westbound track. This grade is maintained for a short distance above Minturn, but throughout most of the distance from Minturn to the Summit [20 miles] the maximum grade is 3 percent, or 158 feet per mile."[31] North of Minturn the line continued to drop along the forty miles to the junction with the Colorado River, and along that master stream a hundred miles westward to Grand Junction.

At Grand Junction not only did the Gunnison River join the Colorado but also the narrow-gauge line passing from Salida over Marshall Pass rejoined the main line. This route was in some ways the epitome of mountain railroading in the United States. With a summit at 10,856 feet, this line rose even higher than that over Tennessee Pass and did so in the open with very stiff grades, 211 feet per mile (4 percent), maintained for a demanding fourteen miles east of the crest. A similar 4 percent grade ruled for nine miles below the crest on the west. Thence this mineral-servicing route passed down the cleft in the plateau cut by the

Summit tunnels were quite common on railroads, as a quite short tunnel under the crest of a pass could considerably reduce grades all year round and snow accumulation in winter. Shown here is the summit tunnel on the highest pass on standard American railroads—Tennessee Pass, at over ten thousand feet on the Denver and Rio Grande Western Railroad. *Source:* Author's photo.

Gunnison in its Black Canyon to turn the western face of the extremely high plateaus of western Colorado to rejoin the main line at Grand Junction. From there the Denver and Rio Grande Western, as it was called once this extension to Salt Lake City was constructed, passed across the high plateaus of eastern Utah before facing its last obstacle, the Wasatch Range.

From a low point at four thousand feet, where the Green River is bridged, the line rose gently for the seventy miles to Helper, gaining only eighteen hundred feet in that distance. But at Helper, as its name suggests, the railroad faced a sharp climb over the main ridge of the Wasatch Plateau. In the twenty-five miles from Helper to Soldier Summit, at 7,440 feet, trains had to be drawn up some 1,600 feet across the Book Cliffs, along a box canyon cut in their 1,500-foot face by the Price River. In this area large coal deposits were found, and mining soon began to produce heavy loads to be carried by the new railroad. "For about 10 miles out of Helper the grade is 127 feet per mile [2.4 percent], and though such a grade is not excessive it necessitates the use of extra engines on some of the heavy trains to get them to the summit."[32] As originally laid out, the Rio Grande dropped quickly down westward from Soldier Summit to Thistle along the Soldier Creek, but a grade of 4 percent (211 feet per mile) was thereby introduced, necessitating the use of four or five engines eastbound per train. "At the turn of the century it was decided to improve the operating characteristics on Soldier Summit so a new alignment, over a longer course, was introduced that dropped the grade to two percent, 106 feet per mile, over a fifteen mile course."[33] From Thistle the railroad used the Spanish Fork to pass with easy grades through the great western face of the plateau, towering here to over ten thousand feet to form the Wasatch Range, to reach the great basin floored with sediments laid down in Lake Bonneville before it dried away. From Spanish Fork—where the river of that name that the railroad follows spreads a fan into this great basin—to Salt Lake City, the Rio Grande could pass through irrigated and productive agricultural lands that formed part of the Salt Lake Oasis the Mormons had shaped after they arrived in Deseret in 1847.

The 735-mile line from Denver to Salt Lake City via the Royal Gorge and Marshall Pass was completed in 1883.[34] Throughout the expansion of interests that brought this line into existence, the Denver and Rio Grande had seen its "natural territory" constantly threatened by other lines, first the Santa Fe and then the Union Pacific when it came under the control of Jay Gould in the late 1870s. The drive to Salt Lake City was as an end run around the UP and between that first transcontinental and its more southerly peer, the Santa Fe.

Once at Ogden, it was assumed that the Rio Grande would have access to the Southern Pacific (as successor to the Central Pacific) and any other lines that might be constructed within the Great Basin. That hope, however, was of short duration. The Union Pacific had in the 1880s gained control of the Oregon Short Line and the north and northwestward connections at Ogden. In 1900 Collis Huntington died, leaving his holdings in the Southern Pacific to his widow and nephew, who were interested in selling that ownership. Edward Harriman soon bought effective control of the California company and added to it an investment in the San Pedro, Los Angeles, and Salt Lake City Railroad sufficient to make certain that Senator Clark could not make effective interchange of traffic with any Gould-owned line, as the Rio Grande then was; and at that point the Denver and Rio Grande company found itself at the same sort of impasse in Salt Lake City and Ogden that it had been in at Pueblo a generation before. Its reaction was predictable: it attempted to secure a new way out under its own control. In this the undertaking was not typical of the Goulds, who had normally added to their increasing empire by buying out existing railroads, often at greatly deflated prices (in whose decline they had commonly played a significant role). At Salt Lake City, however, there was no such line to be had. With Harriman in effective control of the Oregon Short Line, the Utah Northern, the Southern Pacific, and the San Pedro, Los Angeles, and Salt Lake City, there was a phalanx too seamless for Gould to manipulate to his own benefit.

It was in that situation that George Gould, successor to his father as the great manipulator of railroads, decided to complete his empire—which extended from Buffalo in western New York State to Salt Lake City—by building to the Pacific. The Rio Grande segment of this route had been improved and made standard gauge when the Tennessee Pass line was extended to Glenwood Springs in 1887, to Rifle in 1889, and to Grand Junction in 1890. This 745-mile route between Denver and Salt Lake City had better grades and alignment than the earlier narrow-gauge line via Marshall Pass, and it was built at standard gauge so that through trains could now be run west of Denver in Colorado.[35] But with an absolute barrier facing the railroad at Salt Lake City, it seemed that such improvement as had taken place was largely wasted.

The Rio Grande's improvement of its line had come after 1887, when the Union Pacific and Central Pacific had dissolved a longstanding agreement as to interchange at Ogden—for which the UP had substituted a greater use of its Oregon Short Line connection at Granger, Wyoming—making the Central Pacific (Southern Pacific) a potential connection at the Ogden Gateway.[36] The slow rate at which the Denver and Rio Grande was widening its narrow-gauge route kept the Denver and Rio Grande Western (from Grand Junction to Salt Lake) from effectively bidding for an easterly interchange with the Central Pacific. In 1900 the conditions changed in such a way that a realignment of railroad strategies was to be expected: as already noted, Harriman bought Huntington's interest in the Southern Pacific, and in that same year George Gould began to buy stock in the Denver and Rio Grande and that company, in turn, in its connection west of Grand Junction, the Denver and Rio Grande Western.[37] Gould's effort was on behalf of the Missouri Pacific Railroad, which he already controlled.

As early as 1890 General Palmer, promoter and major owner of the Rio Grande Western, had had examined possible extension routes to California, finding the project "premature as regards our financial status."[38] In part that examination considered the Beckwith Pass near the California-Nevada boundary and the Feather River country, both components of one of the several alternative routes that Lieutenant Beckwith had presented in 1854. "In December 1892 M. J. Lorraine, a San Francisco civil engineer, wrote to [the president of the Rio Grande Western], offering to make the necessary surveys. He said that until recently he had been running lines for a project called the San Francisco and Great Salt Lake railway, but the project had fallen through for lack of financial support. After describing the route through Beckwith Pass down the north fork of the Feather River to Oroville and Sacramento, he offered to make a rerun for $10,000 if it were done before timber growth obliterated the earlier work."[39] The Panic of 1893 intervened, and the Rio Grande Western had passed into George Gould's hands before any renewal of interest in a Pacific extension could be reasonably entertained. Starting in 1901 Gould had actively, though clandestinely, pursued his interest in a Pacific connection, but it was only in 1905, when the San Pedro, Los Angeles, and Salt Lake City was nearing completion now under the control of Harriman, that Gould showed his hand, ordering construction to begin and using the Rio Grande as the mentor for this effort.[40] In the process the Rio Grande supplied $31.5 million of the total construction cost of $79.6 million before the line was roughly completed in August 1910, to be opened officially the next year.[41]

The Geography of the North American Railroad Company

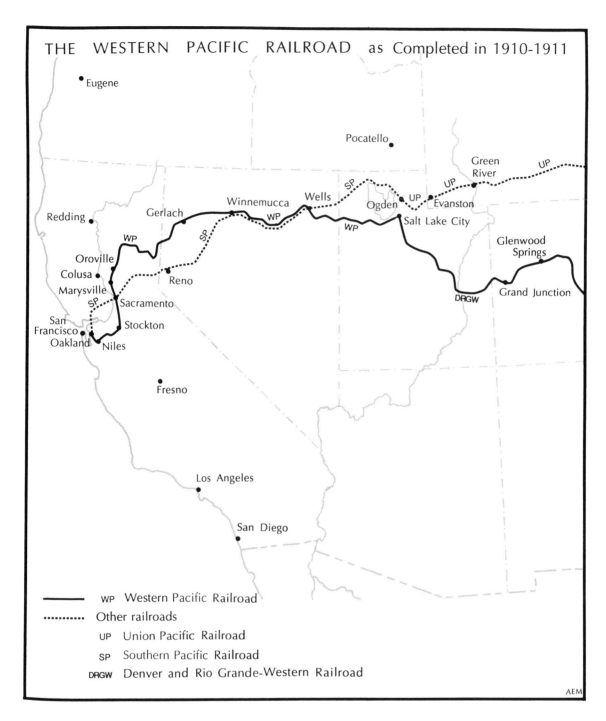

THE WESTERN PACIFIC RAILROAD as Completed in 1910-1911

• Eugene

Pocatello•

Green
River

UP

Redding •

Gerlach

Winnemucca   Wells   SP   Ogden   UP   Evanston

WP   Salt Lake City

WP

WP

Oroville

Colusa •

Marysville

Reno

Sacramento

SP

Stockton

San
Francisco •

Oakland   Niles

Glenwood
Springs

Grand Junction

DRGW

Fresno •

Los Angeles
•

San Diego
•

———— WP Western Pacific Railroad
·········· Other railroads
        UP Union Pacific Railroad
        SP Southern Pacific Railroad
    DRGW Denver and Rio Grande-Western Railroad

AEM

The route taken by the extension—called the Western Pacific Railroad despite the objection of the Southern Pacific, which had used that name for its original line from Sacramento to Oakland via the Altamont Pass and Livermore Valley—was reasonably well graded. Leaving Salt Lake City south of the lake, it passed westward across the Great Salt Lake Desert to Wendover on the Utah-Nevada boundary. The construction of any rail line across the Great Basin would of necessity face the problem of wending its way in a reasonable fashion among the block-faulted basin ranges protruding above the gently sloping alluvial deposits that fill the wide intervening "basins." The Central Pacific had taken the logical route in the late 1800s, when it used the Humboldt River valley to gain a graded course across Nevada, so the Western Pacific rationally set out to follow. But the real problems were to come in reaching the upper Humboldt from Salt Lake City and in finding a passable line through the Sierra Nevada–Cascade range that walls off the coastal valleys of California on the east.

In leaving Salt Lake City the Western Pacific had strong reasons for passing south of the Great Salt Lake, in contrast to the Central Pacific's route around to the north, determined by the Union Pacific's entrance into the Great Basin via the Weber Canyon that debouches near the northern end of the vast inland sea. The Rio Grande approaches Salt Lake City from due south, so to pass around the southern end of the lake was far more direct. In doing so, also, the new line avoided crossing the eastern basin ranges, as had been necessary on the Central Pacific until the Lucin Cutoff, directly across the northern arms of the water body, was completed in 1903 at the behest of Edward Harriman, with a saving of forty-four miles of distance and considerable grades and curves in the passage over Promontory Mountain.[42]

The smooth curve of the south shore of the lake could be followed with only minor filling at the northern end of the Oquirrh Range, which incidentally took the tracks alongside the great Garfield copper smelter, a potential customer of importance. The two parallel ranges to the west, between the Oquirrhs and the Great Salt Lake Desert, could be skirted on the north without any deviation. The desert itself introduced forty miles of absolutely flat and straight track before the boundary range west of Wendover, Utah, was approached, to be passed at its southern end. Within Nevada the Toana Range rose four thousand feet above the salt-flat deposits, right in the path of any direct route. To rise from the valley floor (here at 4,200 feet) to Silver Zone Pass across the Toanas (at 5,800 feet), the railroad was made to climb obliquely up the alluvial deposits until entering the pass where a horseshoe curve had to be introduced to lengthen the line to gain a reasonable grade. To the west almost no elevation was lost, for the floor of the Goshute Valley was only three hundred feet lower than the pass. But farther west lay another basin range directly across the chosen path. These Pequop Mountains were too high to climb but sufficiently narrow to bore through, so a tunnel approaching a mile in length was carried under the ridge just below the six-thousand-foot level. Once in the basin to the west of the Pequops, a clear run to the northwest could carry the railroad to the upper course of the Humboldt River at Wells, formerly Humboldt Wells.

There the Western Pacific began to run for two hundred miles alongside the original transcontinental, a situation that in calmer times permitted the individual single tracks operated by the two companies to be worked as a pair. But while the Western Pacific was being built, Harriman sought in all possible ways to impede its course. Only when the Union Pacific and the Southern Pacific were financially separated by the government did the UP line northward from Wells to the Oregon Short Line in southern Idaho assume any importance as a connection for the Gould line.

The building of the new railroad down the Humboldt needs no explanation until the alignment was located as far west as Winnemucca. There the engineers had to resolve the matter of the Sierra-Cascade crossing, a vexing question that had left Lieutenant Beckwith somewhat irresolute during the

Early practice called for stops at eating facilities such as the Harvey Houses on the Santa Fe. This Currier and Ives print portrays the dispatch of men to compete for service for their wives and daughters. *Source:* Library of Congress picture.

Pacific Railroad Survey. But following on the conclusions drawn from the preliminary surveys of the 1890s, the Western Pacific decided to use Beckworth Pass to cross the last of the basin ranges before reaching the high Sierra Valley, whence flowed the Middle Fork of the Feather River westward to the coastal valleys of California. To make a reasonable approach to Beckworth Pass, the WP line was carried directly westward from Winnemucca across the colluvial basins of the Black Rock and Smoke Creek deserts to approach the pass at just over five thousand feet. To secure as economically operable a route as possible, a tunnel more than a mile long was carried under the crest, which was fairly narrow here, to enter the Sierra Valley with no loss of elevation. Once in that mountain-girt basin, the line could pass across its flat floor to Portola, the gate in the Sierra that leads to the canyons of the several forks of the Feather River. After using the Middle Fork for some twenty miles, the engineers sought through another mile-long tunnel to pass across the interfluve to the North Fork. Entering that valley near its headwaters, the valley floor tended to drop too sharply for a reasonable rail grade, so it was necessary to introduce the Williams Loop whereby more distance was gained to ameliorate the grade.

As the Western Pacific line continued westward, it was carried into a deep cleft in the main mountain range, following one of the three rivers that rise to the east of the Cascades and cross that volcanic range to reach the Pacific. The grades along the North Fork of the Feather were fully reasonable for a rail line, but the construction was difficult, having to be carried on a rock-cut shelf dipping at a continuous rate toward the west and hugging the somewhat circuitous slope of the ledge. As a result, construction was costly and operations had to proceed at rather slow speeds to deal with the curvature. But along this Feather River route

The Santa Fe Railway trains stopped for meals on most schedules until the time of the Second World War. The Hotel Castaneda at Las Vegas, New Mexico, was operated by the Fred Harvey organization until trains with dining cars became standard after 1945. *Source:* Museum of New Mexico photo.

Lamy, New Mexico, 1930. Clarkson buses had replaced local passenger trains on the run to Santa Fe, but the daily freight still carried passengers in the combination baggage-coach seen on the right. *Source:* Photo by Edward A. Kemp. Courtesy Museum of New Mexico, Negative No. 53651.

there was no redundant grade. The tunnel under Beckworth Pass is little above the floor of the basins of western Nevada, and the total drop thence to the Sacramento Valley is little more than the five-thousand-foot elevation of that tunnel.

The Feather River route proved to be a unusually efficient line through a high and wide mountain barrier. Since the Sierra-Cascade barrier is around a hundred miles wide in this part of California, there is no possibility for a tunnel through the mountains, particularly when it is appreciated that the country lying to the east of the crest ranges from forty-five hundred to eighty-five hundred feet in elevation for over a thousand miles. Any transportation movement has to climb eastward about five thousand feet to gain that elevated platform of the Great Basin, Colorado Plateaus, and the Rockies and Great Plains, so the Western Pacific's route, with the climb held to that minimum, was a remarkable accomplishment. With a longer course, the North Fork provided a better ramp up the mountain than that furnished by the shorter and steeper Middle Fork of the Feather River.

The Western Pacific line reached the Sacramento Valley at Oroville at an elevation of about two hundred feet. From there the railroad could be carried in a straight line to Sacramento, where the Southern Pacific sought to bar its entrance, though a city tired of that company's oppressive monopoly gave the newer line the necessary clearances. The WP then faced a difficult problem of gaining an entrance to the San Francisco Bay area, its prime objective. The water-level Carquinez Strait through the Coast Ranges had been effectively occupied by the Southern Pacific in 1879, when it opened its direct route via Benicia and Martinez, so the WP had to adopt the same route that the older carrier had initially built along, as an earlier Western Pacific Railroad, to reach Oakland in 1869. From Sacramento to Stockton the Gould railroad crossed the irrigated floor of the Central Valley of California. At that river port the railroad alignment was turned westward to climb up to Altamont Pass, notched in the eastern rim of the enclosed Livermore Valley whose drainage passes through the narrow Niles Canyon to the alluvial plain of the Bay Area south of Oakland. Building thus a second Western Pacific across the Coast Range, parallel to the first (now renamed) Southern Pacific, the extension of Gould's interests was carried to Oakland in mid-1910, to be formally opened the next year. Thus, the grandest of all expressions of the notion of "natural territory," that for a dynasty of railroad promoters, pirates, and constructors, brought this last of American transcontinentals to completion. Over the years it has proved to be, save for the Altamont Pass stretch, an extremely well located and well built line capable of handling freight at reasonable costs. It has always needed more freight than it has been tendered in an area where the Southern Pacific has been able to maintain the lines of its "territory" more effectively than any other American railroad. But in the flux that now affects those American railroads, the WP is beginning to figure in a new strategy.

That strategy is the culmination of the geographical qualities of the first transcontinental, bestowed by Congress a century and a quarter ago. Because that first transcontinental seemed a herculean task and because it had to be built in two discontinuous sections, two companies were authorized to engage in its construction. That division has continued to the present, but each of those

The hotel at the Hot Spring at Las Vegas, New Mexico, was popular with patients suffering from pulmonary and nervous disorders during the first phase of medical climatology after the completion of the Santa Fe Railway in 1885. *Source:* Museum of New Mexico photo.

companies has sought to devise a "natural territory" of encompassing extent on that original geographical base, but a new one without its restrictions. The Southern Pacific has extended or mergered into its empire lines reaching from St. Louis to Portland, Oregon, effectively making an end run around its eastern partner, the Union Pacific. That partner has, in turn, extended its lines to Seattle and Los Angeles, though for all but the last few years maintaining its eastern terminus where Lincoln placed it in 1862. But at Ogden the SP and the UP have continued to interchange traffic, though often arguing whether agreements as to its volume have been kept. In the early 1980s the argument came into the open, with the Southern Pacific attempting to take over the Rock Island lines that would carry its system in a very direct fashion to the Missouri Gateway at Kansas City, while the Union Pacific has sought to extend its territory by merger with two remnants of Gould's empire—the Missouri Pacific Railroad and the Western Pacific. As now completed, this merger gives the Union Pacific access to its last major Pacific Coast objective (the Bay Area) and all of the articulation points in the midcontinent of the American rail system (Chicago, St. Louis, Cairo, Memphis, Vicksburg, Natchez, New Orleans, Brownsville, Laredo, and El Paso). The Union Pacific now accomplishes what it has always claimed it did: "Serves all the West."

North-South Routes West of the Mississippi

Space forbids a detailed analysis of the other major alignments of lines west of the Mississippi, those extending longitudinally. The Pacific Railroad Survey examined only one of these, and that in a rather brief fashion, when it took up the potential routes for a railroad from Puget Sound in the north to the great interior and coastal valleys of California in the south. Its recommendations were so preordained by terrain that there was little question even before the reconnaissance. The great structural troughs of the Northwest (Puget Sound and the Willamette Valley of Oregon) would be traversed, and between those and the equally grand structural valleys of California (the Central Valley and the Los Angeles Basin) the awkward cluster of mountain ridges in southern Oregon and northern California must be gotten across. The only remaining questions, and they were rather incisively answered, concerned the ranges of southern Oregon and the Tahachapi Range north of the Los Angeles Basin. In the Great Basin and the Columbia Lava Plateau between the Rockies and Sierra-Cascades, no reconnaissance save for Frederick Lander's private survey of the Oregon Short Line was undertaken. A similar disregard for north-south lines in the Great Plains was found in this great exploration, which was after all the *Pacific* Railroad Survey rather than a general western one.

If we take these three bands of land as distinct, divided one from the other by great belts of north-south mountains, we may briefly summarize railroad building in each. The Great Plains lay across the grain of American railroad interest, so no important rail construction was carried out fully longitudinally. On the eastern boundary of the quondam Great American Desert a railroad, initiated as a belt line around the articulation point that grew up at Kansas City, was marvelously extended by Arthur Stilwell in the 1890s to reach to a new port, named in his honor Port Arthur, on the Gulf of Mexico in 1897.[43] On the western boundary of the vast sloping Great Plains a similar border railroad was pushed southward from Denver through Pueblo to the Texas Panhandle and Fort Worth, ultimately to the Gulf of Mexico at Galveston, completed in 1888 over nearly a thousand miles. To this was added another alignment carrying the route northward, along the front ranges of the Rockies to the Wind River Basin of Wyoming, and then on through the water gap of that stream into the Bighorn Basin, and along the stream of that name to its juncture with the Yellowstone River and the Northern Pacific Railway at Billings, Montana.[44]

Within the plains, branches of the Missouri Pacific and the Santa Fe were developed from the latitude of Kansas southward to the Gulf, providing a partial coverage of north-south transport, but north of Kansas no effective longitudinal line within the vast wheat-farming and ranching domain was successfully promoted. To fill that gap one of the early rubber manufacturers in Akron, Frank Seiberling—who contemporaneously played a major role in the development of the Lincoln Highway—had floated the Midland Continental Railroad to be built southward from North Dakota to the Gulf, following what it verbally elevated to the distinction of "the Mid-land Route" (though by 1942 its owned lines reached over only some seventy-two miles in the heart of North Dakota near Jamestown, and its passenger service appeared in the *Official Guide* as "irregular" or by "Motor").[45] We must conclude that there was never any very effective northern plains market for north-south transportation by rail to match that in the South met by the Missouri Pacific and Santa Fe lines and by the independent system of the Missouri, Kansas, and Texas Railroad, which by winning the exclusive right to cross the Cherokee lands of the Indian Territory in a north-south direction created a line from Kansas City to northern Texas, completed in 1874.[46]

There were within the plains several railroad developments that were

somewhat "failed transcontinentals." We have already seen the arrested expansion of the Texas and Pacific at Sierra Blanca short of El Paso. Another promotion of a line beginning in St. Louis to build southwestward to the 35th parallel and then westward along that course to the Pacific, first called the Atlantic and Pacific Railroad, exhausted itself—even despite its corporate name of the St. Louis and San Francisco Railway—at Quanah in the Texas Panhandle. More quixotic was the railroad proposed by Arthur Stilwell, who by then had lost control of the Kansas City Southern leading to his eponymous port. At a banquet in his honor held in 1900 Stilwell described how the "Cannibals of Finance" had failed to defeat him; to demonstrate that, in fact, he launched a campaign, apparently with no forethought, for a bigger and better project. This called for another route to the sea from Kansas City, but this time to the Pacific rather than the Gulf. Just as in creating the Kansas City Southern, Stilwell had used a ruler to determine the most direct route to the Gulf from the Plains Border articulation point, and had established a new Gulf port to serve that geographical abstraction, so in looking toward the Pacific he used a string to show that the ocean approached most closely to Kansas City at Topolobampo, Mexico, on the Gulf of California. But this time the distance was more than twice as far, and a major mountain range intervened.

Undeterred by scale or geography, Stilwell organized the Kansas City, Mexico, and Orient in 1900 and sent out surveyors along its 1,659-mile route. As originally planned, a forty-mile stretch of rack-and-pinion line at a 14 percent grade was included, but later resurveys were said to have found three routes with grades of no more than 2.5 percent through the Sierra Madre Occidental of Mexico. Between 1901 and 1908 729 miles of line was constructed between Wichita and Alpine, Texas, and at several places in Mexico, with some 241 miles more graded. Events, however, overtook the line, and little was accomplished thereaf-

The Geography of the North American Railroad Company

Las Vegas, New Mexico, was near the high point on the Santa Fe Railway, so it was a place where natural ice was cut in large blocks from ponds created to furnish ice over a long season. *Source:* Museum of New Mexico photo.

ter until the company was bought by the Santa Fe in 1928. That carrier completed the railroad to Presidio, Texas, on the Mexican border and sold the Mexican stretches, 289 miles, to B. F. Johnston, a land and sugar investor.[47] There the situation languished for a generation, but in the late 1950s the Mexican government, which had subsequently nationalized the line in Mexico, decided upon completion, and the spectacular stretch between Sanchez, at the edge of the Mexican plateau near Creel, and El Fuerte 160 miles westward at the foot of that great canyon-etched slope was constructed. With that connection opened in 1961, Arthur Stilwell's conception of 1900 was realized, though the great utility of this geographical abstraction has failed to develop. There are so many factors other than simple minimum distance—among the more important of which has been the awkward nature of transshipment across a national boundary to a port of modest size and infrequent marine service—that the Kansas City, Mexico, and Orient has ended up as a minor element in the Santa Fe system in the United States, but a major east-west link in the less dense Mexican rail network. As the Ferrocarril de Chihuahua al Pacifico, this realization of what must have been a quixotic proposal in the after-dinner speech of an intuitive promoter has become the only transverse line in Mexico north of Guadalajara; but its potential as a 585-mile link between the Texas railroads and the Pacific has never been substantially exploited.

Within the Rockies no longitudinal line was practicable, though there were short stretches of longitudinal lines built to serve mining camps, such as some of the Rio Grande narrow-gauge lines of New Mexico and Colorado, parts of the Union Pacific branches in Colorado and Wyoming, and that company's Utah Northern route from Salt Lake City to Butte. Even in the Great Basin there were a few lengths of north-south railroad to tap that center of subtropical irrigation agriculture—among them the Salt Lake–Butte branch already mentioned, the extent of the San Pedro, Los Angeles, and Salt Lake City Railroad between Cajon

THE NORTH
AMERICAN
RAILROAD

Pass and the Mormon city, and the Santa Fe branch southward from Ashfork, on the 35th-parallel route of the main line leading to Phoenix.

Although these stretches of railroad are longitudinal in location, and several were constructed with fundamentally north-south traffic in mind, during the century they have been operated most have become diversion branches of the transcontinental lines used to tap a greater choice of western termini. The Union Pacific has used its system most effectively in this way, gaining traffic in the Pacific Northwest, the Bay Area, and the Los Angeles Basin for its route from Ogden to Council Bluffs. The Butte branch has also served that purpose, as well as the more recently acquired trackage (Spokane International) leading through Spokane to the Canadian border in eastern British Columbia, thus providing a much easier access to the Pacific for coal shipped from the Crowsnest Coal Field than that via the Canadian Pacific Railroad. The Santa Fe has used its Phoenix branch to provide service to southern Arizona from Chicago and the Middle West via northern Arizona.

The final band of north-south rail construction came on the Pacific coast, where the Southern Pacific sought to preserve its "territory" in California by gaining control of the Oregon and California Railroad project, begun by Ben Halladay to be followed by Henry Villard, and completed across the Siskiyous on the boundary between those states in 1887. The resulting railroad, ultimately finished by the Southern Pacific, had numerous faults once it passed southward out of the Willamette Valley beyond Eugene; most notable was that it had to cross three summits, with intermediate loss of elevation in building between the northern structural valley and its geomorphic pair in California's Central Valley. Redundant grade was lengthy, and slopes were very steep. "Eighteen bores were made, of which the summit tunnel [in the Siskiyous] of 3,108 feet was the longest, and the mountains were crossed at an elevation above the sea of 4,135 feet. There were 100 miles of curved track on a distance of 171 miles. Curvatures reached up to 14 degrees on a maximum grade of 3.3 percent."[48] So bad was this route that it was finally decided, during the period of Harriman's control of the Southern Pacific, to replace it by building a new line, the Natron Cutoff, from just south of Eugene (where the Willamette Valley basically pinches out) eastward across the crest of the Cascades, using horseshoe loops and long side-hill cuts to reach a single summit in a tunnel at 4,113 feet bored for 3,108 feet through this great arch of volcanics. From that elevation little height was lost in a rail line carried two hundred miles southward to the head of the Sacramento River Canyon at Dunsmuir, California, south of Mount Shasta, still at nearly four thousand feet. Brought into service in 1926, this Cascade route, though crossing the main range of the Cascades rather than their western shoulders, proved far more economical to operate than the older Siskiyou route.

The southern parts of the longitudinal railroad on the Pacific coast grew out of the Central Pacific's attempt to control its "natural territory" in California. Almost immediately after the juncture at Promontory in 1869, the western company began to organize a subsidiary, the Southern Pacific Railroad, originally incorporated in Kentucky, to construct routes from Sacramento and San Jose southward in the state. An alignment was carried down the Central Valley to its southern end and then in a climb across the Tehachapi Mountains at a single crest to reach the high desert in the Mojave Basin, losing little elevation eastward

Track gang at Deming, New Mexico, ca. 1895. *Source:* Courtesy Museum of New Mexico, Negative No. 14192.

Cerrillos, New Mexico, ca. 1892. Surveyor's gang that surveyed the Santa Fe spur from Waldo to Madrid. The Atchison, Topeka, and Santa Fe was extended to Madrid in 1892. *Source:* Courtesy Museum of New Mexico, Negative No. 5471.

As construction pushed westward, "hells on wheels" (such as this construction camp in Green River, Wyoming) and other beginnings of towns rose at town sites platted on the railroad-owned alternate sections of land. *Source:* Union Pacific photo.

The early stage in Green River, a hell on wheels located such that the railroad could not avoid siting a town there. *Source:* Union Pacific photo.

Gallup, on the high plateau of western New Mexico, was a trading town that grew up as a division point on the Santa Fe. It was the gateway to the Navajo and Zuni reservations. *Source: Museum of New Mexico photo.*

from its four-thousand-foot summit. Using the elevated floor of that desert basin to gain the Santa Clara River valley trending toward the coast, the Southern Pacific line was carried westward before turning through a tunnel at Newhall to gain entrance to the San Fernando Valley forming the headwaters of the Los Angeles River. This longitudinal line had at first been intended to continue across the Mojave Basin to its southeastern edge, where a short climb would have carried it to the crest of Cajon Pass, and a sharp and longer descent into the eastern end of the Los Angeles Basin at San Bernardino. But a $250,000 "payment" from the town of Los Angeles served to divert the route through its present location, causing this first railroad of southern California to reach the incipient metropolis in 1876.

To ensure that no other longitudinal railroad would occupy the more coastal valleys, in 1909 the Southern Pacific completed a Coast Route from San Jose via Salinas, San Luis Obispo, and Santa Barbara to Los Angeles, accepting a stiff 2.2 percent grade at Cuesta Grande in the Santa Lucia Mountains north of San Luis Obispo. Subsequently the Santa Fe, when it managed in the early 1880s to purchase the SP branch from Mojave to the Needles on the Colorado River, began an extension of that line, using trackage rights on the SP from Mojave to Bakersfield, to make juncture with a Central Valley project, the San Francisco and San Joaquin Valley Railroad, which it took over and completed to Richmond on San Francisco Bay in 1900.

The final longitudinal project on the Pacific coast, and the last major railroad constructed in the United States outside of Alaska, was a Great Northern "invasion" of the Southern Pacific's preserve in California. Using one of its own lines southward from the Columbia River through Bend east of the crest of the Cascades, the Great Northern reached Klamath Falls with trackage rights over parts of the SP's Natron Cutoff from Chemult. Beyond Klamath Falls new construction was carried southward across the high volcanic Modoc Plateau into California to join a branch of the Western Pacific built northward from the upper reaches of the Feather River valley on that same plateau. When juncture was made at Nubieber, California, in the mid-1930s, a new Inside Gateway opening California to the Hill Lines, and the Northwest to the Gould Lines, was created, as the last main-line railroad to be built in the United States. There have been relocations of stretches of major railroads, even considerable shifts (as on the Santa Fe near Ashfork, Arizona, or the Harriman Cutoff on the Union Pacific over Sherman Hill in Wyoming). Even major mind changes have occurred, as on the Southern Pacific, where in the 1960s a line from Palmdale in the Mojave

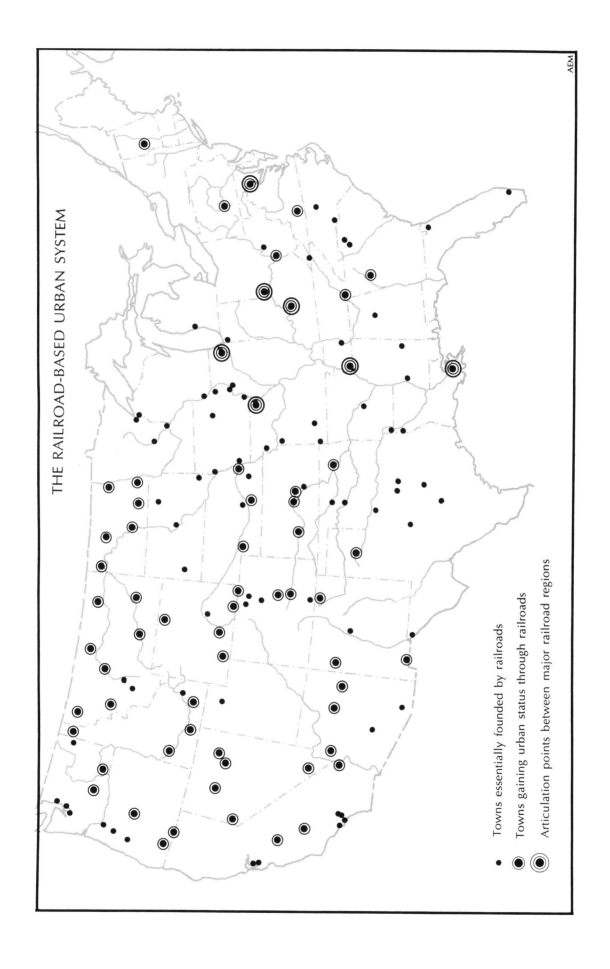

THE RAILROAD-BASED URBAN SYSTEM

•   Towns essentially founded by railroads

◉   Towns gaining urban status through railroads

◎   Articulation points between major railroad regions

AEM

Desert along the northern face of the San Gabriel Mountains and through Cajon Pass to Colton (San Bernardino) at the eastern end of the Los Angeles Basin partially reversed the decision made over a hundred years before, when Los Angeles, at the cost of a $250,000 bribe, diverted the Southern Pacific entrance into the basin through the San Fernando Valley instead of Cajon Pass. A century ago the railroad avoided Los Angeles because of its small size; today it avoids the city, one of the most geographically extensive in the world, because of its crowding. These constructions have cost hundreds of millions of dollars in total, but since the completion of the Inside Gateway in California's Northeast half a century ago, no significant new alignment has been added to the American railroad network. With that completion we may logically consider the major historical geography of the railroad in the United States to have come to a close.

CHAPTER FOUR

A Canadian Postscript

The Essence of the Developmental Railroad

I t is most unfortunately impractical to consider railroad development in Canada in as full detail as we have that industry in the United States, though we should not in any way depreciate the role that the northern Dominion has played. Several things, however, dictate a different organization of our account. To begin with, the small and still quite colonial status of Canada at the dawning of the railroad era in the early 1830s meant that the creation of a distinctive North American railroad came almost entirely within the United States. And it was that specifically American technology that gave the fundamental qualities to Canadian lines just as much as to the American ones. There were English embroideries on that frame, but they remained just that—surface touches to avoid too stark a Yankee outline. Perhaps the most important contribution by a Briton, Stanford Fleming's efforts at the creation of "standard time" were made only after many years in Canada, and certainly fully in relation to North American conditions.

Other factors that dictate a different approach to Canadian railroad geography include the far smaller total mileage of Canadian lines, though they are spread far more extensively in relation to the population of the country. This more demonstrably pioneering and developmental pattern suggests a much longer truly developmental period, and in fact one that has not yet ended. Thus, to add to our total understanding of the North American railroad, it seems more important to consider Canada in the last hundred years, rather than in the fifty years of railroad activity that came before. In fact, during the last fifty years the change that has continued on our continent with respect to railroads has lain almost entirely in Canada. Still another contrast is found in the recent economic history of the two North American democracies: since the Second World War the United States has declined sharply as a raw material supplier to the world beyond the oceans, whereas Canada has increased in that role. In a real sense Canada is still very much influenced by the mercantilist settlement forces that shaped both countries in their first three hundred years of European economic

241

involvement; the United States is now little affected by them. The need for new rail lines oriented toward ports hardly exists in the United States, whereas the recent rise of the port of Prince Rupert argues for different, and traditional, forces still at work in Canada.

The Birth of the Canadian Railroad

The first experiments toward railroad construction in Canada were startlingly similar to those in the United States, except that the Canadians took three steps at once. In the Great Republic, Boston had adopted the horse-operated railway in the 1790s, when that city set about flattening the top of Beacon Hill in order to build the first of what became the distinctive form of the American capitol. Only a generation later, in 1825, did the next step follow, that of using such a tracked way to transport heavy granite blocks on the nearby Granite Railway. Even then, steam as the prime mover was not fully anticipated. In the North the first railway came at Québec City, where in 1830 the Royal Engineers were engaged in the construction of the Québec Citadel. This was a tracked incline, at first operated by a horse windlass but subsequently by a steam winding engine, used to draw granite blocks from the riverbank up to the construction site.[1] Then came the actual attempt to construct a proper railroad, the first being proposed to carry traffic from the Richelieu River, which reached the St. Lawrence from the south some distance below Montréal, across the intervening country directly to the city, much in the fashion of the Boston and Lowell and the South Carolina railroads. The Champlain and St. Lawrence Railroad was organized while those pioneering lines were under construction, and building began in 1835 just as the New England line opened.

When it did open, the twelve-mile Canadian line bought its first engine from Robert Stephenson Ltd., only to continue the parallel by almost immediately abandoning the Newcastle builder in favor of an American one after it was discovered that the delicate English locomotive had trouble staying on the track. The track of the Champlain and St. Lawrence was of ironclad wooden stringers, which once in use proved too rough and flexible for the rigid-framed British locomotive. On July 21, 1836, this first of Canadian railroads opened for service, quickly showing a handsome profit on this essentially portage route around the rapids of the Richelieu, with its diversion of traffic directly to La Prairie across the St. Lawrence from Montréal saving many miles compared with the water route via Sorel.[2] Other portage railroads on the complex of rivers converging around Montréal did come into existence soon thereafter, and proposals were made for longer lines to connect Toronto directly with Lake Huron, to pass around Niagara Falls, and to take the coals from the mines in Nova Scotia to docks on the Northumberland Strait of the Gulf of St. Lawrence. Only the last of these projects was rapidly undertaken. In 1838 one of the previously horse-operated railways near Pictou in Nova Scotia installed a locomotive, beginning thereby the development of railroads in the then quite separate British Atlantic colonies.

Before 1850 there was little coherent development of rail lines in what is now Canada. Short lines for very specialized traffics were present; but no long lines were undertaken, nor any lines aimed at shaping a transportation system

Canada's first railroad was opened between St. Jean-sur-Richelieu east of Montréal and La Prairie opposite that city in May 1836. This scene shows the alignment of the first rails at the time of the centennial in 1936. *Source:* Canadian National photo.

independent of the waterways (which had been both the artery of and the rationale for the Canada of the seventeenth century). It was only in the 1840s, and at first through the effort of John A. Poor, a Maine lawyer, that this parochial pattern was changed. Poor had been present when the first train left Boston in 1834, and from then on he was the great propagandist for railroads in his recently established home state. As he watched the growth of the Boston system of railroads—spreading into northern New England, but not particularly Maine, in the search for a usable new Northwest Passage, as we have seen—he became convinced that Portland and Maine could enter into the general contest of urban mercantilism that was shaping the American railroad pattern only by turning attention to Canada, and especially to Montréal. To that end Poor visited Canada and succeeded there in creating a great deal of interest in a joint undertaking for a railroad from Portland to Montréal. His greatest success came in interesting Alexander Tillock Galt of the British American Land Company in the project. That energetic Scot, who had come to Canada at the age of thirteen, took up the promotion with great vigor, and it was due to him that the Canadian half, the St. Lawrence and Atlantic Railway, was begun in 1848 and ultimately carried to completion.

Because Poor was anxious to project a Portland line to the West, as already noted, he deliberately chose a track gauge different from that of the Boston lines,

243

A Canadian
Postscript

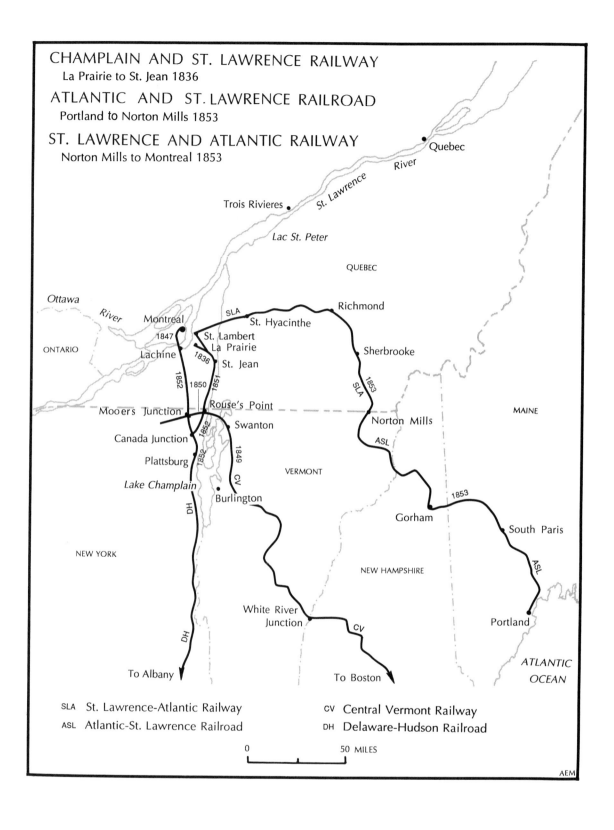

CHAMPLAIN AND ST. LAWRENCE RAILWAY
La Prairie to St. Jean 1836

ATLANTIC AND ST. LAWRENCE RAILROAD
Portland to Norton Mills 1853

ST. LAWRENCE AND ATLANTIC RAILWAY
Norton Mills to Montreal 1853

Quebec

St. Lawrence River

Trois Rivieres

Lac St. Peter

QUEBEC

Ottawa River

Montreal

Richmond

SLA

St. Hyacinthe

1847

St. Lambert
La Prairie

Sherbrooke

Lachine

1836

St. Jean

SLA 1853

ONTARIO

1852   1850   1851

Rouse's Point

MAINE

Mooers Junction

Norton Mills

1852

Swanton

ASL

Canada Junction

1849 CV

Plattsburg

VERMONT

1853

Lake Champlain

Gorham

DH

Burlington

South Paris

NEW YORK

NEW HAMPSHIRE

ASL

White River Junction

CV

Portland

DH

CV

ATLANTIC OCEAN

To Albany

To Boston

SLA   St. Lawrence-Atlantic Railway   CV   Central Vermont Railway
ASL   Atlantic-St. Lawrence Railroad   DH   Delaware-Hudson Railroad

0   50 MILES

AEM

all built on the standard Stephenson gauge. The Atlantic and St. Lawrence Railroad, the Portland-based section—in 1988 called the Grand Trunk Eastern Railway but soon thereafter "privatized" as the St. Lawrence and Atlantic Railroad—adopted a gauge of 5 feet 6 inches to exclude Boston diversions, and that width came thereby to be the gauge of its Canadian partner, and through it of the main lines of Canada for several decades.[3] Others have argued that it was the British desire to have a Canadian gauge different from the American—as had the Russians vis-à-vis the rest of Europe and Spain in contrast to an expansionist France—but the first explanation seems the more believable. In any event, in July 1853 the whole 292-mile line, the first across the United States–Canadian border, was opened.[4]

While all of this was going on, the various colonial governments in Canada were beginning to look toward a rail system of intercolonial purpose. This had been recommended in Lord Durham's report seeking to solve the multifarious problems that seemed to grip Canada at the time of the Rebellion of 1837. What is Canada today was then a string of British colonies, not particularly like-minded and certainly poorly integrated in economic terms. The main attributes they shared were loyalty to Britain and a wish not to be part of the United States politically. That attitude toward the United States did vary considerably in intensity, shifting both with the particular place in Canada and the state of the Canadian economy. On occasion the Montréal merchants did actually adopt a petition calling for joining the Great Republic, and the citizens of the Maritimes saw real need to forge a closer economic tie with the United States. It was in this shifting and unsure context of loyalty without effective nationality that railroad development in Canada had to evolve.

The nature of Canadian settlement, a thin band of towns hugging the American border—placed there first by their dogged loyalty to the crown of Britain, but held there by the climatic limits in an era of agricultural economy—determined that any railroads to be built would be basically east-west in extent and in construction. So thin was the band of farms and towns that in only a few places was any true network of lines at all rational. In Nova Scotia a very small set of lines could be envisioned; New Brunswick, though most sparsely peopled, had two alignments, one on the "North Shore" along the Gulf of St. Lawrence and a second in the St. John River valley, with logical geographical extension through the wilderness both to the east to reach Nova Scotia and to the north through the low sag in the Appalachians to join with a truly Canadian system near Mont Joli in Québec. The final determination of the Maine boundary—which came in 1842, only after railroad development was well under way in New England—had restricted the land corridor tying the Maritimes to the main body of Canada to only about twenty miles between a compromise line boundary with the United States and the south shore of the St. Lawrence. Any intercolonial railroad would have to traverse that narrow belt. Once in the St. Lawrence Valley, conditions did not change all that greatly; any line would, of necessity, tend to pass through the agriculturally developable portions—again a rather narrow band on either bank of the great river, save in the Eastern Townships, where a bit of Vermont-like country with rolling hills and numerous valleys provided a broader scope to Canadian farming settlement. And west of the broad Montréal plain, the most accommodating of regions in physical terms, though arbitrarily cut off in the

A Canadian
Postscript

south by the 45th parallel—badly surveyed, so that the actual boundary lies slightly to the north of the actual parallel of latitude for most of the political divisions based on it—the seemingly usable parts of the British domain narrowed again until the peninsula of Ontario was reached.

The Grand Trunk Railway

It is not surprising that any examination of this band of settlement suggested a single mainline railroad, one that came to be called the "main trunk." In the 1840s, when the agitation for the undertaking was being actively pursued, Canada was a single province—formerly Québec and Upper Canada, now referred to in the union as Canada East and Canada West. Without going into the intricacies of the politics that preceded the actual construction—and if anything those politics were more involved and less careful in separating private undertaking from public office than even such relations in the United States—we can note that on November 10, 1852, twin charters for the Grand Trunk Railway of Canada and the Grand Trunk Railway of Canada East were adopted. These in part grew out of a guarantee of support for the construction issued by the British government. The company was to be organized in London, maintaining its corporate and operating headquarters there. Without that vaunted British understatement, the company prospectus described the railroad to be built as

the most comprehensive system of railway in the world. Protected from the possibility of injurious competition for nearly its entire length by natural causes as well as by legislative enactment, it engrosses the traffic of a region extending for nearly 800 miles in one direct line. . . . The American railroads now in course of construction place the Grand Trunk in the most direct communication with the arterial lines to the Great West and to the Mississippi, a region whose advance in population and in wealth has been regarded as almost fabulous, and yet whose resources are still very partially developed.[5]

The original agitation had been for a rail line from Halifax in Nova Scotia through the several colonies to the western limit of Canada as then constituted, which lay on the St. Clair and Detroit rivers. As chartered, however, the railroad was to be built only from Rivière du Loup, well east of Québec City but on the south shore of the lower St. Lawrence, to Toronto. The promoters could see little hope for any sort of commercially viable line beyond Rivière du Loup until the farming areas of the St. John Valley and the vales of Nova Scotia were reached. Those were to be left to a separate and governmentally based construction, which became the Intercolonial Railway, tied to the lines in Canada itself only by a sharing of the 5-foot 6-inch gauge. There is not space here to recount the slow and excessively politicized spread of those Maritime lines beyond noting that they finally made junctions with the extended Grand Trunk system in 1876, when the 103-mile section from Ste. Flavie (now Mont Joli) in Québec to Campbellton in New Brunswick was opened. This was one of the promises held out to the Maritimes for joining the federal Dominion in 1867.[6] The most important contribution of the Intercolonial Railway may in fact have been that it served as the training ground for the greatest of Canadian railroad locating engineers, Sandford Fleming, who served as the company's chief engineer during its construction.

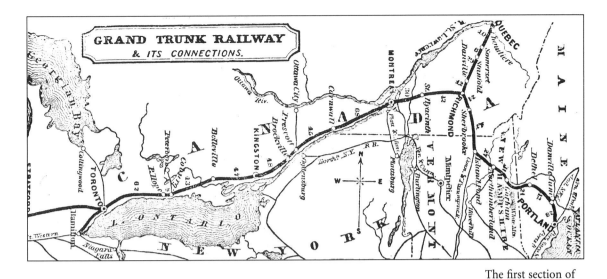

Returning to the Grand Trunk, we should note that there has been an unceasing argument among its historians as to what was wrong with the undertaking. There is no doubt that something was badly amiss. The blame has been widely cast. G. R. Stevens, in his massive history of the Canadian National, seems to blame it most directly on the money the Grand Trunk had to spend to improve the Atlantic and St. Lawrence after it gained control of that New England line, though such a massive impact of such a peripheral and relatively short line seems to me to put in question the actual health of the parent. G. P. de T. Glazebrook, in his standard history of Canadian transportation, presents both an inclusive and a more broadly Canadian view by centering his discussion on the adoption of British financing, management, and construction—by Peto, Brassey, Jackson, and Betts, the premier British railroad contractor—rather than control from Montréal: "Whether or not the Montreal financiers could have found enough capital must remain an open question. The transfer of control to London, the dual position of the Brassey firm as both contractors and promoters, the inexperience of the firm in the conditions of work and climate in North America, and the expensive type of construction adopted, all combined to render the first great railway in Canada an embarrassment almost from its inception."[7] This is not the place to join a historiographic argument, beyond using its existence to set the stage on which to advance a specifically historical-geographical argument as to what the trouble might have been.

The Grand Trunk on the Distant Continent

Owing to its British control, the Grand Trunk became, in a fashion unique to North America, a test of the applicability of the British system of railroad building to a new land, to a region of a developing rather than an accomplished economy. We should call to mind that the essence of the British system is that it came into existence within—and was intended to serve as an improvement to transportation of—an existing market. In truth, it was not a developmental device but rather a remedial device where previous forms of transportation had proved insufficient. Under these conditions heavy investment of capital could both be secured from investors and be justified by logical expectations of profits. Because the remedy was seen to lie in a high level of facilities to overcome

The first section of the Grand Trunk Railway (when that line became the extension of the first railroad built as the Atlantic and St. Lawrence in Maine and the St. Lawrence and Atlantic in Québec) was built at a gauge of 5 feet 6 inches to discourage Boston's domination of that international line. This was in fact extended by a British company westward from Montréal to Toronto and the St. Clair River frontier in 1859. *Source:* Canadian National map.

247

A Canadian Postscript

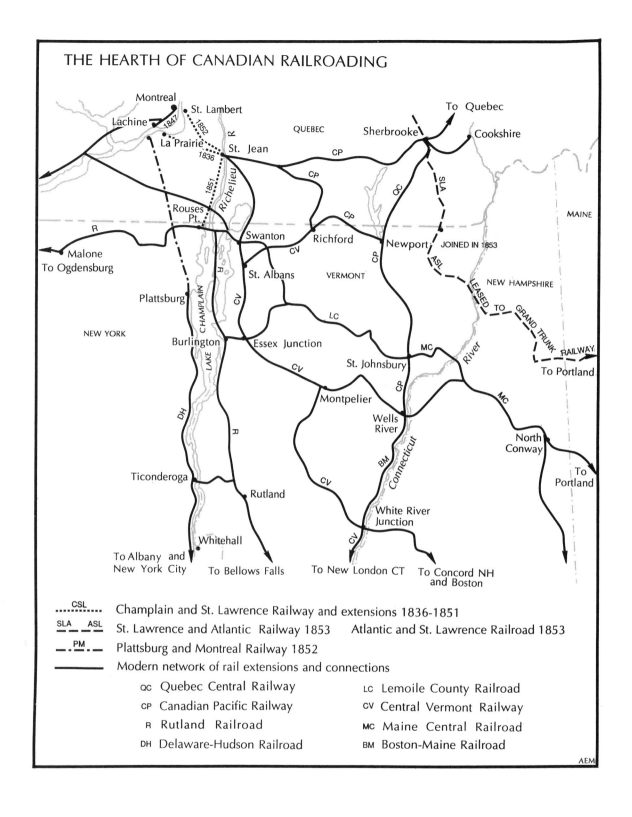

THE HEARTH OF CANADIAN RAILROADING

Montreal
St. Lambert
Lachine
1847
1852
QUEBEC
Sherbrooke
To Quebec
Cookshire
La Prairie
1836
St. Jean
CP
QC
SLA
R
1851
Richelieu
CP
MAINE
Rouses Pt.
CP
Swanton
Richford
Newport
JOINED IN 1853
R
Malone
To Ogdensburg
CV
ASL
NEW HAMPSHIRE
Plattsburg
St. Albans
VERMONT
LEASED TO GRAND TRUNK RAILWAY
NEW YORK
CHAMPLAIN
CV
LC
To Portland
Burlington
Essex Junction
MC
River
LAKE
CV
St. Johnsbury
MC
Montpelier
CP
DH
R
Wells River
BM
North Conway
Connecticut
To Portland
Ticonderoga
Rutland
CV
White River Junction
To Albany and New York City
Whitehall
CV
To New London CT
To Concord NH and Boston
To Bellows Falls

CSL ·········· Champlain and St. Lawrence Railway and extensions 1836-1851
SLA --- ASL --- St. Lawrence and Atlantic Railway 1853   Atlantic and St. Lawrence Railroad 1853
PM —·—·— Plattsburg and Montreal Railway 1852
————— Modern network of rail extensions and connections

QC Quebec Central Railway   LC Lemoile County Railroad
CP Canadian Pacific Railway   CV Central Vermont Railway
R   Rutland Railroad   MC Maine Central Railroad
DH Delaware-Hudson Railroad   BM Boston-Maine Railroad

AEM

existing stress, construction was to be undertaken in a single step, accomplishing the ultimate objective when the first work was completed. In contrast, in America the market was certainly underdeveloped, so it was the anticipation of need rather than actual need that often ruled the undertaking. Even where current modes of transportation were taxed by existing conditions, it was usually only because they were so primitive in their development. Any rational appraisal of costs and benefits called for staged construction: building an initial line as cheaply as possible in order to test the potential market and determine the ultimate level of construction, using earnings to help finance that future rebuilding.

Markets were critical in either case, but under the American system the lineaments of the market were only vaguely sketched, whereas in Britain they were clearly visible. It took more imagination, intuition, and adaptability to succeed under the American system, and I wish to suggest that that was what the Brassey firm, as the promoters of the Grand Trunk scheme, lacked. These were qualities the British system of railroad building normally failed to develop.

There appears to have been some awareness of the difference between Britain and Canada, as evidenced by the prospectus writer quoted above. Having referred to the effulgence of the American Middle West in the mid-nineteenth century, he goes on: "Commencing at the debouchure of the three largest lakes in the world [draining that radiant region] the Grand Trunk Railway of Canada pours the accumulating traffic throughout the entire length of Canada. . . . The whole future traffic between the western regions and the east, including Lower Canada, parts of the state of Vermont and New Hampshire, the whole of the state of Maine, and the provinces of New Brunswick, Nova Scotia, Prince Edward Island and Newfoundland, must therefore pass over the Grand Trunk Railway."[8] It was by including the American Middle West in the potential market for the Grand Trunk that this highly developmental line could be given a more sanguine future, and from the very beginning of the sale of stock such a hinterland was assumed. The impression becomes compelling that the Brassey firm could not envisage railroad building based on so narrow and underdeveloped a market as Canada actually possessed at midcentury; to justify the Brassey firm's activity on this, the largest contract it had ever undertaken, a more developed market must (reasonably or not) be described.

I believe the whole strategy of the Grand Trunk Railway right down to its last two decades, those in the twentieth century, can best be understood in this geographical context. Rather than the Atlantic and St. Lawrence Railroad's being the evil American corruption of the otherwise sound Grand Trunk Railway, as Stevens sees it, I believe the Grand Trunk company perceived that shortest route to the warm ocean as giving it a tremendously enhanced existing, as well as potential, market. And also it was to be through this Grand Trunk line to Portland, Maine, that access to the Maritimes was to be gained, via a proposed European and North American Railway to extend eastward across Maine and the Maritime Provinces from Portland. For the development of these necessary additional markets, the line from Montréal to Portland was critical to the whole endeavor.[9]

Only in 1988 did the line's Canadian proprietors—the government, ever since the First World War—decide that the traditional access to Montréal's

249

A Canadian
Postscript

This board-and-batten structure formed the first railroad station in St. John, New Brunswick, bringing a carpenter gothic look to the port at the mouth of the St. John River. *Source:* Canadian National photo.

The St. Lawrence at Montréal was at first too wide to bridge. In summer a ferry was used to transport passengers and goods to the northern end of the St. Lawrence and Atlantic, now owned by the Grand Trunk. But in winter the ferry could not operate, so once the ice on the river was thick enough, tracks were laid on its surface to serve until the ice became too thin to support it in spring. *Source:* Canadian National picture.

closest ice-free port need no longer remain in Canadian hands in an era when icebreakers could keep the St. Lawrence open in the winter. This dependence upon the American market to justify the more costly construction required by the British rail system was greatly encouraged by the Reciprocity Treaty of 1854 signed by the United States and Great Britain (as the sovereign of Canada), which allowed among other things the much easier passage of goods in bond to and from the American Middle West via Canadian railroads. Thus, Montréal and Québec could serve as ports for the Middle West during the open season, and Portland could do so in the winter.

Much of the criticism of the Grand Trunk came from its very high cost, due to "overbuilding" for the actual existing market. This meant a very heavy subsidy from the Canadian treasury, as well as a necessarily conservative policy in the projection of lines into still developing regions, or even beyond the existing frontier. It seems significant that whenever the Grand Trunk showed audacity in extending its lines, that bravery came in a particularly British fashion, by moving from Canada into the more developed market of the United States. The "main trunk" was the first built. Between 1853 and 1856 the line from Montréal to Toronto was constructed rapidly, if not wholly satisfactorily. The rail used tended to snap in winter, the problem of snow seemed to confound the London managers, and the first British engines proved unworkable on this still too North American railroad. Slowly the company learned to deal with a different physical environment, and engines from Philadelphia were the second and third to be sought (to be followed by many other American engines or Canadian copies). As planned, the Grand Trunk was also carried eastward from Montréal in the agricultural counties south of the St. Lawrence reaching to Rivière du Loup before the thin settlement found beyond there set an eastern terminus. Only a government subvention pushed the line onward to Ste. Flavie (Mont Joli), where it remained for nearly a generation.

Once at Toronto, the company had to think out a policy for further westward expansion, and it was then that the siren call of the American market became particularly compelling. Much as the Great Western Railway of Canada was already in operation in the peninsula between Lake Huron and Lake Erie, and so thought this its privately possessed territory, the Grand Trunk pushed westward, buying the Toronto and Guelph and then extending that company's line all the way to the frontier, reaching Sarnia on the St. Clair River in 1859. Even then, the company was ready to forsake Canadian extension in favor of American. When the line to Sarnia opened on November 21, 1859, there was ready across the river, and the border, an extension built by the Grand Trunk from Port Huron to Detroit, where junction with the Michigan Central was possible and encouraged, as that then Boston-owned company was anxious to avoid having to use the Vanderbilt-controlled Canada Southern extending across the southern peninsula of Ontario to Niagara Falls.[10] During this same period the Grand Trunk set about gaining control of the Great Western Railway, which would give it access from Toronto to Hamilton and Buffalo, and also of the lines toward the New York and Vermont boundaries from Montréal. In 1864 an alliance was established with the Vermont Central Railroad, and by 1883 the tie was so important that the Grand Trunk gained control of that line, which provided yet another tap on the American market, all the way to New York City (using a ferry

In one of the relatively rare contributions of English rail practice to North American railroads, Robert Stephenson (serving as a consulting engineer) designed and built the famous Victoria Bridge at Montréal (1854–60). This bridge was constructed according to the tubular principle that Stephenson had pioneered on the Conway and Brittania bridges in Wales. In 1898 the tubular spans at Montréal were replaced by trusses when this structure was reconstructed using the original piers as the Royal Jubilee Bridge. *Source:* Canadian National photo.

The Royal Jubilee Bridge of 1898 was constructed by placing new trusses on the original piers and subsequently destroying the older tubular spans by pushing them into the river, to be removed later so as not to obstruct passage under the bridge. *Source:* Canadian National photo.

operation from New London, Connecticut, where the St. Albans, Vermont, company reached tidewater).[11]

The Grand Trunk in the Middle West: A British-Style Railroad

This reliance by a British-style railroad operating in Canada on the larger American market did not stop with gaining routes to tidewater in eastern and southern New England. In the 1870s the capture of the Michigan Central by the Vanderbilt interests, with its reorientation of traffic to the port of New York, meant that the natural alliance between that Boston line and the Canadian main stem was no longer very rewarding. The Grand Trunk responded as if torn from its own earth; it set about gaining its own railroad extension to Chicago, where it could work diverse interchanges not merely with the eastern Middle West but with the western lines as well. Virtually no new trackage had to be built; there were so many competing short railroads in the easy terrain of Michigan and Indiana that short lines could be assembled into a through route from Port Huron on the St. Clair River to the outskirts of Chicago. Those bits, assembled into the Chicago and Grand Trunk Railway Company (later and today the Grand Trunk Western) reached to the Burlington railroad, which rented it trackage rights into the Loop. These were ultimately replaced by Grand Trunk trackage to the Belt Railway and over that truly common carrier to Dearborn Station, which remained the Grand Trunk terminus until the coming of Amtrak and the removal of Grand Trunk trains to Union Station. Those trains that first arrived in 1880 still run, and over tracks owned by the Grand Trunk Western.

Canada's Railroads in 1880

The year 1880 assumes great importance in the historical geography of railroads in Canada, so we may well find a place here for a brief summary of where matters stood at that time. In the Maritimes the Intercolonial Railway had been completed to a junction with the Grand Trunk in Québec and provided, along with shorter lines, service to most larger towns. The Grand Trunk furnished the desired main stem westward to Windsor and Sarnia on the Michigan frontier, and extensions thence to Chicago. In addition, the company had branches to Buffalo and Rouses Point on the New York boundary, and lines across New England to tidewater in Connecticut and Maine. Subsequently it began construction of a further line to Providence, Rhode Island, but by the time of the First World War when it was undertaken, the railroad era was passing and the Grand Trunk's bridge abutments were abandoned, leaving a grim reminder that even the American railroad market was fast shrinking.

The Pacific Railroad of Canada

The "main trunk" of Canada could plausibly be established by the Grand Trunk up to the creation of the Dominion in 1867, and even for several years thereafter, until Rupert's Land—which in its southern reaches became most of the settled parts of Manitoba, Saskatchewan, and Alberta—was bought from the Hudson's Bay Company in 1869 and British Columbia was sirened into the Confederation in 1871. Although Ontario (Canada West until 1867) extended basically to the Lakehead at Fort William, all lands west of that point were British territories but

253

A Canadian
Postscript

not Canadian before 1871. It was generally accepted that the Canadian Shield in Ontario, and Québec for that matter, was unsuited to the normal agricultural and industrial settlement that the English had introduced to the continent starting in 1607, so the Grand Trunk as originally aligned served most of the logically defined oecumene of Canada. The tendency of the London company to turn its attention to invasion of the United States rather than to extension in Canada could be indulged so long as it seemed to make economically viable a rail system whose level of construction was more costly than the thin development of the colonies seemed to support. With its trunk line, and some more regional carriers in Ontario, Québec, and the Maritimes, Canada was about as well served as it might hope to be.

The quondam fit of the Grand Trunk disappeared quickly in the face of the majestic expansionism of the new Dominion. Nearly tripling its size in the first two years of the 1870s, though adding no more than twenty-three thousand Europeans in this empire beyond the Lakehead, Canada discovered that a quite different transportation geography was required. The agreement adding British Columbia brought that transformed condition into full view, as the pact called for the construction of a railroad from eastern Canada to tidewater in British Columbia within the period of ten years. The Pacific colony had sought no more than a wagon road, but John A. Macdonald had acted in a fully imperial manner, offering instead the railroad agreement, and the westerners had graciously accepted. In that situation the government of Canada was forced into fairly prompt action if it were to show good faith in its undertaking. Within a year an ostensible Canadian Pacific Railway was established, and Sandford Fleming, from the Intercolonial Railway, was made engineer-in-chief with the responsibility of conducting extensive surveys of possible routes to the Pacific. This was a massive task, requiring the conduct of surveys in a band nearly three thousand miles long east-west and three hundred to four hundred miles north-south at its greatest extent. Beyond the immediate shore of Lake Superior the Canadian Shield in the east was virtually unexplored, and the great chains of mountains in the west were only very partially understood. The fur traders had passed through this country, but their knowledge of traversable terrain for railroads was so scant that little confidence could be placed in their accounts, compiled of course for other purposes.

The Fleming Surveys for the Pacific Railroad

Before we look at the efforts to begin the actual construction of this line, we may best consider the Fleming surveys, since they were responsible both for the first understanding of the Canadian West when viewed in railroad terms and for the outline of the potential routes for development, many of which came ultimately to be built. Upon being given his charge in 1871, Fleming immediately divided his vast realm into three parts: the "Western or Mountain Region," the "Central or Prairie Region," and the "Eastern or Woodland Region." In a preliminary report of 1872 Fleming gave fragmentary accounts of the West, but in 1874 he presented a full report, with elaborate maps, that we may use to portray the state of geographical understanding of the potential routes for a Pacific railroad in Canada.[12] In that report Fleming began with the purpose of the survey:

The undertaking, proposed, is the construction of a railway to connect the seabord of British Columbia with the existing railway system of Ontario and Québec, by the most eligible line that can be found within Canadian territory. . . . The existing railway system of the older Provinces does not extend any great distance northerly or north-westerly from Lake Ontario and the River St. Lawrence; the limit may be defined by drawing a line from the southwesterly angle of the Georgian Bay, Lake Huron, across to a point on the Ottawa River, not far above the city of Ottawa. The exploration may, therefore, be assumed to extend from that line last referred to, near the capital of the Dominion, to that portion of the Pacific Coast lying between Alaska and the Straits of Juan de Fuca. . . . Its extreme limits thus embrace fifty-four degrees of longitude, and ten degrees of latitude, and reduced to miles, the territory under examination will be found to cover fully twenty-seven hundred miles in length, by a breadth ranging from three to five hundred miles. This extensive territory, with an area of one million square miles, drains into three oceans: the Atlantic to the east, the Arctic to the north, and the Pacific to the west.[13]

No one can be unimpressed by the scale of this undertaking—perhaps no greater than that of the American Pacific Railroad Survey of twenty years before, but certainly more striking because of the far less well known nature of that block of one million square miles when the survey began in 1871.

Sandford Fleming set out certain guiding objectives that shaped the survey. After a summary of the broad physical features of the "Western or Mountain Region" he noted, "The foregoing outline of the prominent characteristics of the Rocky Mountain Zone and the shores of British Columbia will give some idea of the difficulties to be overcome in extending the railway system of Canada to the

Canada's greatest terminus was built by the Canadian Pacific and Grand Trunk railroads at Toronto (1914–20) when that city became the most important rail junction in Canada. Following North American practice, the Royal York Hotel (the tall building to the right), constructed by the Canadian Pacific, became the largest hotel in the British Empire. *Source:* Canadian National photo.

255

A Canadian Postscript

Pacific Coast. It will be seen that two important problems are presented. Primarily, it will be necessary to discover the best way of piercing the mountain chains, but it is scarcely less important that the terminating point on the sea board should be easily reached by the largest class of vessels that, now or hereafter, may navigate the Pacific Ocean."[14]

In the "Central or Prairie Region" few obstacles seemed to face the building of a railroad; those that existed were mainly of the order of finding the best bridging place across the broad entrenched valleys cut by the rivers flowing toward the Arctic and Hudson Bay. There was concern about the "fertility" of the prairie, with the citing of the drier triangle in the southwest, Palliser's Triangle, as less likely to provide on-line support than the so-called Fertile Belt extending in a southeast-to-northwest direction between Fort Garry (Winnipeg) and Fort Edmonton (Edmonton). It was clear that the alignment of the rails across the prairies would be determined primarily by two features: the passage of the line south of Lake Manitoba—a water body larger than Lake Ontario—in the eastern prairies, and the opening through the front range of the Rockies to be used in crossing the Rockies to the west.

The "Eastern or Woodland Region" was perhaps not fully perceived at that time as coextensive with the area underlain by the Canadian Shield, but we now know that to be the case, so we may better use that more descriptive term. "Immediately to the east of the Province of Manitoba, begins the woodland region. It extends without much material change in its character, from the prairie region along the north side of Lake Superior and Huron to the settled and cleared portion of Ontario and Quebec, lying on the northerly banks of the St. Lawrence." No part of this belt was mountainous, the highest hills rose to less than two thousand feet, and only along the shore of Lake Superior was "rough and broken elevated ground . . . found. The bank of rocky hills which runs along Lake Superior is variable in width, ranging from forty to seventy miles, and its eastern extension assumes, on the north side of Lake Huron, a width of about fifty miles. Behind the rocky elevated range referred to, the surface is found to be comparatively flat."[15] Fleming succinctly, and accurately, summarized the potential economic value of this Shield stretch: "The agricultural resources of this extensive region of country are not promising. But the timber which covers the surface will every year become more and more valuable, and its geological structure affords indications of mineral wealth."[16]

Even the most preliminary survey suggested to the engineers that "the chief obstacles to be overcome would be found to exist in the Mountain Region to the west, and the Woodland Region to the east." In that context a set of priorities was stated:

First. That every effort should be directed to the discovery of a line through the Woodland Region [the Shield], which would prove the shortest and best possible between the railway system in the two elder Provinces and the Province of Manitoba.

Second. That the above line should touch, or by a branch connect with, Lake Superior, and constitute, as nearly as possible, the shortest and cheapest outlet for transport of natural products from the Prairie Region to the navigable waters of the St. Lawrence [via the Great Lakes].

Third. That the greatest possible energy should be brought to bear on the work of exploring in the Western Region in order to discover, with as little delay as possible, a practicable line for the Railway through the Rocky Mountain Zone; a line which would prove the shortest and least expensive, which would best subserve the interests of the country, and lead to the most eligible harbour on the Pacific Coast.

Fourth. That the route of the Railway through the Prairie Region, which connecting with the lines in the Eastern and Western sections, so as to reduce the distances between the Atlantic and Pacific Oceans to a minimum, should be projected, to avoid the most formidable river crossings, and approach the rich deposits of coal and iron, at the same time to be conveniently near the large tracts of land available for settlement.[17]

This was the prescription for the route over some twenty-eight hundred miles in a vast area largely devoid of European settlement and peopled with fewer individuals than could be found in the larger towns of the "elder Provinces."

It is impossible here to look in detail at the several dozen separate surveys that were run over a five-year period, or even at the wealth of information they produced. We must be content with summarizing the recommendations as to the principal problems facing the location decisions. The most taxing and important of these was the way through the Rockies, for this decision would heavily influence both the route across the prairies and the point of access to the Pacific. Thus, the primary focus of the Fleming surveys became which of the mountain gates to use. As a general guide it was introduced that the pass used should be at least a hundred miles north of the United States border; the bad feelings toward the British during the Civil War had not been removed by the hasty creation of the Dominion. By the time of the 1874 report Fleming was confident that the best pass had been found: "It has been found that of all the "Passes" through the main Rocky Mountain chain, between the International boundary line and the 53rd parallel of latitude, the Yellow Head Pass is the most favourable, and that the approaches to it, from both sides of the Mountain Range, are of such a character as to render the construction of a railway, across the great continental watershed, a far less difficult matter than was previously imagined."[18] That sanguine view was paired with one far more ominous: "The most serious difficulties are found to lie in piercing the Cascade Chain, and in descending from the level of the elevated plateau, in the heart of British Columbia, to the level of the ocean."[19] It was in this Cascade section, which today we would designate as passing through the British Columbia Coast Ranges, that a number of separate routes had to be explored, often at great pain. Seven were examined:

Route No. 1—Begins at Burrard Inlet, near New Westminster. Follows the Lower Fraser River to Fort Hope, passes up the Coquihalla Valley, and thence by Nicola Lake to Kamloops. At Kamloops it enters the valley of the North Thompson, following which it passes over a low water shed at Lake Albreda to River Canoe, and thence crosses by Lake Cranberry to Tete Jaune Cache. From the latter point, it follows the River Fraser to one of its sources, near the Yellow Head Pass, and thence by the Caledonian and Jasper Valleys to the eastern side of the Rocky Mountain Chain, thence easterly by the McLeod and Pembina Rivers to the North Saskatchewan.

The great difficulties on this line are met with between Hope and Kamloops, in a distance of 128 miles. [Several summits reaching to between 2,500 and 3,500 feet must be crossed in series.] From Kamloops to Edmonton, a total distance of 544 miles, very favourable gradients may be had with comparatively light work. It certainly need not exceed the average of work on many of the railways in the Eastern Provinces of the Dominion.

A Canadian
Postscript

On some portions of this line, between Hope and Kamloops, gradients would unavoidably be very steep, ranging as high as 172 feet per mile [3.2 percent], and work would be necessarily heavy. Several tunnels would be required, one of which it is estimated, would be three and three-quarter miles in length. The aggregate tunneling on this rough section would probably be over five miles.

Route No. 2—Begins at Burrard Inlet, and like Route No. 1, follows the River Fraser to Hope, but instead of crossing a depression in the Cascade Chain by the Coquihalla Valley, it continues to ascend the River Fraser to Lytton. At the latter point it passes into the Valley of the River Thompson, and follows the course of that river to Kamloops. From Kamloops to Yellow Head Pass and Edmonton, Routes Nos. 1 and 2 are common. . . . Between Hope and Kamloops the distance is 165 miles. Although no high summit is to be passed over, this section is far from favourable. Long stretches along the canyons of the Fraser and the lower Thompson, occupying about half the whole distance, are excessively rough. On these sections formidable difficulties present themselves; the work would be enormously heavy, and the cost proportionate.

Route No. 3—Begins at Howe Sound, crosses the Cascade Mountains by a series of openings to the River Fraser at Lillooet, and thence passes over the plateau in the centre of British Columbia by the Marble Canyon and Bonaparte Valley to the North Thompson, near the mouth of the Clearwater River; from this point it ascends the Thompson and runs on the same common ground as Routes 1 and 2 to Yellow Head Pass and Edmonton.

From Howe Sound to the North Thompson, by this route, the distance is 284 miles; within this distance the line passes over four main summits, ranging in elevation from 1,610 to 3,847 feet above the sea, and between these summits the ground falls twice to 700 feet and once to 1,847 feet. These great changes in level are suggestive of unusually heavy ascending and descending gradients, as well as equally heavy works of construction. From the point where this route intersects the valley of the River Thompson, it takes the same course to Edmonton as Routes Nos. 1 and 2.

Route No. 4—Commences at Waddington Harbour, on Bute Inlet, and ascends by the valley of the Homathco through the Cascade Chain of mountains to Lake Tatla, thence it passes over the Chilcotin plains to the River Fraser; it crosses the Fraser about 16 miles below Soda Creek, and continuing easterly by Lac la Hacse and Lake Canin, reaches the River Thompson valley, near the mouth of River Clearwater. From the latter point the same course to Edmonton as Routes Nos. 1, 2 and 3. From Bute Inlet to the North Thompson valley, by this route, the distance is 378 miles. On this distance three summits are passed over. . . . There are long stretches on this line where the work would be light, but in some sections it would be very heavy. Ascending the Homathco for a distance of 15 miles through the great canyon, a continuous uniform gradient of 110 feet per mile [2.1 percent] would be required, involving works of excessively heavy character, embracing cuttings in granite, and a great number of short tunnels, amounting in aggregate to about three miles.

The greatest difficulties on this line are undoubtedly met between tidewater and the head of the great canyon; the ascent on this section is 2,285 feet in 34 miles, of which 1,650 feet would have to be overcome in 15 miles.

Route No. 5—[This was a modification of Route 4 in its inland stretches, but the great climb out of Bute Inlet remained unchanged.]

Route No. 6—[This was a modification of Route 4, again in its plateau section, passing northward up the Fraser River to Fort George (Prince George) and then around the great bend of that river to reach Yellowhead Pass via the Fraser rather than the Thompson and Canoe—that is, from the north rather than from the south. Only a rather vague reconnaissance survey was carried out on this route.]

Route No. 7—All parties, who have visited the River Skeena, and acquired from personal observation any knowledge respecting its outlet and the character of the country in that district, seem to unite in an adverse opinion respecting the eligibility of

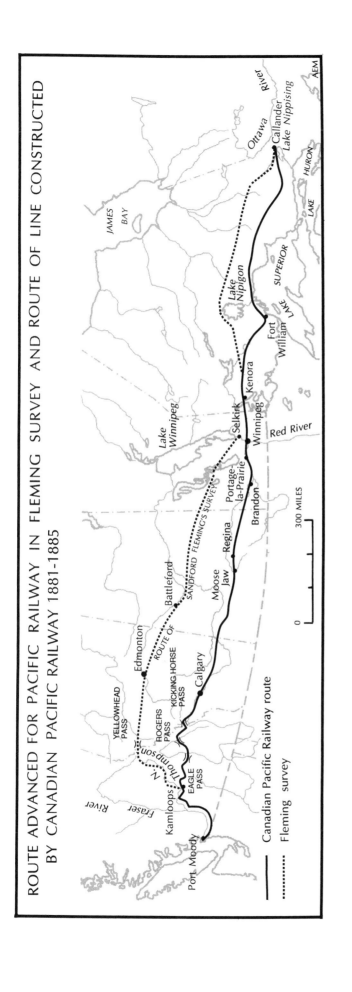

ROUTE ADVANCED FOR PACIFIC RAILWAY IN FLEMING SURVEY AND ROUTE OF LINE CONSTRUCTED BY CANADIAN PACIFIC RAILWAY 1881-1885

Canadian Pacific Railway route
Fleming survey

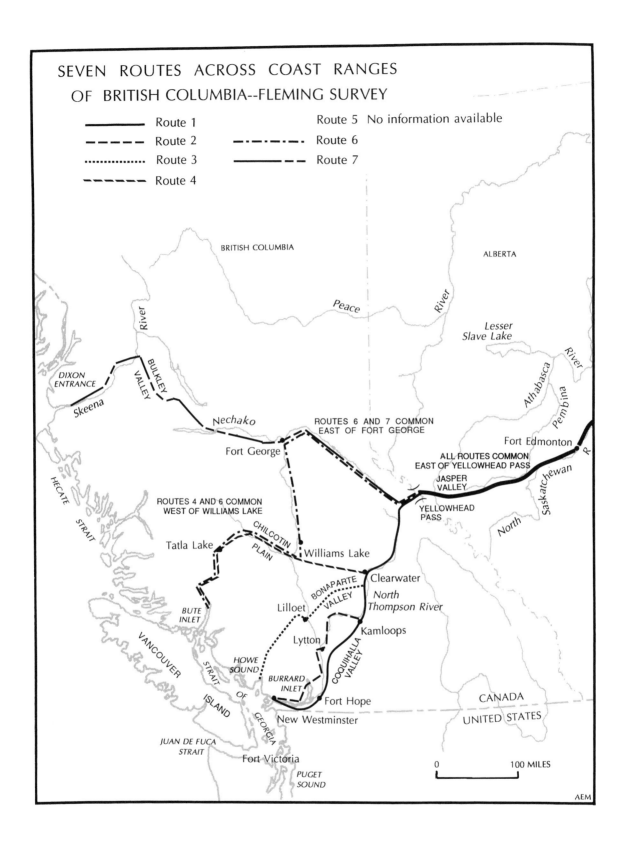

SEVEN ROUTES ACROSS COAST RANGES
OF BRITISH COLUMBIA--FLEMING SURVEY

——————— Route 1   Route 5 No information available
- - - - - - Route 2   -··-··-··- Route 6
·············· Route 3   — — — Route 7
- - - - - Route 4

BRITISH COLUMBIA   ALBERTA

Peace   River

Lesser
Slave Lake

River

DIXON
ENTRANCE   BULKLEY
VALLEY

Skeena

Nechako   ROUTES 6 AND 7 COMMON
EAST OF FORT GEORGE

Athabasca   Pembina

River

Fort Edmonton

ALL ROUTES COMMON
EAST OF YELLOWHEAD PASS

HECATE   Fort George   JASPER
VALLEY

STRAIT   North   Saskatchewan R.

YELLOWHEAD
PASS

ROUTES 4 AND 6 COMMON
WEST OF WILLIAMS LAKE   CHILCOTIN

Tatla Lake   PLAIN   Williams Lake

Clearwater   North
Thompson River

BONAPARTE
VALLEY

BUTE   Lilloet   CANADA
INLET

VANCOUVER   Lytton   Kamloops

HOWE
SOUND   COQUIHALLA
VALLEY

BURRARD
INLET

STRAIT   Fort Hope

ISLAND   OF   New Westminster   CANADA

GEORGIA   UNITED STATES

JUAN DE FUCA
STRAIT
Fort Victoria

PUGET   0   100 MILES
SOUND

AEM

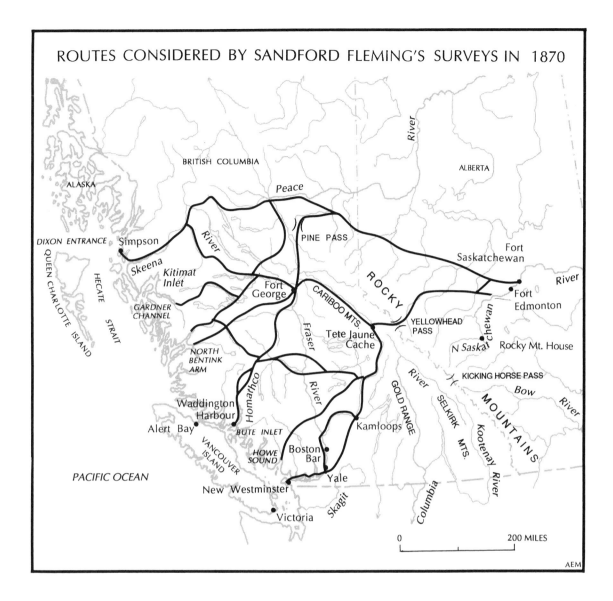

the River Skeena, as route to the seaboard. [It seems that this unfavorable view grew out of the isolation of that outlet (present-day Prince Rupert) more than anything else.][20]

    The appraisal of the routes, with the rather arbitrary rejection of the Skeena opening through the Coast Ranges, fell finally into three basic crossings of the great coastal mountain range: to the south, adjacent to the United States border, the lower Fraser Valley cut across the coastal range and offered a further way through the secondary ranges lying to the east and the western part of the central plateau butting against those coastal ranges; just to the north of the Fraser delta a fjord, Howe Sound, cut well into the coastal mountains and by way of a fairly low saddle, filled with two lakes dammed in this glacial valley, provided a possible connection with the Fraser north of its worst canyons; and still farther north another fjord, Bute Inlet, cut deeply into the ranges giving access over a single summit, reached only up a very narrow and steep canyon, to the interior plateau and the upper Fraser River valley. From each of the inland termini of

261

A Canadian
Postscript

these routes quite easy lines could be run to Yellowhead Pass and what was clearly an efficient crossing of the Rocky Mountains.

The Location of the Pacific Port

The resolution of which of these three basic alignments to employ revolved as much around the potential for the Pacific port at the end of the railroad as around the route across the mountains. Bute Inlet became the logical crossing for those pushing the use of Esquimalt (Victoria) as that terminus, whereas the Fraser crossing became the one self-evident opening to those plumping for the mouth of the Fraser or the less silted harbor lying just away from that mouth at Burrard Inlet. These were respectively the Victoria–Vancouver Island party and the New Westminster–Lower Mainland party. No one seems to have found Howe Sound either a compromise or a first choice.

The choice between the two contending routes came to revolve around the question of carrying a rail line from Bute Inlet across the scattered islands at the north end of Georgia Strait to reach Vancouver Island and thereby Esquimalt and Victoria. Fleming had the Bute Inlet–Vancouver Island extension examined for practicality, and the results were indeed daunting:

For a distance of about 50 miles from Waddington Harbour [the proposed terminus of the Bute Inlet crossing of the Coast Ranges], the only course for the line is to follow the base of the high rocky mountains which extend along Bute Inlet. On this section a great number of tunnels, varying from 100 to 3000 feet in length, through bluff rocky points, would be indispensable, and the work generally, even with unusually sharp curvature, would be very heavy.

Careful examination has established the fact that to reach Vancouver Island from the mainland the following clear span bridges would be required.

At	Arran Rapids		clear span	1100 feet.
"	Cardero Channel	—first opening	"	1350 "
"		—second opening	"	1140 "
"		—third opening	"	640 "
"	Middle Channel		"	1100 "
"	Seymour Narrows	—first opening	"	1200 "
"		—second opening	"	1350 "

The length of the Section across the group of Islands, known as Valdes Islands, lying between the mainland and Vancouver Island is about 30 miles. The channels to be bridged are of great depth, with the tide flowing from four to nine knots an hour.

In crossing the Islands, heavy rock excavation and probably a few short tunnels would be required.[21]

Taking everything into consideration, these eighty miles, lying between Waddington Harbour and Vancouver Island, would be of a most formidable character. The clear span of the required bridges may have lain beyond the technical competence of the time. Railroads have found suspension bridges unstable—John Augustus Roebling's span at Niagara had to be heavily guyed to resist the pounding of the locomotives, and that was hardly practicable at Seymour Narrows—and cantilever bridges had not as yet been utilized on railroads. Even when they were introduced just a few years later in Kentucky, they were of lesser spans than those required of a Vancouver Island bridge. And obviously, any economic justification for such a monumental engineering proj-

ect was totally lacking. In that situation the Vancouver Island route had to be abandoned, leaving the lower Fraser and Fraser Canyon route the clear choice for the "crossing of the Cascade Chain." All that remained to be decided was between Fleming's first and second routes. The excessive climbs and the tunneling resolved that question in favor of the second—cutting benches along the side of a canyon was far quicker than tunneling up to 3.75 miles, as the first route would have required.

The proposed alignment of the Canadian Pacific Railway was falling into place geographically. Burrard Inlet was to be its Pacific terminus, mainly to avoid the silting found on the lower Fraser, which made the earlier landing at New Westminster impractical for the larger oceangoing ships envisioned as the connection at the western end of the Pacific railroad of Canada. Crossing the low ground to the Fraser at the head of its delta, the route would pass eastward to the mouth of that river's canyon and then on benches cut into the side of the gorge until the easterly tributary, the Thompson, was reached. Following up the Thompson, still largely on benches cut into the side walls of the deep valley, the alignment would pass out of the canyons and to the broader, often glacially eroded valleys notched into the plateau surface of central British Columbia.

From Kamloops the route would continue eastward and then northward using the North Thompson and Canoe River valleys to reach a fairly gentle divide between the Canoe and the uppermost Fraser, here flowing northward. Both the Canoe and the upper Fraser in this area are guided in their courses by the great rift valley of the Rocky Mountain Trench, which carried the proposed route to the western end of Yellowhead Pass with little intervening grade. At that portal, here providing a crossing of the Continental Divide at 3,717 feet, quite practicable grades could be secured up both slopes of the gateway and passing

It was the Canadian Pacific Railroad's decision to skirt the north shore of Lake Superior in passing across the Canadian Shield between Sudbury and the Lakehead. *Source:* Canadian Pacific photo, Negative No. A 4247.

263

A Canadian Postscript

eastward to the western extremity of the prairies that lay beyond. First came a transit of the foothill band, here drained northward by the southernmost tributaries of the great McKenzie River. Before Fort Edmonton the Saskatchewan drainage into Hudson Bay was entered over a very gentle divide, and a well-graded line could be built on several possible alignments all the way to the edge of the Canadian Shield east of a crossing of the Red River at Fort Garry in Manitoba. Once these western locations were settled upon, all that remained was to determine the line across the Shield.

The Route across the Shield

In establishing that part of the route, the basic guidelines had been set by Sandford Fleming's original assumptions as to the desirable location. It should be remembered that he called for the most direct route possible between the end of the railroad system of eastern Canada, not far north of Ottawa at Callander on the southeastern corner of Lake Nipissing, and the Red River valley of Manitoba. Furthermore, this line should either directly, or by a reasonable branch, give access to the Lakehead on the northwestern shore of Lake Superior, whence a large traffic with the prairies could be carried from a point of transshipment from lake boats to the stretch of the railroad reaching to Fort Garry. And finally, access to the northern shore of Lake Superior would make it easier to land work crews, materials, and equipment at intermediate points along the line of construction, permitting faster building in this difficult terrain.

Given these criteria, the eastern alignment was fairly narrowly constrained in geographical terms. The jumping-off point for construction was Callander—then the northwestern extremity of the Canadian railway—at the southeastern extremity of Lake Nipissing. The route used the depression containing that large lake to pass westward to what became Sudbury, where it continued northwestward onto the slightly elevated surface of the Shield running in a fairly direct line near the watershed between the short streams flowing into Lake Superior and their longer twins flowing northward into James Bay. At what became Heron Bay, where the straight east-west shore north of Lake Superior begins, the alignment was carried directly westward on that shore to the mouth of the Nipigon River. In this last section heavy construction would be required, as the country for twenty miles back from the lake shore was considerably more hilly than the surface more central to the Shield. Beyond the mouth of the Nipigon River the shoreline turns southwestward, skirting Thunder Bay to reach Fort William. The shortest connection between Lake Superior and the prairies lay in a direct line via Kenora to the edge of the Shield on the Manitoba-Ontario boundary. This was adopted for the proposed route of the Canadian Pacific.

The Construction of the CPR

Fascinating as the construction of the Canadian Pacific Railway is, we cannot detail it here. All we can do is examine the undertaking in its broadest geographical features and the factors that helped to fix its final location. Before construction began there was an instance of the complex political maneuvering that became typical of Canadian railroad building. The explanation lies in the extreme form of developmental railroad that these later transcontinental lines were when built. The Union Pacific–Central Pacific had that quality in the

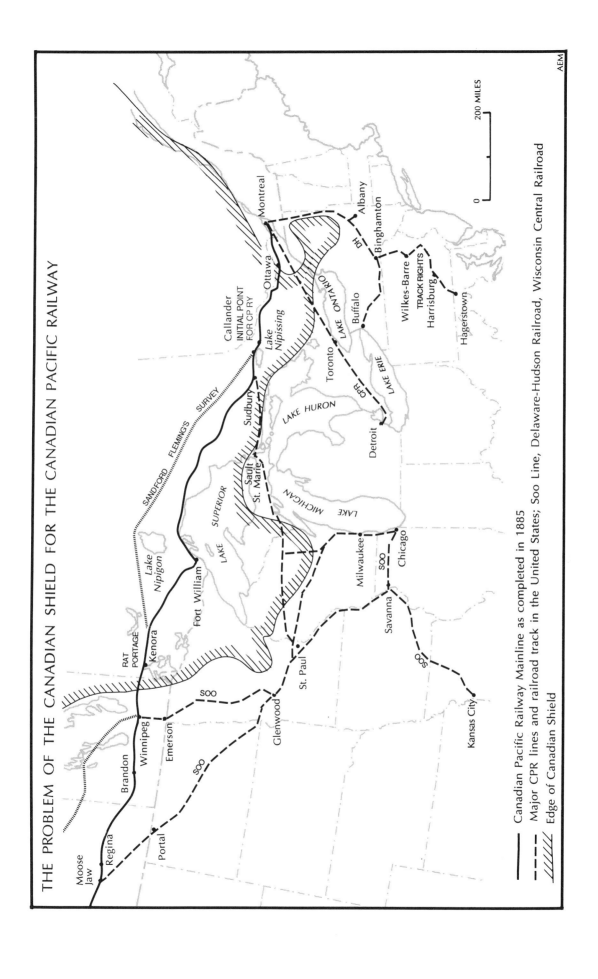

THE PROBLEM OF THE CANADIAN SHIELD FOR THE CANADIAN PACIFIC RAILWAY

Montreal
Albany
DH
Binghamton
Ottawa
Callander
INITIAL POINT
FOR CP RY
Lake
Nipissing
LAKE ONTARIO
Buffalo
Wilkes-Barre
TRACK RIGHTS
Harrisburg
Hagerstown
Toronto
CPR
LAKE ERIE
SANDFORD FLEMING'S SURVEY
Sudbury
LAKE HURON
Detroit
Sault
St. Marie
LAKE
SUPERIOR
LAKE MICHIGAN
Milwaukee
SOO
Chicago
Lake
Nipigon
Fort William
Savanna
RAT
PORTAGE
Kenora
St. Paul
SOO
SOO
Winnipeg
Glenwood
Emerson
Kansas City
Brandon
SOO
Portal
Regina
Moose
Jaw

_____ Canadian Pacific Railway Mainline as completed in 1885
- - - - Major CPR lines and railroad track in the United States; Soo Line, Delaware-Hudson Railroad, Wisconsin Central Railroad
/////// Edge of Canadian Shield

AEM

200 MILES
0

When Chapleau, midway between Sudbury and the shore of Lake Superior, was selected as a division point in CPR operations, these boarding houses and cottages were constructed for housing employees. *Source:* Canadian Pacific photo, Negative No. A 191791.

United States and experienced a similarly strong political component in its history. Later American transcontinental lines had complex corporate histories but normally somewhat less national political involvement. In the case of the Canadian Pacific there are several distinct phases in its evolution, one of which was totally governmental in nature.

Without going into what is essentially historical detail, we should recall that the proposed route was fairly well fixed by the mid-1870s and the tendering of Sandford Fleming's reports. The government of John A. Macdonald was anxious to get under way on construction, so it set about trying to find a private company to do the job. The self-evident choice was the Grand Trunk Railway Company, for that firm dominated Canadian railroading in a way no American company ever had dominated the industry in the United States. When approached, the London company promptly stated that it was not interested in the project and that "it was ready to fight to protect its own territory from Sarnia easterly from invasion." It soon became clear that the "Grand Trunk's economic interest cut squarely across the national interests of Canada. It had been designed to carry U.S. western traffic to Portland, Maine. Chicago was its logical western teminus, and it wanted no part of the Canadian ambition. Not until after 1900 did it move from that position."[22] With the obvious front runner hanging to the rear, Macdonald's government had to accept the fact that the Grand Trunk was very much a British presence in Canada; its mentality was that of British construction and British operation within a developed market. The peculiar situation of using a Canadian base to legitimize an interloping involvement in the American market did not endear the British company to its host country. The rigidity of the British conception of railroading could not encompass the Grand Trunk's advancing Canadian goals in distinction to those peculiarly British ones of its investors. But Americans fully understood what were clearly North American conceptions of railroad construction and purpose, and there were a number of capitalists and railroad managers from the United States anxious to participate in the building of the Canadian Pacific. For the Canadian government a major problem was the quasi-political one of keeping effective control in Canada while drawing on American money and experience.[23] Canada at that time just did not have the body of railway-building experience or the organization that was available in the United States. More important, it was doubtful whether Canada could raise even the initial capital necessary to set so large a project in motion. To be able to draw upon the experience and the resources of American capitalists would be a very great help. When earning power had been developed, it would be possible to raise further money in London; but a substantial and dependable equity interest, fully established in the property, was a first necessity.

Canadian domicile for the company and the absence of Americans on the board of directors became the basis of the government's policy. Given that there were only some thirty thousand white settlers in all of Canada between Lake Nipissing and the Pacific, it is not surprising that the American capitalists proved lukewarm to making massive investments in a company over which they would have little effective say.[24] It was one thing to be conversant with the nature of the developmental railroad, quite a different one to be stripped of any effective role in advancing the development that would justify the considerable risk involved in that sort of undertaking.

Having effectively excluded the Americans, the Macdonald government began to try to organize a Canadian group to take their place. The result was the "Pacific Scandal" that drove the Conservative party from office in 1873, just at the time the panic of that year pretty much ruled out any effective investment for several years to come.

The Alexander Mackenzie government, which replaced Canada's less Olympian version of George Washington, could raise no private interest in the Pacific railroad, and yet the ten years promised to British Columbia were passing. In desperation the government turned to direct construction. Fleming had made the actual location of the line as far west as Yellowhead Pass by 1876, so building could commence that year on the two sections that seemed most likely to justify the initial investment: the stretch from Fort William to Selkirk on the Red River of Manitoba, and that from Selkirk southward via Winnipeg to Pembina on the United States border.[25] But even on this limited project progress was slow. When Macdonald returned to power in 1878 attempts were made to speed up building by laying out a new line in Manitoba—shifting the crossing of the Red River from Selkirk to Fort Garry, now Winnipeg, to conform more to the pattern of settlement that had actually taken place in the Red River valley.

By 1880 it was clear that government construction was not proving satisfactory, as to either speed or substance. At that juncture Macdonald decided that the best course was to seek instead a private syndicate to undertake the building and operation of the Canadian Pacific. Still eschewing the largely historical details of the search for undertakers, we may merely note that he again rejected active American involvement—in the form of the group that had pushed the Northern Pacific across the Dakotas—turning instead to Canadians, or to Britons. Puleston Brown and Company of London sought the charter and the government subvention that would go with it, involving the French Société Générale as a major source of funds. George Stephen and the Bank of Montréal

267

A Canadian
Postscript

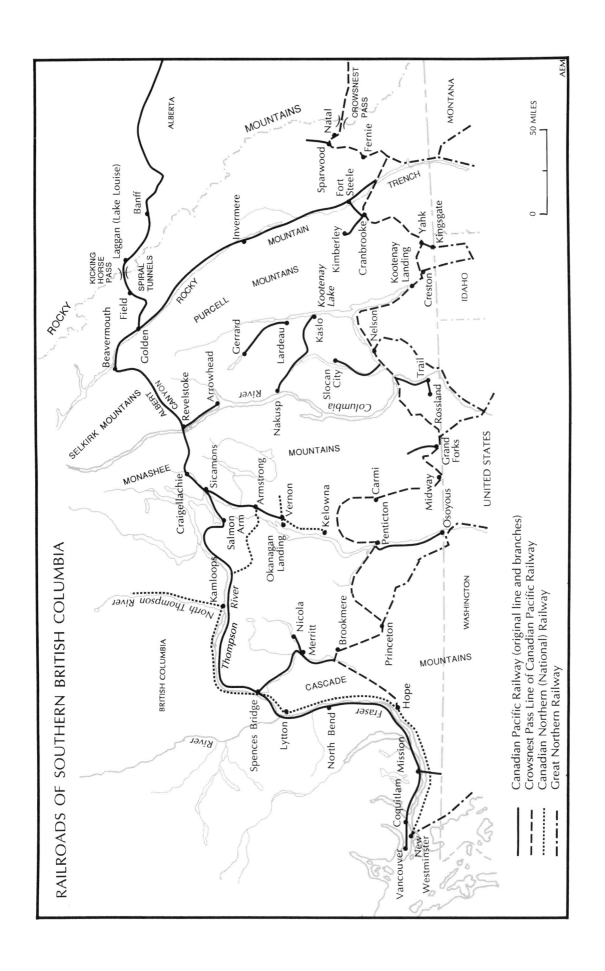

RAILROADS OF SOUTHERN BRITISH COLUMBIA

Canadian Pacific Railway (original line and branches)

Crowsnest Pass Line of Canadian Pacific Railway

Canadian Northern (National) Railway

Great Northern Railway

ALBERTA

BRITISH COLUMBIA

MONTANA

IDAHO

WASHINGTON

UNITED STATES

ROCKY MOUNTAINS

PURCELL MOUNTAINS

SELKIRK MOUNTAINS

MONASHEE MOUNTAINS

CASCADE MOUNTAINS

TRENCH

CROWSNEST PASS

KICKING HORSE PASS

SPIRAL TUNNELS

ALBERT CANYON

Banff

Laggan (Lake Louise)

Field

Beavermouth

Golden

Invermere

Natal

Sparwood

Fort Steele

Kimberley

Cranbrooke

Yahk

Kingsgate

Creston

Kootenay Landing

Kootenay Lake

Nelson

Kaslo

Lardeau

Gerrard

Arrowhead

Revelstoke

Nakusp

Slocan City

Trail

Rossland

Grand Forks

Craigellachie

Sicamons

Armstrong

Vernon

Kelowna

Carmi

Midway

Osoyous

Penticton

Salmon Arm

Okanagan Landing

Kamloops

Nicola

Merritt

Brookmere

Princeton

Spences Bridge

Lytton

North Bend

Hope

Coquitlam

Mission

New Westminster

Vancouver

Fraser River

Thompson River

North Thompson River

Columbia River

Fernie

50 MILES

0

AEM

attempted at the same time to form a true Canadian syndicate. Neither group was particularly pleased with what the government seemed to offer in subsidies, and eventually the London syndicate withdrew because it would have to be general contractor, and it feared the potential loss on the actual construction. In that situation Stephen and his Montréal group became the undertakers by default.[26]

The Organization of the CPR

The organization of the Canadian company to construct and then operate the Pacific railroad took some time and was very complex. This has so frequently been recounted in histories of transportation in the Dominion that there is no need here to repeat the story. It should be noted that in 1878 Sandford Fleming had made a formal recommendation to the government that the Burrard Inlet terminus on the Pacific be adopted and that the route via the Fraser and Thompson rivers through the Coast Ranges be used.[27] We should also remember that a considerable amount of construction had already been accomplished before the private Canadian Pacific Railway Company undertook the completion of the transcontinental line. Over 700 miles was nearing completion—410 miles from Fort William to Selkirk, 85 miles from Selkirk to Emerson (near the United States border), 100 miles westward from the Red River at Fort Garry (Winnipeg), and 127 miles eastward from Port Moody on Burrard Inlet in British Columbia.[28] The proposed route from Lake Nipissing (Callander) to Fort William seems to have been viewed rather differently by participants in the construction. George Stephen and James J. Hill (then a large investor in the company), both of whom had major financial interests in the St. Paul, Minneapolis, and Manitoba Railway already reaching to Fargo in the Dakotas, and soon to be extended to the Canadian border at Pembina (Emerson), seem to have intended to delay any serious effort at constructing across the Shield from Callander to Fort William for some considerable period of time. The man they recommended for heading the construction effort, then the general superintendent of the Chicago, Milwaukee, and St. Paul Railroad, William Van Horne, thought otherwise when he accepted the invitation to become general manager of the Canadian Pacific Railway.[29] Van Horne prevailed, causing Hill to withdraw from the CPR, and to set about his own course of transcontinental railroading that brought his Great Northern Railway to Seattle in the 1890s.

Problem Areas of the CPR

Three areas posed the most severe problems to the builders of the Canadian Pacific: the passage across the Shield to Fort William; the transit of the Rockies and Selkirks from the prairies to Kamloops; and the line from Kamloops westward through the Thompson and Fraser gorges to Emory's Bar, where the valley opens out into the "Lower Mainland" of today's British Columbia. The first two of these were the responsibility of the company, and thereby of Van Horne, whereas the third remained the responsibility of the government, which had commenced construction there in British Columbia in the late 1870s and continued its section (to Kamloops) even after the company took over the rest of the line.

Sandford Fleming's basic route from Callander to Fort William was

269

A Canadian
Postscript

The completion of
the Canadian Pacific
Railway was signaled
for workers when
Onderdonk, the
contractor for the
western section of
the line, posted this
notice in 1885. *Source:*
Canadian Pacific picture.

NOTICE!

YALE, B. C., SEPT. 26, 1885.

AS OUR LAST RAIL FROM THE PACIFIC HAS BEEN LAID IN
Eagle Pass to-day,

And the balance of work undertaken by the CANADIAN PACIFIC RAIL-WAY COMPANY between Savona and point of junction in Eagle Pass will be Completed for the Season on WEDNESDAY,

ALL EMPLOYEES WILL BE DISCHARGED

On the Evening of September Thirtieth.

Application for position in the Operation Department for the present may be made to M. J. HANEY, but the above portion of line will not be operated until Notice is given to that effect by the VICE PRESIDENT.

ALL ACCOUNTS

Should be liquidated before the TENTH PROXIMO, at Yale, as the books of the Company should be closed on that day.

A. Onderdonk.

adopted by Van Horne, though there were major shifts in the precise location of the line. The seemingly endless alternation of rock knobs and rock basins (filled with swamps or lakes) made construction slow, costly, and seemingly unrewarding, since little on-line support could ever be envisaged. It was for this reason that Stephen had wanted to put off this construction, but Van Horne did not want to be dependent on anyone for his connections, even Hill, the man who had first raised his name for the general manager's job. So blasting and filling followed its slow progression once construction on the company section began in 1882.

During 1883 a hundred miles were completed west of Callander and thirty-five miles around Port Arthur (a twin town to Fort William laid out by the CPR to match the earlier Hudson's Bay Company post on the site). The next year some 300 miles of track in this Shield section were completed, with 193 miles of grade without track in addition. By then trains were running as far west as Sudbury. In May 1885 the track was finally completed to the Lakehead and passenger service began to Port Arthur, having already run from there westward to Winnipeg in 1883.[30] On this "Eastern or Woodland" section the amount of rock to be dealt with was almost prodigious, more by the continuity of ledge over hundreds of miles than by any great hills and valleys that had to be crossed. Only along the shore of Lake Superior were there any considerable hills, with cliffs, though they added to the burden of rock work on this section, raising its per-mile costs well above those of most developmental railroads.

In the prairie section work was reasonably light, though Van Horne questioned the categorizing of the region as "prairie": "The so-called Prairie section is not prairie at all, it is broken, rolling country, with a great deal of heavy work, and the line we are building is a very different thing from [the] standard fixed [by the government survey] and costing double the price of a poor Prairie road."[31] One senses his middle-western training in railroad construction in this comment. In western Canada the semiarid land of thin glacial cover and heavy erosion was certainly in contrast to the flat-lying and till-cover lands of Illinois and Iowa. Also, Van Horne was talking about a very different route from that proposed by Sandford Fleming. When the company undertook its contract, it made one absolutely fundamental change in Fleming's proposed route: moving it southward from the Fertile Belt extending generally northwestward from Winnipeg to Edmonton to run much closer to the 49th parallel. Having shifted the line to cross the Red River valley well to the south of Selkirk, at Winnipeg, carrying the alignment due westward could shorten the route significantly, as Burrard Inlet lay only a short distance north of the international boundary. "Such a position would bring two benefits: it would enable the company to compete for American traffic, and protect its American connections after the twenty-year restrictions had run out," a restriction forbidding the building of any competing railroad between the CPR and the boundary for a period of twenty years.[32] Thus, there was in the transcontinental project some of the strategy of the Grand Trunk: trying to enhance the meager development of Canada by invading the American market, or at least by keeping out branches of American railroads.

It has been argued in addition that one of the prime investors in the CPR, Donald Smith of the Hudson's Bay Company, may have sought by shifting the line southward to protect that company's fur-trapping areas from immediate settlement. That settlement was still problematic, as the wheat varieties then being planted could not ripen in the more northerly parts of the prairies; thus, in the 1880s southern Manitoba and Saskatchewan seemed the better land for immigrants, even if less naturally "fertile."

This decision to move the route southward in the prairies away from the line surveyed by Fleming has puzzled all those looking into the matter. Some have argued that it was the naturalist John Macoun, who had accompanied the Fleming expedition in 1872, who brought it about; he certainly was a strong proponent of the idea that Captain John Palisser and others had painted the picture of the fertility of the southern prairies in too somber tones. But if the company was convinced of that fact, and that is why the southerly route was adopted, it is hard indeed to explain why the company in turn took much of its land grant not along this route in southern Alberta but rather in the Fertile Belt to the north. It seems to me that Pierre Berton has supplied the most plausible explanation. He has argued that the decision was motivated by the company's desire to build through absolutely unsettled country, in order to control all the potential town sites, and in a region where no competing transportation was in existence, or could (under the charter) be introduced for a period of twenty

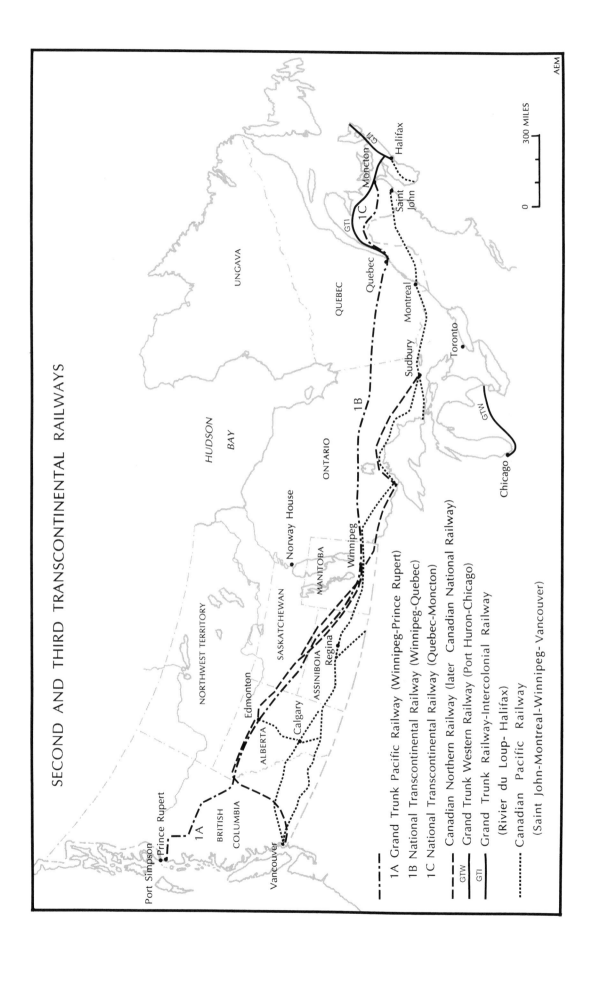

SECOND AND THIRD TRANSCONTINENTAL RAILWAYS

1A Grand Trunk Pacific Railway (Winnipeg-Prince Rupert)

1B National Transcontinental Railway (Winnipeg-Quebec)

1C National Transcontinental Railway (Quebec-Moncton)

Canadian Northern Railway (later Canadian National Railway)

GTW — Grand Trunk Western Railway (Port Huron-Chicago)

GTI — Grand Trunk Railway-Intercolonial Railway
(Rivier du Loup-Halifax)

Canadian Pacific Railway
(Saint John-Montreal-Winnipeg-Vancouver)

300 MILES

0

AEM

years. To back up that view Berton notes that it was James J. Hill—while he was still part of the syndicate—who pushed through the decision, and that he was consistently a proponent of the notion of avoiding all competition in transport and making the major return on invested capital from utter domination of all shipments, inbound and outbound. In other words, Hill was a dedicated latter-day mercantilist and fully part of the now North American practice of building economically, laying out a line ahead of the market, and then totally controlling both line and market for a long period of time.[33]

The CPR in the West

The original contract between the Canadian government and the syndicate that formed the Canadian Pacific Railway company called for the construction of the line up to the standard of the Union Pacific when first built. This meant that in shifting the alignment to the southern prairies no section might exceed the grade of 116 feet per mile (2.2 percent) that had been adopted almost at the beginning when the Baltimore and Ohio was assaulting the Allegheny Front west of Cumberland. Thus, once the Canadian Parliament had accepted the change in prairie alignment, merely specifying that a pass no less than a hundred miles north of the United States border must be used, the company was committed to finding a route through the Rockies at no greater a grade than 2.2 percent, and in addition a similarly good alignment across the Selkirk Range, which in this latitude lies across the potential route. Still, the syndicate accepted those challenges and began building westward from Winnipeg and laying out absolutely new towns where the potential for growth appeared good. Brandon was the first, to be followed by Regina, Moose Jaw, Calgary, Revelstoke, and paramountly Vancouver. The construction on the prairies continued apace, and by the onset of winter in 1882 nearly five hundred miles had been built.

This push due westward was an almost incredible gamble: when the decision for it was made, there was no assurance that there was a usable mountain pass anywhere near that latitude. James Hector had passed in a trying fashion through Kicking Horse Pass—he was the one who was kicked—a generation earlier, but there was no reasonable assurance that a railroad might be laid out in his tracks. And the Selkirk Range, lying to the west across the Rocky Mountain Trench, was seriously believed to be unbroachable. If a British or Canadian historian were to describe this state of geographical knowledge and a decision of this sort made by an American company, I believe the adjective *irresponsible* would automatically be applied. Better, it seems, would be the terms *brave* and *sanguine*.

Rogers Pass

In the summer of 1881 Major Albert Bowman Rogers, hired by James Hill for the Canadian Pacific Railway, did conduct preliminary surveys in the Selkirks that held out some hope for a usable pass. The next summer he conducted a detailed survey of Kicking Horse Pass and, after severe trials, did manage to find a seemingly practicable route through it, though it later had to be rebuilt because snows and avalanches proved a real difficulty and its grade was nearly double the acceptable maximum. During that same survey season, 1882, he finally confirmed the existence of Rogers Pass in the Selkirks, which with very heavy

In the 1970s it became clear that the traffic flow on the Canadian Pacific Railway was shifting, with a rapid increase in transpacific trade and a decline in transatlantic trade. The Rockies and the mountains of British Columbia were less favorable to westbound movement, with grades of over 2 percent facing shipments toward Vancouver and Robert's Bank. In that situation, the CPR decided to undertake a costly tunneling project at Rogers Pass, to lower the height of the crest to a grade of just under 1 percent compensated, so that trains might operate there with no additional pusher or helper engines. With this project finished, the power required to run up the high plains (prairies) would suffice to carry freights across the Selkirks (using a nine-mile tunnel). *Source:* Canadian Pacific map.

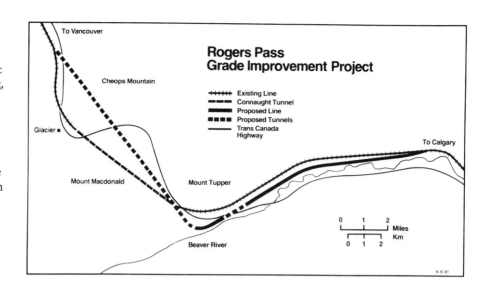

Rogers Pass
Grade Improvement Project

++++++ Existing Line
----- Connaught Tunnel
▬▬▬ Proposed Line
▪▪▪▪ Proposed Tunnels
——— Trans Canada Highway

To Vancouver

Cheops Mountain

Glacier ▪

Mount Macdonald   Mount Tupper

Beaver River

To Calgary

0   1   2 Miles
0   1   2 Km

6 6 81

engineering could be held to the 2.2 percent ruling grade adopted, though again it had later to be improved with a five-mile tunnel and a considerable relocation to overcome snow and avalanches. More recent construction of a nine-mile tunnel under the pass has finally made available a compensated 1 percent grade in the direction of heaviest movement in the Selkirks, which opened to freight service in 1989. It seems basically true that the Yellowhead Pass was a far preferable route for a pioneering railroad—it had a bit of settlement along its course, it did prove to pass through better land for agricultural settlement, and it was vastly ahead in grades, and thereby in continuing costs of operation. The Canadian aphorism has always been, "The Canadian Pacific [Kicking Horse Pass] has the scenery, while the Canadian National [Yellowhead Pass] has the gradients!"

The key does seem to lie in the matter of town-site development and monopoly of transportation. The CPR came early to realize that only upon completion was there likely to be any appreciable economic support for the line, given the essentially unsettled nature of this route between Winnipeg and the Pacific coast, where even its terminal city was built on a site at first literally no more than a sawmill in a dense forest. In that situation speed in construction was essential. Even though the company had ten years to fulfill the contract, it set about doing so in five and ended up completing the track less than four years after actual construction had commenced. By June 1883 rails had reached the Continental Divide in Kicking Horse Pass, but the greatest engineering trials still faced the company virtually all the way to the already established juncture with the government-built line moving eastward from the British Columbia coast. In the interests of that speed of construction, the company rejected the preliminary line Major Rogers had located down Kicking Horse Pass to the flat where Field, British Columbia, now stands and substituted a "Big Hill" with grades of 232 feet per mile (4.4 percent) for four miles plus an additional three and a half miles at 4 percent beyond Field. Going up took an hour for the eight miles, and going down, if slightly faster, was totally harrowing. Trains all too often ran away, so safety shunt lines were built and the switches were manned at all times, but even that expedient was not sufficient. Trains had to be broken into short segments, all brakes were set, and emergency water brakes were added. It was only after

1909 that the CPR decided to return to Major Rogers's plan and drill the necessary tunnels, among which was the famous double circular tunnel drilled into
the mountainside to lengthen the line, and thereby reduce the grade, in a great
subterranean figure eight. But the expediently steep original line permitted
William Van Horne to carry his track from the summit down to the Columbia
(at present-day Golden, British Columbia), between June and September 1884.[34]

    Once on the Columbia, the crews faced an even more daunting task, that of
crossing the highly Alpine Selkirk Range. From the Columbia a steep west-bank
tributary, Beaver River, was used to gain elevation on a practicable grade. Twenty
miles up its valley a further tributary heading from the west, now Beaver Creek,

275

A Canadian
Postscript

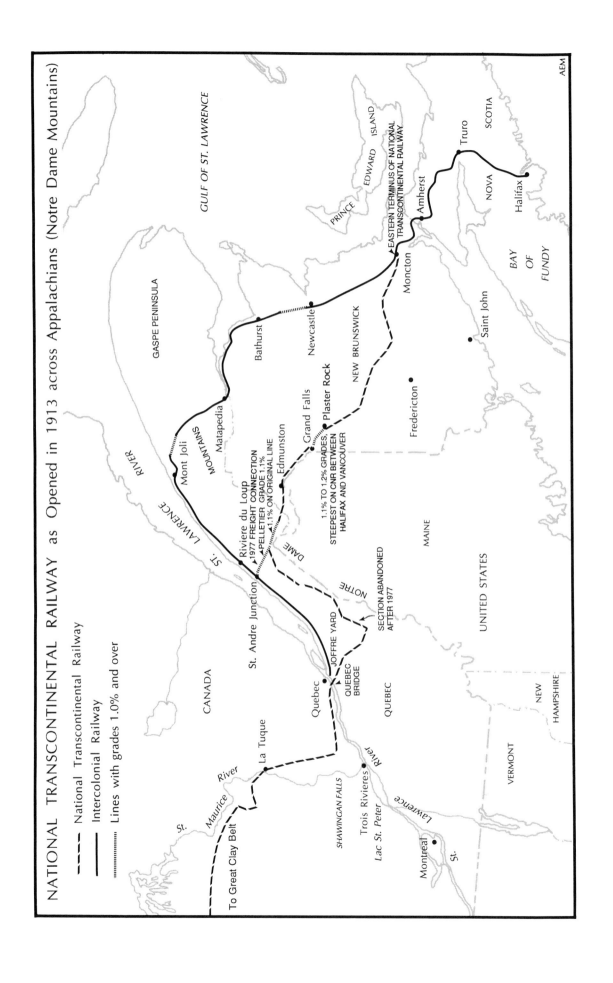

NATIONAL TRANSCONTINENTAL RAILWAY as Opened in 1913 across Appalachians (Notre Dame Mountains)

National Transcontinental Railway
Intercolonial Railway
Lines with grades 1.0% and over

carried the rail line toward Rogers Pass, but only at the cost of high wooden trestles carried over the torrents crashing down the northern slope of this narrowing valley. Finally the crest was reached, and the Illecillewaet River flowed south of west toward the Columbia, here returned from its great sweep around the northern end of the Selkirks. But conditions became even more difficult— from extremely heavy vegetation and very high water, the meltwater from the forty-odd glaciers ringing this valley in summer. Winters were even more frightful. The snow in the pass averaged fifty feet a winter, and up to eight or nine feet could fall in a single storm. Avalanches were frequent, torrents from the glaciers grabbed at the weak grades scrabbled out of the mountainside, and the pitch of the track was more than the contract called for. But until 1910 this line had to suffice for a railroad not overly endowed with capital and still passing through mostly thinly settled areas. Still, the track was pushed westward to a second crossing of the Columbia (at what became Revelstoke). The problems of this Rogers Pass stretch were such that in 1910 the company decided to invest in a five-mile tunnel under the pass, lowering the summit level by 540 feet and greatly reducing the dangers of avalanches and the constant problem of extremely heavy snows. The tunnel was straight, so not only was the line reduced by four and a half miles but also curves amounting to seven circles were removed.[35] More will be said about this Rogers Pass stretch at the conclusion of this chapter.

From this second crossing of the Columbia the country became more kindly, though hardly gentle. Yet another crest faced the westward progress, the Gold Range of that time, now called the Monashees, but the glaciers had carved a deep, wide valley, Eagle Pass, through it and the track could advance rapidly. By November 1885 rails were west of the Gold Range, while the slow progress of track construction under way since the mid-1870s in the Fraser and Thompson canyons and along the shores of Kamloops and Shuswap lakes was carrying the rails from the Pacific eastward. On the morning of November 7, 1885, on the very western slopes of the Gold Range, at a section house called Craigellachie, the final spike—steel, like the millions of others already set—was driven and the Canadian Pacific railroad was initially complete.[36]

The line from Montréal to Port Moody at the eastern end of Burrard Inlet in British Columbia extended for 2,893 miles. Van Horne had already determined that Port Moody was too cramped a site for the great city he anticipated as his terminus, so he decided upon Coal Harbour, just inside the First Narrows of Burrard Inlet, as his terminus. The fourteen additional miles were constructed, and in 1886 the absolutely pristine city of Vancouver began to grow as the Pacific port for the Pacific railroad of Canada. But the absence of any appreciable population in this vast realm west of Winnipeg meant that the CPR was a true archetype of the developmental line. In 1886 it earned $2,357 per mile of line; that same year the St. Paul, Minneapolis, and Manitoba Railway earned $4,978 and the Northern Pacific $4,316 per mile, and these were at best highly developmental lines in their own right.[37] For twenty years the Canadian Pacific was short on earnings, and thus short on money for capital improvements or massive extensions of its lines. Only in the late 1890s and the first decade of the twentieth century did the picture begin to change. Wheat boomed in that period, acreages expanded greatly, and there was a large immigration into Saskatchewan and Alberta, heavily American in the first decade of the twentieth century, all of

A Canadian
Postscript

which lifted the company's fortunes. But only then did the market begin to take on the character that truly justified the construction that for political reasons had been carried out in the 1880s. The CPR was just as premature and equally political as the Union Pacific and the Central Pacific had been.

The Later Transcontinentals of Canada

The brightening market of the prairies in the 1890s rapidly kindled interest in other railroads in the West, and those thoughts led fairly quickly to notions of a second, and soon a third, transcontinental railroad. The story is complicated and must be only briefly summarized here. It all began in 1887, when the Canadian Pacific Railway had concluded that the "monopoly clause" in its charter that forbade the chartering of any other line between the Canadian Pacific main line and the United States border was actually a disadvantage to the company. George Stephen, soon to resign as president of the CPR, proposed that it be replaced by a sizable federal money grant and permission from the Canadian government to gain control of the Minneapolis, St. Paul, and Sault Ste. Marie Railway, familiarly known as the Soo Line. Ultimately the government agreed, and what is now by its denizens called the Upper Midwest of the United States became a field of operations for Canada's Pacific railroad. In turn, Manitoba was opened to others, and the Northern Pacific entered the fray in 1888. The Soo Line gave the CPR access to Duluth from the west, and by picking up the ailing Duluth, South Shore [of Lake Superior], and Atlantic the company gained a second transcontinental route—from Sudbury to Sault Ste. Marie, Ontario, on a CPR branch—skirting the southern edge of the Canadian Shield and reaching Winnipeg and the West south of Lake Superior. This had been a routing proposed by the Grand Trunk when it was approached by the Canadian government in the 1870s as the potential builder of a Pacific railroad, but one soundly rejected by John A. Macdonald as not in any way a *Canadian* Pacific railroad.[38] George Stephen was reported to have considered gaining entry into the Upper Midwest while shedding the monopoly in the prairies as his "last, . . . greatest service to the maintenance of the power and the independence of the national highway," that is, the CPR.[39] Despite its impeccably Canadian birth, the Canadian Pacific came quite promptly to follow the Grand Trunk's course of borrowing some of the Great Republic's market to make ends meet north of the border.

The Canadian Northern Railway

With the monopoly clause removed, other promoters could begin to push lines into the prairies, something encouraged by the rapid settlement of the more productive areas of Manitoba and Saskatchewan and the quick rise in wheat production and sales. The most significant of these promotions was one that began as a short line connecting from Portage la Prairie on the Canadian Pacific in western Manitoba to Dauphin in the burgeoning wheat country west of Lake Manitoba, which would have been served by Sandford Fleming's original alignment of the transcontinental that passed from Selkirk on the Red River across the narrows of Lake Manitoba to the Dauphin country. With the CPR line having been moved south of the lake, there was a strong feeling in Manitoba that a line to Dauphin was required, and the provincial government offered a bond

A survey crew on
the Canadian Shield
section of the
Canadian Northern
Railway. *Source:*
Canadian National photo.

Grading on the prairies for the line of the Canadian Northern Railway. *Source:* Canadian National photo.

guarantee to get it built. In 1895 the government succeeded in interesting two temporarily unemployed railroad contractors, Donald Mann and William Mackenzie, in the needed line. Starting with a peculiar $5,000 loan from the mother superior of a Montréal convent, this partnership eventually managed to carry out its objectives, which became transcontinental, by borrowing more than $300 million from Canadian, American, and British investors.[40]

It is impossible here to recount the detail of the Canadian Northern Railway, which began with this short line in Manitoba in 1895. After having rapidly spread lines to the more productive parts of the Fertile Belt in the eastern prairies, Mackenzie and Mann formed the Canadian Northern Railway and began to look beyond their nursery region. As fundamentally wheat carriers, they were intrigued with the idea of gaining access to the Lakehead whence the grain could be carried by lake boat to the port of Montréal. In this push for the point of articulation of transportation on Lake Superior they were greatly encouraged by the Manitoba government and by prairie farmers who wished to break the functional monopoly of the Canadian Pacific. By New Year's Eve, 1901, trains were leaving both Port Arthur at the Lakehead and Winnipeg, thus bringing about the desired competition with "the company."[41] The Canadian Northern did not rest long on this success. Mackenzie and Mann were bitten by the same bug that had infected James J. Hill in the 1880s: they wanted their own transcontinental railroad, and to get it they had to continue on to eastern Canada from Port Arthur and westward in the prairies to the Rockies and beyond. Already at Port Arthur, any eastern extension was logically to be located around the northern side of Lake Superior, and that remained a daunting project even in 1901. Instead, Mackenzie and Mann began by gaining control of smaller companies already operating in the eastern part of Ontario, and in Québec and the Maritimes. In this way they came into possession of a fairly well integrated eastern Canadian railroad system, but one obviously totally detached from the system they were developing in the prairies. "Initially Mackenzie and Mann hoped to use a joint water-and-land route from Port Arthur to Montreal and Quebec City. In order to do this they acquired an interest in several Great Lakes shipping ventures and began serious negotiations with several eastern railway promoters. . . . The most desirable eastern railway [they] tried to acquire was the Canada Atlantic [which] . . . had a completed line from Depot Harbour on Georgian Bay to Coteau Junction near Montreal."[42] The Grand Trunk tried to block the sale and in 1904 bought the line for itself.[43]

Mackenzie and Mann felt betrayed by the Wilfrid Laurier government in Ottawa, and they turned their attention to the provincial government of Ontario, which in 1908 guaranteed the bonds for building a five-hundred-mile route from Port Arthur to Sudbury and gave four thousand acres of land per mile for what was a logical continuation of the Canadian Northern of the prairies. This was still not enough to encourage Mackenzie and Mann to push ahead across the Canadian Shield, an undertaking that had nearly bankrupted the better-subsidized Canadian Pacific. The eastern link remained unbuilt, and it seemed that the only way for the Canadian Northern to gain a tie with the thousand miles of line it owned in eastern Canada was by means of cooperation or consolidation with American railroads passing from the Upper Midwest to the Middle West south of Lake Superior. When that eventually was bruited in

A track-laying machine used to place track on the right-of-way of the Canadian Northern Railway in the crossing of the Canadian Shield. *Source:* Canadian National photo.

The pioneering track of the Canadian Northern Railway on the Canadian Shield. *Source:* Canadian National photo.

Grain elevators on
the Canadian
Northern Railway in
the prairies. *Source:*
Canadian National photo.

1910, the Canadian government finally produced the necessary bond guarantee.[44] In 1911 Canadian Prime Minister Laurier stated,

It is in the interests of Canada as a whole that another line of railway designed to assist
in the direct and economic interchange of traffic between the eastern and western
portions of Canada, to open up and develop portions as yet without railway facilities,
to promote the internal and foreign trade of Canada, to develop commerce through
Canadian ports, and to afford the Government system of railways in Quebec, New
Brunswick, and Nova Scotia and Prince Edward Island an interchange of through
traffic, should be constructed from the Pacific Ocean to the City of Montreal.[45]

This act caused Mackenzie and Mann to put men to work in 1911, and construction between Port Arthur and Montréal was rapid. The line had fine grades, 0.5
percent at the maximum, excellent curvature (6 degrees), and a sound infrastructure. To reach downtown Montréal the promoters undertook a costly tunnel under Mount Royal, and at the northern end of this tunnel they laid out the
new town of Mount Royal. The line selected was to run from Capreol at the edge
of settlement north of Lake Nipissing along the watershed between Lake Superi-
or and James Bay, thus to the north of Lake Nipigon, and then southwestward
to Port Arthur. This was opened to transcontinental traffic in 1915, when the
western extension was completed.

While the Canadian Northern was seeking to tie its system together in the
east, it also turned its eyes toward the Pacific. The line having been extended to
Edmonton from Winnipeg, by 1905 the railroad officials began to think of a
Pacific terminus to match that on the St. Lawrence. There was already at hand a
fully explored route, the one Sandford Fleming had recommended for the
Canadian Pacific. "In 1908 surveys were begun through the Yellowhead Pass to
Vancouver, following the line traced by Fleming."[46] Building toward the pass
from Edmonton began soon thereafter, and in 1910 a subsidiary aided by British
Columbia, called the Canadian Northern Pacific, began construction of the

section from Yellowhead Pass (the provincial boundary) to Vancouver. This line had the same very favorable grades as the stretch north of Lake Superior (0.5 percent) and could, on completion, be operated without helper engines, a luxury the CPR western line has enjoyed only since 1989. Only in the Thompson and Fraser canyons, where the Canadian Northern Pacific occupied the opposite side from the CPR, was heavy construction required. It was money rather than terrain that slowed the course, but gaining successive governmental subsidies, the Canadian Northern was completed in September 1915—an excellent line, certainly the best transcontinental route in Canada, but it was by then an exhausted company.

The Grand Trunk Pacific Railway and the National Transcontinental Railway

That exhaustion was further compounded by the fact that during 1914 another Canadian transcontinental railroad had been completed, so the Canadian Northern was the third to enter the field. It may be recalled that in the late 1870s, and again just before the Canadian Pacific syndicate was organized in 1882, the Grand Trunk was approached by the Canadian government to explore the possibility of the London company's undertaking the national project. The proprietors firmly rejected both tentative invitations and continued to maintain their view that the only economic role for railroads in eastern Canada was to serve as the outlet for the American Middle West. But the increasing numbers of settlers heading to the Canadian West in the 1890s, and the enlarging amounts of wheat they started to send east, began to shake the company's objection to participating in a transcontinental project. By 1910 the Grand Trunk Railway had come to the conclusion that the company should enter the western portion of the country, though it still as firmly shied away from the notion of constructing a line north of Lake Superior. In what seems a distinctly inside deal with the government, the Grand Trunk organized a separate company to build a "western division" from Winnipeg to the Pacific in a manner "not inferior to the main line of the Grand Trunk Railway Company of Canada between Montreal and Toronto, so far as may be practicable in the case of a newly constructed line of railway."[47] From Winnipeg eastward a "National Transcontinental Railway" was to be built to Québec City and onward to Moncton in New Brunswick. Because that eastern section had to conform to the infrastructure of the Grand Trunk Pacific, its western partner, the whole thing was conducted at a level considerably more costly than either the original Canadian Pacific or the contemporary Canadian Northern.

The route chosen for this pair of railroads was certainly reminiscent of the original CPR, passing for the major distance beyond the contemporary limit of settlement in Canada. From Moncton to Québec the National Transcontinental passed largely through the infertile stretches of the Appalachians, which still remained in forest. At Québec a great bridge, still the world's longest railroad span, would be required to carry the line across to the northern shore of the river. After the unaccustomed urbanity of the province's capital city, the National Transcontinental headed into the fastness of the Canadian Shield, then virtually unsettled and in parts even unexplored all the way to the edge of the prairies in eastern Manitoba. There was no rational understanding of what the country

The great railroad
junction city of the
prairies was
Winnipeg, where an
impressive station
was built by the
Canadian Pacific's
incoming
competitors, the
Canadian Northern
and the Great
Northern. The
CPR's earlier station
has now been
abandoned. *Source:*
Canadian National photo.

284

THE NORTH
AMERICAN
RAILROAD

held for the builders, beyond the fact that there was absolutely no on-line market at the time. When construction began around 1905, no more quintessentially developmental line could have been found. It did open up a new settlement area in western Québec and eastern Ontario, when fine clay sediments were found in an east-west band along the road's alignment. This great Clay Belt almost immediately became the locale of a pioneer movement, but even then its produce never rose to great sum. Mineral development did eventually assume considerable importance, but it was too slow in coming to save the railroad economically. When completed in 1913, the National Transcontinental was a well-built line extending for over a thousand miles on a watershed between the St. Lawrence and Arctic drainage through a nearly unbroken forest. Eighty years later there has been spectacularly little change.

The Grand Trunk Pacific was undertaken in earnest in 1903, and again its course was direct and well constructed. It passed in a nearly straight line from Winnipeg through the Fertile Belt to Edmonton, tapping the more productive parts of the prairies but not in any sense having the sort of exclusive market that the CPR enjoyed for a generation. Branches from the older line were repeatedly headed northward from its more arid course across the southern prairies into the Fertile Belt, and in the early 1900s the somewhat sinuous route of the Canadian Northern was built basically parallel to the Grand Trunk. To compound this crowding of a still fairly modest market, the Grand Trunk, after

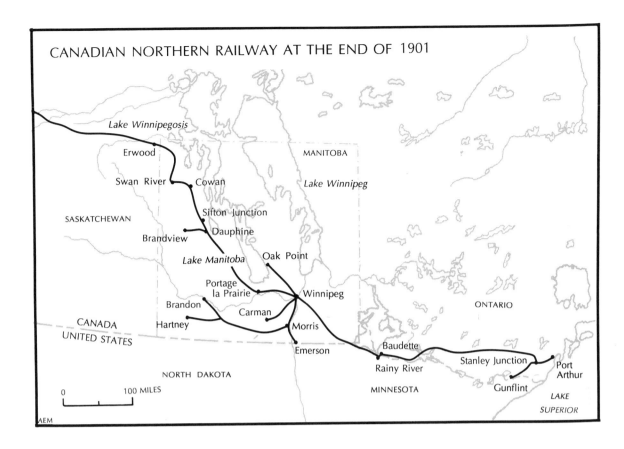

CANADIAN NORTHERN RAILWAY AT THE END OF 1901

dithering as to which pass it would use to cross the Rockies, settled on Yellow-head and built in close proximity to the advancing rails of the Canadian Northern. Only the shortage of steel during the First World War kept two lines from being completed; after 1914 the second track west of Edmonton (the Canadian Northern's) was torn up and sent to the front in France. The Canadian Northern had tried to set up a joint trackage agreement with the Grand Trunk, here and elsewhere in the West, but that still rather arrogant senior company failed even to respond to the proposal.

West of the prairies the Grand Trunk Pacific adopted Sandford Fleming's largely unexplored route, using the upper Fraser River as far as Fort George, where the river turns to flow due south. Continuing westward the Grand Trunk Pacific then crossed a low, rolling plateau country until the upper Skeena was encountered and its graded valleys could be used to reach the Coast Ranges. There was some heavy construction along the Skeena, but only in the sense of finding the way through a narrow cleft, and also the problem of finding a western terminus. The Hudson's Bay post at Fort Simpson (Port Simpson) had been proposed, but the railroad company settled on an island, Kaien, just along the coast a bit north of the Skeena for its port, Prince Rupert. The rails were joined in September 1914, just a year before the completion of the Canadian Northern to Vancouver.

A Rash of Railroad Building

At this remove it is hard to understand the optimism that led to the contemporaneous construction of the Canadian Northern and the Grand Trunk's Pacif-

285

A Canadian
Postscript

When the second crossing of the front range of the Canadian Rockies was undertaken at Crowsnest Pass, with the idea of opening up the coal mines in the vicinity, there were rivers that trenched the high-plains strata, making east-west lines awkward to build until the practice of constructing high viaducts across longitudinal valleys was developed. In the case of the Old Man River at Lethbridge, the highest railroad bridge in the British Empire resulted. *Source:* Canadian Pacific photo.

When the plan for the combined National Transcontinental Railway (Moncton, New Brunswick, to Winnipeg) was advanced and construction was undertaken directly by the dominion government, a major bridge was required across the St. Lawrence River. The site chosen for it was at the lowest point on the river where a cantilever bridge was feasible. Just upstream from Québec City, where the St. Lawrence cuts across Cape Diamond, an eighteen-hundred-foot cantilever could jump from the heights on the south shore of the St. Lawrence to the heights of Cape Diamond on the north. Only in 1917 was a bridge carried between the two shores (after the first and second tries led to failure when the central truss span collapsed while being raised into position from a floating barge). *Source:* Author's photo.

ic extension. Certainly earnings were up at the turn of the century, the Canadian government proved receptive to requests for subsidies of one sort or another, and it was still possible to threaten shippers with the notion that the United States might withdraw its permission to send goods in bond via the Upper Midwest or through northern New England. But to us none of these seems a rational basis for *two* additional lines. The Canadian Northern did obtain the best route across Canada, but as a company in a state too weakened to continue to develop it. The Grand Trunk certainly concluded its transcontinental line little educated in the realities of developmental railroad construction and operation. Its Pacific branch was the most irrational undertaking of private railroad construction in Canada, and only the public National Transcontinental could be placed in the same league. The result was that the trying financial times of the First World War threw both these later transcontinentals into bankruptcy, forcing the government to intervene, and a nationalized system emerged in the early 1920s to salvage what it could from this enormous effort and investment.

With the completion of these two transcontinental lines in 1914–15 the private construction of developmental railroads in Canada essentially came to an end. The simple truth is that 90 percent of the Canadian population even today resides within two hundred miles of the United States border. That means that the band for "developed railroading" is very thin and elongated. The competition is of necessity corporate, and no company can dominate such a region. The governmentally controlled line—the Canadian Northern, Grand Trunk, National Transcontinental, and Intercolonial combined into the Canadian National Railways—had to share virtually all its territory with the Canadian Pacific, so there is nearly absolute competition. Only on Prince Edward Island, in Newfoundland (after 1949), and in the Northern Frontier areas does the Canadian National have a monopoly, though hardly an enviable one. The historical geography of transportation in Canada was such that two national systems emerged, competitive but chained together like the classical wrestlers, each unable to get away from his enemy. Starting even with the Canadian Pacific, the truth had been that the character of settlement in Canada was such that for a major private line to survive, it had to tap the entire national market—quite unlike the situation in the United States, where no private company seemed large enough to serve the full national market.

The Developmental Railroad Lives on in Canada

There have been lines built since 1915, virtually all of them developmental and of a public or quasi-public nature. Ontario evolved an "emigrant railway" from the turn of the century into the Ontario Northern Railway northward to the Clay Belts and even to James Bay in 1932.[48] In 1929 a Manitoba-subsidized line northward from the Fertile Belt to Hudson Bay at Churchill, the Hudson Bay Railway, was opened. In Alberta north of Edmonton, the Edmonton, Dunvegan, and British Columbia Railway was carried into the Peace River Country, an outlier of the more productive prairies. Between 1912 and 1930 a 496-mile line was built to Dawson Creek, there reaching to the southern edge of that fertile outlier of the prairies in the Peace River block of British Columbia.[49] The Pacific Great Eastern Railway at first commenced from Squamish on Howe Sound (at

287

A Canadian
Postscript

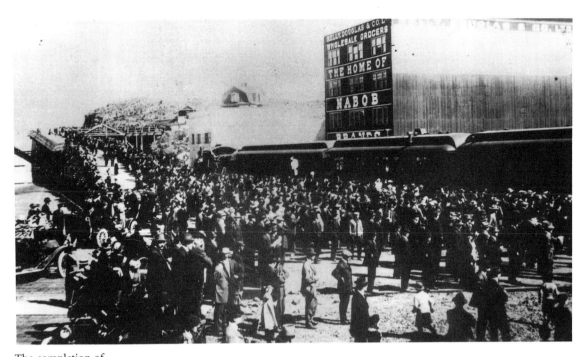

The completion of the Grand Trunk Pacific Railway from Winnipeg to Prince Rupert on Kaien Island near the mouth of the Skeena River in British Columbia allowed the first transcontinental train to arrive at Prince Rupert on April 9, 1914. In harness with the National Transcontinental, opened from Moncton to Winnipeg, the Grand Trunk Pacific made available a second Canadian transcontinental in 1914. *Source:* Canadian National photo.

last brought in to use as a route across the Coast Range) to Quesnel. The PGE was subsequently, at a great cost, completed to junction with the Northern American network at North Vancouver on Burrard Inlet to the Canadian National Railway (Grand Trunk Pacific Railway) at Prince George, as well as to the ED&BC at Dawson Creek. At the present time this public developmental line, now the British Columbia Railway, has been extended nearly to the Yukon boundary at Fort Nelson and is slowly creeping toward Dease Lake. In Québec the development of iron mining after 1945 brought the Québec, North Shore, and Labrador Railway and another short mineral line from Port Cartier to Gagnon, Québec. Western Canada has seen similar "railways to resources" in the line from the Peace River Country to Hay River and the Pine Point lead-zinc mines in the Northwest Territories, and in the newly constructed railroads in the foothills of the Rockies developed in the 1970s and 1980s to tap coal resources for export to Japan.

The Canadian railroad era is not over, but its growth has become limited and specific as to purpose. Any general railroading in Canada must tap an entire national market and for sweetening add some tasty bits of the American one. The combination of a small domestic market and a vast realm makes any other strategy uneconomical. Where railroads are needed outside this compelling oecumene, they have had to come as publicly supported lines seeking ports (Churchill and James Bay) or resources (Pine Point or Wabush in Labrador).

Oddly enough, in light of later events, the first hundred years of the developmental railroads in Canada were mostly concerned with the opening up of farming areas, first in Québec and Ontario but later in a more encompassing way in the prairies. The larger role that the Canadian Pacific played in the development of the three prairie provinces came in recognition of the spread there of the great carpet of wheat that became Canada's largest export—a source of external earnings and a means to the end of the prairie settlement that was

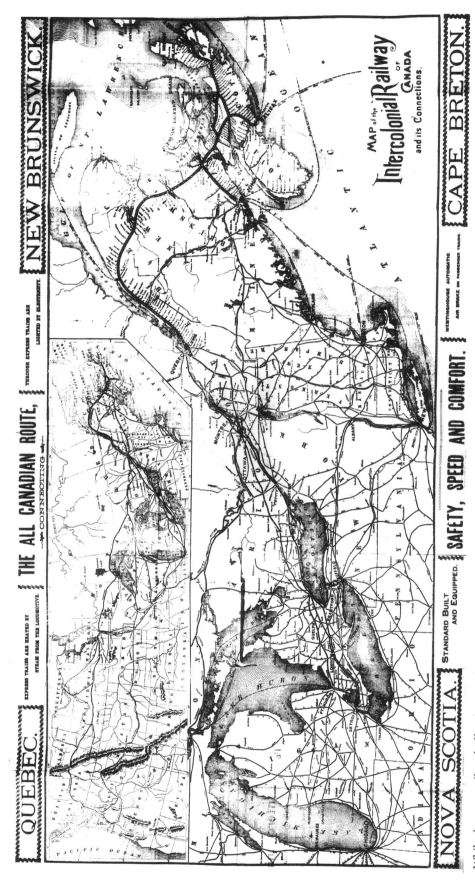

Source: Canadian National map.

While the great railroad effort in Canada after 1870 had always been the construction of a transcontinental line, and then a second and a third, the earliest national effort had been to shape an Intercolonial Railway to tie together Nova Scotia and New Brunswick on the one hand with Québec and Ontario on the other. This map shows that Intercolonial Railway after it was finished across the Notre Dame Mountains to the south shore of the St. Lawrence at Mont Joli in 1876. This line met the requirement in the British North America Act of 1867 that the several provinces be joined by rail.

The Grand Trunk Railway Company, after great reluctance with respect to a transcontinental line in the first decade of the twentieth century, chose to reverse its course, agreeing to build a rail line from Winnipeg to the Pacific, where it chose a terminus at the mouth of the Skeena at Kaien Island (Prince Rupert) and to lease the publicly built line from Moncton to Winnipeg (National Transcontinental Railway) to be operated in connection with the western section that was called the Grand Trunk Pacific Railway. Just prior to the First World War Prince Rupert was hacked out of the heavy coastal forest. Here is shown the Grand Trunk Pacific's version of a railway hotel, the Prince Rupert Inn in that port. *Source:* Canadian National photo.

ultimately to be cited as justifying a second and third transcontinental railroad. We can take note of the close of this great historical spread of rails and settlement in the 1930s, but we should not think that the end of that association meant the end of the developmental railroad. When the construction of these lines recommenced in 1945, after the Second World War, their main purpose had shifted: from support of immigration and the spread of the agricultural settlement frontier, toward support of mineral and forest exploitation.

When we sum up the experience of that first century of the Canadian developmental railroad, what dominates is the role the railroads played both in creating a settlement pattern for a British Canada and in achieving the political integration of those British colonies into a single dominion. Certainly lines were constructed that served mines and forests—New Glasgow to Pictou in Nova Scotia was a coal-carrying line and one of the earlier railroads in Canada—but political and settlement objectives determined the building of most lines. If strictly economic purposes intruded, they showed up in two ways: in the early attempts to "borrow" some of the American market to support Canadian lines by moving middle-western agricultural products toward Britain and Europe through Canadian ports, or in the later efforts to move the now more developed Canadian crops to the same destinations. In the late 1930s Canada produced virtually no iron ore, little export coal or oil, and only very modest tonnages of nonferrous and precious metals.

The fact that the agricultural settlement pattern in Canada was largely fixed by 1939 meant that when construction of transportation routes began again after 1945, a new phase was entered, that of the "railways to resources," now seen as mineral production and, in a more extensive though geographically less intense pattern, as forest production. Cars and trucks could provide transportation for the small bits of settlement resulting from further agricultural expansion into

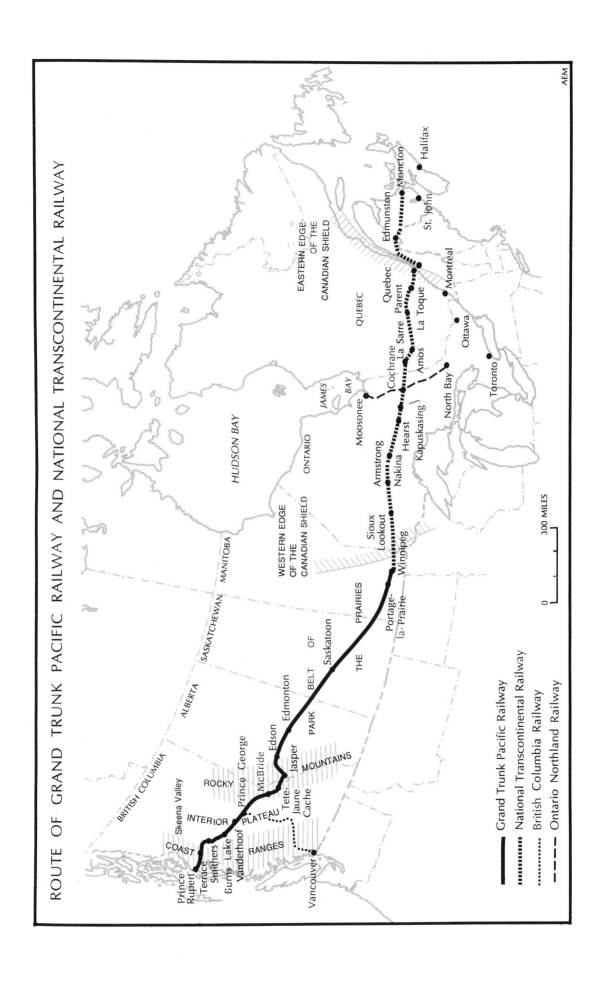

ROUTE OF GRAND TRUNK PACIFIC RAILWAY AND NATIONAL TRANSCONTINENTAL RAILWAY

Grand Trunk Pacific Railway
National Transcontinental Railway
British Columbia Railway
Ontario Northland Railway

300 MILES

0

HUDSON BAY

JAMES BAY

EASTERN EDGE OF THE CANADIAN SHIELD

WESTERN EDGE OF THE CANADIAN SHIELD

QUEBEC

ONTARIO

MANITOBA

SASKATCHEWAN

ALBERTA

BRITISH COLUMBIA

THE PRAIRIES

PARK BELT OF THE

ROCKY MOUNTAINS

COAST RANGES

INTERIOR PLATEAU

Halifax
Moncton
St. John
Edmunston
Quebec
Parent
La Toque
La Sarre
Amos
Cochrane
Montreal
Ottawa
Toronto
North Bay
Moosonee
Kapuskasing
Hearst
Nakina
Armstrong
Sioux Lookout
Winnipeg
Portage-la-Prairie
Saskatoon
Edmonton
Edson
McBride
Prince George
Jasper
Tete-Jaune Cache
Vanderhoof
Burns Lake
Smithers
Terrace
Prince Rupert
Skeena Valley
Vancouver

AEM

the vastness of the forest frontier, but the increasing scale of mineral and timber shipments still called for rails to do the job economically.

The earlier of these "lines to resources" came into being in the late 1940s, when American steel companies turned to the Canadian Shield for iron ore after the severe taxing of the Lake Superior ores during the war. First the Québec, North Shore, and Labrador Railway was constructed from the port of Sept Iles northward onto and then across the low plateau of Labrador for 350 miles to Schefferville in Québec, where the first of these mines was opened in 1954 as a massive open-pit facility. Subsequently a branch was constructed to Wabush and Labrador City in Labrador, and then a second port was created at Port Cartier on the St. Lawrence River, from which the 193-mile Quebec Cartier Mining Company line was carried to its mine on the Shield. These mines and the rail lines that carried their ores to the northern shore of the St. Lawrence, whence they could be handled on ore ships sailing up the river and into the Great Lakes on the St. Lawrence Seaway, were in the long tradition of the internalized North American shipment of mineral products. For more than a hundred years bituminous coal and anthracite had moved from the Middle Atlantic states to Ontario and Québec; now it was Canadian iron ore moving southward by rail and boat to northern Ohio and to other Great Lakes smelters. But by 1983 Schefferville had been largely mined out and was abandoned by the iron ore company of Canada.[50]

There was no fundamental change, save in the net direction of movement, in these iron ore shipments. A major shift came, however, with the rise of Japan as a major steel producer in the 1950s and 1960s. In support of that development Japan had to find a reliable source of large tonnages of coking coal. Traditionally Canada had depended upon Nova Scotia coal, mined at Sydney and New Glasgow, to care for that small part of domestic needs supplied within the country. The much larger and richer coal deposits associated with the Rocky Mountain orogeny remained only modestly tapped. At the turn of the century the Canadian Pacific had constructed a second line across the Rockies, through Crowsnest Pass just north of the American border, which could be used particularly to tap the coal deposits near Fernie in British Columbia. At the time, however, the market lay mostly in the prairies and on eastward, so coal from the Appalachians of the United States could be set down more cheaply in Toronto or Hamilton. With the rise of the Japanese market in the 1950s and 1960s these western coal resources gained great value. Large deposits of good-quality coking coal were to be found in a band running along the eastern side of the Rockies from the American border to the Peace River, and at places in the valleys west of the mountain crest in southeastern British Columbia. The Crowsnest Pass line did pass across the coal belt, but no other railroad—neither the main line of the Canadian Pacific nor the Canadian Northern—actually served potential mining areas.

Using the Crowsnest Pass line as an initial outlet, in the postwar years, the first effort at reorienting the outward flow of resources in western Canada came in the building of a major deepwater, mainly coal-shipping port at Robert's Bank between the mouth of the Fraser River and the boundary at the 49th parallel. Although the Crowsnest Pass line had been extended westward by a major piece of mountain railroad, the Kettle Valley line of the Canadian Pacific, its steep

grades and tight curves discouraged use of that route for massive coal hauling. The Coquihalla section of this route, first opened in 1916, was abandoned in 1973, cutting the through nature of rail transportation in the southern tier of British Columbia and forcing all flow of freight northward from Cranbrook to Golden, and thus through Rogers Pass in westward movement. Rather quickly the direction of flow of that freight on the main line of the Canadian Pacific shifted from eastbound to dominantly westbound. In 1921 bulk shipment of grain had already begun from Vancouver, but it remained modest until after the Second World War, when the Asian market commenced its rapid growth. By 1987 this Pacific-port shipment of grain had come to exceed that from the Lakehead eastward, further reorienting the "economic geography" of western lines. The original Canadian Pacific main line through Kicking Horse and Rogers passes; the later Crowsnest Pass and Kettle Valley route the CPR built closer to the American border; the Canadian Northern (later Canadian National) line through Yellowhead Pass and the Fraser Gorge; and the original Grand Trunk Pacific, later the Prince Rupert line of the Canadian National Railway—this set of rail lines, constructed in terms of an economic geography that emphasized the transatlantic sale of Canadian staples, has had to be transformed to shift that overseas sale increasingly across the Pacific. In addition, the production of energy and metal resources in the West has been vastly expanded. The United States and Canada remain one another's largest trading partner so transborder rail connections are in total more important than port-bound rail shipments in either country.

The Developmental Railroad in Western Canada

The iron-ore carrying railroads of Labrador and other resource lines such as that from Lac St. Jean via Chibougamau to the Clay Belts of Québec, built to give access to mines and timber, might be examined to see the most recent phases of the developmental railroad. These, however, lack some of the more geographical qualities of the western lines, as well as their experiences of opening up previ-

Canadian railroads frequently extended their transportation lines by putting boats on rivers. These shallow-draft stern-wheelers operated extensively during the open season on the broadly encompassing river system. *Source:* Canadian National photo.

293

A Canadian Postscript

ously underdeveloped lands and also shaping a further phase of mercantile settlement. For these more general qualities of western developmental rail lines, we shall conclude our discussion of that great instrument of historical economic geography, the North American railroad, by looking at three recent or impending constructions in Alberta, British Columbia, and the Northwest Territories of Canada.

In the 1960s the restless frontier of nonferrous-metal production, which had earlier brought developmental railroads to Montana, Arizona, and southeastern British Columbia, began to affect the edge of the Canadian Shield. The Chibougamau mine of Québec, the Porcupine District mines of Ontario, and the Tompson and Flin Flon operations in Manitoba all gave a greater geographical spread to nonferrous-metal production in Canada. Initially these operations were within reasonable branch-line reach of developmental railroads that had earlier been constructed to aid in the spread of the immigrant and agricultural frontier. The Lac St. Jean spread of the habitant agriculture of the province of Québec, which came in the late nineteenth century, brought railroads northward that could be lengthened to reach Chibougamau, just as the Hudson Bay Railway in Manitoba passed reasonably near Tompson and well toward Flin Flon, thus furnishing rail transport to mines on the Shield. But in the 1960s one mineral project, the lead and zinc mines at Pine Point in the Northwest Territories, lay well beyond the most northerly reach of the Northern Alberta Railway near Peace River in Alberta. Looking at the construction of the Great Slave Lake Railway northward from Roma Junction to the lake for which it is named and eastward to Pine Point, we can see the complexity of the modern developmental railroad.

The mineral site at Pine Point stands out not as the totality of interests that brought about that project, but rather as the necessary "market" that justified hazarding the considerable investment involved in a railroad. As the Peace River agricultural frontier was developed, rail transport became virtually essential because the utility of that large stream for transportation was limited by the fact that it flows into the Mackenzie River and thence to the sea on Canada's northern coast. No market was available there at the turn of the century when pioneers went to "the Peace." The wheat they had begun to produce had to be carried out by rail, crossing the rough and unproductive band of country that separates the Peace River Country from the main plains that make up the settled part of the Canadian prairies. By the time of the First World War the limit of wheat farming was being reached where summers were too short for the maturing of a crop. By the time tracks were extended to the town of Peace River in 1916, the northern agricultural frontier appeared to have been reached. When access farther north was sought for trade with the Indians (Dene) and the service of mostly precious-metal mines, the traditional means of pioneering transportation of North America, river- and lake boats, were revived. Northward from Edmonton a line was pushed into the bush to Fort McMurray and to Waterways, where riverboats could navigate down the Athabaska–Slave River to Great Slave Lake, across that broad lake to its outlet above Fort Providence, and then down the Mackenzie River to the various native settlements near its mouth. The connections with the North were in existence, though they had of necessity to be relatively cheap natural expedients that required little capital investment.

294

THE NORTH AMERICAN RAILROAD

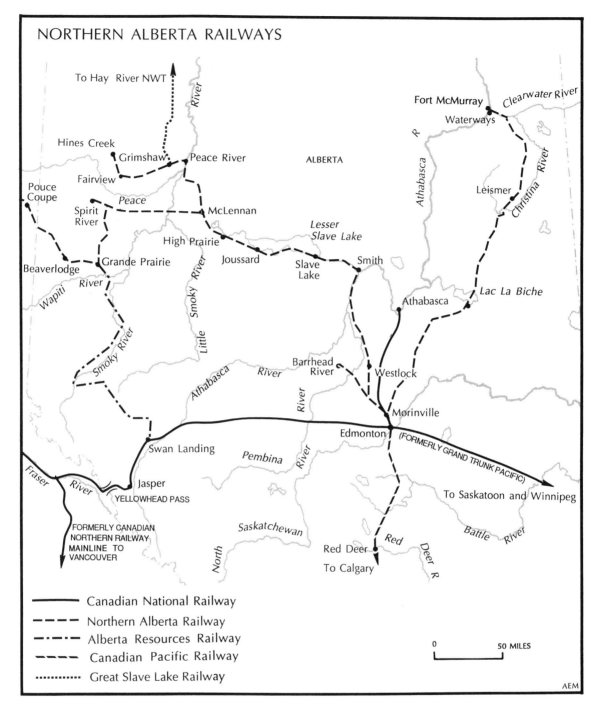

NORTHERN ALBERTA RAILWAYS

To Hay River NWT

Hines Creek

Grimshaw

Peace River

Fairview

Pouce
Coupe

Spirit
River

Peace

McLennan

High Prairie

Joussard

Lesser
Slave Lake

ALBERTA

Fort McMurray

Clearwater River

Waterways

Athabasca R

Leismer

Christina River

Beaverlodge

Grande Prairie

Wapiti River

Smoky River

Little Smoky River

Slave
Lake

Smith

Lac La Biche

Athabasca

Barrhead
River

Westlock

Athabasca River

Morinville

Edmonton

(FORMERLY GRAND TRUNK PACIFIC)

Swan Landing

Pembina River

To Saskatoon and Winnipeg

Fraser River

Jasper
YELLOWHEAD PASS

FORMERLY CANADIAN
NORTHERN RAILWAY
MAINLINE TO
VANCOUVER

Saskatchewan

North

Red Deer

To Calgary

Red

Deer R

Battle River

—————— Canadian National Railway

– – – – – Northern Alberta Railway

–·–·–·– Alberta Resources Railway

– – – – Canadian Pacific Railway

·········· Great Slave Lake Railway

0   50 MILES

AEM

With the coming of the projected nonferrous mining, which produces heavy tonnages over a number of years, these expedients could not very well continue. Roads served in some places, as for the former Clinton Creek asbestos mine in the Yukon Territory, which was served by the long road via Dawson City to the railhead at Whitehorse; but such working was always relatively expensive. For truly economical full-scale operation, continuous waterways or railroads were needed. In the case of Pine Point in the Northwest Territories the Canadian government decided to undertake to build a new rail line in the early 1960s from Roma Junction, just west of the town of Peace River on the Northern Alberta

295

A Canadian
Postscript

branch ending at Grimshaw, some 377 miles northward to the port of Hay River on the southern shore of Great Slave Lake, with a 54-mile branch leading from the main line to the lead-zinc mines that lie to the east. Because this line would be constructed on the rolling surface of eroded flat-lying sedimentary rocks, grades were very light save for several rivers that were cut into that surface and might be crossed by reasonable bridges. In only one place was it necessary to drop down into a wide valley and recover the elevation on the opposite side. The construction suffered more from infirm ground, due to muskeg and permafrost, than from difficult terrain. When put in service in 1965, the Great Slave Lake Railway became the northernmost line in the integrated North American railroad system. Only the Alaska Railroad reached closer to the pole, and it was quite isolated from all other lines on the continent.

Twenty years after opening for service, the Great Slave Lake Railway, operated by Canadian National Railways, remains a developmental line. Because the line passes northward from Peace River, it crosses the northern section of the original Peace River Country around Manning, Alberta, and then the northernmost outlier of prairie agriculture, which is located between High Level on the railroad and Fort Vermilion on the Peace River. In both those areas the presence of a railroad has encouraged agricultural expansion, so both acreage and production have grown since the mid-1960s when the line opened.

Change along the route has come perhaps more clearly at Hay River in the Northwest Territories, where the major port for the northern inland waterways of Canada has emerged. Based first on the road built from Peace River to Hay River soon after the Second World War, the arrival of rails shifted northern transportation fundamentally. Now heavy commodities for the North are brought by freight train or truck to Hay River. From there barges can distribute those loads around Great Slave Lake or down the Mackenzie River to Norman Wells and other outposts, and to Aklavik or Inuvik in the Mackenzie delta. As a result, Hay River has taken on the sort of transportation functions that distinguished Buffalo, Pittsburgh, and St. Louis in the nineteenth century. Clearly the northern market did not bring the railroad, any more than the canola and wheat production of the Fort Vermilion area brought the Great Slave Lake Railway into existence. That initiator was the Pine Point lead-zinc mines. But once the railroad was available, general development—which in this region meant the further poleward extension of the agricultural frontier and the improvement of the marginal transportation previously available beyond the regular settlement frontier—came to be advanced by it.

It now appears that the mining operation at Pine Point will not last much longer. The question then arises: Once it has lost its original generating market from mineral transportation, what will happen with the railroad? If only the small farming region between High Level and Fort Vermilion were involved, trucking might well be substituted. But with the movement of goods for the North having been diverted from Fort McMurray on the Athabaska to Hay River on the Great Slave Lake, and with the North standing as an area of critical concern to the Canadian government—for maintaining sovereignty, for developing other mineral productions, and particularly for pursuing oil exploration—it seems that the Great Slave Lake Railway to the port of Hay River will have to be maintained for its crucial developmental function. That role is to ensure the

economic attachment of the North to Canada in terms of freight in the same way
that the North is tied to the oecumene of the state for passenger purposes by
Edmonton, particularly its downtown airport.

The Special Case of the Western Coal Railroads

Although Canada was similar to the United States in having a short line for the
transport of coal among its earliest railroads, the association of railroading and
coal mining was of rather small importance in the Dominion. In the lands that
were to become Canada in 1867, coal was found in appreciable quantities only in
peninsular Nova Scotia and its island of Cape Breton. These reserves were
generally modest and of a gassy nature that made exploitation dangerous and
difficult. Rails reached to mining areas in Nova Scotia, but the isolation of these
workings meant that those rails played a role of only localized importance,
unlike the situation in the Appalachians of the United States. Canadian coal had
to wait for its role until a later act, when the transcontinental railroads came on
the scene. In the foothills of the Rockies coal measures had been discovered at
quite an early time, but none lay directly along the route that was adopted for
the Canadian Pacific. Instead, when it shifted from wood to steam coal in the
years after its opening, the company depended on coal landed from the east—
probably mostly of Pennsylvania provenance—and from the Vancouver Island
mines around Nanaimo. When the Mackenzie and Mann interests began to
reach into Saskatchewan and Alberta, coal mining presented a fresh appeal as a

A Canadian
Postscript

source of traffic. At Drumheller in Alberta local coal mining led to the construction thence from the Goose Lake branch of the Canadian Northern (the line from Saskatoon to Calgary) as a coal branch. The coal at Drumheller proved so soft and cindery that it was not used for locomotives, but other coal workings at Noregg, Alberta, were more useful for steam coal. Still, in 1915 the Canadian Northern loaded just over a quarter of a million tons of coal there. This was, however, a small undertaking compared with the large ore and coal dock Mackenzie and Mann built at Port Arthur at the head of Lake Superior for Pennsylvania coal, and also their investments in the coal mines around Nanaimo.[51]

Coal was not the initial attraction that led to the building of a railroad over the southernmost of Canada's important passes through the Rockies. Instead, it was the far more traditional appeal of gold and silver, now with the added attraction of important deposits of nonferrous metals, that turned the locating engineer's sight toward southwestern Alberta and southeastern British Columbia. Soon after the spike was driven at Craigellachie in 1885, prospectors began to discover indications that led to the creation of mining towns in southeastern British Columbia. American prospectors were very active in the region, and it was far easier to reach the deep north-south trenches of eastern British Columbia from south of the border, causing a resurgence of that perpetual Canadian fear in the nineteenth century, American domination of still loyally British territory.

To develop this region in southeastern British Columbia, a railroad was seen as essential. The only way Rossland and other mining towns could be effectively tied into the Canadian economy was to build a railroad across this southern tier of the province, an area where the drainage was mainly to the south into the United States. Only a railroad could carry the heavy tonnages of mining and do so in the west-east alignment that was necessary to keep the flow truly Canadian. Particularly as production increased and smelting was introduced, coal was needed to provide the heat for the enrichment processes. In the early stages of the boom that coal had to be brought by water, rail, and then again water from the coal mines on Vancouver Island to the smelters such as that vast one at Trail operated for so long by a subsidiary of the Canadian Pacific Railway. Good coking coal was available in the Crowsnest Pass area, where Canada had its southernmost reasonable crossing of the Rockies. If a railroad could be built through the pass and on westward to the Kootenay and upper Columbia valleys, two objectives could be secured: the Crowsnest Pass coal could reach the smelters and mines where gold, silver, lead, zinc, and bismuth were being produced in increasing quantities; and this area could be firmly tied into the Canadian economy by commencing the line at Medicine Hat to continue across the higher parts of the prairies to Lethbridge and then westward across the foothills and into Crowsnest Pass to breast the Rockies at the eastern boundary of British Columbia in the region of important coal deposits. By the mid-1890s the line had been constructed as far as Lethbridge, but the heavier and more costly climb into and through the pass remained to be built.

At first the British Columbia provincial government had hoped to accomplish its ends by issuing a provincial charter for the B.C. Southern Railway. That line, however, could call on little capital in a land where many deep and repeating valleys had to be crossed at considerable expense. As an only recently completed

developmental line, the Canadian Pacific had little available capital, though it had more than any other line anywhere around. In 1892 the CPR took over a coal road that had been built from Dunmore on the CPR main line (just east of Medicine Hat) to Lethbridge. This line of the Alberta Railway and Coal Company was the logical beginning of any through route passing through the southern tier of British Columbia. Onward through Crowsnest Pass was obviously the route of any railroad seeking to cross the Canadian Rockies this far south. In its upper sections potential coal fields would be close, and once in the Pacific drainage a number of nonferrous mineral sites suggested the likelihood of considerable numbers of heavy carloadings. Thus, the Crowsnest Pass line of the CPR was not specifically and exclusively a coal line when it was opened in sections in 1898 and 1899. Coal mining began in the summit section immediately. As the alignment was occupied by rails pushing westward toward Nelson and the metal-mining camps, the initial purpose of the line was increasingly accomplished. In addition, for the first time in the West a specialized notion of the purpose for railroads was enunciated, to open to economic exploitation resources that stood landlocked in the vastness of little-developed Canada west of the Lakehead. Before the Second World War making such an opening meant two things: (1) giving western consumers access to the burgeoning coal mines of the region, and (2) providing western mines with reasonable transportation to market. As yet, fish and forest products from the area moved in only modest quantities, and coal produced in the West mostly remained there. After the First World War petroleum was produced near Calgary, but not in quantities sufficient to encourage a proliferation of rail lines.

The great change in the resource railroads of the West, particularly those associated with coal mining, came when the rapid industrialization of East Asia took place. Japan had begun its industrialization between the two world wars, but in the rebuilding after the second of those conflicts such momentum was accomplished that the search for the necessary raw materials spread across the Pacific, notably to the only modestly developed regions of western Canada. Such was the scale of this search that by the 1980s the centuries-old tradition of transoceanic trade had been transformed, with service between Asia and North

Temporary housing could be provided to construction crews by turning boxcars into shedlike dormitories that could be moved with the head of construction. *Source:* Canadian National photo.

299

A Canadian Postscript

America displacing that between Europe and North America as the largest sea link in the world.

Before we take up that more recent situation, it is desirable to complete our view of the more characteristic evolution of the Canadian railroad. At the turn of the century the Canadian Pacific was pursuing the more longstanding strategy of opening the West to the East. That purpose was best served by a continuation of a line westward to open up direct service thence from the more westerly parts of interior British Columbia. The Crowsnest Pass line was completed to Nelson, though with a thirty-four-mile gap along Kootenay Lake that was connected by ferry until a rail line was opened in 1930.[52] From Nelson other forces seem to have taken over, most notably the effort to contain the incursions of James J. Hill's railroads into the Lower Mainland of British Columbia and the southern tier of valleys in that province's interior. For the lower Fraser Valley Hill had announced in 1901 that he intended to have built a line from Vancouver to the Kootenays, thus competing directly with the Canadian Pacific's monopoly of the tonnage originating in that mining area on the western side of Crowsnest Pass. The line passed back and forth across the international boundary, a feature generally viewed with distrust by British Columbians. Many believed that Hill's funneling of the rich Kootenay and Boundary trade to the United States was severely retarding the economic development of the southern interior. Such a sentiment was echoed by the *Victoria Colonist,* which described Hill's line as being "like so many fingers on a hand, with the State of Washington as the palm."[53]

Thomas Shaughnessy, William Van Horne's successor as president of the Canadian Pacific Railway, decided in 1910 to fight Hill directly. He rapidly extended what began as the Crowsnest Pass line by taking over the Kettle Valley Railway and extending that line through extremely difficult terrain (using the Coquihalla Pass) to reach the CPR's main line at Merritt in the Fraser Gorge in 1916.[54] In this manner the Crowsnest became a second route across the interior of British Columbia and the Rockies—one never very profitable to operate, whose abandonment, in pieces, commenced in 1961 and was brought to completion west of Midway, essentially on the American border. There construction of the Kettle Valley Railway began in the first decade of the twentieth century, thus leaving that railroad almost completely a ghost by 1980. Extremely difficult terrain for railroading and the then weak westerly flow of coal and other minerals beyond Trail and its smelter defeated the "second transcontinental," now freed of any role in containing a long-dead James J. Hill.

British Columbia Looks North

Railroading in Canada, as in the United States, has consistently shown how the development of what was often a true wilderness has played a leading role in the promotion of railroad companies. Certainly the Canadian Pacific Railway was fully as pioneering as had been the Union Pacific, which so clearly had been its model. The building of the CPR continued a pattern that had begun with the UP developmental lines building westward from an eastern oecumene toward an enclave of settlement by Europeans originally planted by sea on the Pacific coast of North America. The absolute quality of the wilderness in the intervening country had been reduced by the time the Grand Trunk Pacific and the Canadian

As a second transcontinental sought to use the lower Fraser River canyon of British Columbia, only one line could occupy each side of the river. Here the earlier Canadian Pacific Railway shifts from the right to the left bank of the stream (the lower bridge), forcing the Canadian Northern (the high line) and later construction to cross to the left bank. *Source:* Canadian National photo.

The change that has taken place in construction technology can be judged by comparing this picture of building being done using earth-moving machines with that using horses shown in the figure on page 279. *Source:* Canadian National photo.

Northern came into operation a generation later; but the east-west orientation of these later lines—finished respectively in 1914 and 1915—remained the same. Much of the explanation of such a persistent alignment in rail construction relates to the broad geography of Canada. In agricultural terms, terms that determined the widespread settlement of both the United States and Canada, the northern dominion was then and has remained a rather thin band of habitable territory extending little more than 250 miles north of the United States boundary. Thus, any geographical scope in railroad development had to be sought in longitudinal growth. It was only as the frontier approached the moderating climatic effect of the Pacific that an agricultural (or major forestry) settlement could assume much latitudinal breadth. We have already seen how northern Alberta, where the climatic moderation gained from Pacific air moving inland begins to be felt, witnessed a northward spread of productive agriculture into the Fort Vermilion–High Level area once the originally mineral-based Great Slave Lake Railway was built through the area in the early 1960s. It is in British Columbia that the moderating effect of the Pacific is strongest and the east-west construction of developmental railroads has been greatest.

Climate did not pose the only barrier to the northward spread of agriculture and settlement in eastern Canada; the presence of the rocky and water-logged Canadian Shield on the border or not very far north of it until the western prairies are reached has meant that in the first phase of developmental railroading in Canada—that phase associated with agricultural-based settlement—there was little interest in "developing" the areas underlain by the Shield. Only well into the twentieth century did interest arise with regard to mineral-based development, first with gold mines such as those on the southern edge of the Québec-Ontario Clay Belt, in the region opened to railroading by the government-built Ontario Northland Railway (begun in the first decade of the century to encourage both agricultural settlement in the Clay Belt and mineral exploitation of the Porcupine mining district). The deep southward penetration of Hudson Bay and James Bay geographically constrained the Ontario Northland when it reached Moosanee on James Bay in 1932. Turning westward, the Hudson Bay Railway was originally drawn beyond the rather narrow band of agricultural settlement in southern Manitoba neither by farming prospects nor by mineral expectations, but rather by the geographical abstraction of a port on the northern and innermost reaches of the Atlantic and its potential role in the traditional eastward flow of agricultural exports for Canada to Europe. That expectation has borne stunted fruit, but the presence of a longitudinal line crossing the Shield has given to mining on that worn-down surface an economical route for exports, via the rail system of the Dominion, to the industrial areas of North America and the truly Atlantic ports. Along with the Great Slave Lake Railway and the now largely outmoded rail connection at Fort McMurray (and Waterways) with the Mackenzie River navigation, these represent the rather limited examples of longitudinal railroads in Canada between the two iron-ore-carrying railroads of Labrador (Quebec Cartier Railway and Québec, North Shore, and Labrador Railway) and the cordillera. West of the Rockies, where the Shield now lies far to the east and the maritime moderation of the higher-latitude climate becomes strongest, the potential for north-south developmental railroads in Canada reached its peak.

The general drive to construct three transcontinental railroads in the Dominion had resulted in the utilization of two of the major Rocky Mountain passes (Kicking Horse by the CPR, and Yellowhead by the Grand Trunk Pacific and the Canadian Northern) and two of the discerned routes across the Coast Range (the Fraser Gorge and delta by the CPR and the Canadian Northern, and the Skeena valley by the Grand Trunk Pacific). Yet another latitudinal rail line was added by later construction through Crowsnest Pass and thence through the several north-south-trending trenches and valleys of interior British Columbia and over the Coquihalla Pass to the Lower Mainland of the western province. At the outbreak of the First World War the province found itself far less well served longitudinally. The only rail component that afforded significant transportation north-south was that section of the Canadian Northern extending from the northern crossing of the Rockies at Yellowhead Pass southward across the interior plateau to Kamloops, where it joined the southern transcontinental alignment coming over Kicking Horse Pass. Thus, to go by rail from Vancouver was nearly nine hundred miles to Prince George, and nearly fifteen hundred to Prince Rupert.

In this situation the potential promoters of railroad construction began to argue forcefully that British Columbia needed a north-south developmental line commencing at Vancouver and passing northward through the interior to Prince George. Any extension beyond there seemed too chimerical to imagine at that time. But a line from Vancouver to Prince George would tie the provincial transportation system together as none of the transcontinentals did, cutting the distance by rail between the two essentially in half, to 464 miles, and it would provide an independent connection from the Grand Trunk Pacific to Vancouver. In the process, an additional crossing of the Coast Ranges as discerned by Sandford Fleming—that through Howe Sound and the glacial valley opening

The port of Prince Rupert as built just before the First World War. In an all-wooden town, even including streets and sidewalks, the Fire Hall shown became a critical component. *Source:* Canadian National photo.

A Canadian Postscript

from it toward the northeast—would be occupied, and the beginning of a longitudinal line toward the great undeveloped wilderness north of Prince George would be made. Although the interior plateau in these reaches was mostly given over to cattle raising, there was enough agricultural and forestry potential to encourage a developmental railroad.

Modest construction began in 1912 in accordance with an agreement with the provincial government worded as follows:

[The Pacific Great Eastern Railway] shall, will, truly and faithfully, acquire, lay out, build, construct, complete, etc., a line of standard gauge railway from the city of North Vancouver and thence running north along the margin of Howe Sound thence following the general course of Squamish River and continuing north easterly to Lillooet, and by the most feasible route to a junction with the Grand Trunk Pacific at or near Fort [later Prince] George. . . . [The] line when completed, shall in all respects, apart from grades and curvatures, be equal to the standard of the main line of the Canadian Northern as constructed between the City of Winnipeg and the City of Edmonton, as the condition of that when first completed and ready for operation. The Company shall sufficiently equip such a line of railway, and shall make the sleeping cars, dining cars and day coaches thereon equal to those in use on the first class railway system of America.[55]

This, then, was to be a south-north line with the purpose not of opening a specific resource-producing area to exploitation, but rather of opening a great wilderness area to settlement in the traditional mode of Canadian general development—first perhaps as a ranching region, but later as an agricultural belt with occasional mining and timber production interspersed within it. This anticipation was accurate; it remained just up to half a century later.

It is easy to understand why first private promoters and later the provincial government saw both a rosy and an immediate prospect for the Pacific Great Eastern Railway. Between the turn of the century and the year 1912, two vast and truly transcontinental systems had been under construction in the Dominion. Since Canada's West Coast was restricted to British Columbia, those two transcontinental systems had to find their western terminus there, one heading for the Lower Mainland (the Canadian Northern Railway) already pioneered by the Canadian Pacific, and the other finding its own virgin frontier (the Grand Trunk Pacific Railway) at Prince Rupert via the only other river valley along a stream rising east of the Coast Ranges and reaching the Pacific wholly within Canada, the Skeena. Within two years, 1914–15, these main lines had added massively to the province's network of modern transportation. But being the traditional Canadian railroads that they were, this addition to that network was characteristically east-west in orientation and of little use to a province that saw its future in the north. The early subsidy given the PGE was to gain that route to the north; the ultimate provincialization of the company was entirely with that end in mind, particularly when in 1913 a recession caused high unemployment in the province and Richard McBride, the premier, envisaged relieving the stress by announcing that not only would the PGE be completed forthwith to Prince Rupert, but in addition the line would then be completed to Dawson Creek in the Peace River Block of British Columbia, where traditional agricultural pioneering could be anticipated. The PGE seemed a critical part of the traditional objective of rail construction in Canada, to open an agricultural frontier. Part of it ultimately was to become the sort of "railway to resources" that could pay for itself from its opening. Instead, the Pacific Great Eastern Railway became such a drain that the provincial treasury was emptied ahead of normal inflow.

Before that drain became alarming, the construction began in two places. First, from the southern terminus at North Vancouver the line was constructed rapidly along the moderately sloping shore of Burrard Inlet to the end of the peninsula forming its northern shore at Horseshoe Bay (called Whytecliff as a railroad station). Thence along the eastern shore of the fjord to the north, Howe Sound, construction was extremely heavy, requiring much blasting to carve a narrow shelf for the tracks. Meanwhile, at the northern head of the sound a lumber dock, Newport, had come into existence, subsequently to be more romantically renamed Squamish, and from there the main construction effort was launched. It became a major undertaking almost immediately, for the Squamish River valley rose steeply toward a pass through the first range of the Coast Ranges. Money was consumed rapidly in this effort and in cutting another bench along the shores of Seton and Anderson lakes, water bodies that occupied a great groove cut by the glaciers in the main crest of the Coast Ranges. Money continued to be spent at a rate far ahead of investments, and on a line that had support only at its very western end where there had already been a short logging railroad inland from Squamish. To deal with that situation the British Columbia government assumed outright ownership of the PGE in February 1918.[56]

Construction continued under government control. Clinton had been reached, and forty-two miles north thereof construction was put under contract. Williams Lake, a new town site, was reached in the beginning of September 1919, and a year later the line was approaching Quesnel eighty miles south of the original northern terminus at Prince George. And there the money ran out. To the north of Quesnel a major bridge was needed, and the constant drain on the provincial treasury finally prompted an investigation. John G. Sullivan, a former consulting engineer employed by the Canadian Pacific, in his report stated, "As a local line the country between Prince George and Squamish will not produce enough traffic to a reasonable rate to pay operating and fixed charges." Sullivan blamed the initiation of the PGE on business groups in Vancouver and Victoria seeking for selfish reasons to encourage such a line without obvious market, and on the desire of the Grand Trunk Pacific Railway to secure independent access to Vancouver. He held, "If the peoples of British Columbia are not prepared to continue paying $2,000,000 or $2,500,000 per year on the investment already made and to do what will be necessary in the next ten years, it is recommended that the company be ordered at once to abandon the whole system and recover what salvage is possible, and in this way slightly reduce the liability and also prevent any further increase in their obligations."[57]

Faced with the costly section between Horseshoe Bay and Squamish and the expensive bridge north of Quesnel, the government abandoned construction in 1922. The PGE stood as a suburban line from North Vancouver to Horseshoe Bay and a detached line of 344 miles from Squamish to Quesnel, a railroad "from nowhere to nowhere" through country producing and consuming little. The wonder is that it was not torn up for scrap, as it neither connected important

305

places in the classic bridge-road sense nor produced the requisite resources that allowed such thrusts into the bush to anticipate long-term goals or advance obvious resource development.

The story of the PGE in the interwar years reads rather like a Saturday-afternoon movie serial: peril stalked its path. On a number of occasions various boards of inquiry recommended that the line be scrapped, but it was always saved by the bitter political embarrassment its abandonment (So much public investment!) would cause the government in power. It continued to exist as the great railroad joke—the "Please Go Easy," the "Past God's Endurance," the British Columbia "Premier's Great 'Eadache," the "Prince George Eventually"—and to creep toward financial survival. By the late 1930s its earnings were overtaking its expenses, and the provincial government could begin to see the possibility of completing the line between its original termini at North Vancouver and Prince George. This experience demonstrated clearly that in the era of the automobile, the developmental railroad had become a "railway to resources," that is, to existing, currently utilizable resources with a certain market.

At first that more demanding definition of the practicable frontier railroad eluded the directors of the PGE. But with the outbreak of the Second World War for the United States in 1941, and the war's obvious threat to Alaska, that necessary market was more confidently envisaged in tying Alaska to the rest of the United States by land, thus avoiding the submarine threat in the Pacific. But the prospect of success for the PGE was again withdrawn. It was concluded that the Alaska Highway (commencing at Dawson Creek) could be built more quickly, using little essential steel, and would be of broader utility in the age of automotive transportation.

It was this conclusion—that the motor truck and the automobile, operating on paved highways, could provide frontier transportation for most demands —that nearly killed our hero in the next-to-last installment. By the time of the Second World War, when that conclusion was reached, the PGE had begun to break even financially, so it was saved from abandonment, in fact, by the ultimate correctness of the initial justification offered for its construction—that it would open up a viable northern regional economy to development. And at the conclusion of the war the developmental fervor in general was growing. The construction from Quesnel to Prince George resumed after a quarter of a century of waiting, and the line was completed from Quesnel to the junction with the Canadian National in September 1952.[58] Even then the southern connection was missing, to be made firm only when the heavy construction along the shore of Howe Sound was completed to North Vancouver on August 26, 1956, forty-four years after the PGE commenced construction. Now the railroad could undertake at least part of the role for which its construction had been undertaken, that is, to serve as a bridge railroad connecting the former Grand Trunk Pacific Railway to Vancouver. Unfortunately for the PGE, in the same year that it had been halted at Quesnel, the Grand Trunk Pacific had been joined with the Canadian Northern to form the Canadian National Railway. The Canadian National thus gave the former Grand Trunk a shorter connection into Vancouver by turning trains south at Red Pass Junction (just west of Yellowhead Pass) and using the former Canadian Northern main line to reach a station at False Creek in Vancouver.

Even though the PGE was now completed, this loss of bridge function

clouded the future of the provincially-owned railroad. That loss, combined with
the rise of automotive highway transportation during the two generations that
had intervened since the commencement of the project, forced the provincial
management of the railroad to reexamine its probable future function. The
conclusion reached was that the PGE should be extended to Dawson Creek in the
Peace River Block of British Columbia. That construction would greatly shorten
the distance by rail from that major wheat-growing area to the British Columbia
ports of Vancouver and Prince Rupert, thus earning for the PGE the western
Canadian railroad function of serving as a granger line to the port. In addition,
much was made in the resource surveys carried out in the late 1940s of the
massive coal deposits found in the foothills lying east of the Rockies, that is,
marginal to the Peace River Block. At the time the Dawson Creek extension was
agreed to, however, the coal had only a very small demonstrable market. The
Crowsnest Pass coal fields were already developed on existing rail lines and could
produce enough for any then demonstrable demand in western Canada. Thus,
the Peace River extension had to be justified by the expectations of increased
settlement in the Peace River agricultural belt, which might enlarge flows of
grain to coastal ports. It was also realized that over the years since the PGE first
began construction, the forest resources of interior British Columbia had gained
a place in the ever-expanding market for lumber and paper. That lumber, like
grain, was a product traditionally sent great distances by rail, so the extension to
Dawson Creek seemed justified.

A Canadian
Postscript

Such proved the case. On October 1, 1958, junction was made at Dawson Creek with the Northern Alberta Railway, which possessed a network of feeder lines in the southern Peace River Country, and traffic on the PGE grew. But this was traditional western Canadian business, and the margins of the agricultural settlement appeared to have been essentially reached. The north-south developmental line in British Columbia, the PGE, could be seen as finally completed, and in the "normal" fashion, even though the pace of its growth could have been called rather too deliberate to live up to North American developmental standards. The question now faced was, Can any future development for railroading be expected on Canada's northern frontier, particularly in the Northwest, where climate and geomorphology seemed most hospitable to an outward spread of the frontier?

The favorable experience with the Peace River extension was not as fully developmental as such a northern thrust might seem, because the Northern Alberta Railway (originally the Edmonton, Dunvegan, and British Columbia Railway) had reached Dawson Creek from Edmonton via the Peace River Country of Alberta in 1931. But the success was such that the provincial government of British Columbia looked favorably on further northward construction. As opened in 1958, the PGE line to the Peace River Block had two termini: the main one at Dawson Creek on the Alberta border where junction was made with the Northern Alberta Railway, and a second one at Fort St. John, a rival regional center lying on the Peace River somewhat to the north. North of Fort St. John continued a third of British Columbia's expanse, still served only by the gravel-paved Alaska Highway constructed as a war measure in 1942. In the 1970s the W. A. C. Bennett government undertook a 250-mile extension from Fort St. John to Fort Nelson, a line whose main justification was found in the immediate prospects for lumber development in the northeastern forest block of the province. Also at that time, the government advanced what might be seen as a grand design for a full-scale provincial development railroad, soon to be redesignated the British Columbia Railway to be founded on the original PGE North Vancouver–Prince George line of 464 miles and its considerable initial extension of 327 miles to Dawson Creek and Fort St. John. Next came the 250-mile extension to northeastern British Columbia at Fort Nelson. Earlier, in the 1950s (when the Peace River Block extension was under construction), a seventy-five-mile branch off that trunk line was carried from Odell to the late-eighteenth-century fur post at Fort St. James, a jumping-off place to north-central and west-central British Columbia. When the following stage of system growth arrived, with the line from Fort St. John to Fort Nelson, this original thrust to the northwest, consequent on the grain of the country in northern interior British Columbia, was further extended another eighty miles to the important timber-producing region around Takla Lake. The grand design then called for carrying that extension yet another 260 miles to Dease Lake, a center of an increasingly important mining region, and perhaps ultimately another 140 miles to the boundary of the Yukon Territory. There, vague thinking foresaw tying that ultimate provincial rail terminus to Whitehorse and finally to Fairbanks, for junction with the existing Alaska Railroad. In such a strategy was seen the seemingly ultimate expansion of the North American rail net. The exigencies of the British Columbia provincial treasury halted this thrust to the northwest near Takla Lake, a halt

The typical view of railroad towns was that they could bring wealth almost instantly, with promoters selling lots for hard cash as soon as the corner stakes could be driven. Prince Rupert in 1914. *Source:* Canadian National photo.

conditioned upon the seeming wisdom of waiting a while for mineral development in the northern part of the province to become imminent. By 1990 active prospects for gold mining in northwestern British Columbia had begun to restore interest in a rail line to Dease Lake or even Watson Lake in the Yukon Territory.

The Developmental Railroad Today

This consideration of the growth of railroads in Canada since the Second World War allows us to see where the North American railroad stands today and what its future is likely to be. It takes no true prescience to be aware that the traditional role of the railroad in North America—first as the joiner of cities, and second as the mover of agricultural and forestry products—has probably been essentially completed. The agricultural frontier has been reached, and the forest frontier lies no more that a couple of hundred miles beyond the railheads in most areas outside northwestern British Columbia. Even there, the possible spread of economic forestry is geographically limited. The Dease Lake extension surveyed for the British Columbia Railway, and certainly its further push to the southern tier of the Yukon Territory and thence into central Alaska, would seem to represent the extent of reasonable traditional railroading. Beyond that quite limited band representing a rational zone for traditional frontier development in Canada and southern Alaska, only a rather adventitious pattern of mineral production would seem to portend rail expansion.

Western Canadian rail expansion during the last fifty years has been fostered by a major revolution in economic geography since the Second World War: the reorientation of North American trade from dominantly eastbound and transatlantic to dominantly westbound and transpacific, and the encouragement thereby of western increases in coal production to serve peripheral parts of Asia deficient in coal reserves. The shift of manufacturing from Europe and North America to East Asia has been consequent upon the postwar economists' argument that reductions in restrictive tariffs in western Europe and Canada and

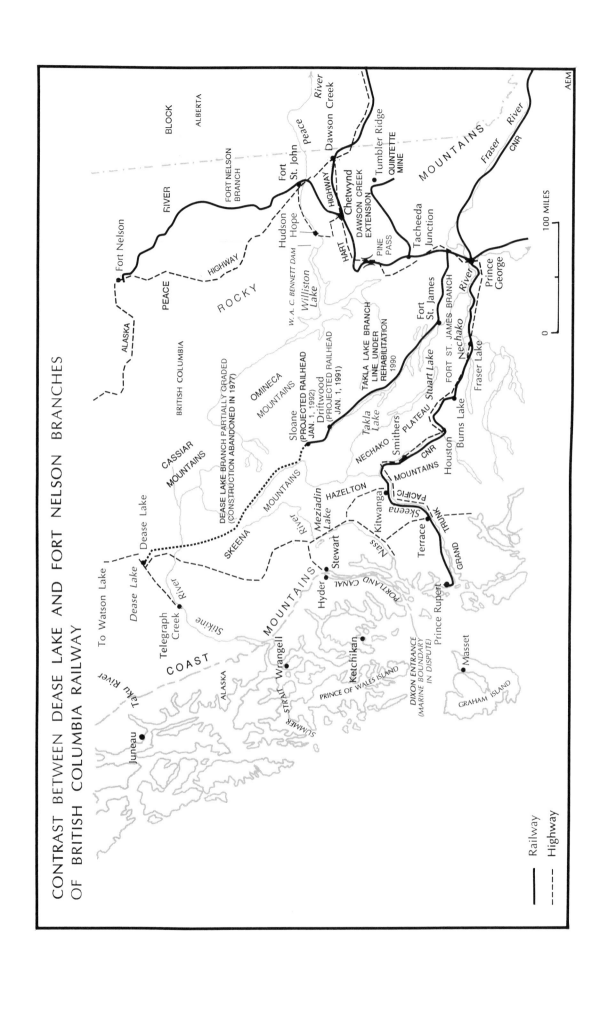

CONTRAST BETWEEN DEASE LAKE AND FORT NELSON BRANCHES
OF BRITISH COLUMBIA RAILWAY

Railway
Highway

the United States would be met with a commensurate opening of East Asia's markets to goods and raw materials from North America in particular. In the latter case the geographically abstract thinking of economists has been considerably borne out by increases in the purchase of grains, coal, other minerals, and timber from Canada. But for the United States, with its much more "mature" industrial economy, the thinking was faulty and unbalanced to begin with—notably so in the extremely biased markets of East Asia where tariffs are not by any means the only, or perhaps even the dominant, restrictive trade practice, and where the manufacturing exports that dominate American foreign trade directly conflict with the determined trade-restriction practices of those Asian countries. Given the geographically blind nature of most economists' analysis, it was little appreciated in the 1960s and 1970s that Canada's experience with postwar efforts to "free" trade would be so very much more favorable than the experience in the United States. That contrast in experience with this new "Pacific-oriented" world has also meant that the country still using the railroad in a highly developmental way—Canada—has gone on building railroads to fulfill its traditional staple-supplying role, while in the United States, where the railroad exists within a manufacturing economy, the era for railroad evolution has been truncated by the severely restrictive and discriminatory practices of the East Asian countries. In the United States there is no sizable development occurring to bring about further railroad evolution; in Canada that traditional staple development has continued and been aided by the construction of railroads to resources.

*Railroads to Resources Carry forward the Tradition
of the North American Railroad*

The contrast between the postwar continuation of staple production in Canada and the sharp decline in similar staple production in the United States hardly needs detailed proof. The massive decline of iron mining in the United States since the Second World War is widely understood, as it is for copper, lead, gold, and a number of other minerals. In that same period Canada became a producer of iron on a major scale, after having produced hardly any iron ore at all in 1939. In a similar way Canada produced only very small amounts of coal in 1939 but has become a world-class producer since 1945. In that same period American coal mining has fared quite well, but mainly in satisfying a growing domestic demand rather than in supplying a large foreign trade in fuels. In timber, in wheat, in paper, and in a number of other basic resources or manufactures Canada has grown, particularly by satisfying foreign demand, in the mid-1980s running over a $20 billion trade surplus against the United States even before the Free Trade Agreement of 1989. To continue this enviable export growth Canada has had to depend upon the export of staples, as it has done since the sixteenth century. Those often far-spread staple resources have come into distance trade through improvements in the cost and competence of transportation. In contrast, in the United States what growth in exports has occurred, proportionately far less, has come along three lines with far different transportation needs. First, America's largest-value export has been capable of self-transport: commercial aircraft have long been flown directly to the customer without the intervention of other means of transport. Second, the shift of American exports from goods to services means that postwar American transportation is increasingly electron-

311

A Canadian
Postscript

ic rather than physical. And finally, physical trade has grown ever more heavily unidirectional, with a vast inflow of manufactures into the United States and a recklessly large compensating outflow of money and eventual debt. Ships return westward to Asia from the United States riding high in the water with the empty containers that must thus return so that yet more goods may be dispatched toward America. But for Canada the bulk carriers pass westward toward Asia fully loaded and tend to return in ballast.

To observe how the continuance of this great trade in staples also maintains the growth of the North American railroad, we may in conclusion look at the projection of new lines in Canada in the last forty years and the fundamental transformation of earlier construction that has been required.

It is impossible here to look at all postwar construction and evolution on Canadian railroads; it is sufficient, however, merely to examine a quite specific trade, and one in a clearly defined and limited geographical area. That trade is the export of coal to East Asia, and the area conducting the Canadian part of this movement is the cordilleran portion of Canada with its ties to the Pacific coast, whence ocean shipping carries the trade farther on across the Pacific. Although this is not our main concern, it might be noted that conditions of trade have so changed in four hundred years that the carrying trade between producer and consumer has become almost entirely monopolized by Asians rather than by the British or their North American heirs. One cannot help but give thanks that Canada's vast coal deposits lie in the Rockies, granting to Canadians at least a small role in that carrying trade, the part cared for by the newest examples of the North American railroad.

The Tumbler Ridge Project

We have already reviewed the evolution of British Columbia's developmental line northward from Vancouver, originally called the Pacific Great Eastern Railway when first undertaken in 1912, but renamed the British Columbia Railway in more recent years as it became the provincewide structure for a final developmental railroad system on Canada's western frontier. To this system fell the responsibility of dealing with the geographical turnabout that has seen East Asia become North America's largest trading partner, with a two-way flow in Canada's case. Because the Dominion has maintained the traditional exchange of staples or manufactures, this transformed direction of trade has required further elaboration of the rail net in the West, particularly as the greatest tonnage increase in the exchange has been experienced with respect to Canadian coal headed for East Asia. All the railroads serving the West—the Canadian Pacific, the Canadian National, the British Columbia Railway, and even the Burlington Northern through its Great Northern lines and junctions in British Columbia—have been affected. In the foothills of the Rockies in Alberta the Alberta Resources Railway has been constructed from Swan Landing just east of Jasper to Grande Prairie in the Peace River Country. This "railway to resources" financed by public money has been taken over for operation by the Canadian National Railway (with which it makes junction at either end, and over which coal is shipped to the Pacific coast, both at the new coal dock at Ridley Island just south of Prince Rupert, and at the deepwater installation at Robert's Bank just north of the 49th parallel on the Strait of Georgia south of the Fraser delta, where some protection is afforded against the silt carried to sea by the Fraser River); thus, the nationalized rail system is strongly involved. The Burlington Northern is only marginally involved, however; it provides rather modest tonnage to Robert's Bank over its Great Northern lines from the coal fields near Crowsnest Pass, and some of the trackage used for coal trains in metropolitan Vancouver. It is the Canadian Pacific Railway and the British Columbia Railway that have been most directly concerned with the continuance of the traditional staple export, so we may best focus on the transformation of existing CPR and BCR lines and the expansion taking place.

When demand for Canadian coal, particularly by the Japanese steel industry, rose sharply, the closest appropriate coal resources were to be found adjacent to the Rockies, in eastern British Columbia and western Alberta. In 1981 a contract was entered into by the Japanese steel industry and two mining companies in Vancouver. The project called for development of the Tumbler Ridge mines in the foothills of the Rockies in east-central British Columbia. These were located some fifty miles to the south of Chetwynd on the British Columbia Railway extension into the Peace River Block and eighty miles across the Rockies from the signboard station of Tacheeda on that same Prince George–Dawson Creek line. Chetwynd was the closer station, and on the same eastern side of the chain of the Rockies here; but it was decided instead to construct two long tunnels, the 5.6-mile Table Mountain Tunnel and the 3.8-mile Wolverine Tunnel—the first when completed was the longest rail bore in Canada—and to carry a branch from Tacheeda on the western side of the range directly eastward through the tunnels to the location of the Tumbler Ridge mines. This was a Can$455 million undertaking, so it could be constructed only in anticipation of extremely large shipments. It was decided that the six hundred miles to Ridley Island from the mine made it essential to carry the coal in "unit trains," preassembled trains of approximately 125 gondola cars, with a total weight of up to twelve thousand tons. These were run as a unit, both moving loaded toward Ridley Island and returning empty to Tumbler Ridge. These cars were loaded under huge coal silos, with the train moving slowly forward as each set of empty cars was filled; later, as the train drew across a bridge, the cars would be inverted in pairs and emptied into chutes leading to large coal ships bound for Japan. In this way, it was concluded, some 120 million tons could be moved annually at a reasonable cost. The route had much to recommend it: the shortening of the overall distance to port from the mine; the better crossing of the Rockies offered by the two long tunnels compared with the higher crest found at Pine Pass on the Peace River main line; the greater ease of handling unit trains this way; and the easier winter working afforded by a tunnel compared with an open crossing of the Rockies. Just twenty-three months after the signing of contracts, the line was opened.

The speed of this construction, truly remarkable for such extensive tunneling, was due in part to the decision to electrify the line. In recent long rail-tunnel projects in North America—the Great Northern in Montana and the Mount MacDonald project on the Canadian Pacific—diesel-electric traction was adopted from the beginning of construction, mainly because the capital cost is considerably less than that for electrification. But in long tunnels in which diesel-electric locomotives are operated, it is necessary to install massive ventila-

A Canadian
Postscript

tion systems, using doors to direct the forced-air movement, and the tunnels must be lined with concrete to reduce frictional drag on the forced air. At Table Mountain Tunnel and Wolverine Tunnel 50,000-volt electrification was adopted, permitting the rock tunnel drilled and blasted through the mountain to be used without further lining. The result is a very wet tunnel, with cascades of highly sulfurous water pouring from the roof—like a tunnel to the Underworld, from the viewpoint of a passenger on a "speeder" (handcar). But the tunnel was bored very quickly and serves admirably for the massive transport of coal.[59]

Once the unit-train service was established on the Tumbler Ridge branch on November 1, 1983, this truly impressive developmental railroad began to contribute importantly to the successful operation of the BCR. It had been justified in the beginning as a project to stabilize the business of the railroad, then predominantly dependent upon the forest industries for its freight-car loadings. Commercial forestry operations are particularly sensitive to the general level of economic activity, and to restrictions that might be imposed by foreign markets, so such support is problematic. Coal production, particularly under a very long-term contract with the Japanese steel industry, seemed the ideal diversification of loading that the BCR needed. By 1985, of the 211,000 carloads originated at or north of Williams Lake, almost 40 percent (83,400 carloads) were of coal shipped from Tumbler Ridge.[60] The future seemed assured; but in 1986 the general market for steel declined sharply, leading the Japanese to seek, essentially to demand, a downward renegotiation of the contract, on the argument that under Japanese practice contracts are normally renegotiable if market conditions decline. In 1990 a Canadian arbitration court awarded the Japanese Can$46 million, taking much of the blush off this project.

Whatever we may think of the legal practices involved, there can be no question that the Tumbler Ridge line represents a very healthy survival of the traditional North American developmental railroad down to our time. The project differs greatly from its predecessors in the speed of construction and in capital cost—Can$455 million (current values), compared with about US$60 million for the Union Pacific construction in 1862–69; and the line was built entirely in terms of freight operation, and that by unit trains. But the developmental railroad is still to be found and remains important in permitting and encouraging the shaping of resources and trade.

The Mount MacDonald Project on the CPR: The Evolution of the Selkirk Crossing

A new line leading to a new coal-mining project can easily be seen as a developmental project, with resource and railroad interacting intimately. Thus, the Tumbler Ridge project continues the traditional role of the railroad in North America. Another aspect of this "developmental" railroad appears, in a quite contrasting manner, as the reconstruction of an existing line so as to deal with a growing and changing market. The eighty-one-mile branch to the mine site is the highly visible part of the development of the coal resources at Tumbler Ridge, but in addition there had to be a major reconstruction of the Grand Trunk Pacific Railway route from Prince George to Prince Rupert, a distance of 467 miles. As originally opened in 1914, this line was supposed to have been built to the standards of the GTP in the prairies. Such was the case, but this truly pioneering railroad—built through most sparsely settled country to a port that came into existence only with the completion of the line—was not up to the standards of a heavy rail line in certain respects, such as the width and depth of the ballast, the weight of the steel rails, and the signaling system. To operate unit trains over the same route and to carry the 120 million tons of coal a year foreseen—this required a true reconstruction of the successor Canadian National Railways Skeena route.

Even more dramatic an example of such developmental reconstruction is found in the project of the Canadian Pacific to improve the grade on its line over the Selkirk Mountains in southeastern British Columbia. As originally located in 1881 by Major Albert Bowman Rogers, an American railroad-locating engineer, the eastern approach to the only usable pass to be found through the Selkirks used the Beaver River valley westward from the first rail crossing of the upper Columbia River near Golden, British Columbia. At Beavermouth the ten-mile climb to the top of Rogers Pass lifted the railroad almost eighteen hundred feet for an average grade of 1.7 percent, with some steep bits at 2.5 percent. On the western slope of Rogers Pass, loops to lengthen the line to reduce the grade kept that figure to a maximum of 2.2 percent and an average of 1.8 percent.

Not only were the grades relatively steep in this section; the snows were extremely heavy as well, and snowsheds nearly five miles long were constructed. Even so, great avalanches closed the line for a time each winter. And on March 4, 1910, a series of disastrous avalanches killed sixty-two men clearing the rails. That event, combined with the need to secure more capacity for running the increasing number of freight trains moving over the CPR, encouraged the construction of a tunnel over five miles long and located 550 feet below the open summit of the pass. The tunnel reduced most of the severe snow conditions and provided a double track over the pass, but it left a stiff 2.2 percent grade to be dealt with on both sides of the pass. The double tracking of the Selkirk crossing, from Connaught station east of the pass to Glacier station on the west, a distance of 5.3 miles, was all that was accomplished during the First World War until the Connaught Tunnel was opened in 1916. The double-tracking program on the CPR in the West never resumed, and "the introduction of higher capacity steel railway cars and much heavier and more powerful locomotives—allowing more tonnage per train—eliminated the need for the double track program."[61] The size of freight cars continually increased, particularly with respect to height. The result was that it was decided to remove the second track from the Connaught Tunnel—as had been done in the first of the long North American railroad tunnels, that at Hoosac Mountain in Massachusetts—and to move the single remaining track to the middle so as to gain the greatest clearance in an arched tunnel. "An ever-increasing grain crop, the addition of new bulk commodities such as potash and sulphur, and the conclusion of contracts with Japan which necessitate the uninterrupted movement, on a regular year-round schedule, of millions of tons of coal from the Crowsnest Pass area to a new superport at Roberts Bank south of Vancouver, forced new studies to be undertaken in the late 1960s, to increase line capacity [through the Rogers Pass area]."[62] It was found that these very large tonnages were preponderantly being carried west-

A Canadian
Postscript

bound, and so attention was turned to double-tracking the line "in areas where long grades were against westbound trains." Rogers Pass was consummately such an area. And furthermore,

In the 1970s four major bottlenecks were identified on the Calgary-Vancouver mainline. At each bottleneck, grades of more than one percent necessitated smaller trains of pusher type locomotives to assist trains over these heavy grade sections. By 1979 the projects at Salmon Arm and Revelstoke were completed and that at Lake Louise was completed in 1981. In each case, a second main line track was constructed to a maximum grade of one percent. The existing track [with a grade over 1 percent] continues to be used for eastbound trains while heavy westbound traffic moves on the new track.[63]

What remained was the long, stiff grade up from Beavermouth on the Columbia River in the Rocky Mountain Trench to the eastern portal of the Connaught Tunnel, a climb that sometimes requires up to six large pusher (diesel) engines attached to a train already heavily powered.

It was in this context that the Canadian Pacific undertook to build, at a cost of Can$600 million, a new westbound track of twenty miles from the eastern foot of Rogers Pass up the slope to a new tunnel of nine miles, with a second tunnel a mile long just before it. The new bores, finished in 1988, allow the maximum opposing grade to be 1 percent, compensated for curves. Of the twenty miles of new line, ten were in tunnel and the other ten on a great side-hill bench climbing up the side of the Beaver Valley and secured by 220 square feet of concrete retaining wall, mostly bolted to the hillside. Since this track was to be used by diesel-electric locomotive operation westbound, ventilation was required and was afforded by a shaft near the midpoint of the tunnel. Not only is the tunnel approach along the side-hill grade reduced to a maximum of 1 percent; the entrance portal is also more than four hundred feet lower in elevation than the portal of the earlier Connaught Tunnel. As a result, both grade and total climb are reduced, producing great savings by reducing the total elevation to which freight trains have to be raised, and by holding the grade down sufficiently that pusher engines can be dispensed with. The long trains and heavy tonnages contained in a file of some 100 to 125 cars will still require multiple locomotives, both on the head end and as "drones" or "slaves" in a midtrain position. But by limiting all opposing track to a maximum of 1 percent, it becomes economically efficient to run throughout the Calgary-Vancouver journey with the same complement of engines. At the time of the construction of this project it was not thought economical to undertake the electrification of the new line. But for possible future service by overhead-fed electricity, all tunnels were built with head room for a catenary wire.

The physical evolution of the Selkirk Crossing—first breasting the summit of Rogers Pass in the open, from 1885 to 1916; next through the Connaught Tunnel, from 1916 to January 1, 1990; and finally through the Mount MacDonald Tunnel almost a thousand feet below the natural pass—is a striking example of the phased growth that must be envisaged under developmental railroading. In 1884–85, the period of the discovery and completion of the line through the pass, money was very scarce for the CPR, and the market for its services was at best highly conjectural. A hundred years later, when the Mount MacDonald project was under construction, money became more plentiful, though the railroad could agree to spend the Can$600 million for the project only after being finally relieved of the burden of reduced rates on grain transportation first introduced in the Crowsnest Pass Agreement (an agreement with the federal government worked out at the turn of the century to bring into being the rail line that could open up the coal production of that region, still the main source of coal tonnage carried through Rogers Pass). The $600 million is still a large sum, but it is assumed that the long-term contract with Japan for coal purchases will be honored and that the cost of the "developmental improvement" of the CPR can be both amortized and justified.

Thus, the developmental line retains an active role in Canadian railroading, though the mercantilist stimulation of resource development that first came to Canada at the beginning of the seventeenth century has been greatly transformed in its geography. This new economic geography, now more focused on the Pacific than the Atlantic, of necessity has its own pattern of the North American railroad.

Railroad Maturation: Pioneering Progress

A final point that should be made concerning the North American railroad is the presence in its construction phase of two convergent but distinct cycles of "development," the second distinguished from the more common and more general first purpose of developing markets. The second cycle of development relates to the improvement of the line itself, financed by earnings. Even in England it was clearly perceived that success in operating a railroad would lead to the development of the local economy of the region through which the line passed. In this sense there would be a geographical internalization of effects— but only in the matter of market enhancement, not of the infrastructure of the rail line. The pattern of rail development in North America was quite different. The earlier years saw rail lines of truly submarginal quality, as attested to in the accounts of Robert Louis Stevenson, Charles Dickens, and other British travelers. Only relatively profitable early operations could lead to the second cycle of development, the cycle whereby the company could shape an ultimately satisfactory basic fabric for its line. In this sense the North American railroad was doubly developmental, both in the fabric of the line and in the nature of the country through which it would ultimately pass.

To test the fundamental duality of development in the North American railroad, I recently investigated the situation at the end of twenty years of "development" on a modern developmental railroad, the British Columbia Railway reaching close to the boundary of the Canadian North, the 60th parallel, the northern boundary of British Columbia. In the late 1960s, during the premiership of W. A. C. Bennett, it was decided to seek to open up the virtually undeveloped northern part of British Columbia, by projecting two lines toward the edge of the Yukon Territory. The first line was to be carried northward from Fort St. John (in the Peace River Block), where the province's developmental railroad had come to rest in the early 1960s. This development was to extend 250 miles farther on to Fort Nelson (located on the tributary of that lake behind the Bennett Dam) leading first to the Liard River and then to the Great River of the North, the Mackenzie. In this region extensive forest resources seemed to promise significant expansion of Canada's oecumene. A second northern branch was also proposed from the railhead on the short Fort St. James spur of the BCR north of Prince George. This route projected northwestward via Takla Lake and Dease Lake to the valley of the Stikine River, reaching the sea near Wrangell in the Alaska Panhandle; a possible extension was also projected to Watson Lake in the Yukon Territory.

Both these lines were undertaken at the same time in the sanguine business climate of the late 1960s. The relatively easy construction across the rolling country northwest of the Peace River Block, where no major rivers had to be bridged except the Fort Nelson near the post, progressed rapidly in raw developmental construction opened to Fort Nelson at the end of the 1960s. The 420-mile line to north-central British Columbia at Dease Lake, undertaken at the same time, encountered harder construction and a more problematic future. The undertaking stalled well short of the mark (adjacent to Takla Lake, where the railhead languishes still). Fort Nelson had already shown some development in timber and oil production before construction of the Fort Nelson branch began; it had been reached by the Alaska Highway in 1941. In contrast, Dease Lake remained quite isolated and was considerably less established when the railroad line thence was begun. We may well argue that the Dease Lake branch was so premature in "development" that it continued to be seen as stillborn even in the 1980s, whereas the Fort Nelson branch, though perhaps somewhat less than fully robust, was viewed as viable.

Because the Fort Nelson branch was completed promptly, it could thus begin to earn a return on investment; the classical situation on North American railroads obtained. This led to two related consequences: there were gross earnings that could justify a plowback of funds into the line, and such a plowback would, if extended over a long enough period, bring the particular stretch of rail line up to a satisfactory basic infrastructural level for operation. In July 1989, just twenty years after the original construction on the Fort Nelson branch, I had the opportunity to ride in a locomotive cab over this line and observed what is hoped to be the final phase of the building of this railroad. Drainage, ballasting, correction of the grade, and other "improvements" were still under way. For essentially a generation such fundamental improvements were needed and were incrementally supplied, at least in part, from earnings. Thus, 160 years after the system for building North American railroads was first devised, it is of necessity still being used to permit the construction of truly developmental lines. In this way the route becomes usable earlier than might otherwise be the case while pushing beyond the existing economic frontier. The two branches of the British Columbia Railway reaching toward the Canadian North serve to demonstrate the advantages of this North American rail system. In the case of the Dease Lake branch, we can see that it is quite easy to overstep the limits of economic practicality, even accepting that all new lines carry risk and trial. Inability to give the best chance for success by completing even a most marginal railroad to the most distant rationally expectable market can mean delay, or even ultimate defeat. The Fort Nelson branch is working and gaining a satisfactory physical structure; the Dease Lake branch is a weak, little-used, and entirely unrealized project.

The North American Railroad

Not only is there a geography *of* railroads, a geography with which this book has been primarily concerned, but there is also a massive component of geography *in* railroading; the nature of the land through which the tracks pass is deeply reflected in the form of the line and in its operation. The case could hardly be otherwise; ultimately, it takes a market to bring railroads into being and an investment responsive to that immediate (and eventual) support to create the line. Thus time, as measured in a staged evolution of market and economy, is a substantial factor in determining what a rail line will be like as built; in addition, subsequent stages in the economic geography of the region served will be reflected in physical changes in the railroads passing through and providing service. In truth, there is both a historical economic geography of the region and a historical geography of the transportation therein to consider. The second of those studies is what has been attempted here, but the evolution of economic geography in the region considered cannot be disregarded, particularly because some regions evolve over a long period and experience diverse stages of economic activity, whereas other regions experience little more than the entry stage of economic and transportation geography. The railroad was the great transportation advance of the nineteenth century, but not of times before then. Any evolution of economic geography accomplished before 1825–30 must have depended on transportation other than railroads; and in the presence of such prior evolution, when rail service was finally introduced it could be initiated at a fairly advanced level. Where the market is well developed, the railroad can enter the scene in more developed form, and can expand further, than it can where the market is yet to come.

From these general relationships it follows that the stage of the economic geography of a region must strongly affect the form of the railroad (or other transportation medium) that services it. The technology of rail-guided and rail-supported transport, originally using steam traction in trains of cars, was initially introduced in Britain at the turn of the nineteenth century. All of the essential components of that technology as stated in the previous sentence were around some years before Richard Trevithick ran his, and the world's, first train in 1804. Not all of the components were first used in Britain; it was in Wales that they were first combined successfully. From that first successful trial word spread rapidly of a new potential medium of transport, one that during the succeeding quarter-century was effectively experimented with in France and the United States as well as in Britain. In the three countries mentioned, practicable systems of railroad transportation were constructed, and each was regionally associated with coal mining during the 1820s. It must be emphasized that each country took the idea of the railroad, an idea certainly gained from Trevithick's successful running on the Penydarren Tramroad in 1804, and evolved from it a distinct technology for a geographically and stage-separated market. Marc Sequin in his work in the Stephanoise in France was in engineering terms rather more advanced than George Stephenson in Britain. Similarly, the locomotive builders in Philadelphia, Paterson, and Lowell created much stronger and more versatile locomotives than Robert Stephenson did at Newcastle. There can be no question that the *idea* of the railroad is British, but there is also no doubt that in France

The problems of trying to operate ferries across the St. Clair River during a long winter caused the Grand Trunk Railway to have constructed the first underwater tunnel for a North American railroad.
Source: Canadian National photo.

and the United States separate and distinct technologies and concepts drawn from that idea were evolved.

It was particularly in the United States that the technical and geographical distinction from British practice was most clearly drawn. By 1830 a separate railroad was coming into existence based on concepts of civil and mechanical engineering that were indigenous to the United States. It could hardly have been otherwise. America was at a different stage of economic geography from Britain (and also, by the way, from France); it required a railroad appropriate for true pioneering conjoined with continuing development. That development was showing in the obvious need in the United States and Canada for potential markets to be found and exploited. Development also appeared in the necessity for a new technology of railroading—a new form of railroad, less costly than the capital-intensive British version, that would lend itself readily to the job of hacking an economic geography of development out of a continent with a primitive economy.

The evolutionary stages of American economic geography have given to the North American railroad its own stages. As markets grew, so did the rail lines that had brought them into being. The rail net was spread across a continent of well over six million square miles, but again with the same recognition of these facilities as developmentally differentiated. By the time of the First World War about one-third of the railroad mileage in the world was in North America, a quarter of it in the United States alone. Within such a vast total the physical

THE NORTH
AMERICAN
RAILROAD

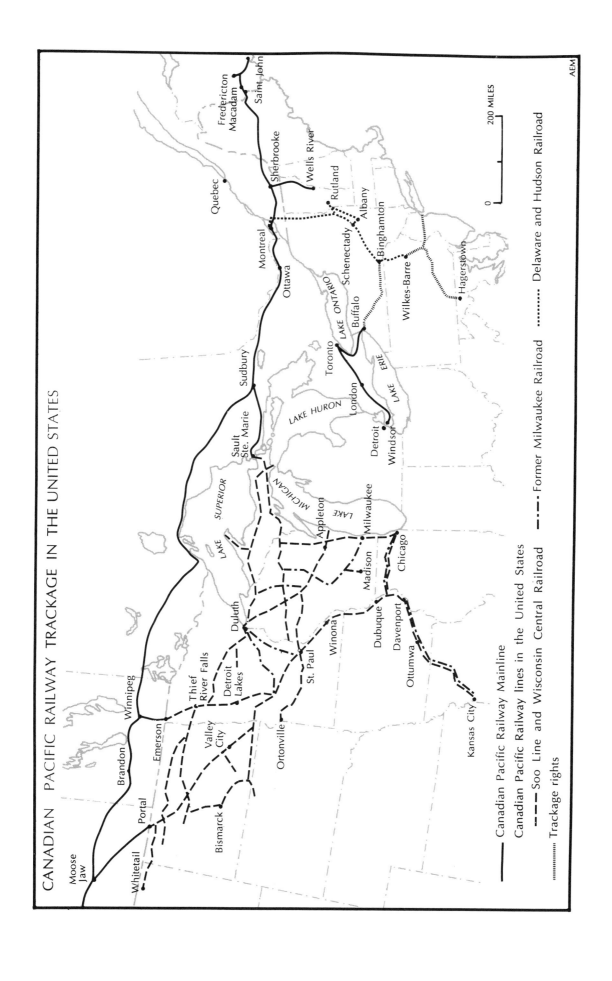

CANADIAN PACIFIC RAILWAY TRACKAGE IN THE UNITED STATES

Moose Jaw
Whitetail
Portal
Brandon
Winnipeg
Emerson
Bismarck
Valley City
Thief River Falls
Detroit Lakes
Ortonville
Duluth
St. Paul
Winona
Dubuque
Davenport
Ottumwa
Kansas City
Chicago
Madison
Milwaukee
Appleton
LAKE MICHIGAN
Sault Ste. Marie
LAKE SUPERIOR
Sudbury
LAKE HURON
London
Detroit
Windsor
LAKE ERIE
Toronto
LAKE ONTARIO
Buffalo
Wilkes-Barre
Hagerstown
Binghamton
Schenectady
Albany
Rutland
Wells River
Ottawa
Montreal
Quebec
Sherbrooke
Macadam
Fredericton
Saint John

AEM

200 MILES
0

—— Canadian Pacific Railway Mainline

—— Canadian Pacific Railway lines in the United States

– – – Soo Line and Wisconsin Central Railroad

–·–·– Former Milwaukee Railroad

········· Delaware and Hudson Railroad

············ Trackage rights

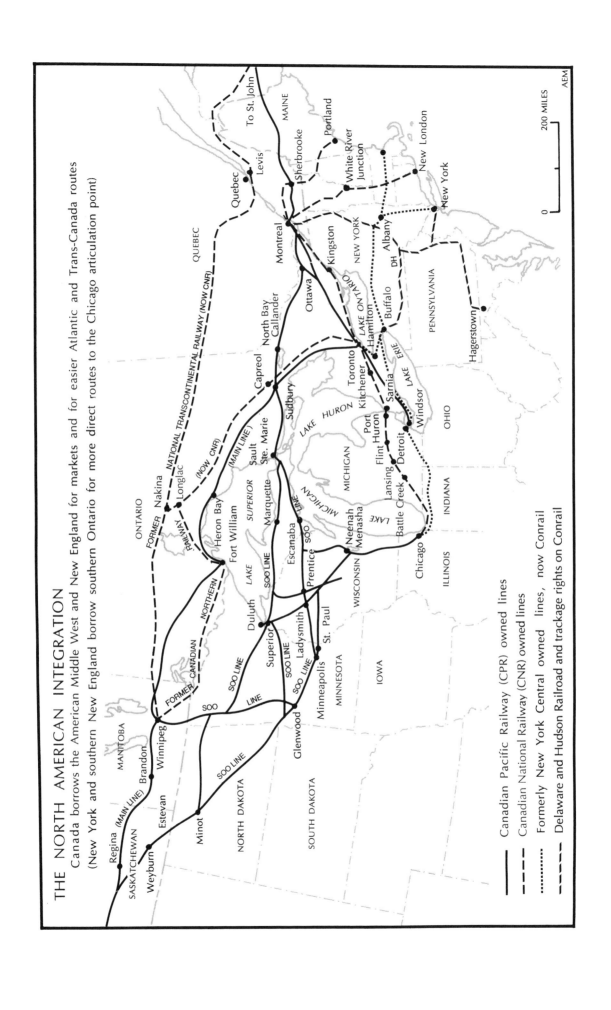

THE NORTH AMERICAN INTEGRATION
Canada borrows the American Middle West and New England for markets and for easier Atlantic and Trans-Canada routes
(New York and southern New England borrow southern Ontario for more direct routes to the Chicago articulation point)

Canadian Pacific Railway (CPR) owned lines

Canadian National Railway (CNR) owned lines

Formerly New York Central owned lines, now Conrail

Delaware and Hudson Railroad and trackage rights on Conrail

200 MILES

AEM

nature of the railroad varied from the truly pioneering lines such as the Edmonton, Dunegan, and British Columbia Railway of the Peace River Country to the very heavily capitalized and highly engineered lines of the Pennsylvania Railroad just recently brought into Manhattan. The evolution, however, was clearly visible in the latter when one compares Manhattan's earliest horse-drawn line with that opened in 1910 at a cost of over $400 million.

Certainly there was evolution in French and British railroading, particularly in the first of these. But by the final third of the nineteenth century, most of that evolution was technical rather than geographical. Electric traction was introduced, though first actually at Baltimore in the United States; diesel-electric traction followed, though first more importantly in the United States, where this less capital-intensive technology was more critically needed for evolution; and certainly increasing emphasis on speed in passenger and freight came to the fore, though again before around 1950 more in the United States than in Britain and France. In geographical terms, however, the railroad has had a continuous expansion in North America, even up to the very present, though there has been some contraction in actual total miles of track since the First World War. It is this continuing role for geographical development and market expansion that distinguishes the North American railroad from that of Britain and Western Europe. North America was the first continent to have its economy and settlement pattern massively shaped by the railroad. From that beginning there has always been a specifically separate meaning to the term *railroad* in North America. I hope that here I have been able to make the case that when we talk about railroads we must recognize a fully genetic separation of the British and North American railroads from the very beginning. As in so many things, there is a cultural debt owed to Britain for the idea of the railroad. But in geographical purpose and detailed technology, the two railroads are widely separated. It is my hope that the North American railroad can be accorded the individuality and independence its historical geography makes clear.

A Canadian
Postscript

ABBREVIATIONS

BCR   British Columbia Railway

B&O   Baltimore and Ohio

CP   Central Pacific

CPR   Canadian Pacific Railway

D&H   Delaware and Hudson

GTP   Grand Trunk Pacific

L&N   Louisville and Nashville

M&M   Milwaukee and Minnesota

M&O   Mobile and Ohio

M&P   Milwaukee and Prairie du Chien

NAR   Northern Alberta Railway

NP   Northern Pacific

N&W   Norfolk and Western

O&W   New York, Ontario, and Western

PFW&C   Pittsburgh, Fort Wayne, and Chicago

PGE   Pacific Great Eastern

T&P   Texas and Pacific

UP   Union Pacific

WP   Western Pacific

NOTES

Introduction

1. For a discussion of the mercantile model of settlement, see James E. Vance, Jr., *The Merchant's World: The Geography of Wholesaling* (Englewood Cliffs, N.J.: Prentice-Hall, 1970).

Chapter 1. The North American Railroad Rises in the East

1. Evans, who had successfully constructed fairly high pressure steam engines even before 1800, in 1804 completed a steam dredge, which he equipped with wheels as well as paddles. This ran over the streets of Philadelphia under its own power before reaching its launching site. In 1812 Evans sought to still the critics of his proposals for steam road vehicles "by answering that I would make a carriage, to be propelled by steam for a bet of $3,000, to run upon a level road against the swiftest horse they would produce. I was then as confident as I am now that such velocity could be given to carriages. . . . I am still willing to make a steam carriage that will run fifteen miles an hour, on good, level railways, on condition that I have double price if it shall run with that velocity, and nothing for it if it shall not come up to that velocity." Seymour Dunbar, *A History of Travel in America* (New York: Tudor Publishing, 1937), pp. 875–76.

2. John Stevens, *Documents Tending to Prove the Superior Advantages of Steam Rail-ways and Steam Carriages over Canal Navigation* (New York: T. and J. Swords, 1812). Reprinted with an introduction by Charles King (president of Columbia College) in 1852 (New York: Stanford and Swords) and again by *The Magazine of History, with Notes and Queries,* extra number no. 54, 1917 (Tarrytown, N.Y.: William Abbatt). All references here are to this 1917 printing.

3. Ibid., p. 51.

4. Although Stevens somewhat qualifies this conclusion as "merely possible," with probable speeds more likely to be twenty to thirty miles an hour, he adds, "I should not be surprised at seeing steam-carriages propelled at the rate of forty or fifty miles an hour." Ibid., pp. 5–6.

5. Ibid., p. 19.

6. Ibid., p. 22.

7. Ibid., pp. 37–38.

8. Dunbar, *History of Travel in America,* pp. 876–80.

9. *The First Railroad in America: A History of the Origin and Development of the Granite Railway at Quincy, Massachusetts* (privately printed for the Granite Railway Company, 1926), p. 27).

10. Perkins was a man of sufficient substance that when offered the secretaryship of the navy by President Washington, he declined, "saying that he owned a larger fleet of vessels than the United States Navy and believed he could do more good by continuing to manage his own property." Ibid., p. 21.

11. Alvin F. Harlow, *Steelways of New England* (New York: Creative Age Press, 1946), p. 17; Edward C. Kirkland, in *Men, Cities, and Transportation* (Cambridge: Harvard University Press, 1948), 1:100, gives slightly varying dimensions, making the iron strap three-eighths of an inch thick and placing the one-ton granite crossties at eight-foot intervals under the pine "rails."

12. Kirkland, *Men, Cities, and Transportation* 1:119.

13. Quoted in Harlow, *Steelways of New England*, p. 26.

14. For an elaboration of this theme, see James E. Vance, Jr., *The Merchant's World: The Geography of Wholesaling* (Englewood Cliffs, N.J.: Prentice-Hall, 1970).

15. Portland, Maine; Portsmouth, New Hampshire; Boston; Providence; New London, Hartford, and New Haven, Connecticut; New York; Philadelphia; Baltimore; Alexandria and Norfolk (Richmond), Virginia; Wilmington, North Carolina; Charleston; and Savannah.

16. Frederic J. Wood, *The Turnpikes of New England* (Boston: Marshall Jones, 1919), p. 7.

17. Caroline E. MacGill, *History of Transportation in the United States before 1860*, prepared under the direction of Balthasar Meyer (Washington, D.C.: Carnegie Institution, 1917), p. 406.

18. Quoted in Edward Hungerford, *The Story of the Baltimore and Ohio Railroad, 1827–1927* (New York: G. P. Putnam's Sons, 1928), 1:19.

19. Quoted, ibid., pp. 20–21.

20. Quoted, ibid., pp. 21–22.

21. Quoted, ibid., pp. 23–24.

22. Quoted, ibid., p. 24.

23. Quoted, ibid., p. 25.

24. William Strickland, *Reports on Canals, Railways, Roads, and Other Subjects, Made to "The Pennsylvania Society for the Promotion of Internal Improvement"* (Philadelphia: H. C. Carey and I. Lea, 1826), p. 31.

25. Hungerford, *Baltimore and Ohio* 1:27.

26. Strickland, *Reports on Canals, Railways, Roads,* pp. 23–24. This location practice of using grades favoring the flow of goods was first noted in North America by Strickland in 1826, but it was applied fundamentally to the construction of the Western Hemisphere's longest tunnel, opened by the Canadian Pacific Railway in 1989.

27. B&O Passenger Department, *Book of the Royal Blue* (Baltimore, 1898), 2:8–9.

28. Hungerford, *Baltimore and Ohio* 1:52.

29. Ibid.

30. Ibid., p. 53.

31. Ibid., pp. 52–64.

32. Quoted, ibid., p. 70.

33. Ibid., p. 78.

34. John H. White, Jr., *A History of the American Locomotive: Its Development, 1830–1880* (1968; rpt. New York: Dover, 1979), pp. 4–7.

35. Arthur M. Wellington, *The Economic Theory of the Location of Railways* (New York: John Wiley, 1902), pp. 421–22.

36. Quoted, ibid., p. 180.

37. Quoted, ibid., p. 184.

38. Quoted, ibid., pp. 185–86.

39. Ibid., pp. 207–10.

40. MacGill, *Transportation in the United States,* pp. 387–92.

41. Ibid., pp. 252–67.

42. Ibid., p. 387.

43. Ibid.

44. Ibid.

45. Francis B. C. Bradlee, *The Boston and Lowell Railroad, the Nashua and Lowell Railroad, and the Salem and Lowell Railroad* (Salem: Essex Institute, 1918), pp. 3–4; Harlow, *Steelways of New England,* pp. 73–93; Kirkland, *Men, Cities, and Transportation* 1:111–12.

46. Quoted in Harlow, *Steelways of New England,* pp. 73–74.

47. Louis P. Loring, "Early Railroads of Boston," *The Bostonian,* 1894, pp. 299–309.

48. Harlow, *Steelways of New England,* p. 87.

49. [William Gibbs McNeill], *Report of the Board of Directors to the Stockholders of the*

Boston and Providence Rail-road Company, Submitting the Report of their Engineer (Boston: J. E. Hinckley, 1832).

50. It was for Patrick Tracy Jackson that one of the earlier Boston and Lowell locomotives was to be named; but with Andrew Jackson in the White House, the "Cotton Whigs" of northeastern Massachusetts, who were eager participants in the rail line, insisted that it be made clear that only a Massachusetts Jackson was being honored by naming the engine *Patrick.*

51. McNeill, *Report of the Board of Directors to the Stockholders of the Boston and Providence,* p. 8.

52. Ibid., p. 10.

53. Ibid., p. 37.

54. Ibid., p. 43.

55. Quoted, ibid., p. 44. Robert Stevenson was the famous author's father.

56. A detailed account of the American track system and its predecessors is given in J. Elfreth Watkins, "The Development of the American Rail and Track, as Illustrated by the Collection in the U.S. National Museum," *Report of the National Museum, 1888–1889,* pp. 651–708. Citation is to pp. 657–61.

57. Ibid., p. 663.

58. Ibid.

59. Ibid., pp. 666–67.

60. Quoted, ibid., p. 670.

61. Ibid., pp. 670–74.

62. *Report of the Directors of the Boston and Worcester Rail-road,* January 1833 (Boston: Stimpson and Clapp, 1833), p. 23.

63. James E. Vance, Jr., "Labor-shed, Employment Field, and Dynamic Analysis in Urban Geography," *Economic Geography* 36 (1960): 189–220.

64. *Report of the Directors of the Boston and Worcester Rail-road,* January 1833, p. 23.

65. *Report of Boston and Worcester Directors to General Court of Massachusetts* (Boston: Stimpson and Clapp, 1833), p. 2.

66. Ibid., pp. 2–3.

67. Ibid., pp. 9–10.

68. *Report of Boston and Worcester Rail-road,* 1838, p. 7.

69. *Report of Boston and Worcester Railroad,* 1840, p. 7.

70. Quoted in Harlow, *Steelways of New England,* p. 132.

71. Kirkland, *Men, Cities, and Transportation* 1:130.

72. Alvin Harlow, *Road of the Century* (New York: Creative Age Press, 1947), pp. 4–24.

73. Kirkland, *Men, Cities, and Transportation* 1:136–37.

74. Harlow, *Steelways of New England,* p. 129.

75. *Second Annual Report of the Directors of the Western Rail Road Corporation* (Boston: A. N. Dickinson, 1837), pp. 5–7.

76. Ibid., p. 15.

77. *Report of the Delegation to Albany to the Stockholders of the Western Rail-road Corporation* (Boston, 1840), pp. 12–14.

78. Ibid., p. 16.

79. Ibid., p. 17.

80. *Proceedings of the Western Railroad Corporation, with a Report of the Committee of Investigation* (Boston, 1843), pp. 28–30.

81. John Kellett, *The Impact of Railways on Victorian Cities* (London: Routledge and Kegan Paul, 1969).

82. Quoted in Kirkland, *Men, Cities, and Transportation* 1:142, 140–41.

83. Ibid., pp. 148–49.

84. Charles Francis Adams, Jr., "Boston," *North American Review* 106 (1868).

85. MacGill, *Transportation in the United States,* p. 338.

86. Ibid., p. 337.

87. Ibid., pp. 335–36.

88. Reported in a paper read by Henry A. Willis before the Fitchburg Historical Society, April 1892. Quoted in William Bond Wheelright, *Life and Times of Alvah Crocker* (Boston, 1923), p. 17.

89. Ibid., p. 46.

90. Ibid., p. 47.

91. Harlow, *Steelways of New England*, p. 250; Kirkland, *Men, Cities, and Transportation* 1:411.

92. Kirkland, *Men, Cities, and Transportation* 1:203–15; Harlow, *Steelways of New England*, pp. 309–17.

93. G. R. Stevens, *Canadian National Railways* (Toronto: Clarke, Irwin, and Company, 1960), 2:414–17.

94. Kirkland, *Men, Cities, and Transportation* 1:190.

95. Ibid.

96. Ibid., p. 191.

97. Frank Walker Stevens, *The Beginnings of the New York Central Railroad* (New York: G. P. Putnam's Sons, 1926), pp. xi–xii.

98. MacGill, *Transportation in the United States*, p. 367.

99. Ibid.

100. Edward Harold Mott, *Between the Ocean and the Lakes: The Story of Erie* (New York: John S. Collins, 1900), pp. 4–5.

101. Ibid., p. 7.

102. Ibid., p. 16.

103. Quoted, ibid., pp. 17–18.

104. Ibid., p. 19.

105. Quoted in toto, ibid., pp. 25–31. All further quotations are from this citation.

106. Ibid., p. 149.

107. Edward Hungerford, *Men of Erie* (New York: Random House, 1946), pp. 180–99, 204.

108. New York, Lake Erie, and Western Railroad, *Suburban Homes on the Picturesque Erie* (New York, 1886), pp. 24–25.

109. Stevens, *Beginnings of the New York Central*, p. x.

110. Ibid., pp. 106–14.

111. Ibid., pp. 115–46.

112. Ibid., p. 299.

113. Ibid., pp. 317–30.

114. Harlow, *Road of the Century*, p. 271.

115. H. W. Schotter, *The Growth and Development of the Pennsylvania Railroad Company* (Philadelphia: Pennsylvania Railroad, 1927), pp. 5–6.

116. Ibid., p. 7.

117. "Horseshoe Curve and Approach to Gallitzin Tunnels, Notable Feats in Railroad Engineering," *Trains and Travel* 12 (May 1952): 28–29.

118. Ibid., p. 15.

119. Quoted in U. B. Phillips, *A History of Transportation in the Eastern Cotton Belt to 1860* (1908; rpt. New York: Octagon Books, 1968), p. 136.

120. Samuel Melanchton Derrick, *Centennial History of South Carolina Railroad* (Columbia, S.C.: The State Company, 1930), p. 27.

121. Ibid., pp. 29–33.

122. Ibid., pp. 39–42.

123. Allen's report, quoted, ibid., p. 41.

124. Phillips, *Transportation in the Eastern Cotton Belt*, p. 145.

125. Ibid., p. 148. Phillips makes the mistake of locating the West Point Foundry at the site of the United States Military Academy rather than at New York City.

126. Derrick, *South Carolina Railroad*, p. 43.

127. Quoted, ibid.

128. Ibid., p. 61.

129. Ibid., p. 104.

130. Phillips, *Transportation in the Eastern Cotton Belt*, pp. 162–63.

131. Ibid., p. 177.

132. Ibid., p. 178.

133. *Trains* 32 (October 1972): 51–52.

134. Phillips, *Transportation in the Eastern Cotton Belt*, pp. 252–63.

135. Ibid., p. 263.

136. Ibid., pp. 229–43, 263–72.

137. Ibid., p. 308.

138. Ibid., p. 318.

139. MacGill, *Transportation in the United States*, p. 392.

140. Harlow, *Steelways of New England*, p. 221.

141. Elmer F. Farnham, *The Quickest Route: The History of the Norwich and Worcester Railroad* (Chester, Conn.: Pequot, 1973), p. 9.

142. Ibid., p. 73.

143. Harlow, *Steelways of New England*, pp. 217–18.

144. Quoted, ibid., p. 185.

145. Eugene Alvarez, *Travel on Southern Antebellum Railroads, 1828–1860* (University: University of Alabama Press, 1974), p. 10.

146. George Behrend, *Pullman in Europe* (London: Ian Allen, 1962).

147. Ibid., p. 5.

148. Frank P. Morse, *Cavalcade of the Rails* (New York: E. P. Dutton, 1940), pp. 257–59.

149. For a detailed account of the Louisville and Nashville, see Maury Klein's comprehensive *History of the Louisville and Nashville Railroad* (New York: Macmillan, 1972).

150. Ibid., pp. 60–61.

151. Julius Grodinsky, *Transcontinental Railway Strategy, 1869–1893: A Study of Businessmen* (Philadelphia: University of Pennsylvania Press, 1962), p. 105.

152. David B. Steinman and Sara Ruth Watson, *Bridges and Their Builders* (New York: Dover, 1957), pp. 25–26.

153. George R. Taylor and Irene D. Neu, *The American Railroad Network, 1861–1890* (Cambridge: Harvard University Press, 1956), pp. 43–45.

154. Ibid., p. 47.

155. Ibid., p. 53.

156. Ibid., p. 55.

157. Ibid., p. 54.

158. Ibid., p. 62.

159. Ibid., p. 63.

160. Ibid., p. 77.

161. Ibid., pp. 77–78.

162. Ibid., pp. 77–83.

163. Jim Shaughnessy, *Delaware and Hudson* (Berkeley: Howell-North, 1967), pp. 31–41.

164. Ibid., p. 61.

165. William F. Helmer, *O. & W.: The Long Life and Slow Death of the New York, Ontario, and Western Railway* (Berkeley: Howell-North, 1959), pp. 9, 22.

166. Ibid., pp. 63–64. That bridge remains a derelict reminder of that valuable anthracite trade extinguished by the oil burner in the 1930s.

167. Ibid., p. 95.

168. Ibid., p. 129.

169. Ibid., pp. 136–66.

170. Quoted in Joseph Daughen and Peter Binzen, *The Wreck of the Penn Central* (Boston: Little, Brown, 1971), pp. 57–58.

171. Ibid., p. 59.

Chapter 2. The Drive for Ubiquity

1. Caroline E. MacGill, *History of Transportation in the United States before 1860*, prepared under the direction of Balthasar Meyer (Washington, D.C.: Carnegie Institution, 1917), pp. 494–95.

2. Ibid., p. 496.

3. Ibid., pp. 503–9; Alvin Harlow, *Road of the Century* (New York: Creative Age Press, 1947), pp. 274–76.

4. G. P. de T. Glazebrook, *A History of Transportation in Canada* (1938; rpt. Toronto: McClelland and Stewart, 1964), 1:160.

5. Ibid. 2:96.

6. Harlow, *Road of the Century,* pp. 341–400.

7. Edward Hungerford, *Men of Erie* (New York: Random House, 1946), pp. 166, 204, 205.

8. H. W. Schotter, *The Growth and Development of the Pennsylvania Railroad Company* (Philadelphia: Pennsylvania Railroad, 1927), pp. 36–38; Edwin P. Alexander, *The Pennsylvania Railroad: A Pictorial History* (New York: Bonanza, 1947), p. 24.

9. Schotter, *Pennsylvania Railroad,* p. 82.

10. Edward Hungerford, *The Story of the Baltimore and Ohio Railroad, 1827–1927* (New York: G. P. Putnam's Sons, 1928), 2:106.

11. Ibid., pp. 299–305.

12. Ibid., pp. 107–8.

13. Maury Klein, *History of the Louisville and Nashville Railroad* (New York: Macmillan, 1972), p. 10.

14. Ibid., p. 16.

15. MacGill, *Transportation in the United States,* p. 471.

16. Klein, *Louisville and Nashville,* p. 110.

17. John F. Stover, *History of the Illinois Central Railroad* (New York: Macmillan, 1975), pp. 38–57.

18. Ibid., p. 150.

19. Ibid., p. 151.

20. European figures are from B. R. Mitchell, *European Historical Statistics, 1750–1970* (New York: Columbia University Press, 1978), p. 319.

21. Harold M. Mayer and Richard C. Wade, *Chicago: Growth of a Metropolis* (Chicago: University of Chicago Press, 1969), p. 44.

22. *The Railway Passenger Terminal Problem in Chicago* (Chicago: City of Chicago, City Council, Committee on Railway Terminals, 1933), p. 12; Mayer and Wade, *Chicago: Growth of a Metropolis,* p. 126.

23. *Railway Passenger Terminal Problem,* pp. 12–14; Mayer and Wade, *Chicago: Growth of a Metropolis,* p. 298.

24. *Railway Passenger Terminal Problem,* pp. 14–15.

25. Robert E. Riegel, *The Story of Western Railroads* (Lincoln: University of Nebraska Press, 1964), p. 100.

26. *Railway Passenger Terminal Problem,* p. 15.

27. Ibid., p. 18; Taylor Hampton, *The Nickel Plate Road: The History of a Great Railroad* (Cleveland: World Publishing, 1947), pp. 23–31.

28. *Railway Passenger Terminal Problem,* pp. 18–20.

29. Ibid.

30. John A. Droege, *Passenger Terminals and Trains* (1916; rpt. Milwaukee: Kalmbach, 1969), p. 123.

31. Quinta Scott and Howard Miller, *The Eads Bridge* (Columbia: University of Missouri Press, 1979), p. 130.

32. Wyatt W. Belcher, *The Economic Rivalry between St. Louis and Chicago, 1850–1880* (New York: Columbia University Press, 1947), pp. 174–75.

33. Ibid., p. 167.

34. Ibid., pp. 142–43.

35. Stewart Holbrook, *The Story of American Railroads* (New York: Crown Publishers, 1947).

36. Reigel, *Western Railroads,* p. 11.

37. William H. Goetzman, *Army Exploration in the American West: 1803–1863* (New Haven: Yale University Press, 1959), pp. 265–66.

38. Howard Stansbury, *Exploration and Survey of the Valley of the Great Salt Lake of Utah, Including a Reconnaissance of a New Route through the Rocky Mountains* (Washington, D.C.: Robert Armstrong, 1853).

39. Ibid., p. 262.

40. I. I. Stevens, *Narrative and Final Report of Explorations for a Route for a Pacific Railroad Near the Forty-seventh and Forty-ninth Parallels of North Latitude from St. Paul to Puget Sound,* in *Reports of Explorations and Surveys to Ascertain the Most Practicable and Economical Route for a Railroad from the Mississippi River to the Pacific Ocean,* vol. 12 (Washington, D.C., 1855).

41. Ibid., p. 331.

42. Ibid., p. 337.

43. Ibid., pp. 345–46.

44. E. G. Beckwith, *Report upon the Route Near the Thirty-eighth and Thirty-ninth Parallels, Explored by Captain J. W. Gunnison, Corps of Topographical Engineers*, in *Reports of Explorations and Surveys to Ascertain the Most Practicable and Economical Route for a Railroad from the Mississippi River to the Pacific Ocean*, vol. 2 (Washington, D.C., 1855), p. 38.

45. Ibid., pp. 47–48.

46. Frederick W. Lander, *Synopsis of a Report of the Reconnaissance of a Railroad Route from Puget Sound via South Pass to the Mississippi River*, in ibid., p. 11.

47. Ibid., p. 14 (emphasis removed).

48. Ibid., p. 18.

49. McClellan, quoted, ibid., p. 31.

50. Ibid., pp. 31–36.

51. E. G. Beckwith, *Report of Explorations for a Route for the Pacific Railroad, on the Line of the Forty-first Parallel of North Latitude*, in *Reports of Explorations and Surveys to Ascertain the Most Practicable and Economical Route for a Railroad from the Mississippi River to the Pacific Ocean*, vol. 2 (Washington, D.C., 1855), p. 59.

52. Ibid., p. 11.

53. Ibid.

54. Ibid., p. 13.

55. Ibid., p. 14.

56. Ibid., pp. 14–15.

57. Ibid., p. 38.

58. Ibid., p. 63.

59. Ibid., p. 66.

60. *Extracts from the [Preliminary] Report of Lieutenant A. W. Whipple, Corps of Geographical Engineers, upon the Route Near the Thirty-fifth Parallel, with an Explanatory Note by Captain A. A. Humphreys, Corps of Topographical Engineers*, in *Reports of Explorations and Surveys to Ascertain the Most Practicable and Economical Route for a Railroad from the Mississippi River to the Pacific Ocean*, vol. 3 (Washington, D.C., 1856), pp. 3–4.

61. Ibid., p. 12.

62. Ibid., p. 19.

63. Ibid., p. 21.

64. Ibid., p. 22.

65. Ibid., pp. 23–27.

66. Ibid., pp. 39–41.

67. Ibid., p. 42 (original paragraphing removed).

68. Ibid., pp. 41–44.

69. John G. Parke, *Report of Explorations for That Portion of a Railroad Route Near the Thirty-second Parallel of North Latitude, Lying between Doña Ana, on the Rio Grande, and Pimas Villages, on the Gila*, in *Reports of Explorations and Surveys to Ascertain the Most Practicable and Economical Route for a Railroad from the Mississippi River to the Pacific Ocean*, vol. 7 (Washington, D.C., 1854), pp. 3–19.

70. Act of 1862, quoted in Charles Edgar Ames, *Pioneering the Union Pacific: A Reappraisal of the Builders of the Railroad* (New York: Appleton-Century-Crofts, 1969), p. 12.

71. Ibid., p. 15.

72. Ibid., p. 17.

73. Ibid., pp. 31–32.

74. Ibid., p. 45.

75. Major-General Grenville M. Dodge, *How We Built the Union Pacific Railway* (privately published, n.d.), pp. 142–43.

76. Quoted in Ames, *Pioneering the Union Pacific*, pp. 130–31.

77. Dodge, *How We Built the Union Pacific*, pp. 108–9.

78. Dodge, *Autobiography*, p. 410, quoted in Ames, *Pioneering the Union Pacific*, pp. 117–18.

79. James E. Vance, Jr., "The Oregon Trail and Union Pacific Railroad," *Annals of the Association of American Geographers* 51 (December 1961): 369.

80. Ibid.

81. Ibid., pp. 369–72.

82. Ibid., p. 374.

83. Ames, *Pioneering the Union Pacific*, p. 161.

84. Ibid., pp. 295, 336.

85. Ibid., p. 119.

86. Quoted in Ward McAfee, *California's Railroad Era: 1850–1911* (San Marino, Calif.: Golden West Books, 1973), pp. 35–36.

87. Ibid., p. 51.

88. Quoted, ibid., p. 53.

89. Quoted in Neill C. Wilson and Frank J. Taylor, *Southern Pacific* (New York: McGraw-Hill, 1952), pp. 13–14.

90. Ibid., p. 17.

91. Dr. H. Latham to the New York Herald, January 9, 1871, quoted in Ames, *Pioneering the Union Pacific*, p. 14.

92. The awkward name for the stream bordering the ramp on the north comes from a fact of physiography: the Yuba captured the upper course of the Bear, making the joint term necessary.

93. Ames, *Pioneering the Union Pacific*, p. 92.

94. Wilson and Taylor, *Southern Pacific*, p. 23.

95. Ibid., p. 26.

Chapter 3. The Geography of the North American Railroad Company

1. Julius Grodinsky, *Transcontinental Railway Strategy, 1869–1893: A Study of Businessmen* (Philadelphia: University of Pennsylvania Press, 1962).

2. Neill C. Wilson and Frank J. Taylor, *Southern Pacific* (New York: McGraw-Hill, 1952), p. 125.

3. Grodinsky, *Transcontinental Railway Strategy*, pp. 136–37.

4. Merrill D. Beal, *Intermountain Railroads: Standard and Narrow Gauge* (Caldwell, Idaho: Caxton, 1962), p. 185.

5. Glenn Chesney Quiett, *They Built the West: An Epic of Rails and Cities* (New York: D. Appleton-Century, 1934), p. 418.

6. Ibid., p. 420.

7. Ibid., pp. 295–97.

8. Robert Athearn, *Rebel of the Rockies: A History of the Denver and Rio Grande Western Railroad* (1962; rpt. Lincoln: University of Nebraska Press, 1977), pp. 131–33, 226–28.

9. Quoted, ibid., p. 312.

10. Ibid., p. 313.

11. Quoted, ibid.

12. Quoted, ibid., p. 315.

13. Beal, *Intermountain Railroads*, pp. 184–85.

14. Wilson and Taylor, *Southern Pacific*, p. 77.

15. Ibid., p. 71.

16. *The Great Northwest: A Guide-book and Itinerary for the Use of Tourists and Travelers over the Lines of the Northern Pacific Railroad* (St. Paul: Northern News, 1888), p. 259; Marius Campbell et al., *Guidebook of the Western United States: Part A, The Northern Pacific Route*, in U.S. Geological Survey *Bulletin* 611 (1915): 94–95.

17. USGS *Bulletin* 611:124.

18. *The Great Northwest*, p. 94.

19. Quiett, *They Built the West*, p. 459.

20. Marshall Sprague, *The Great Gates: The Story of Rocky Mountain Passes* (Boston: Little, Brown, 1964), p. 161.

21. Ibid., p. 290.

22. Quoted, ibid., p. 291.

23. Quoted in Michael P. Malone and Richard B. Roeder, *Montana: A History of Two Centuries* (Seattle: University of Washington Press, 1977), p. 135.

24. The data quoted are from an article in *Trains* magazine, September 1952.

25. H. Craig Miner, *The St. Louis-San Francisco Transcontinental Railroad: The Thirty-fifth Parallel Project, 1853–1890* (Lawrence: University Press of Kansas, 1972), p. 40.

26. August Derleth, *The Milwaukee Road: Its First Hundred Years* (New York: Creative Age Press, 1948), p. 165.

27. Ibid., p. 173.

28. Athearn, *Rebel of the Rockies*, pp. 13–15.

29. Ibid., p. 100.

30. This detail, like much of the factual material on this line, is from Marius R. Campbell, *Guidebook of the Western United States: Part E, The Denver and Rio Grande Western Route*, in U.S. Geological Survey *Bulletin* 707 (1922): 111.

31. Ibid.

32. Ibid., p. 217.

33. Ibid., p. 220.

34. Athearn, *Rebel of the Rockies*, p. 122.

35. Ibid., p. 162.

36. Ibid., p. 166.

37. Ibid., p. 191.

38. Quoted, ibid., p. 196.

39. Ibid.

40. Ibid., pp. 206–9.

41. Ibid., p. 210.

42. Wilson and Taylor, *Southern Pacific*, p. 111.

43. Henry Sampson, *World Railways*, 3d ed. (Chicago: Rand McNally, 1954–55), p. 130.

44. Richard C. Overton, *Gulf to Rockies: The Heritage of the Fort Worth and Denver-Colorado and Southern Railways, 1861–1898* (Austin: University of Texas Press, 1953).

45. *Official Guide of the Railways*, August 1942, p. 965.

46. Miner, *St. Louis-San Francisco Transcontinental Railroad*, p. 78.

47. L. L. Waters, *Steel Trails to Santa Fe* (Lawrence: University of Kansas Press, 1950), pp. 366–70.

48. Wilson and Taylor, *Southern Pacific*, pp. 90–92.

Chapter 4. A Canadian Postscript

1. G. R. Stevens, *Canadian National Railways* (Toronto: Clarke, Irwin, and Company, 1960), 1:23.

2. Ibid., pp. 26–30.

3. Ibid., pp. 52–58.

4. Alvin F. Harlow, *Steelways of New England* (New York: Creative Age Press, 1946), p. 315.

5. Quoted in Stevens, *Canadian National Railways* 1:87.

6. Ibid., p. 194.

7. G. P. de T. Glazebrook, *A History of Transportation in Canada* (1938; rpt. Toronto: McClelland and Stewart, 1964), 1:162.

8. Quoted in Stevens, *Canadian National Railways* 1:88.

9. Ibid., p. 63.

10. Ibid., p. 285.

11. Ibid., p. 352.

12. Sandford Fleming, *Report of Progress on the Explorations and Surveys up to January, 1874, the Canadian Pacific Railway* (Ottawa: MacLean, Roger, and Company, 1874).

13. Ibid., pp. 2–3.

14. Ibid., p. 6.

15. Ibid., p. 8.

16. Ibid., p. 9.

17. Ibid., pp. 10–11.

18. Ibid., p. 16.

19. Ibid.

20. Ibid., pp. 17–21.

21. Ibid., p. 23.

22. J. Lorne McDougall, *Canadian Pacific: A Brief History* (Montréal: McGill University Press, 1968), p. 20.

23. Ibid., p. 21.

24. Ibid., p. 16.

25. Ibid., p. 26.

26. Ibid., pp. 33–37.

27. Glazebrook, *Transportation in Canada* 2:79.

28. Ibid., p. 70.

29. McDougall, *Canadian Pacific,* p. 52.

30. Glazebrook, *Transportation in Canada* 2:82–83.

31. Quoted, ibid., p. 83.

32. Ibid.

33. Pierre Berton, *The Last Spike,* vol. 2, *The Great Railway, 1881–1885* (Toronto: McClelland and Stewart, 1971), pp. 11–22.

34. Ibid., pp. 292–95.

35. Ibid., pp. 331–35.

36. Ibid., p. 412.

37. McDougall, *Canadian Pacific,* p. 67.

38. T. D. Regehr, *The Canadian Northern Railway: Pioneer Road of the Northern Prairies, 1895–1918* (Toronto: Macmillan of Canada, 1976), pp. 13–14.

39. Ibid., p. 14.

40. Ibid., p. 29.

41. Ibid., p. 104.

42. Ibid., p. 128.

43. Ibid., p. 129.

44. Ibid., p. 314.

45. Preamble of the act authorizing assistance, quoted, ibid., p. 317.

46. Stevens, *Canadian National Railways* 2:88.

47. Quoted in Glazebrook, *Transportation in Canada* 2:136.

48. Patrick C. Dorin, *The Ontario Northland Railway* (Burbank, Calif.: Superior Publishing, 1989), p. 12.

49. Colin K. Hatcher, *The Northern Alberta Railway* (Calgary: RRMNA, 1981), p. 1.

50. Nick and Helma Mika, with Donald M. Wilson, *Illustrated History of Canadian Railways* (Belleville, Ont.: Mika Publishing Co., 1986), p. 274.

51. Regehr, *Canadian Northern Railway,* pp. 248–53.

52. McDougall, *Canadian Pacific,* pp. 73–88.

53. Barrier Sandford, *The Pictorial History of Railracing in British Columbia* (Vancouver: Whitecap Books, 1981), p. 59.

54. Ibid., p. 67.

55. Bruce Ramsey, *PGE: Railway to the North* (Vancouver: Mitchell, 1962), p. 57.

56. Ibid., p. 127.

57. Quoted, ibid., pp. 149–52.

58. Ibid., p. 244.

59. *Annual Report,* British Columbia Railway, 1983. Additional information was secured from field investigation along the line most generously assisted by the British Columbia Railway in September 1986.

60. *Annual Report,* British Columbia Railway, 1985, p. 34.

61. Publicity release of Canadian Pacific Railway, "Canadian Pacific and Rogers Pass" (n.d.), p. 10.

62. Ibid., p. 14.

63. Ibid.

INDEX

Entries and page numbers in italics indicate illustrations or maps.

347

Index

ABOUT THE AUTHOR

James E. Vance Jr. is emeritus professor of geography at the University of California, Berkeley. He has also taught at the universities of Arkansas, Wyoming, Nebraska, Wisconsin-Madison, Cambridge, Natal, and the Negev. He has seriously studied railroads on five continents for over five decades, and he is especially concerned with the evolution of the railroad since 1825. He is the author of *The Continuing City: Urban Morphology in Western Civilization* (1990), *Capturing the Horizon: The Historical Geography of Transportation since the Sixteenth Century* (1986), and *The Merchant's World: The Geography of Wholesaling* (1970), among other works. Born and raised in Natick, Massachusetts, Vance has lived in Berkeley since 1958 and spends his summers in a medieval timber house in the Queen Charlotte Islands of British Columbia. He rides the rails—passenger and freight—whenever he can.

Library of Congress Cataloging-in-Publication Data

Vance, James E.
    The North American Railroad : its origin, evolution, and geography /
James E. Vance, Jr.
        p.   cm.—(Creating the North American landscape)
    Includes bibliographical references and index.
    ISBN 0-8018-4573-4
    1. Railroads—United States. 2. Railroads—Canada. I. Title. II.
Series.
TF23.V36 1995   94-16306

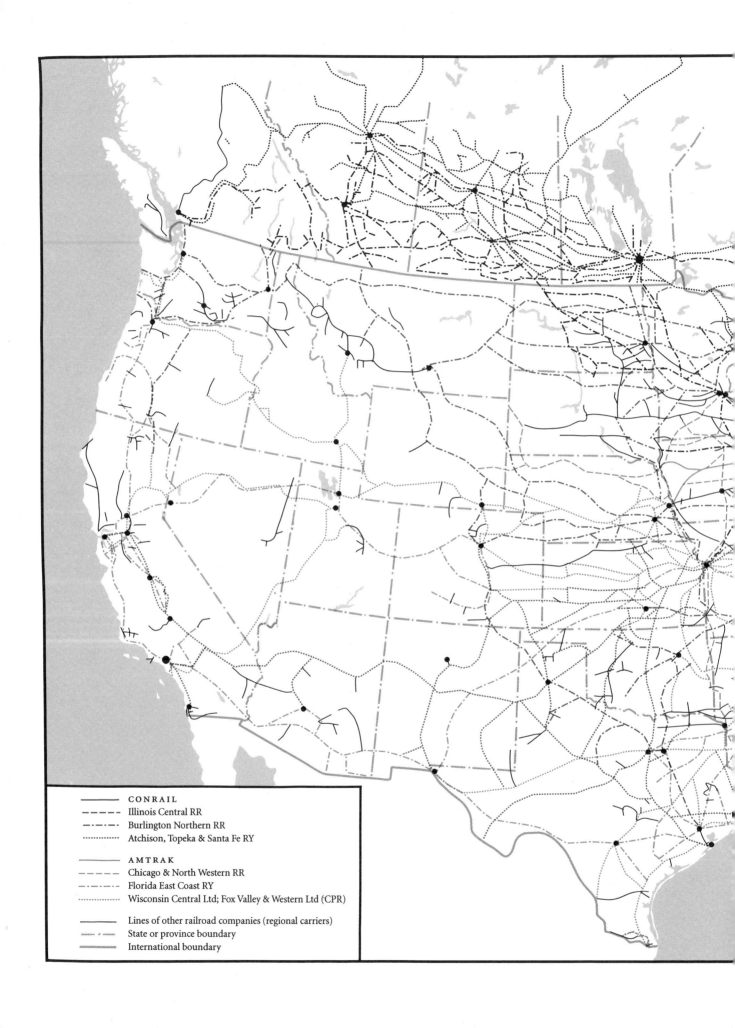